Contemporary Discourses of Hate and Radicalism across Space and Genres

Benjamins Current Topics

ISSN 1874-0081

Special issues of established journals tend to circulate within the orbit of the subscribers of those journals. For the Benjamins Current Topics series a number of special issues of various journals have been selected containing salient topics of research with the aim of finding new audiences for topically interesting material, bringing such material to a wider readership in book format.

For an overview of all books published in this series, please see *http://benjamins.com/catalog/bct*

Volume 93

Contemporary Discourses of Hate and Radicalism across Space and Genres
Edited by Monika Kopytowska

These materials were previously published in *Journal of Language Aggression and Conflict* 3:1 (2015)

Contemporary Discourses of Hate and Radicalism across Space and Genres

Edited by

Monika Kopytowska
University of Łódź

John Benjamins Publishing Company
Amsterdam / Philadelphia

The paper used in this publication meets the minimum requirements of the American National Standard for Information Sciences – Permanence of Paper for Printed Library Materials, ANSI Z39.48-1984.

DOI 10.1075/bct.93

Cataloging-in-Publication Data available from Library of Congress:
LCCN 2017020008 (PRINT) / 2017042120 (E-BOOK)

ISBN 978 90 272 4281 5 (HB)
ISBN 978 90 272 6498 5 (E-BOOK)

John Benjamins Publishing Company · https://benjamins.com

Table of contents

INTRODUCTION

Discourses of hate and radicalism in action

Monika Kopytowska
University of Łódź

Recent debates on freedom of speech triggered by the *Charlie Hebdo* attacks in Paris, on the one hand, and by the resurgence of European far-right parties along with their nationalist and populist discourses on the Other, inescapably bring to the limelight the role of language as a social agent and the material effects of speech. After all, as argued by Searle (1995, 2010), social reality is co-constructed by language. Its performative potential, together with collective agreement, are behind the attribution of status functions and creation of institutional facts. The linguistic representations of individuals, groups, events, issues, phenomena and relations are essential for the continued maintenance of these status functions and, thus, the socio-political status-quo of social actors and institutions. Hence, for Foucault (1985, 74), discourses are practices which systematically form the objects of which they speak, while Jäger (2001, 32) emphasizes the fact that the knowledge discourses transport "is the basis of individual and collective action and the formative action that shapes reality." Such a perspective has been invariably reflected in Critical Discourse Analysis's view of discourse as "a form of social practice" (Fairclough and Wodak 1997), seen as both socially constituted and socially constitutive.

Contemporary public discourse — in its various forms and contexts — abounds in messages of hate and radicalism. Political speeches, mainstream and social media, which are meant to be a platform for political debate within the Habermasian public sphere allowing for "critical public discussion of matters of general interest" (Habermas 1989, xi), become a vehicle for hateful political beliefs, ideologies and actions. The objective behind this volume, originally published as a special issue of *Journal of Language Aggression and Conflict* 3(1), is thus to bring together various academic voices and critical reflections on hate and radicalism in public discourse, to explore the ideological motivations which underlie such messages and the implications they might have for social actions on both an individual and a collective level. The contributors examine various instances of texts studied under the terms of "hate speech" (Boromisha-Habashi 2011, 2013; Waltman and Haas 2011), discourse of populism (Kienpointner 2006), or "New Populism" (Panizza

DOI 10.1075/bct.93.001ed

2005), "right-wing extremism" (Taggard 1995), "racist discourse" (Van Dijk 1987, 1991, 1993), "fascist discourse" (Reisigl and Wodak 2001, Wodak and Richardson 2013), white supremacist discourse (Bostdorff 2004, Brown 2009, Daniels 1997), "homophobic discourse" (Harvey 2012, Leap 2011, Vasu 2002), and, last but not least, "paranoid style" in politics (Hofstadter 2008). What all these texts share and perpetuate are extreme negative feelings and beliefs about groups of individuals, linked to their race, religion, gender or sexual orientation (Perry 2001). What they reflect and impact, if we adopt a perspective on discourse as "a social practice" (Fairclough and Wodak 1997, 273), are various dimensions of social life, including representations of the world, social relations among people, and personal identities.

In their recent book *The Communication of Hate*, Waltman and Haas (2011, 7) refer to hatred as "a problem that results in isolated acts of murder and more systematic and coordinated genocide [...] a problem that knows no geographical boundaries". Indeed, recent decades have produced numerous examples of hateful and radical discourses and their social "enactment" in the form of social movements, political actions and individual instances of verbal and physical violence. They have been used with various intentions and for different purposes: to intimidate the out-group and influence (unite) the in-group, to discriminate against minorities and promote ethno-violence, and to preserve or challenge existing power structures. Additionally, they have often been linked, directly or indirectly, to ideologies embedded in Christian identity, white supremacy, xenophobia, sexism/heterosexism, and anti-statism (Perry 2001). Being produced by both religious-hate groups and secular hate-groups and having their manifestations in both inter- and intra-state conflicts, they have relied on similar metaphorical conceptualizations, patterns of argumentation and rhetorical strategies, and have perpetuated a similar "hate stratagem" (Willcock 1995, 4). They have thrived on myths constituting the collective memory and have made use of individual experiences. Technologies and the existence of the virtual public sphere have made discourses of hate and radicalism available to mass publics (Duffy 2003). Cyberspace has endowed them with a new dimension by removing the boundaries of time and space, by exploiting the potential of intertextuality and interdiscursivity, and, as argued by Waltman and Haas (2011, 5), by creating "congenial environments", which "have played an important role in the radicalization of individuals who go 'Lone Wolf' and take it upon themselves to commit horrific acts of hate-motivated violence" (see also: Lee and Leets 2002, Schafer 2002, Williamson and Pierson 2003).

The present collection of papers sets out to identify what we might call a pragma-semantic and pragma-dialectic profile of discourses of hate and radicalism. The authors venture into various socio-political contexts, genres and public spaces, providing a compelling overview of similarities and divergences, continuities and discontinuities. They take under scrutiny outward hatred and the "politics of denial", collective symbols and individual identities. Several genres are examined — viz. blogs, discussion fora, internet websites and newspaper coverage, political speeches and debates, news reports and broadcast interactions — with a view to capturing themes and pragma-rhetorical strategies, the motivations behind them and the implications they have for "public opinion, dominant ideologies and consensual everyday practices (van Dijk 1993, 8–9). While reflecting upon the discourse dynamics and the underlying logic of the texts studied by the contributors to this volume, and perhaps more broadly, of radical and hateful discourses as such, we can observe the following regularities and tendencies.

1. *Diversity and common ground.* Whether it is about far-right discourses or homophobic messages, they draw upon a common inventory of linguistic and rhetorical tools and strategies that enable the construction of *us* vs. *them* dichotomies. Time- and space-wise, the "vocabulary of motives" (Ivie 1974, 1980), "good terms" and "devil terms" (Burke 1969, 298–301), displays universality and consistency of use. Likewise, van Dijk's "ideological square" meant to present the "we" group favourably and the "they" group unfavourably (van Dijk 1998, 33), and similar topoi — collective symbols shared by members of a given society (Jäger 2001, 32) — seem to be applied universally in the construction of the Other in the messages of hate and radical discourses, irrespective of historical, geographical and cultural context. Mediating between the conscious and the subconscious to create a moral perspective on things, and providing access to the underlying social and cultural value system, metaphor, and the resulting frames, emerge as a central strategy. For example, as demonstrated by Musolff and Sotiris in this volume, *parasite* metaphors, with their dehumanizing potential, play an important role in the anti-immigration discourse, both in the UK and Greece. In a similar way, Kopytowska, Grabowski and Woźniak examine other dehumanizing metaphors as epistemic, axiological and emotional proximization triggers in the anti-refugee online discourse. Despite this common inventory, however, context, in all its dimensions, determines the choice of final strategies. Several contributors to this collection highlight the importance of the historical and socio-economic conditions. Szilágyi, for example, points to ideological differences between Western and Eastern far-right movements and variations in the construction of "external"and "internal" others. Kampf demonstrates the peculiarities of the Israeli discourse, while Hodges elucidates why the U.S. constitutes a fertile ground for the "paranoid style" in politics. And there is yet another contextual determinant, as Musolff demonstrates in his paper, namely the structural and functional features of a given genre. We can see, for instance, that in Musolff's study of *parasite* metaphors, only the blogosphere "appears to exhibit a relatively consistent xenophobic and

polemic bias". As shown by Kopytowska et al., also online comments following press articles about refugees abound with explicit manifestations of hate and verbal violence, further inflamed by other Internet users (to which phenomenon they refer to as "discursive spiral of hate").

2. *Denial and implicitness.* In the post World War II reality with people cognizant of the Holocaust, the Rwanda genocide and the Kosovo atrocities, the "never again" imperative is reflected in legal rulings and social-moral principles. Hence, in many countries, explicit manifestations of racist, anti-Semitic, anti-Muslim, and xenophobic attitudes are punishable by law and taboo. Similarly, Holocaust denial and Nazi glorification are banned "out of a desire to prevent a reemergence of fascism" (Oboler 2015). Faced with legal consequences and social disapproval, the authors of hateful messages opt for more implicit forms of expression in order to be able to refute allegations of committing a criminal offence. And languages offer several ways of linking explicit content with relevant aspects of background information so as to convey implicit meaning which can be strategically exploited (Verschueren 1999). Presuppositions, for example, can become a powerful tool for the organisation of social approval, combining "common sense, false conscience and other heterogenous socio-cultural or evaluative assumptions into a mixture which, conveyed with the complicity of norms of discourse, seems to evade critical analysis" (Sbisa 1999, 506). Since the propositions they express are not made explicit, it is difficult for people to identify and reject them (Fairclough 1989, 153). The authors of this collection demonstrate that the strategic avoidance of explicitness can have many forms and functions. In her chapter, Wodak shows how, despite legal sanctions, politicians of the far-right have managed to implement implicit discursive-pragmatic strategies to deny the Holocaust, even during parliamentary debates and official speeches. In a similar fashion, Leezenberg reflects on how it is possible to avoid language that indiscriminately targets particular ethnic or religious groups, and yet successfully perpetuates hatred and prejudice. Baker and Love, also point to the shift from explicit homophobia to more indirect and implicit forms of expressing anti-gay attitudes.
3. *Performativity of hate speech.* Although the cause and effect link between messages of hate and acts of violence has been widely debated (see Leezenberg, this issue for a comprehensive overview), with various opinions as to the scale of perlocutionary effects, history has presented us with numerous examples of the implementation of the call-for-action messages. In the words of Searle (1995, 1) "there are things that exist because we believe them to exist", as X becomes Y in context C. The authors of hateful messages construct such a context for their audiences, proximizing potential threats and legitimizing actions to eliminate them. Demonizing and dehumanizing others creates the

possibility, or even probability, of perpetrating atrocities against them, as many cases of genocide and ethnic violence have demonstrated. As argued by Leezenberg in this issue, "language use may help in performatively bringing about what it appears to be describing". Finally, it can become an inspiration for others who, taking on their "lone wolf" mission,[1] may make an attempt to eliminate the Other. Leezenberg, for example, points to the link between Breivik's terrorist act and the radical discourse of PVV's Islamophobes. But in addition to inciting violence, as the authors here demonstrate, hate speech can become "violence in action", as it polarizes and excludes, sometimes even in the name of liberty and equality.

4. *Mediatized hate speech and radicalism.* Back in the 1920s, Walter Lippmann made his now famous statement that the media are a major source of definitions and "pictures in our heads" and thus influence our reception of the external world that is "out of reach, out of sight, out of mind" (Lippmann 1922, 29). Since that time "mediatization" has become one of the key words in the literature discussing the functioning of contemporary media and their interface with society (Agha 2011; Bennet and Entman 2001; Ekström 2001; Schulz 2004). In this process, media transform society on both the collective and individual levels, firstly, by creating a common spatiotemporal, cognitive and axiological sphere of shared experience (Hepp 2013; Kopytowska 2013, 2014, 2015a, 2015b, 2015c; Krotz 2007, 2009), and, secondly, by substituting for social activities, which previously took place face-to-face (Schulz 2004). Since September 11, the mediatization of terrorism (and the subsequent war on terror) has played a key role in constructing the threat coming from the distant Other and justifying preventive actions. In their contribution to this issue, Evans and Schuller show how, as a result of this, the concept of terrorism has been transformed and eagerly used by the media in support of various political agendas.

With new technical solutions, new forms of expression and new public spheres, there is no doubt that mediatized hate speech reaches wider audiences and is likely to have more substantial effects. McLuhan's claim that "the medium is the message" gains particular relevance in this case. The near-instantaneous, dialogic, and decentralized nature and interactivity of cyberspace make it an ultra-attractive site for extended political debate, citizen participation, and a more direct and effective communication between political elites and the rest of the society (Coleman and Blumler 2010; Keren 2006, 2010; Street 2011). At the same time, however, the anonymity and global accessibility have transformed it into a tool for promoting

1. The term "lone wolf", currently used in the context of terrorist activities to refer to terrorists acting alone or in small groups, was coined in the 1990s by white supremacists, Curtis and Metzger.

messages of hate and radicalism, by enabling previously diverse and fragmented groups to connect and providing them with the sense of a community that shares values, ideologies and fears (Perry and Olsson 2009). The discursive integration of multimodal forms results in the unique intertextual and interactive character of online communication, with its potential to unite and divide, include and exclude members of the groups addressed (Kopytowska 2013). As demonstrated by Musolff in his study, blogs turned out to be a most effective vehicle for xenophobic messages. Leezenberg comments on the extreme right politician's extensive use of twitter to perpetuate messages of hate and ideas of anti-Islamism. Likewise, comments analyzed by Kopytowska et al., become a potentially fertile ground for the perpetuation of hateful anti-refugee messages. Last, but not least, what has to be mentioned and what resonates in several chapters in this collection is the observation that media offer hate speech perpetrators and radical discourse makers worldwide visibility, thereby increasing their impact. Whether it is through mainstream television and newspaper coverage, or through discussion in the social media, their words and the sentiments along with the underlying radical messages are thrown into public eye and inculcated into public consciousness.

This edited monograph comprises ten chapters exploring a variety of themes, devices and strategies, as well as socio-political consequences of what might be termed as discourses of hate and radicalism. Analysing their texts from discourse analytic, pragmatic, and stylistic perspectives and drawing on the insights from political studies, sociology and corpus linguistics, the authors provide a compelling overview of the discourses in question, along with their continuities and discontinuities across time and space.

The first contribution, by Ruth Wodak, focuses on "discourses about Holocaust denial" in Austria and the UK. Adopting a Discourse-Historical Approach to CDA, the author examines the strategies of "saying the unsayable", employed by the presidential candidate of the Austrian Freedom Party (FPÖ), Barbara Rosenkranz and the leader of the British National Party (BNP), Nick Griffin. Wodak demonstrates how these two politicians, known for their racist and anti-Semitic stance, skilfully exploit various strategies of provocation and calculated ambivalence to convey their radical messages, while, at the same time, denying their denial. Placing this discourse in its socio-historical context, including the legal status of hate speech, Wodak sheds light on the dynamics of "a globalised *politics of denial*".

Andreas Musolff's chapter discusses the power of metaphor in enacting an us versus them dichotomy. The author focuses on British debates about immigration and their use of dehumanizing and stigmatizing metaphors, specifically *parasite* metaphors. The way these metaphors conceptualize the socio-political relations between insiders and outsiders, clearly positions the latter as a threat to the national wellbeing in the form of the destruction of the host (bio-parasite scenario) or, at least, damage to the host (socio-parasite scenario). After examining texts from different media genres, viz. blogs, online fora and articles from mainstream newspapers, Musolff concludes that the aggressive potential (related to the bio-parasite scenario) of such metaphors is most effectively exploited and most visibly manifested in blogs.

In the chapter that follows, Kopytowska, Grabowski and Woźniak also set out to explore the dynamics of the online construction of the Other and the phenomenon of hate speech within cyberspace. Adopting the Media Proximization Approach (MPA), originally developed by Kopytowska (2013), the authors study keywords and word-co-occurrence patterns in online refugee-related discourse of *Niezalezna.pl* articles and comments that follow them (2015–2016) in order to establish their spatiotemporal, epistemic, axiological, and emotional proximizing potential and to identify the recurrent linguistic means, as well as the underlying cognitive and discursive mechanisms, of representing refugees as the Other to be rejected and annihilated. The results of the quantitative and qualitative analysis of questionnaire and corpus data, conducted to examine the public perception of online hate speech in Poland and discursive representation of refugees on the Internet respectively, shed new light on the interface between cyberhate and othering by identifying and describing the most salient exponents of hate speech attested in the Internet users' comments.

Forms of radical homophobia-related discourse are explored in the next contribution by Robbie Love and Paul Baker. Using corpus-based methods, the authors scrutinize British Parliamentary arguments against LGBT equality and the degree of their explicitness. The comparison of the argumentation employed in the debates over the equalization of the age of consent for anal sex (1998–2000) and over same-sex marriage (2013) demonstrates clearly that previously *explicit* homophobic speech has given way to more *implicit* or indirect forms of homophobia. The authors conclude that in the context of the battle against discriminatory language in public discourses, hate speech directed against minority groups inescapably assumes more subtle forms that are more difficult to detect, criticize or remedy. Hence, although, on the surface, discourses revolving around LGBT equality are harder to interpret as homophobic, they are still far from acknowledging equal rights for this group.

In his chapter, Adam Hodges examines yet another example of radical discourse, along with its ideological motivations and socio-political consequences. What comes under scrutiny is the American debate over gun rights and its leading voice, the National Rifle Association (NRA). The data, which includes speeches delivered by the NRA's Executive Vice-President, Wayne LaPierre, during the organization's annual membership meetings over the past decade, is analyzed within a CDA framework. This *discourse of Second Amendment absolutism*, as Hodges calls it, is highly polarized between the in-group of "freedom fighters" struggling to save the Second Amendment and the out-group, considered the "enemy of freedom." As an element of a "paranoid style", such a polarization, not only incites fear and hatred, but also precludes any form of reasonable debate over issues of public safety.

The next chapter is a reflection on the perlocutionary effects of hostile, or otherwise ofensive, discourse. Zohar Kampf explores here the meta-pragmatics of "hurt feelings" and the dynamics of *politically unacceptable acts* (PUA) with the intention to demonstrate how responses to insults can be strategically employed within two models of public discourse: the confrontational and the emotional type. His analysis, focusing on the instances in which various public figures stated their feelings towards insults in Israeli public discourse (1997–2012), shows that hurt feelings are frequently resorted to as a means for expressing one's discontent with or dissent from the disrespectful behavior of others.

Discourse on terror and media representation of terrorist acts are also prone to radical rhetoric and relapse into "us versus them" hostility. Matthew Evans and Simone Schuller adopt a critical stylistics approach to analyze the way in which the British press used the term "terrorism" in the coverage of the Woolwich attack in 2013. Discussing the media construction of this event as a terrorist act against the background of academic literature on the phenomenon itself and an overview of its definitions, the authors conclude that journalists are far too willing to adopt the terrorist frame, prevalent in the reporting on this particular event. In the chapters analyzed, categorical assertions used to make connections to previous Islamic terrorist attacks and speculations about links to al-Qaeda helped to position the attack within the familiar frame of Islamic terrorism, bringing forth a potential for similar inferences concerning the causes, solutions, and moral judgements about the perpetrators.

In the next chapter, the discussion on the European far-right parties is situated in a transnational context, since, as the author argues, such a perspective can provide important insights into both common elements and ideological diversity of Eastern and Western radicalism. Anna Szilágyi puts under scrutiny the representation of China as an emerging political and economic power in the discourse of the British National Party (BNP) and the Hungarian Jobbik party in the early 2010s. In order to compare and contrast the "othering" strategies of these two far-right parties, she applies a CDA framework to study naming and reference, argumentation schemes as well as metaphors and framing. This ideologically embedded and historically determined representation of the "external other" has, as the study shows, important implications for the internal identity construction and legitimization of state policies.

Remaining within the theme of extremist politics, Panagiotis Sotiris's chapter explores the ideology and discourse of Golden Dawn in Greece. Situating them within their socio-economic and historical context and adopting a Marxist orientation inspired by Gramsci and Althusser along with principles of Critical Discourse Analysis, Sotiris examines major policy documents together with chapters from Golden Dawn's websites on subjects such as globalization, the Greek crisis, racism, and the role of women in society. The analysis of the main themes and discursive strategies reflecting and constituting racism, anti-Semitism, authoritarianism, admiration of leadership, and anti-parliamentarism leads him to the conclusion that the discourse of Golden Dawn displays a strong allegiance to fascist ideology, but, at the same time, involves elements of the anti-austerity discourse in Greece.

The problem of denial and reversal of the victim-perpetrator roles also surfaces in Michiel Leezenberg's chapter, where the lexical and discursive strategies of the Dutch Freedom Party (PVV), known for its populist and Islamophobic stance, are examined. Using Speech Act Theory and Butler's ideas about the performativity of hate speech, the author substantiates the claim that the PVV leader Geert Wilders's language is not only a discourse *about* violence, but is itself a discourse *of* violence. In his use of war rhetoric and vocabulary denoting physical violence, the politician concerned not only fabricates justifications for state violence against Muslims, but also constructs a dividing line between Muslims and non-Muslims, which acts as a frontier between civilisation and savagery. Importantly, as Leezenberg points out, Wilders's exclusionary practices are preformed in the name of normative ideals such as liberty and equality.

References

Agha, Asif. 2011. "Meet Mediatization." *Language & Communication* 31: 163–170. doi: 10.1016/j.langcom.2011.03.006

Bennett, Lance, and Robert Entman. 2001. *Mediated Politics: Communication in the Future of Democracy*. Cambridge: Cambridge University Press. doi:10.1017/CBO9780511613852

Boromisza-Habashi, David. 2011. "Dismantling the Antiracist "Hate Speech" *Agenda in Hungary: An Ethno-rhetorical Analysis*." *Text & Talk* 31(1): 1–19.

Boromisza-Habashi, David. 2013. Speaking Hatefully. Culture, Communication, and Political Action in Hungary. University Park: The Pennsylvania State University Press.

Bostdorff, Denis M. 2004. "The Internet Rhetoric of the Ku Klux Klan: A Case Study in Web Site Construction of Whiteness Ideology." *The Howard Journal of Communications* 2: 189–208.

Brown, Christopher. 2009. "WWW.HATE.COM: White Supremacist Discourse on the Internet and the Community Building Run Amok." *Communication Studies* 55: 340–361.

Burke, Kenneth. 1969. *A Rhetoric of Motives*. Berkeley: University of California Press.

Coleman, Stephen, and Jay Blumler. 2009. *The Internet and Democratic Citizenship: Theory, Practice and Policy*. Cambridge: Cambridge University Press. doi: 10.1017/CBO9780511818271

Daniels, Jessie. 1997. *White Lies: Race, Class, Gender, and Sexuality in White Supremacist Discourse*. New York: Routledge.
Duffy, Margaret E. 2003. "Web of Hate: A Fantasy Theme Analysis of the Rhetorical Vision of Hate Groups Online." *Journal of Communication Inquiry* 27: 291–312. doi: 10.1177/0196859903252850
Ekström, Mats. 2001. "Politicians Interviewed on Television News." *Discourse and Society* 12: 563–584. doi: 10.1177/0957926501012005001
Fairclough, Norman. 1989. *Language and Power*. London: Longman.
Fairclough, Norman, and Ruth Wodak. 1997. "Critical Discourse Analysis." In *Discourse Studies. A Multidisciplinary Introduction. Discourse as Social Interaction*, edited by Teun A. van Dijk, 258–284. London: Sage Publications.
Foucault, Michael. 1985. *The Archaeology of Knowledge*. London: Tavistock. doi: 10.1177/053901847000900108
Habermas, Jürgen.1989. *The Structural Transformation of the Public Sphere: An Inquiry into a Category of Bourgeois Society*. Cambridge: MIT Press.
Harvey, Andy. 2012. "Regulating Homophobic Hate Speech: Back to Basics about Language and Politics?" *Sexualities* 15(2): 191–206. doi: 10.1177/1363460712436539
Hepp, Andreas. 2013. *Cultures of Mediatization*. Cambridge: Polity Press.
Hofstadter, Richard. 2008[1965]. *The Paranoid Style in American Politics*. New York: Vintage Books.
Ivie, Robert. 1974. "Presidential Motives for War." *Quarterly Journal of Speech* 60: 337–45. doi: 10.1080/00335637409383241
Ivie, Robert. 1980. "Images of Savagery in American Justifications of War." *Communications Monographs* 47: 279–291. doi: 10.1080/03637758009376037
Jäger, Siegfried. 2001. "Discourse and Knowledge: Theoretical and Methodological Aspects of Critical Discourse and Dispositive Analysis." In *Methods of Critical Discourse Analysis*, edited by Ruth Wodak, and Michael Meyer, 32–62. London: Sage Publications.
Keren, Michael. 2006. *Blogosphere: The New Political Arena*. Toronto: Lexington Books.
Keren, Michael. 2010. "Blogging and Mass Politics." *Biography* 33: 110–126. doi: 10.1353/bio.0.0148
Kienpointner, Manfred. 2006. "Racist Manipulation within Austrian, German, Dutch, French and Italian Rightwing Populism." In *Manipulation and Ideologies in the Twentieth Century: Discourse, Language, Mind*, edited by Louis de Saussure, and Peter Schulz, 213–36. Amsterdam: John Benjamins. doi: 10.1075/dapsac.17.11kie
Kopytowska, Monika. 2013. "Blogging as the Mediatization of Politics and a New Form of Social Interaction." In *Analyzing Genres in Political Communication*, edited by Piotr Cap, and Urszula Okulska, 379–421. Amsterdam: Benjamins. doi: 10.1075/dapsac.50.15kop
Kopytowska, Monika. 2014. "Pictures in Our Heads: Crisis, Conflict, and Drama." In *Why Discourse Matters: Negotiating Identity in the Mediatized World*, edited by Yusuf Kalyango, and Monika Kopytowska, 89–109. New York: Peter Lang.
Kopytowska, Monika. 2015a. "Ideology of 'here and now'. Mediating distance in television news". *Critical Discourse Studies* 12(3): 347–365. doi: 10.1080/17405904.2015.1013485
Kopytowska, Monika. 2015b. "Covering conflict: between universality and cultural specificity in news discourse genre and journalistic style". *International Review of Pragmatics* 7: 308–339.
Kopytowska, Monika. 2015c. "Mediating identity, ideology and values in the public sphere: towards a new model of (constructed) social reality". *Lodz Papers in Pragmatics* 11(2): 133–156.

Krotz, Friedrich. 2007. "The Meta-process of Mediatization as a Conceptual Frame." *Global Media and Communication* 3: 256–260. doi:10.1177/17427665070030030103
Krotz, Friedrich. 2009. "Mediatization: A Concept with which to Grasp Media and Societal Change." In *Mediatization: Concept, Changes, Consequences*, edited by Knut Lundby, 21–40. New York: Peter Lang.
Leap, William L. 2011. "Introducing the Special Issue." *Gender and Language* 4(2): 179–185.
Lee, Elissa, and Laura Leets. 2002. "Persuasive Story by Hate Groups Online." *American Behavioral Scientist* 45: 927–957. doi:10.1177/0002764202045006003
Lippmann, Walter. 1922. *Public Opinion*. New York, NY: Harcourt, Brace and Co. doi: 10.2307/2263833
Oboler, Andre. 2015. *Je Suis Humain: Responsible Free Speech in the Shadow of the Charlie Hebdo Murders*. Online Hate Prevention Institute. Available at: http://ohpi.org.au/jesuishumain/#report. [Accessed 20 February 2015].
Panizza, Francisco. 2005. "Unarmed Utopia Revisited: The Resurgence of Left-of-centre Politics in Latin America." *Political Studies* 53(4): 716–734. doi:10.1111/j.1467-9248.2005.00553.x
Perry, Barbara. 2001. *In the Name of Hate: Understanding Hate Crimes*. Routledge: New York
Perry, Barbara, and Patrick Olsson. 2009. "Cyberhate: The Globalization of Hate." *Information and Communications Technology Law*. 18(2): 185–199. doi:10.1080/13600830902814984
Reisigl, Martin and Ruth Wodak. 2001. *Discourse and Discrimination*. London: Routledge.
Sbisa, Marina. 1999. "Ideology and Persuasive Presuppositions". In *Language and Ideology: Selected Chapters from the 6th International Pragmatics Conference, vol. 1*, edited by Jef Verschueren, 492–509. Antwerp: International Pragmatics Association.
Schafer, Joseph A. 2002. "Spinning the Web of Hate: Web-based Propagation by Extremist Organization." *Journal of Criminal Justice and Popular Culture* 9: 69–88.
Schulz, Winfried. 2004. "Reconstructing Mediatization as an Analytical Concept." *European Journal of Communication* 19: 87–101. doi:10.1177/0267323104040696
Searle, John. 1995. *The Construction of Social Reality*. London: Penguin Books.
Searle, John. 2010. *Making the Social World: The Structure of Human Civilization*. Oxford: Oxford University Press.
Street, John. 2011. *Mass Media, Politics & Democracy* (2 edn.). Basingstoke: Pallgrave Macmillan.
Taggart, Paul. 1995. "New Populist Parties in Western Europe." *West European Politics* 18(1): 34–51. doi:10.1080/01402389508425056
Van Dijk, Teun A. 1987. *Mediating Racism. The Role of the Media in the Reproduction of Racism*. In *Language, Power and Ideology*, edited by Ruth Wodak, 199–226. Amsterdam: Benjamins. doi:10.1075/ct.7.15dij
Van Dijk, Teun A. 1991. *Racism and the Press*. London / New York: Routledge.
Van Dijk, Teun A. 1993. *Elite Discourse and Racism*. Newbury Park, CA, USA: Sage Publications.
Van Dijk, Teun A. 1998. *Ideology*. London: Sage Publications Ltd.
Vasu, Reddy. 2002. "Perverts and Sodomites: Homophobia as Hate Speech in Africa." *Southern African Linguistics & Applied Language Studies* 20(3): 163–175. doi: 10.2989/16073610209486308
Verschueren, Jef. 1999. *Understanding Pragmatics*. London: Arnold.
Waltman, Michael, and John Haas. 2011. *The Communication of Hate*. New York: Peter Lang.
Whillock, Rita K. 1995. "The Use of Hate as a Stratagem for Achieving Political and Social Goals." In *Hate Speech*, edited by Rita Kirk Whillock, and David Slayden, 28–54. Thousand Oaks, CA: Sage.

Williamson, Lisa, and Eric Pierson. 2003. "The Rhetoric of Hate on the Internet: Hateporn's Challenge to Modern Media Ethics." *Journal of Mass Media Ethics* 18: 250–267. doi: 10.1080/08900523.2003.9679667
Wodak, Ruth and John Richardson. eds. 2013. *Analysing Fascist Discourse. European Fascism in Talk and Text.* New York: Routledge.

Saying the unsayable

Denying the Holocaust in media debates in Austria and the UK

Ruth Wodak
Lancaster University

After 1945 and the end of WWII, denying the Holocaust became an explicit taboo in most European countries. More specifically, in Austria, denying the Holocaust in public implies legal consequences: the so-called *Verbotsgesetz* persecutes any public utterances which even insinuate National Socialist ideology (utterances, symbols, songs, images) and the Holocaust denial. Naturally, it remains difficult for the courts to substantiate any accusations and to prove that somebody has actually uttered Holocaust denial if the meanings are only implied, inferred, or alluded to. Thus, in spite of such explicit sanctions, politicians of the far-right have found many coded and implicit discursive-pragmatic practices and devices of denying the Holocaust, even during parliamentary debates and official speeches. In this chapter, I compare the "discourses about Holocaust denial" in Austria and the UK, in two case studies: the first one relates to the controversy about some utterances of Barbara Rosenkranz who stood as candidate of the Austrian Freedom Party (FPÖ) for election to Austrian Presidency in April 2010. Secondly, I focus on the debates triggered by Nick Griffin from the British extreme right party BNP, in and after his appearance in the prominent BBC 1 weekly show *Question Time*, in 2009. I apply the Discourse Historical Approach in CDA for the detailed analysis of such recurring debates and foreground the patterns of a globalised *politics of denial*.

Keywords: hate speech, Holocaust denial, far right, implicitness, Discourse Historical Approach, topos, right-wing populist rhetoric, taboo, antisemitism

DOI 10.1075/bct.93.01wod

1. Hate speech and Holocaust denial[1]

1.1 Defining hate speech

In a recent book, *Speaking Hatefully* (2013), the anthropologist David Boromisza-Habashi defines hate speech as utterances "directed against groups of people and arous[ing] fear in them in a strategic and conscious manner" (Boromisza-Habashi 2013, 23). Thus, the expression of hatred per se does not qualify as hate speech. Importantly, communicative acts have to be performed intentionally and strategically. Moreover, the author provides a useful typology which includes: a) the *type of speaker* (usually from a specific political party); b) the relative *social influence of the speaker and target* (an aggressive attack is performed in the public sphere and disseminated); c) the *variety of communicative acts* which can be interpreted and classified as hate speech (usually associated with antisemitic, racist and discriminatory beliefs and attitudes, threatening others with serious harm); d) *insinuations and references to historical patterns and events* (usually, historical events are redefined from a revisionist perspective); and finally e) existing *legal (and moral) sanctions* against the producers of hate speech (Boromisza-Habashi 2013, 25).[2] This typology enables classifying the range of expressions of hate speech for comparative purposes.

The definition above draws on Article 4 of the *International Convention on the Elimination of all Forms of Racial Discrimination* (ICERD), which condemns all propaganda and organizations that attempt to justify or legitimize discrimination or which are based on the idea of a so-called "racial supremacy". The ICERD obliges parties, "with due regard to the principles embodied in the Universal Declaration of Human Rights", to adopt "immediate and positive measures" to eradicate these forms of incitement and discrimination. Moreover, it obliges parties to *criminalize hate speech, hate crimes and the financing of racist activities*, and to prohibit and criminalize membership of organizations that "promote and incite" racial discrimination.

1. In this chapter, I also draw on research about Holocaust denial in Austria, partly conducted together with Jakob Engel, published elsewhere in much greater detail and with a different focus (Engel and Wodak 2013, Wodak 2015). Ana Tominc transcribed the BBC *Question Time* episode; Sten Hansson helped in researching the media reactions to this episode. I also thank Gerard Hearne for editing my English. Of course, I am solely responsible for the final version.

2. See, for example, International Convention on the Elimination of all Forms of Racial Discrimination (ICERD), a United Nations Convention, first signed on 21 December 1965. As of 2013, it has 87 signatories and 176 parties http://www.ohchr.org/EN/ProfessionalInterest/Pages/CERD.aspx (accessed 28 February 2014).

Obviously, in line with various constitutional rights which guarantee "free speech", a number of countries and parties have expressed reservations about this chapter, arguing that such a regulation would infringe on freedoms of speech, association or assembly. Accordingly, the ICERD has frequently and repeatedly criticized parties for failing to abide by it and views the provisions as necessary to prevent organised racial violence or the "political exploitation of ethnic difference" (General Recommendation, No 15, § 1).[3]

From a linguistic, argumentative and pragmatic-rhetorical point of view, it becomes apparent that no linguistic indicators are explicitly presented in the various international and national conventions and laws which cover detecting and substantiating allegations of hate speech occurrences. Indeed, this is impossible, as languages offer different resources to realise racist, antisemitic and xenophobic prejudices which are context-dependent and frequently uttered indirectly. Moreover, explicit manifestations of racist and antisemitic attitudes are taboo in many countries post World War Two and the Holocaust, after the huge numbers of war crimes and mass murders committed and huge levels of institutional racism and discrimination implemented (Delanty et al. 2011; Engel and Wodak 2009, 2013; Heer et al. 2008; Judt 2007; Wodak 2007; Wodak and Richardson 2013). But hate speech continues to exist both globally and locally, and it is still functionalised for political ends.[4] Hate speech can but does not necessarily have to lead to violent and physical acts as, inter alia, the socio-psychologist Gordon Allport evidenced in his seminal book *The Nature of Prejudice* (1979). Thus, it seems both timely and relevant to focus on the range of linguistic, pragmatic and rhetorical devices and argumentation schemes employed in different cultural and sociopolitical contexts which convey such agonistic and exclusionary meanings.

1.2 Holocaust denial

Officially, Holocaust denial is defined as the claim that the mainstream historical accounts of the Holocaust are either highly exaggerated or wrong, whereas historians, experts and witnesses almost universally regard Holocaust denial as untrue

3. See the overview about different signatories and salient cases as well as recommendations in http://en.wikipedia.org/wiki/Convention_on_the_Elimination_of_All_Forms_of_Racial_Discrimination (accessed 2 January 2014); Regulation 2000/43/EG of the European Commission, 29 June 2000 http://ec.europa.eu/justice/discrimination/files/com_2014_2_en.pdf (accessed 28 February 2014).

4. See, for example, the recent polarised debate triggered by the *Daily Mail* in the UK, directed against the leader of the opposition Labour Party (and his father, Ralph Miliband) (Stögner and Wodak 2014, 2016); or the hate crimes and hate speech enacted almost daily by the Neo-Nazi party *Golden Dawn* in Greece (Angouri and Wodak 2014).

and as obvious expression of antisemitic hate speech. Usually, Holocaust deniers emphasise that they do not deny per se that Jews, Roma, disabled people, homosexuals and political opponents were persecuted under the Nazi regime; they also usually do not deny that Jews were deprived of civil rights or that Jewish ghettos or concentration camps existed. And they normally admit that Jews died for a great number of reasons. But they *do* deny that there were mass murders; and they provide many fallacious arguments concerning the numbers of victims and the specific means of death, particularly related to the gas chambers and crematoria. Holocaust denials are frequently disguised as legitimate challenges to hegemonic historical theories and established facts; moreover, typically, such utterances pertain to freedom of opinion and freedom of speech, as realised in naive rhetorical questions, such as "Why cannot one re/investigate the gas chambers — were they really built in a way that so many people could have been killed?" (See Engel and Wodak 2013).

At this point, it is important to provide some brief information related to various dimensions of Freedom of Speech: Freedom of Speech is covered in Article 19 of the *Universal Declaration of Human Rights*, adopted in 1948: "Everyone has the right to freedom of opinion and expression; this right includes freedom to hold opinions without interference and to seek, receive and impart information and ideas through any media and regardless of frontiers."[5] The right to freedom of speech, however, is also subject to limitations, as with libel, slander, obscenity, sedition (including, for example, inciting ethnic hatred), copyright violation, revelation of information that is classified or otherwise. For example, Freedom of Speech may be legally curtailed where it is found to cause religious or racial offence, such as by the Racial and Religious Hatred Act 2006 in the United Kingdom.[6]

In many countries, Holocaust denial is regarded as a criminal offence — for example in Austria, France, Germany, Israel, Belgium, Poland, Lithuania, and Switzerland — and punishable by fines and/or jail sentences. Because of such pending sanctions, denials of the Holocaust, an extreme case of hate speech, are uttered indirectly in order to be able to refute allegations and accusations of committing a criminal offence.[7] This is why a critical discourse-analytic perspective

5. http://www.un.org/en/documents/udhr/ (accessed 5 January 2014).

6. http://en.wikipedia.org/wiki/Racial_and_Religious_Hatred_Act_2006 mostly concerned with expressions of religious hatred.

7. See recent incidents of Holocaust denial: in Hungary, 27 May 2013, when a MP of the extreme right-wing Jobbik Party claimed that the Auschwitz Death Camp museum "may not reflect real facts" (http://www.eurojewcong.org/hungary/9492-jobbik-mp-in-holocaust-denial.html, accessed 16 February 2014); or the huge scandal in Poland, following publication of the extreme right-wing Polish historian Dariusz Ratajczak's book, "*Dangerous themes*", in which he claims, inter alia, that the gas Zyklon B was only used for disinfection in the concentration camps, and

is salient, as it facilitates deconstructing "the unsayable" when it occurs in official settings, in the media, or on front stage in politics.

The aim of the following is to compare two such incidents systematically and thoroughly, as case studies, in the public media and political spheres: in Austria, where Holocaust denial is criminalized with a law that is justified by the National Socialist past of many Austrian perpetrators during World War Two; and in the UK, where such criminalization does not exist in the same way and where Freedom of Speech is regarded very highly and institutionalised in a different way.

I will first briefly summarise the theoretical and methodological approach employed in this chapter: the Discourse Historical Approach (DHA). Then, I will provide two recent examples of "saying the unsayable": the first occurred during the last election campaign for the Austrian presidency in spring 2010 and refers to specific utterances made by the presidential candidate of the Austrian Freedom Party (FPÖ), Barbara Rosenkranz. The second occurred during a discussion on the prominent BBC 1 TV programme "*Question Time*", in the UK, in October 2009, when the leader of the British National Party (BNP), Nick Griffin, was invited to be a discussant on the panel, the first time a member of the BNP had ever officially been invited to participate. Both parties, FPÖ and BNP, are well-known for their well-established racist and antisemitic beliefs which continue to appear in various contexts in more or less implicit or explicit ways.[8]

The two incidents are quite similar as the main protagonists, Rosenkranz and Griffin, breached taboos by insinuating Holocaust denial during TV appearances. However, their status differs significantly. In the Austrian case, we are dealing with an official candidate for President of the Republic. In the British case, the scandal was already initiated by inviting Nick Griffin onto a prominent BBC TV show, which — as alleged by many politicians and journalists alike — constitutes

other similar lies. He was suspended from teaching in 1999. Ratajczak was supported by some members of the far-right League of the Polish Families Party. Many utterances by Jean-Marie Le Pen, since 1978, were classified as Holocaust denial and widely accepted within the extreme-rightwing party *Front National* in France (http://mondediplo.com/1998/05/08igou). Marine Le Pen, however, has recently strategically distanced herself, in respect to antisemitic and racist hate speech, from her father's usage in order to open the party up to a bigger electorate. Thus, one can conclude that, even nowadays, antisemitism and Holocaust denial are part and parcel of extreme and populist right-wing rhetoric across Europe (Wodak, KhosraviNik and Mral 2013; Wodak and Richardson 2013; Wodak 2015).

8. There exists a vast amount of research on antisemitism in Austria and in the UK, both historically and also referring to present-day incidents. Due to space limitations, it is impossible to cover the range of antisemitic manifestations in this chapter. I refer readers to Wodak et al. (1990), Billig (1978), Richardson and Wodak (2009a, b) and Stögner and Wodak (2014; forthcoming).

transcending a *cordon sanitaire,* i.e. never to allow space to members of the BNP on such programmes. Analysing the unfolding interactions and interdependencies between politics and media is thus, in both cases, at the centre of this chapter, though in different historical, media, legal and political contexts. In the conclusion, I discuss what such media events might imply for pluralistic Western democracies.

2. The Discourse Historical Approach (DHA)

The DHA focuses, first, on how audio, spoken, visual and/or written *texts,* as they relate to structured knowledge (*discourses*), adhere to specific *genres* and how they must be viewed in terms of their situatedness. That is, texts cannot be fully understood without considering different layers of context, following a *four-level model* of context, such as the historical context of the Austrian Freedom Party (FPÖ) or the British National Party (BNP) (*socio-historical context*), the debates which dominated the Austrian/ British public spheres after the incidents (*current context),* a *text-internal co-text* as well as *intertextual and interdiscursive relations* (Reisigl and Wodak 2001, 40f). The former two are of particular significance as they allow deconstructing *interdiscursive* and *intertextual* relations, presuppositions, implicatures and insinuations in text and talk, and following a debate, as arguments, topics and opinions are recontextualised from and by the media in newspaper articles, interviews and so forth. Interdiscursivity / intertextuality — established via explicit or implicit references — denote the linkage between discourses and texts across time and space. If text elements are taken out of their original context (de-contextualisation) and inserted into another one (recontextualisation), a similar process occurs which causes the element (partly) to acquire new meaning(s) (Wodak 2011a, b).

The DHA views *discourse* as "context-dependent semiotic practices", as well as "socially constituted and socially constitutive", "related to a macro-topic" and pluri-perspective, i.e. linked to argumentation (Reisigl and Wodak 2009, 89). Taking such a perspective, the media incidents analyzed below can be understood as texts which draw on existing opinions and collective memories about Austrian or British history, while also *mobilising* and *radicalising* these discourses. Positive self- and negative other-presentation is realised via *discursive strategies* (Reisigl and Wodak 2001, 45–90). Here, I primarily focus on *nomination* (how events/ objects/ persons are referred to) and *predication* (what characteristics are attributed to them). Finally, *argumentation strategies* concern the justification and legitimation of specific claims, in our case related to the Holocaust. Within the DHA (Reisigl and Wodak 2001, 74f), the notion of *topos* designates both formal and content-related "conclusion rule[s] that connect[s] the argument or arguments with the conclusion, the claim". Here, the DHA draws on Wengeler's (2003) and Kienpointner's (1996) context-specific notion of *topos*, defined as semiotically manifested "figures of thought in approaching a political issue" (Wengeler 2003, 67). Kienpointner (quoted in Wengeler 2003, 65) similarly, views *topoi* "as being typical for arguments by speakers of a speech-community or at least bigger groups of not especially trained speakers". These conclusion rules are either sound or fallacious, enabling or preventing the *more or less* undistorted exchange of standpoints through particular ways of representing events, objects or persons (for this normative distinction, see: Forchtner 2011; Forchtner and Tominc 2012; Wodak and Forchtner 2014).

In sum, the DHA focuses on ways in which power-dependent semiotic means are used to construct positive self- and negative other-presentations (US and THEM, in our case in this chapter, the pro and contra about US and the Jews). This also captures the ability to select specific events in the flow of a narrative as well as increased opportunities to convey messages by opening up space for "*calculated ambivalence*" (Engel and Wodak 2009, 2013). The latter is defined as a phenomenon whereby one utterance carries at least two more-or-less contradictory meanings, oriented towards at least two different audiences. This not only increases the audience, but also enables the speaker / writer to deny any responsibility: after all, "it wasn't meant that way". Finally, the power of discourse creates regimes of quasi "normality", i.e. what is deemed "normal", e.g. with regard to the political messages circulating during heated debates.

At this point, it is important to emphasize that "antisemitic language behaviour" may, though not necessarily, imply explicitly held and/or articulated hostility towards Jews, and it certainly does imply the presence of prejudicial assumptions about the *Jews as a group* (see Boromisza-Habashi's typology above). For example, the slogan "Kill Jews" painted on the Sigmund Freud monument in Vienna (1988) clearly contains an explicit, though anonymous, imperative call for the most hostile of actions against Jews. On the other hand, a Jewish joke, which can have various meanings depending on such dimensions as the setting, the participants and the function of the utterance, also forms part of what we term "antisemitic language behaviour", but only in circumstances where the joke expresses anti-Jewish prejudices. Thus, analysing the *context of an utterance* is indispensable in determining whether that utterance expresses antisemitic prejudice or not. What antisemitic content is expressed depends, among other things, on the setting (public, private or media), the formality of the situation, the participants, the topic, and the presence or absence of Jews. Antisemitic language behaviour, moreover, covers a wide range of speech acts, from explicit remarks or appeals for action to mere allusions. Antisemitic language behaviour includes all levels of language, from text or discourse to the individual word, or even sounds, e.g. the Yiddish intonation of certain words or phrases.

Ideally, the systematic in-depth linguistic analysis of hate speech and antisemitic utterances of Holocaust denial should draw on, inter alia:

- Historical analysis of antisemitism and its verbal expressions (i.e. "coded language");
- Socio-cognitive analysis of collective memories and frames guiding the acquisition of specific knowledge so as to be able to understand "coded language";
- Socio-political analysis of ongoing debates, and political parties taking part in them; these two dimensions form the broad context;
- Genre theory; the functions of TV interviews and TV discussions (persuasive strategies; positive self-presentation/ negative other-presentation; populist rhetoric, etc.);
- The setting, speakers, etc. of concrete utterances; this is the narrow context;
- The co-text of each utterance;
- And finally, verbal expressions have to be analysed in terms of linguistic pragmatic / grammatical approaches (presuppositions, insinuations, implications, etc. as characteristics of specific "coded antisemitism").

Due to space restrictions, I will of necessity have to neglect some of these dimensions in my analysis below (for more details see Wodak 2007, 2011b, 2015; Engel and Wodak 2013).

3. The Austrian case[9]

3.1 The *Verbotsgesetz*

Central to the case being examined in this chapter is the complex history of Austrian de-nazification, and particularly the *Verbotsgesetz*, a body of post-war legislation in Austria known simply as "the prohibition law", which effectively prohibits the glorification, mystification or denial of National Socialist crimes. De-nazification measures were passed in the immediate aftermath of World War Two, on 8 May 1945, and were reformulated in 1947. The laws forbid, among other things, any National Socialism-related activity. De-nazification measures also required the registration of all NSDAP, SS and SA members, the payment of fines, and participation in reconstruction works projects. Moreover, former Nazis were

9. More details about this and other cases can be found in: Engel and Wodak (2009, 2013), Wodak and Reisigl (2002), Wodak et al. (1990).

barred from public sector employment as well as from high-level private sector positions. However, in 1957, following an amnesty, many of the more punitive measures were lifted.

As already mentioned above, in many other European countries, there have been significant controversies around the *Verbotsgesetz*, most notably in its relationship to freedom of speech.[10] The European Court of Human Rights has, however, consistently rejected any claims against the law, arguing that it "can be justified as necessary in a democratic society in the interest of national security and territorial integrity as well as for the prevention of crime".[11]

The most relevant part of the *Verbotsgesetz*, §3, has been repeatedly amended since 1945 — most recently in 1992 — and it states that "even outside of these organisations, no one may be active for the NSDAP or its aims in any form". While § 3a to §3f focus primarily on the re-establishment of organisations that disseminate National Socialist propaganda, or the dissemination of such materials in print or similar means, §3g states that:

> Anyone who becomes active in the National Socialist sense in ways other than those specified in §§3a-3f — unless the offence carries a harsher sentence under other legislation — is punishable with imprisonment of one to ten years, and in case the offender is of exceptional danger of up to 20 years.

§3h of the *Verbotsgesetz*, which became most relevant in the case studies examined, includes the following passage:

> Prosecution according to §3g also applies to anyone who seeks to deny, flagrantly downplay [*gröblich verharmlost*], glorify or justify the National Socialist genocide or other National Socialist crimes against humanity in print material, a broadcast or other medium, or in any other form accessible to many people.

§3h, specifically, punishes public denial of the Holocaust, or other extreme revisionist views pertaining to National Socialist crimes.[12] The emphasis on the

---

10. See, for example, Lipstadt (1993) or Kahn (2005) for an overview of comparative legislation and controversies pertaining to Holocaust denial. Particularly, Lipstadt's *Denying the Holocaust* is notable not only for its thorough treatment of the subject, but also for the suit filed by David Irving against Deborah Lipstadt and her publisher, Penguin Books, in which he alleged that Lipstadt had libeled him in her book. Irving lost the case and in the trial judge's 333-pages-long opinion in favour of the defendant, he detailed Irving's systematic distortion of the historical record of World War Two.

11. Cited at: http://www.menschenrechte.ac.at/orgi/98_5/Nachtmann.pdf.

12. Benz (1995) defines revisionism in the narrow sense as "the denial of the proven historical fact that in the course of the Second World War millions of European Jews were murdered in gas chambers".

word "flagrant" (*gröblich*) has in the past frequently allowed for the dismissal of Holocaust denial lawsuits, particularly against prominent individuals, since while the downplaying or mitigation of Nazi crimes could be established, these were found to not be flagrant (Wodak 2007).

In recent years, there has been an increase in the number of trials for violations of the *Verbotsgesetz*, with 153 in 2010 (as opposed to 104 in 2009 and 17 in 2008).[13] Despite this, the number of convictions has remained relatively constant over the past two years, implying that a growing number of lawsuits have been dismissed or resulted in acquittal.

3.2 The "Rosenkranz affair"

On 28 February 2010, the leader of the Austrian Freedom Party (FPÖ), HC Strache, announced publicly that the FPÖ would nominate Barbara Rosenkranz as its presidential candidate[14] — even before the federal executive board had actually approved her. The rationale behind nominating a national-conservative candidate was, according to Strache, to thematise the so-called "unresolved question of immigration" ("*ungelöste Zuwanderungsfrage*").[15]

Barbara Rosenkranz was elected to the Parliament of Lower Austria in 1993; she also became deputy chair of the FPÖ in the state of Lower Austria in 1996, and chaired her party group from 2000 onwards. The mother of ten had studied history and philosophy, was secretary general of the state party FPÖ from 1998 to 1999, and in 2003 was elected chair of the FPÖ. In the 2008 election, she was her party's top candidate in Lower Austria, where she now serves as Minister of Construction Law and Animal Protection of the State of Lower Austria. Between 2002 and 2008, she was a member of the Austrian Parliament. In 2007, Rosenkranz was awarded the *Decoration of Honour for Services to the Republic of Austria* (*Ehrenzeichen für Verdienste um die Republik Österreich*).[16]

13. Considerable international attention was attracted by the conviction of the (now released) British Holocaust denier David Irving, who was sentenced to three years of prison in Austria on 21 February 2006 (the verdict was confirmed on 4 September 2006). Controversies around Irving's conviction led to a number of editorials in leading British and Austrian conservative newspapers objecting to the law for its limitations on the freedom of speech and its allegedly ineffective preventative effect.

14. [14]See: http://www.krone.at/Oesterreich/Strache_schickt_Rosenkranz_ins_Rennen_um_Hofburg-Seite_an_Seite-Story-187536.

15. See: http://derstandard.at/1267131932485/Rosenkranz-wird-fuer-FPOe-kandidieren.

16. Incidentally, on 13 November 2003, the European Court of Human Rights in Strasbourg decided that the journalist Hans-Henning Scharsach (*News*) was found to not be in contraven-

Her husband, Horst Rosenkranz, is a publisher of extreme-right books and pamphlets and a former member of the now banned right-wing extremist *National Democratic Party* (NDP). She herself is the author of a book that criticises feminism and efforts promoting gender mainstreaming.[17] She opposes civil partnerships for homosexual couples because — she argues — the legal definition of marriage also addresses the assumed intention to produce and raise children.[18]

Moreover, Rosenkranz has predominantly associated questions of migration policy with criminality. During the 2008 election campaign for the Lower Austria provincial legislature, she spoke of "unbridled mass immigration" and "imported criminality", and demanded a moratorium on naturalisation (*ZurZeit*, "Die Einbürgerung stoppen", February 2008). During her candidacy for Austrian President, one of the main issues she raised was the question of "to what extent immigration into the country should be possible" and whether "the Austrians even want that" (*Die Presse*, 2.3. 2010).

Rosenkranz finally became widely known in the course of her candidacy for the Austrian presidential election in 2010. She also received significant support from the far right.[19] Most importantly, however, on 1 March 2010, Hans Dichand, owner and editor-in-chief of the tabloid *Neue Kronen Zeitung*, announced in his paper, under his pseudonym CATO (page 3), his pro-Rosenkranz campaign, while stressing primarily her "motherhood". Hence, it seems that being a good mother to her children implies that she would also be a "good mother" to the "Austrian family"; on the other hand, the praising of motherhood certainly relates to conservative and Christian family values:

tion of libel laws for calling Rosenkranz a "*Kellernazi*" (the term, literally 'cellar Nazi', describes a person who supports National Socialist/ anti-democratic ideas through clandestine activities).

17. *MenschInnen. Gender Mainstreaming — Auf dem Weg zum geschlechtslosen Menschen* (2008): "Es ist klar, dass der Rang der Frau in unserer Gesellschaft ein gänzlich gleichberechtigter sein muss, da kann es keine Abstriche geben. Ebenso aber ist es eine Tatsache, dass erfolgreiche Weiblichkeit und Mütterlichkeit nicht auseinanderfallen dürfen, wenn wir im Gesamten eine Zukunft haben wollen" (ibid.).

18. Rosenkranz argues that such partnerships contravene the contract between generations to ensure that the state has sufficient revenue to provide social services. She also opposes the right of homosexual couples to adopt children.

19. See: http://derstandard.at/1267132251749/Kandidatur-Rechtsextreme-NVP-unterstuetzt-Rosenkranz, http://derstandard.at/1268700952546/Rosenkranz-ist-eine-nationale-Sozialistin; cf. also http://www.kleinezeitung.at/nachrichten/politik/bundespraesident/2307151/zwei-gesichter-kandidatin.story.

Text 1:

> A brave mother (…) A new federal president is up for election. A mother of ten children, who has already demonstrated what she is capable of in her political career, is in the running for a very high position. Let us vote for her; she will be a good president for Austria.

On 2 March 2010, she was officially presented as candidate for the federal presidency by the FPÖ. On the same day in the evening news, on 3 March 2010 in a radio interview (Ö1 *Morgenjournal)* and on 4 March 2010 in *Neue Kronen Zeitung* (cf. Figure 1), Rosenkranz challenged the *Verbotsgesetz* (she had already done so in 2006 when commenting on the so-called "Gudenus affair"; see Engel and Wodak 2013). Similar to Gudenus, she claimed that challenging the existence of gas chambers should fall under "freedom of expression".[20]

Text 2:

> *Kronen Zeitung*: You have, however, repeatedly demanded that the *Verbotsgesetz* should be repealed?
> *Rosenkranz*: This is a question of freedom of speech: if one is in favour of this, one has to allow opinions to be voiced that one finds wrong, absurd or repulsive.
> *Kronen Zeitung*: Should Holocaust denial be permitted?
> *Rosenkranz*: I have repeatedly taken a stand on this issue. Laws against defamation and libel exist, and these of course keep freedom of speech within the bounds of civilised cooperation.

In this way, Rosenkranz draws on the *topos of freedom of speech* ("if freedom of speech exists, then wrong opinions can also be voiced/ every opinion can be voiced"). When asked specifically about Holocaust denial, she redefines this offence implicitly (she does not mention Holocaust denial explicitly but refers to it vaguely as "this issue") as libel or defamation. Thus, she avoids further explicit discussion about the Holocaust and Nazi crimes.

When asked in an interview with Ö1 *Mittagsjournal* on 3 March 2010 whether she actually believed in the existence of gas chambers in the concentration camps during World War Two, she replied that she had the typical knowledge of an Austrian "who attended Austrian schools between 1964 and 1976 — this is the extent of my knowledge of history and I do not intend to change this".

As stated in a dossier collected by the Green Party on Barbara Rosenkranz (2010, 15), this utterance seems to be part of a coded language amongst radical right-wing party members indicating a revisionist perspective of contemporary history, and most specifically a positive view of National Socialism: *Blaming the*

20. See: http://www.vol.at/news/politik/artikel/bundespraesident — rosenkranz-steht-weiterhin-zu-umstrittenen-aussagen/cn/news-20100303–12292321, http://www.krone.at/Oesterreich/FPOe-Kandidatin_Rosenkranz_gegen_NS-Verbotsgesetz-Meinungsfreiheit-Story-188096.

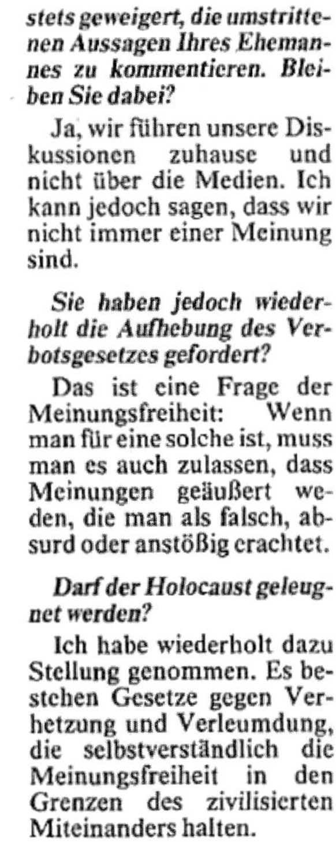

stets geweigert, die umstrittenen Aussagen Ihres Ehemannes zu kommentieren. Bleiben Sie dabei?

Ja, wir führen unsere Diskussionen zuhause und nicht über die Medien. Ich kann jedoch sagen, dass wir nicht immer einer Meinung sind.

Sie haben jedoch wiederholt die Aufhebung des Verbotsgesetzes gefordert?

Das ist eine Frage der Meinungsfreiheit: Wenn man für eine solche ist, muss man es auch zulassen, dass Meinungen geäußert weden, die man als falsch, absurd oder anstößig erachtet.

Darf der Holocaust geleugnet werden?

Ich habe wiederholt dazu Stellung genommen. Es bestehen Gesetze gegen Verhetzung und Verleumdung, die selbstverständlich die Meinungsfreiheit in den Grenzen des zivilisierten Miteinanders halten.

Figure 1. Rosenkranz and freedom of speech, *Neue Kronen Zeitung*, 4 March, 2010.

schoolbooks is obviously regarded as a suitable defence strategy, i.e. of avoiding blame. Rosenkranz assumes (rightly) that nobody would check the schoolbooks which she might have used many decades ago; secondly, it is also common knowledge that many Austrian schoolbooks in the 1960s and 1970s did not elaborate on World War Two and Nazi crimes. This period was frequently summarised very briefly; war crimes were reported, but only if they had happened far away and thus, not in Austria (see Loitfellner 2003). She emphasises the unchallenged and unchallengeable "authority of schoolbooks" (*topos of authority*) as a legitimation device. All these meanings are coded in this statement, which thus clearly establishes its calculated ambivalence.

Of course, superficially, the statement does not breach any norms of political correctness. One might wonder though why she states explicitly that she would never change her views or be open to new insights (particularly during her studies of history and philosophy at the University of Vienna during the late 1970s and early 80s). This clause serves, as stated in the aforementioned dossier, as a salient implicit indicator of revisionist ideology, for those "in the know".

Following this remark, Vienna's Archbishop Cardinal Christoph Schönborn labelled Rosenkranz ineligible for the presidency on 4 March 2010, a most unusual move for a representative of the Church in a secular state: "When someone is running for high office in this country and simultaneously leaves room for ambiguity over the question of the *Verbotsgesetz* or the *Shoah*, then they are unelectable for me." This remark indicates that Rosenkranz's repeated statements had been well understood, in spite of the use of calculated ambivalence. On the same day, the then leader of the *Austrian People's Party* (ÖVP) and former Foreign Minister, Michael Spindelegger (a devout Catholic), supported the Cardinal's move: "For me someone who has this kind of relationship to questions that affect our past is unelectable." Through her strategy of provocation, Rosenkranz's nomination monopolised the agenda; thus the media and most public debates revolved around her utterances and not about the characteristics of other candidates and their programmes.

However, on 6 March 2010, Hans Dichand, again under his pseudonym CATO, demanded a serious and honest *declaration of distance* from National Socialist beliefs and ideology (Figure 2).

Text 3:

> As an independent newspaper, *Kronen Zeitung* has always attempted to give outsiders a fair chance and to not exclude them. This is also the case in the ongoing presidential campaign, where we have provided Barbara Rosenkranz with the opportunity to present her ideas and views. Among these, there were also some that led to doubts. Therefore it is currently necessary that Barbara Rosenkranz distance herself under oath from all National Socialist ideas. Anything else would disqualify her as a presidential candidate.

The same day, under obvious pressure, in an interview with the conservative broadsheet *Die Presse*, Rosenkranz was asked the question: "Do you believe there is such a thing as an Austrian nation?" This question is linked to a similar question once posed to the former leader of the FPÖ, Jörg Haider, many years ago, to which he responded that Austria was an "ideological miscarriage" (*ideologische Missgeburt*); of course, Haider triggered a huge scandal with such a negative predication (Wodak et al. 2009). Rosenkranz responded by stating, "Of course the Austrian nation-state exists."[21] Again, we are confronted with a factually and politically correct statement; however, she avoids answering the question, if she actually "believes" in the Austrian nation. This move is another example of calculated ambivalence.

21. See: http://diepresse.com/home/politik/hofburgwahl/544630/Rosenkranz_Kein-Zweifel-an-Gaskammern?_vl_backlink=/home/politik/hofburgwahl/544587/index.do&direct=544587.

Unabhängig

Als unabhängige Tageszeitung hat die „Kronen Zeitung" stets versucht, Außenseitern eine faire Chance zu geben, sie nicht auszugrenzen.

So ist es auch im gegenwärtigen Präsidentschafts-Wahlkampf, wo wir Barbara Rosenkranz Gelegenheit geboten haben, ihre Ideen und Einstellungen darzulegen. Darunter waren allerdings auch solche, die Zweifel aufkommen lassen. Daher ist es ein Gebot der Stunde, dass sich Barbara Rosenkranz von allen nationalsozialistischen Gedanken eidesstattlich distanziert.

Alles andere würde sie als Präsidentschafts-Kandidatin disqualifizieren. **Cato**

Figure 2. Cato's demand, *Neue Kronenzeitung*, 6 March, 2010

Finally, on 8 March 2010, at a public press conference, Rosenkranz signed a declaration distancing herself from National Socialism, as demanded by CATO (http://newsv1.orf.at/100308-48803/index.html), which, however, had no legal significance.[22] Thus, paradoxically, the eligibility of Rosenkranz's candidacy was re-established in the eyes of the most widely read Austrian populist tabloid, which exerted and manifested more power than any court, law or politician. On 9 March 2010, this declaration was reprinted in the *Kronen Zeitung*, including a personal letter from Rosenkranz to Dichand (Figure 3). In this letter, she states, inter alia, that "I condemn the crimes of National Socialism out of conviction and distance myself vehemently from the ideology of National Socialism."[23]

22. See: http://derstandard.at/1268402692605/Kommentar-der-anderen-Die-Nullnummer-des-Onkel-Hans.

23. See: http://newsv1.orf.at/100308-48803/index.html for the precise wording of the letter.

Figure 3. Rosenkranz distances herself from National Socialism, *Neue Kronenzeitung*, 9 March, 2010.

On 18 March 2010, Rosenkranz, for the first time, explicitly acknowledged the existence of gas chambers: "Of course, gas chambers existed. Of course, awful crimes took place. No reasonable person questions this."[24] This utterance seems not to contain any indicators of calculated ambivalence. However, her statement does not mention any perpetrators (actually no human beings are mentioned), nor does it mention any specific territory or historical period. Hence, this statement could have been employed for any period of time and for any similar event in the entire world. In this way, abstraction and vagueness reinforce calculated ambivalence. On 25 April 2010, Rosenkranz received 15.62% of the vote (voter turnout: 49.2%). FPÖ party leader HC Strache had initially envisaged 35%.[25]

24. See: http://diepresse.com/home/politik/hofburgwahl/547110/Rosenkranz_Selbstverstaendlich-gab-es-Gaskammern.

25. See: http://diepresse.com/home/politik/hofburgwahl/543588/Rosenkranz_Ueber-Identitaet-des-Landes-diskutieren?direct=543061&_vl_backlink=/home/politik/index.do&selChannel=101.

4. The British case

4.1 The BBC Programme "Question Time"

The second example concerns an episode of *Question Time*, a weekly British television programme that stages topical debates including representatives from at least three different political parties as well as other public figures. The audience can direct questions to the invited speakers who are not told in advance which questions to expect. The programme is currently broadcast on BBC 1 every Thursday from 10.30 pm to 11.30 pm and has been moderated by the prominent and very well-known journalist David Dimbleby since the mid-1990s.

"*Question Time*" was first broadcast in 1979 and has become very popular over the years. The literary meaning of "*Question Time*" is: "a period of time set aside each day for members to question government ministers".[26] David Dimbleby as moderator exerts much power in inviting turns, closing turns, inviting members of the audience to speak or disregarding them. He also determines the sequence of answers by inviting the panelists to respond directly to a specific question; he is thus the key figure of this show and keeps the discussions going, intervenes if politicians do not answer questions properly or digs deeper. Dimbleby sits in the middle of the panel at a table that faces the audience. The issues discussed are usually major political events currently taking place or other prominent news of the week. The programme is recorded in front of a live audience, approximately two hours before it is broadcast. Thus, the BBC guarantees a convenient recording slot for the panel as well as for the audience and claims that this is the only reason for not broadcasting this programme live. The specific episode analysed in this chapter was broadcast on 22 October 2009 and triggered much scandal and public uproar. Nick Griffin, leader of the BNP, was caught in the crossfire between the audience, the panel and the host, Dimbebly, for his statements about World War Two, the Holocaust, British identity, and homosexuality (amongst other topics).[27]

26. http://dictionary.reverso.net/english-definition/question%20time; accessed 10 January 2014

27. See, for example, "BNP on Question Time: Nick Griffin uses BBC appearance to attack Muslims and gays", *The Telegraph*, 22 October 2009, published immediately after the show was broadcast (http://www.telegraph.co.uk/news/politics/6410764/BNP-on-Question-Time-Nick-Griffin; accessed 24 October 2013); "Keeping Nick Griffin off air is a job for parliament, not the BBC" was the tenor of Mark Thompson, BBC's director, when justifying the invitation (*The Guardian*, 21 October 2009; http://www.theguardian.com/commentsisfree/2009/oct/21/question-time-bbc-bnp-griffin; accessed October 24, 2013).

4.2 British National Party

The BNP is an extremist right-wing political party founded in 1982 (and successor to the so-called fascist "Black shirts" from the 1930s) which, according to their leader Nick Griffin, "is a patriotic, democratic alternative to the old parties that have wrecked our great country" (http://www.bnp.org.uk/introduction; see: Billig 1978, Richardson 2013a, b, Solomos 2013). In an introduction on their homepage, the BNP presents its opinions about the political system and the life in Britain today in a provocative way by defaming and bad-mouthing the actual situation. This part is followed by their official standpoint: "We will put British people first in their own country. We demand British jobs go to British workers! We say NO to an EU superstate, and YES to keeping Britain free. We will stop paying foreign aid and give that money to pensioners, and we will bring British troops home from Afghanistan.".[28] In 2009, the BNP had two representatives in the European Parliament and ten out of 28,871 representatives in local government (recently, they lost many representatives at by-elections; see Wodak 2015). In the United Kingdom general election of 2005, the BNP received 192,746 votes, i.e. 7% of the overall vote. In the general election (2010), the BNP gained more than 530,000 votes (6.26%).

4.3 The broadcast and panellists

Nick Griffin, born in 1959, has been the leader of the BNP since 1999 and was a member of the European Parliament for northwest England until 2014. He was invited onto *Question Time* for the first time on the said date, which caused a huge and polarised controversy amongst politicians, media and the public.[29] Before the show, Nick Griffin told the broadsheet *The Times*: "I thank the political class and their allies for being so stupid … [this invitation] gives us a whole new level of public recognition."[30] In this interview, he also labelled his fellow panelist and the former Minister of Justice, Jack Straw, a "very effective advocate" (ibid.). This label is of interest here as, on the one hand, it might have insinuated something about

28. http://www.bnp.org.uk/introduction; accessed 3 August 2011; since 2011, the website has been closed.

29. Peter Hain, Secretary of State for Wales, made a final appeal to the BBC Trust to have the appearance blocked but this failed after an emergency meeting of the BBC Trust, held on 21 October 2009, which "cleared" the way for Nick Griffin's participation. *The Guardian* cited former Home Secretary Alan Johnson, who also condemned the decision of the BBC to invite Nick Griffin (21-10-2009); and Conservative leader David Cameron who stated that the BBC should not have invited him (*The Times*, 21-10-2009).

30. See: http://news.bbc.co.uk/1/hi/uk_politics/8319596.stm (from 22-10-2009).

Jack Straw's profession as secretary of justice; on the other, it might also have been directed against Jack Straw as a Jew, as "advocate" could be perceived as a negatively connoting label used for Jewish lawyers who are alleged to be "tricky and cheating".

Apart from Nick Griffin, the panel also consisted of: Jack Straw, former Labour justice secretary and previously home and foreign secretary; Sayeeda Warsi, then Conservative shadow minister for community cohesion; Chris Huhne, then spokesman for the Liberal-Democratic party on home affairs; and Bonnie Greer, an African-American playwright and deputy chair of the British Museum.

The programme began with the following question from the audience: "Is it fair that the BNP has hijacked Churchill?" After approximately ten minutes of discussion about World War Two, the Holocaust and other issues concerning racism and antisemitism, Dimbleby took some comments from the audience, all of which were directed against Nick Griffin, before turning to the next main question, again addressed to Griffin: "Why is Islam a wicked and vicious faith?" The following question also concerned the BNP: "Can the recent success of the BNP be explained by the misguided immigration policy of our government?" A couple of short questions including attacks on Nick Griffin followed. Later on, the British immigration policy system was discussed, and Jack Straw was forced to justify the Labour Party's policies. The last question was: Might this programme be viewed as an early Christmas present for the BNP?

It becomes obvious that almost the entire programme was oriented towards issues related to the BNP and Nick Griffin. Although Dimbleby tried to change the topic several times, questions from the audience again and again were directed at Nick Griffin.

4.4 Holocaust denial and blame avoidance

Extract 1: Nick Griffin on race and Churchill

Peter Loge: Given that the Second World War was fuelled by the need to disarm oppressive and racist regimes is it fair that the BNP has hijacked Churchill as its own?

DD: Is it fair that the BNP has hijacked Churchill? Jack Straw.

JS: Certainly not fair, and one of the extraordinary things about the Second World War and the First World War was not only that we fought Nazism in the Second World War and defeated it, a party and an ideology based on *race*, just like another party represented here today, based on race, fundamental to its constitution, and it's that difference, by the way, the fact that BNP defines itself on race, which distinguishes it from every other party that I can think of and what is common about every other political party that I can think of regardless of the difference is, that they have each have a moral compass and they show respect and recognisable, moral compass for them based on longstanding cultural and philosophical and religious values of western society. Nazism didn't and neither I'm afraid does the constitution of the BNP. The other thing I just say is this. We only won because of the black and Asian people from around the world. [Applause and woo]

JS: My constituency is twinned with a little town in northern France called Péronne, it was *massacred* in the First World War, the battle of the Somme, hundreds of people from East Lancashire, young lads from East Lancashire were killed and if you go to the Péronne military cemetery, just outside Péronne, you'll find 577 young men buried there. 257 of those come from East Lancashire, they' we got names like Ainsworth and Barnes. The others, more than half, have Indian and Pakistani sounding names like Mohammed Khan, from the 18th King's own Lancers, or Sheik Mohammed. These people died together to fight for *us* [*DD*: OK] and that's why having a multiracial society and ensuring that race based politics has no place in our society is *fundamental* to the decent British values which are held by most people in this country.

[*Applause*]

[…]

DD: Nick Griffin, you said if Churchill were alive today his own place would be in the British National Party. Why d'you say that? Why did you hijack his reputation?

NG: I said that Churchill belonged to the British National Party because no other party would have him for what he said in the early days of mass immigration into this country or the fact that quote, 'they're only coming for our benefits system' and for the fact that in his younger and in his earlier days he was extremely critical of the dangers of fundamentalist Islam in the way that would now be described as islamophobic. I believe that the whole the effort in the Second World War and the First a lot of effort was designed to preserve British sovereignty, British freedom which Jack Straw's governments is now giving away lock, stock and barrel to the EU and to prevent this country being invaded by foreigners. Finally, my father was in the RAF during the Second World War while Mr Straw's father was in prison for refusing to fight Adolf Hitler. that's it, that's it

[from the public, small applause and boooo]

DD: What, sorry, what what's that got to do, what's that got to do with it?

NG: Mr Straw was attacking me and I've been relentlessly attacked and demonised during the last few days but the fact is that during the Second World War my father was in the RAF.

I can't believe this [from the public]

I am not a Nazi, I've never have been.

DD: The man there [*points towards audience*]

A man in the audience: Emmm, yeah, just to say to Nick Griffin on the whole issue of Europe and how you seem to be against Europe while 80% of our trade is with Europe.

After a first very clear answer to Peter Loge's question that it is certainly unfair to "hijack Churchill", Jack Straw then immediately focuses on the BNP's racist policies which exclude diversity. Nick Griffin is asked to respond, both to the first question and to Jack Straw's evidence that Britain is a diverse, multiracial society and that many Pakistanis and Indians fought on Britain's side in World War Two.

Nick Griffin's overall argumentation in this passage can be deconstructed according to Toulmin's scheme of argumentation in the following way: That "Churchill belonged to the British National Party" (l. 58.) provides the claim.

"Because no other party would have him for what he said in the early days of mass immigration into this country" (l. 58–59) "and for the fact that in his younger and in his earlier days he was extremely critical of the dangers of fundamentalist Islam" (l. 61–62) are used as *data*. "In the way that would now be described as Islamophobic" serves as *warrant*. The warrant is supported by the *topos of burden*: "they're only coming for our benefits system" (using the conditional: "If foreigners come, they are only here for our benefits, and thus they should be kept out of the country"). This warrant leads, in Nick Griffin's argument, to the *conclusion* that Churchill, were he alive today, would belong to the BNP.

Of course, the merging of past and present in this case is fallacious. Griffin continues with a *topos of history* in that he claims "I believe that the whole effort in the Second World War and the First a lot of effort was designed to preserve British sovereignty, British freedom" (l. 62–64). This is the second attempt at a fallacious reconstruction of British history, as no evidence for such a claim exists. The latter could be interpreted as *argumentum ad ignorantiam,* i.e. an argument that is regarded as true as it has not been refuted. Griffin continues this line of argumentation with another *topos of history* in order to attack the Labour Party and its pro-European position: "which Jack Straw's government is now giving away lock, stock and barrel to the EU" (l. 64–65).

At this point, Griffin's argumentation shifts and he attacks Jack Straw directly: "Finally, my father was in the RAF during the Second World War while Mr Straw's father was in prison for refusing to fight Adolf Hitler" (l. 66–67) — *argumentum ad hominem* used by Griffin to personally attack his opponent Straw by criticizing his father, a conscientious objector. Here, Dimbleby intervenes and defends Jack Straw. He asks Griffin: "What, sorry, what what´s that got to do, with it?" (l. 69). Griffin answers: "Mr Straw was attacking me and I've been relentlessly attacked and demonised during the last few days but the fact is that during the Second World War my father was in the RAF."

Hence, Griffin did not reply to the question. He uses *argumentum ad misericordiam,* i.e. an appeal to pity or related emotions to gain the acceptance of other people or of one's antagonist. He constructs himself as a victim so that everybody should have mercy on him. Griffin provokes harsh criticism from the audience with his revelations. One man speaks up: "See I think it's an absolute disgrace that you can't even sort of take on board what Jack Straw has said", and continues: "yes you are, poison politics and poison the minds of people in this country. The vast majority of this audience, the vast majority of this audience, fine, would find what you stand for to be … completely disgusting".

Griffin, instead of referring to and dealing with the accuser's points, uses another *argumentum ad misericordiam*: "if you look at some of the things I'm quoted as having said in the *Daily Mail,* and so I'd be a monster. Those things are outrageous lies…". Griffin offers no proof for his claim; Dimbleby digs deeper and asks for the specific quote. However, Griffin tries to avoid answering but Dimbleby insists on an answer:

Extract 2: Calculated ambivalence and Holocaust denial

110 *NG*: No doubt, I appreciate that but if you look at some of the things quoted as having said in the
111 *Daily Mail* and so, I'd be a monster. Those things are outrageous *lies*.
112 *DD*: Which is the untrue quote? The Holocaust denial possibly
113 [*general laugh, people speaking*]
114 *NG*: The. hh [*smile*]. the *vast* majority of them, far too many to go into, but
115 [*general laugh*]
116 *DD*: But denying, denying of Holocaust,
117 did you deny the Holocaust? Yes you did
118 *NG*: I . I do not have a conviction for Holocaust denial
119 *DD*: But you did deny it. Why are you smiling? It's not particularly amusing you see.
120 [*NG smiles*]
121 *NG*: I was, I was very much critical for the way Holocaust was and is in fact abused to prevent serious
122 discussion of immigration.

Instead of answering the question of whether he denied the Holocaust, Griffin replies with a strategy of calculated ambivalence: "I do not have a conviction for Holocaust denial" (l. 118), which serves two aims: first, stating — after a second question by Dimbleby (l. 116) — that he was "very critical of the Holocaust"; however, the statement, that he was never convicted, does, of course, not exclude that he has actually denied the Holocaust. This claim provokes his opponents even more; Dimbleby angrily points to Griffin's inappropriate behaviour, i.e. smiling when talking about a very serious issue concerning millions of people losing their lives (l. 120). Dimbleby does not let Griffin get away with his technique of blame avoidance and cites some quotes to prove that Griffin's claims of being incorrectly quoted are simply wrong and reprimands him yet again: "D'you know what I'm saying? I can't find misquotations and apparently nor can you".

Extract 3: Griffin and the KKK

238 A male voice: Absolutely. [*and applause*]
239 *NG*: I was… I was sharing a platform with David Duke, who was a head of KKK
240 who was once a leader of the Klu Klux Klan and almost a totally non-violent
241 organization, incidentally, no no no …
242 *DD*: oooo, wow
243 [*noise in the public, boooo*]

Griffin keeps on trying to ignore facts about him, e.g. that he was in a video standing next to the head of the Ku Klux Klan, and at the point where he realises that he cannot deny the truth anymore, he states that the "KKK is an almost non-violent organization" (l. 240). At this point, the audience boos and the panel utters its disgust. The debate at this point is dominated by many turn-takings from the panelists. Dimbleby continues to take comments and questions in order to avoid an escalation of the discussion. Probably, the most controversial moment is reached when Griffin suggests that he has changed his mind about the Holocaust and yet can give no reason for this, while implying possible negative sanctions because of laws against Holocaust denial:

Extract 4: Changing his opinion

297	Audience:	So…
298	*DD*:	You've got white shirt, alright… Go on.
299	Man from audience:	So Winston Churchill put everything on the line so that my ancestors wouldn't get
300		slaughtered in the concentration camp. But here sits a man who says that that's
301		a myth just like a flat world was a myth. How could you say that, how could you?
302	*NG* [*to DD*]:	Can I answer these three points, very briefly?
303:	*DD*:	Yes.
304:	*NG*:	First the first one, I cannot explain why I used to say those things, I can't tell you.
305		[*booooooooooo*]
306		anymore than I can tell you why I've changed my mind, I can't tell you the
307		extent to which I've changed my mind, because European law prevents
308	*JS*:	This is rubbish, this is rubbish… there is no law *here* that stops you from
309		explaining yourself
310		[*NG*: The European law prevents from]
311	*CH*	And we refused to a European arrest warrant from precisely this country
312		that does require a Holocaust denial to be an offence and we refused
313	*JS*:	that as a justice minister, I promise you, if you want to explain why you
314		[*audience wooo and applause*]
315	*BG*	[*during applause*]: Nick, tell them, tell them, you gadit.
316	*JS* and *CH*	[*interchangeably, during applause*]: go on, come on…
317	*DD* [to *NG*]:	You have, you have the freedom now to explain it.
318		[*laughter in audience, NG smiles too*]
319	NG:	But unfortunately, the French courts and German courts would not recognise
320		me that [*talks*]
321	*BG*	and *another male voice*: ooo ooo oooooo, woow…
322	*BG*	This isn't justified
323		[*laughter, incl. NG*]
324	*Male voice*:	[*talks loudly and non-understandably*]
325	*DD*:	I have I have I have wait wait I have a question here. Have you actually changed
326		your mind or do you only say you've changed your mind because a law says it is
327		illegal to be a Holocaust denier?
328	*NG*:	I I I *have* changed my mind, yes, a lot's of it about the figures, and one of the
329		yes, yes one of the key things that made me change my mind is British radio
330		intercepts of German transmissions about the *brutal* mass murders of innocent
331		Jews on the Eastern border during anti-partisan warfare which changes the

332		figures very much
333	*JS*:	What about Holocaust? Does that not require an [...]? What about Auschwitz?
334	*NG*:	Can I go back to my other point?
335	*JS*:	Can people not see with their own eyes what happened at Auschwitz? It didn't
336		need subsequent radio intercepts to find out that people were gassed.
337		[*applause and a voice saying 'absolutely' and more talk*]

This extract illustrates strategies of both calculated ambivalence and blame avoidance. Even though both Dimbleby and justice minister Jack Straw clarify that nothing would happen to Nick Griffin if he explains what he means when staying in the United Kingdom where no legal measures against Holocaust denial exist, he just does not answer. Finally, he admits to having changed his mind (after an ironic question by Dimbleby, l. 325–326), but avoids talking about concentration camps and the gassing of Jews. He shifts to another topic, the Eastern border and the "anti-partisan" warfare, thus employing a Nazi concept used to refer to civilians and resistance fighters (l. 331; see Heer et al. 2008). Jack Straw intervenes with much emotion and emphasis that one does not need any figures or facts when referring to Auschwitz (l. 335).

Nick Griffin employs strategies of blame avoidance via calculated ambivalence, shifting blame, switching topics, not answering questions and the fallacy of *ignoratio elenchi* (ignoring counter-proof or counter argument) (see Reisigl and Wodak 2001, 73). Griffin does not deny everything; however, he continuously uses fallacious analogies and comparisons (*topos of history*) and emphasises his right of freedom to speak. Implied throughout is the fact that he does not want to state or repeat the denial explicitly as otherwise, he would possibly not be able to travel to France anymore where laws against Holocaust denial exist. His smirk (smile) indicates to his core voters that he is well aware of his strategy.

5. Conclusion: provoking media scandals

In *Le Monde Diplomatique,* Valérie Igounet states, while exposing Jean Marie Le Pen and his party *Front National*'s manifold denials of the Holocaust, that "Holocaust denial is a convenient polemical substitute for antisemitism".[31] This is certainly the case when considering the two incidents analysed in this chapter. In both cases, implicit and explicit denials of the Holocaust were made on public television, in Austria and in the United Kingdom, by well-known politicians and members of far-right parties. In both cases, the main protagonists succeeded in using various strategies of provocation and calculated ambivalence, while denying

31. May 1998, http://mondediplo.com/1998/05/08igou; accessed 2 March 2014

their denial, but simultaneously signalling to their core constituencies what they really believed in. In both cases, strategies of provocation served to obtain wide media attention and to set the agenda for a couple of weeks, at least in the media.

Rosenkranz's relatively brazen xenophobia was acceptable to the public, also to mainstream media and politicians. She had, as mentioned above, even received an important decoration from the Austrian state. However, her coy attempts to question historically established facts about the history of the *Third Reich* went too far for her supporters in the tabloid media and she was required to distance herself publicly — via a legally irrelevant oath — from National Socialist ideology in order to be accepted in the mainstream of right-of-centre Austrian politics. However, this was only relevant as she was a candidate for the presidency; otherwise, she presumably would have not attracted the level of attention she did. In this way, one could speculate that the scandal she provoked had the intended or unintended benefit of allowing her to set the agenda in the ongoing election campaign in which, predictably, she had little chance of winning against a very popular incumbent president running for a second term.

The specific *Question Time* programme analysed in this chapter was watched by more than eight million viewers. Protesters gathered outside BBC Television Centre and regional BBC offices. The BBC was closed down so that people invited to other shows were not able to enter. Six people were arrested, and some protesters and police officers were wounded.[32] Moreover, in an interview given to *The Telegraph* on 23 October 2009, Griffin demanded a repeat of the programme, as he felt unfairly treated by the panel and argued that the show had not been a typical *Question Time* event but rather a "lynch mob against him". A typical conspiracy theory was set in motion, many postings on various online fora agreed, and in this way, Griffin succeeded in turning the tables.[33]

References

Allport, Gordon. 1979 [1954]. *The Nature of Prejudice*. New York: Perseus Books.

Angouri, Jo, and Ruth Wodak. 2014. "'*They became big in the shadow of the crisis*' The Greek Success Story and the Rise of the Far Right." *Discourse & Society* 25(4): 540–565. doi: 10.1177/0957926514536955

32. See: http://www.socialistworker.co.uk/art.php?id=22373.

33. "Nick Griffin on Question Time: BNP boss squirms as audience laugh" (*Mirror Online*; http://www.mirror.co.uk/news/uk-news/nick-griffin-on-question-time-bnp-426538). http://www.mirror.co.uk/news/uk-news/nick-griffin-on-question-time-bnp-426538) (*The Guardian* 23-10-2009; http://www.theguardian.com/politics/2009/oct/23/bnp-nick-griffin-question-time).

Benz, Wolfgang.1995. "Realitätsverweigerung als antisemitisches Prinzip: Die Leugnung des Völkermords". In *Antisemitismus in Deutschland. Zur Aktualität eines Vorurteils*, edited by Wolfgang Benz, 121–139. Stuttgart: DTV.
Billig, Michael. 1978. *Fascists. A Social Psychological View of the National Front*. London: Harcourt, Brace, Jovanovich.
Boromisza-Habashi, David. 2013. *Speaking Hatefully*. Philadelphia: Penn. State University Press.
De Cillia, Rudolf, and Ruth Wodak (eds.) 2009. *Gedenken im „Gedankenjahr": Zur diskursiven Konstruktion österreichischer Identitäten im Jubiläumsjahr*. Innsbruck: Studienverlag
Delanty, Gerard, Ruth Wodak, and Paul Jones (eds.) 2011. *Migration, Identity, and Belonging*. Liverpool: LUP. doi:10.5949/UPO9781846314537
Engel, Jakob, and Ruth Wodak. 2009. "Kalkulierte Ambivalenz, „Störungen" und das „Gedankenjahr": Die Causen Siegfried Kampl und John Gudenus." In *Gedenken im „Gedankenjahr": Zur diskursiven Konstruktion österreichischer Identitäten im Jubiläumsjahr*, edited by Rudolf de Cillia, and Ruth Wodak, 79–100. Innsbruck: Studienverlag.
Engel, Jakob, and Ruth Wodak. 2013. "'Calculated Ambivalence' and Holocaust Denial in Austria". In *Analysing Fascist Discourse. European Fascism in Talk and Text*, edited by Ruth Wodak, and John E. Richardson, 73–96. London: Routledge.
Forchtner, Bernhard. 2011. "Critique, the Discourse-Historical Approach and the Frankfurt School." *Critical Discourse Studies* 8(1):1–14. doi:10.1080/17405904.2011.533564
Forchtner, Bernhard, and Ana Tominc. 2012. "Critique and Argumentation: On the Relation between the Discourse-Historical Approach and Pragma-Dialectics." *Journal of Language and Politics* 11(1): 31–50. doi:10.1075/jlp.11.1.02for
Heer, Hannes, Walter Manoschek, Alexander Pollak, and Ruth Wodak (eds.) 2008. *The Discursive Construction of History. Remembering the Wehrmachts War of Annihilation*. Basingstoke: Palgrave (transl. from the German version 2003).
Judt, Tony. 2007. *Postwar*. London: Penguin.
Kahn, Robert A. 2005. *Holocaust Denial and the Law: A Comparative Study*. Basingstoke: Palgrave.
Kienpointner, Manfred. 1996. *Vernünftig argumentieren: Regeln und Techniken der Diskussion*. Hamburg: Rowohlt.
Lipstadt, Deborah. 1993. *Denying the Holocaust: The Growing Assault on Truth and Memory*. New York: Free Press.
Loitfellner, Sabine. 2003. "'Furchtbar war der Blutzoll, den Österreich entrichten musste...'. Die Wehrmacht und ihre Soldaten in österreichischen Schulbüchern." In *Wie Geschichte gemacht wird. Zur Konstruktion von Erinnerungen an Wehrmacht und Zweiten Weltkrieg*, edited by Hannes Heer, Walter Manoschek, Alexander Pollak, and Ruth Wodak, 171–191. Vienna: Czernin.
Reisigl, Martin, and Ruth Wodak. 2001. *Discourse and Discrimination. Rhetorics of Racism and Antisemitism*. London: Routledge.
Reisigl, Martin, and Ruth Wodak. 2009. "The Discourse-historical Approach (DHA)." In *Methods of Critical Discourse Analysis*, edited by Ruth Wodak, and Michael Meyer, 87–12. London: Sage.
Richardson, John E. 2013a. "Ploughing the Same Furrow? Continuity and Change on Britain's Extreme Right Fringe." In *Rightwing Populism in Europe: Politics and Discourse*, edited by Ruth Wodak, Majid KhosraviNik, and Brigitte Mral, 105–120, London: Bloomsbury.
Richardson, John E. 2013b. "Racial Populism in British Fascist Discourse: The Case of COMBAT and the British National Party (1960-1967)." In *Analysing Fascist Discourse. European*

Fascism in Talk and Text, edited by Ruth Wodak, and John E. Richardson, 181–202. London: Routledge.
Richardson, John E., and Ruth Wodak. 2009a. "Recontextualising Fascist Ideologies of the Past: Right-wing Discourses on Employment and Nativism in Austria and the United Kingdom." *Critical Discourse Studies* 4:251–267. doi:10.1080/17405900903180996
Richardson, John E., and Ruth Wodak. 2009b. "The Impact of Visual Racism - Visual Arguments in Political Leaflets of Austrian and British Far-right parties." *Controversia* 2:45 -77.
Solomos, John. 2013. "Contemporary Forms of Racist Movements and Mobilization in Britain." In *Rightwing Populism in Europe: Politics and Discourse*, edited by Ruth Wodak, Majid KhosraviNik, and Brigitte Mral, 121–134. London: Bloomsbury.
Stögner, Karin, and Ruth Wodak. 2014. "Nationale Einheit" und die Konstruktion des "fremden Juden", *Osnabrücker Beiträge zur Sprachtheorie* 24: 131–160.
Stögner, Karin, and Ruth Wodak 2016. 'The Man who Hated Britain'. The Discursive Construction of National Unity against 'the Jewish Alien'. *Critical Discourse Studies* 13(2): 193–209.
Toulmin, Stephen E. 1958. *The Uses of Argument*. Cambridge: Cambridge University Press. doi:10.1017/CBO9780511840005
Wengeler, Martin. 2003. "Argumentationstopos als sprachwissenschaftlicher Gegenstand. Für eine Erweiterung linguistischer Methoden bei der Analyse öffentlicher Diskurse." In *Sinnformeln. Linguistische und soziologische Analysen von Leitbildern, Metaphern und anderen kollektiven Orientierungsmustern*, edited by Susanne Geideck, and Wolf-Andreas Liebert, 59–82. Berlin/New York: Mouton de Gruyter.
Wodak, Ruth. 2007. "Pragmatics and Critical Discourse Analysis." *Pragmatics and Cognition* 15(1):203–225. doi:10.1075/pc.15.1.13wod
Wodak, Ruth. 2011a. *The Discourse of Politics in Action. Politics as Usual*. Basingstoke: Palgrave.
Wodak, Ruth. 2011b. "Suppression of the Nazi Past, Coded Languages, and Discourses of Silence: Applying the Discourse-Historical Approach to Post-War Anti-Semitism in Austria." In *Political Languages in the Age of Extremes*, edited by Willibald Steinmetz, 351–379. Oxford: OUP.
Wodak, Ruth 2015. *The Politics of Fear – What Right-Wing Populist Discourses Mean*. London: Sage.
Wodak, Ruth, Peter Nowak, Johanna Pelikan, Helmut Gruber, Rudolf de Cillia, and Richard Mitten. 1990. *'Wir sind alle unschuldige Täter!' Diskurshistorische Studien zum Nachkriegsantisemitismus*. Frankfurt a.M: Suhrkamp.
Wodak, Ruth, Rudolf de Cillia, Martin Reisigl, and Karin Liebhart. 2009. *The Discursive Construction of National Identity*. Edinburgh: EUP.
Wodak, Ruth, and Martin Reisigl. 2002. "'*Wenn einer Ariel heißt...*': Ein linguistisches Gutachten zur politischen Funktionalisierung antisemitischer Ressentiments in Österreich." In *Dreck am Stecken. Politik der Ausgrenzung*, edited by Anton Pelinka, and Ruth Wodak, 134–172. Vienna: Czernin.
Wodak, Ruth, and Bernhard Forchtner. 2014. "Embattled Vienna 1683/2010: Right- wing Populism, collective memory and the fictionalization of politics." *Visual Communication* 13(2): 231–255.
Wodak, Ruth, and John E. Richardson (eds.) 2013. *Analysing Fascist Discourse. European Fascism in Talk and Text*. London: Routledge.
Wodak, Ruth, Majid KhosraviNik, and Brigitte Mral (eds.) 2013. *Right-wing Populism in Europe: Politics and Discourse*. London: Bloomsbury.

Dehumanizing metaphors in UK immigrant debates in press and online media

Andreas Musolff
University of East Anglia

Some Internet genres, in particular weblogs and discussion fora, have a dubious reputation for giving voice to strongly polemical discourses or hate speech. This chapter investigates the use of dehumanizing metaphors, specifically *parasite* metaphors, in British debates about immigration. It compares the range of metaphors used in blogs with that used in online fora and in mainstream newspaper coverage and concludes that despite substantial variation, they can be categorised into four main scenarios, of which one includes dehumanizing metaphors such as depictions of immigrants as *parasites, leeches,* or *bloodsuckers*. Whilst this kind of stigmatizing imagery occurs across the three different media genres, the samples also show significant quantitative and qualitative differences: dehumanizing metaphors occur most often and their potential for aggressive argumentation and polemics is exploited in more detail in blogs than in the fora, and least in the mainstream press. It is then asked what cognitive import this differential usage has in view of a) the discourse histories of such metaphors and b) their most likely present-day semantic motivation. The chapter concludes that while it is unlikely that present-day users have detailed knowledge of the etymological and conceptual histories of such metaphors, it is also improbable to assume a wholly "unconscious" or "automatic" use or reception in the respective community of practice, and that instead it is more likely that they are used with a high degree of "deliberateness" and a modicum of discourse-historical awareness.

Keywords: dehumanization, discourse history, immigration, metaphor, scenario

1. Introduction

The use of dehumanizing and stigmatizing metaphors in political polemics and, in particular, in immigration debates has been analysed and commented on in Critical Discourse Analysis (CDA)-oriented research on many occasions (Böke 1997; Bosmaijan 1983; Chilton 2005; Cisneros 2008; Hart 2010, 2011; Hawkins

DOI 10.1075/bct.93.02mus

2001; Hönigsperger 1994; KhosraviNik 2010; Musolff 2012). One of the methodological hallmarks of this research tradition has been a focus on the "production side" of metaphors, i.e., demonstration of their occurrence, frequency and intensity in texts produced by political leaders, journalists, and other commentators. The quantity of text material considered in these studies differs greatly, depending on the focus of the analysis, and the data range from imagery used in a few texts that are deemed to be exemplary of a particular type of discourse to large research corpora of "instantiations" of metaphor use, which have often been assembled electronically from even larger general corpora that can be subjected to statistical analysis. Despite such variation, most of these corpora fulfil one of the fundamental methodological demands of empirical linguistic research, namely the need to document the evidence for the qualitative and quantitative hypotheses and explanations put forward by the researcher (Cameron and Low 1999; Deignan 1999, 2005; Steen 2007). On the other hand, research on how metaphor production is understood by recipients has so far focused mainly on psycholinguistic studies of comprehension speed, comparability and metaphor identification (Cienki 2008; Gibbs 1994, 2007, 2011; Gibbs and Tendahl 2006; Giora 2003; Glucksberg 2001; Steen 2007). Speakers' self-interpretations, i.e. interpretations of their own intentions when uttering metaphors, are even less researched. In the case of polemical discourse, which may be ethically contentious or lead to legal prosecution (e.g. for libel, insult or incitement to violence), it is unlikely that a speaker would admit to having such intentions. Disclaiming statements by media-savvy politicians that deny xenophobic or racist implications of their utterances have become notorious (Beauzamy 2013; Wodak 2013). On the other hand, debates between metaphor-producers and –recipients about contentious imagery *do* reveal at least the deliberateness of its use and provide a valuable source of information for CDA-research that compares and "triangulates" production and reception data with media studies, social and political science research, and discourse-historical data (Wodak 2001).

The present chapter follows this approach by comparing the use of one type of dehumanizing metaphors, i.e. the stigmatization of immigrants as (social) *parasites* across different genres of immigration debates in Britain, (i.e. the press, and blogs) and by including readers' "comments" as far as they are documented in blog comments and online discussion fora. In this way, we hope to gain a more representative picture than one based solely on studying one genre of metaphor use/production. In addition reception/"comment" data in particular provide evidence on how this use of metaphors is received by readers (as long as we bear in mind that these data too have to be interpreted critically and cannot be taken at face value).

2. Data and methodology

The data for this analysis consist of three samples: a press sample, a sample of three online discussion fora that are maintained on the BBC under their popular "Have your say" website (http://www.bbc.co.uk/news/have_your_say/) and 40 Internet weblogs (blogs) with readers' comments, as far as these have been kept accessible by the blog managers (comments on online fora and blogs that were removed by the website managers are thus excluded from the analysis.).

The following table gives an overview over the range and size of the whole corpus (NB: word counts for blogs have been established through conversion into word documents, which exclude extra website material to a greater or lesser extent; their word count is therefore not as exact as that for the other media).

Table 1.

Media	Newspaper and magazine articles (2003–2013)	*Have your say* Online fora (April-June 2010)	blogs (accessed December 2013)
Titles/key words	*Daily Express, Daily Mail, Financial Times, Guardian, Independent, Observer, Scotsman, Spectator, Sun, Telegraph, Times.*	(1) Should politicians be talking about immigration? (2) How should immigration be tackled? (3) Are immigration rules fair?	40 websites, searched on WWW by key words: *immigration, parasites, UK*
No. of items	138 articles	2473 postings (566, 881, and 1026 for the respective for a; with altogether 81 postings removed by BBC online forum management	40 websites
No. of words	100.756	333.518	89.950

The first sample consists of press articles that have appeared in mainstream UK media, which have been sampled from the online sites of the respective newspapers or magazines; however, they have appeared also in print. This sample does not contain any readers' comments, even if the respective media operate comment sites attached to the online versions. The *Have Your Say* sample, on the other hand, consists exclusively (with the obvious exception of the forum theme question) of comments by members of the public who participate in the forum debates. As is evident from the increase in comments from 566 to 1026 between the first and the third forum debate on immigration-related topics within three months, these fora attracted a fast growing audience. This rise in interest has also of course to do with the fact that in May 2010 a general election took place in Britain, in which the competing parties highlighted immigration control as one of their main vote-winning strategies. The third sample, i.e. blogs, was collected by a Google search for keywords, with the specific goal of finding websites that contained *parasite*-metaphors in texts relating to immigration. The three samples are so different in elicitation procedure, respective time frame and size that they cannot be regarded as balanced, let alone validated in a statistical sense. They are solely intended to provide a heuristic basis for the comparative analysis of different media and, in particular, for relating press discourse as produced by journalists (and, via the press, also by politicians) to readers' reactions to and, in the case of comments, "uptake" of metaphors.

The methodology to be employed is that of corpus-based metaphor analysis (Deignan 1999; Musolff 2004; Zinken 2007; Zinken, Nerlich, and Hellsten 2008; Zinken and Musolff 2009), specifically "scenario analysis" as applied to political metaphors (Musolff 2006; Semino 2008, 220–222). The category of *scenario* serves as an analytical construction to capture clusters of conceptually related metaphor formulations in a corpus, which add up to mini-narratives, with default participants, action schemas, outcomes, and attached "standard" evaluations/stances. In actual text corpora, scenarios can be (and are) linguistically "realised" also by non-metaphorical lexis (e.g. by a literal paraphrase in the target terminology). In some cases a formulation may contain both metaphorical and non-metaphorical lexis such as the statement, "Sham marriages are a 'massive loophole' in Britain's border controls and amount to a 'golden ticket' into the country for immigrants [...]" (*The Daily Telegraph,* 23 January 2014). Its main scenario aspects are that of a CONTAINER and of MOVEMENT, which frame both its source domain (*loophole, golden ticket*) and target domain terminology (*border control, into the country...*).

Scenarios are not directly comparable to "metaphor fields" or "domains", which denote large semantic and encyclopaedic areas of knowledge; rather, as framing devices, they combine snippets of encyclopaedic knowledge to arrive at a default conclusion or evaluation that is based on common sense experience, e.g., that it is "good to become healthy again after an illness", or that "in a family all members should show solidarity to each other", or that on "a ship someone has to be in command to guarantee everybody's safety". These conclusions are applied to the target notion, e.g. a state that needs to "recover from a crisis", or "have more cohesion" or "have a firm leadership". Such default conclusions or outcomes are not logically binding but they are assumed or taken for granted under normal circumstances — any deviation from them is understood as an exceptional, "marked" case. This scenario-based approach has the advantage to account for a range of lexical variation and collocation patterns in a corpus sample, which otherwise have to be laboriously summarised under "domains". The scenarios that are identified here are not assumed on the basis of some grand conceptual architecture and then imposed in a top-down procedure to the data; rather, they are based on the corpus evidence itself. Scenario-analysis can thus serve to explore the range of metaphors in a relatively wide data collection and to investigate specific scenario aspects or formulations in detail.

3. Analysis

3.1 Overview of general metaphor scenarios relating to immigration in British public discourse

In the case of the British immigration debate, the press and online forum samples show a high degree of consistency in the use of a limited set of standard scenarios that are used time and again. They account for more than 90% of all ideologically relevant metaphors in the corpus; many of them have been analysed and commented on in research literature on (im)migration discourse (Böke 1997; Charteris-Black 2006; Cisneros 2008; Hönigsberger 1991; Jung, Niehr and Böke 2000; KhosraviNik, Krzyżanowski and Wodak 2012; Musolff 2011), which may be taken as evidence that they have been established for a long time. They can be summarised as follows (italicised items are lexemes or phrases that reoccur with high frequency):

1. The SPACE-CONTAINER scenario: the nation(-state) is conceptualised as a *container* with distinct *boundaries*, which distinguish those *on the outside* from those *inside*: immigrants are *outsiders* that want to *come/move into the container*. The *container* has *doors* or other openings that can be *closed, open* or *half-open* and it is seen as having a *limited capacity* to include people; if too many immigrants come in, this increases the *pressure* inside to *bursting point* and necessitates the erection of new *barriers*.

2. The MOVEMENT scenario (specific to immigrants as PARTICIPANTS): the most famous (or rather infamous) scenario version is that of a *flood, tide* or *wave* that *pours/rushes* into the container. It fits into the wider concept complex of a *mass movement,* which is also indicated by verbs such as *flock, pass through, overwhelm*. However, there are also instances of single immigrants being pictured as *swimming over*, which is most probably motivated by Britain being an island

3. The ACTION scenario, which is specific to CONTAINER-insiders as PARTICIPANTS: the latter fall into two distinct groups: on the one hand, those politicians and social groupings who are viewed as (and mostly condemned for) *inviting, letting, allowing, bringing* immigrants into the country, and on the other side those who try to *send them home, round them up, chuck* or *kick them out* or at least *limit, target,* and *control* immigration. Even the lexical pair of *importing* and *exporting* is used. In this scenario, "ordinary" insider-citizens are depicted as victims of an unwanted change in their living circumstances; one popular formula is the construction *when I/you walk down the street and see ….*, which always precedes a negative evaluation of immigrants as having changed a familiar living environment for the worse. A further sub-scenario is that of VIOLENT ACTION, as indicated by terms such as *backlash, combustible issue, dangerous game, invasion, rivers of blood, start a revolution, storm troopers, time bomb, weapon,* which portrays immigration as a wilful violation of the INSIDERS' rights and their predicted response to this perceived aggression. The *rivers of blood* phrase alludes to the conservative politician Enoch Powell's speech of 20 April 1968 (Charteris-Black 2011, 27–28). In press articles, this speech is referred to only as an exemplary case of dangerous xenophobic rhetoric; the online commentaries and blogs sample include both positive and negative evaluations.
4. The EFFECT scenario has three sub-scenarios: MIX, GAIN, and SCROUNGE. The first one is most strongly represented in the online commentaries and in tabloid anti-immigrant press articles, referring as it does to an alleged blending of cultures that makes them interchangeable or even *submerges, dominates* or *subjugates* the traditional British culture, i.e. the effect that insiders recognize when they "go out in the street" (see above). This sub-scenario includes colorful formulations such as the supposed vision of *Coronation Street* (a TV soap opera set in a "typical" terraced street, supposedly in the Manchester area) having been *moved to Pakistan;* it is particularly frequently used in debates about the pros and cons of "multiculturalism". The GAIN sub-scenario is confined to the quality press and small sections of the fora that report and comment on debates about those immigrants that *benefit UK Plc,* i.e., those who are among the *best and brightest* of their respective home countries and may provide an *economic benefit* to Britain. It is mostly used in arguments made by centre-left leaning journalists and public figures in defence of continued emigration of certain specialised groups (e.g., foreign students, skilled workers, business people). The last sub-scenario, which is of particular interest here, is that of the IMMIGRANT-AS-SCROUNGER who *sucks, drains or bleeds the country dry, aims for freebies* and *lives off* or *sponges from Britain,* thus exploiting it as a *treasure island.* Its references to immigrants range from relatively moderate

depictions as *welfare-tourists* (since 2013 also, *NHS-tourists*) to their dehumanizing stigmatization as *leeches, bloodsuckers* and *parasites*, which will be analysed in detail in the following section.

3.2 Immigrants as "parasites"

A closer view at the stigmatization of (im)migrants as *parasites* reveals a differentiated picture of the immigration debate in Britain, which in part relativizes the above-given overview. As part of the SCROUNGE sub-scenario, *parasite* imagery does indeed occur across all the genres of press articles, blogs and online fora but its frequency, collocation patterns and argumentative contexts are markedly different. The press sample, even though it includes strongly anti-immigration texts from tabloids and broadsheets has only one single text (out of 12 altogether) in which *parasite* is used in an assertive sense to denote immigrants, and even this is a qualified statement that distinguishes "beneficial" from "non-beneficial" immigrants, accusing as it does the Conservative-Liberal government of "letting in parasites, [but] turning away entrepreneurs" (*The Daily Telegraph,* 25/03/2013). The article gives no unambiguous indication of exactly who the *parasite* immigrants are supposed to be. All other articles in the press sample quote *parasite* imagery (or allege to quote it) as used by xenophobes, e.g. "The attempt of the far right to present the citizens of these countries as parasites [...] is as absurd as it is repellent (*The Scotsman,* 04/01/2014); "The government is telling us that the coming Romanians and Bulgarians are ill-educated, parasitic benefit tourists. These people deserve better" (*The Guardian,* 05/02/2013); "people like me: non-EU immigrants [...] are all viewed as grasping parasites" (*The Spectator,* 27/04/2013). In the mainstream press, *parasite* imagery is evidently too ideologically loaded to be used uncritically; instead, they report and quote it as being employed by the xenophobic part of the political spectrum in Britain. There appear to be only a few press texts that could serve as models for readers to "learn" the use of *parasite* imagery from, even though the SCROUNGE scenario of the UK being exploited by immigrants is represented in about 20% of all articles.

The percentage of texts invoking the SCROUNGE scenario is even smaller in the online-forum sample, where this scenario is present in just 251, i.e. about 10% of all 2473 postings. In 90% of all these occurrences, however, the scenario is used in an assertive-aggressive way to depict immigrants as scroungers, in some cases in elaborate, sarcastic versions. This use of the SCROUNGE scenario overlaps in many cases with the INSIDER-ACTION scenario, so that radical measures against *sponging* illegal immigrants are advocated, e.g. using the army to "round up imigrants [*sic*] who are not working & deport them immediately" (BBC, HYS-1, 29/04/2010).[1] As regards the use of dehumanizing lexemes such as *parasites, leeches,* or *sucking blood/life out of [the host society],* the picture becomes more complicated: in the first place they appear to be rare in general, amounting as they do to just 15 instances in the sample; of these 50% are directly targeted at immigrants, e.g. in postings such as the following:

> [...] the willy nilly entry into this country of immigrants who come to do harm or to simply suck a living out of hard working middle income earners?? (BBC, HYS-1, 30/04/2010).

> If they haven't been detected for ten years then they are either living via the proceeds of crime or tax dodging. And that makes them parasites and criminals (BBC, HYS-2, 30/04/2010).

> [...] the sort of immigrants who Labour has been busy encouraging are precisely the sort whose existence guarantees that quality, skilled immigrants don't consider the UK a worthy destination. These dregs naturally become potential Labour "clients" of lazy spongers and parasites, almost guaranteed to vote for the party who will keep feeding them benefits (BBC, HYS-3, 09/06/2010).

The remaining 50% of instances, however, include critical thematisations of such uses within the context of arguments defending the right of immigrants and promoting counter-usage, so to speak, which applies the *parasite/scrounger* image to "indigenous" UK benefit receivers to whom the immigrants are compared favourably, as in these quotations:

> Let's tackle the real problems of a lazy bunch of parasites feeding of the life blood of our hard working people, who consider benefits to be a God given right and work to be beneath them and stop bashing the hard working immigrants, just because they are fulfilling a vital place in our farms and factories (BBC, HYS-1, 29/04/2010).

> [...] there are far more work-shy benefit scrounging and criminal indigenous Brits [than immigrants] who suck the life out of the public services. (BBC, HYS-3, 10/06/2010).

Like the press, such online comments ascribe either explicitly or implicitly the discriminating use of *parasite* imagery against immigrants to xenophobic parts of the British public and the political establishment. Unlike the press, however, the

1. Quotations from the online fora have been anonymized and are identified here only by reference to the respective *Have Your Say*-sample (numbering 1–3) and the date of the posting. Omissions are indicated by "[...]" and all special notations, highlighting, typographic and other errors in the postings have been preserved.

commentators' critical perception of allegedly typical xenophobic users of such imagery does not seem to frighten them off using such metaphors themselves against different target-groups (see above: "benefit scrounging and criminal indigenous Brits").

In the blog sample, on the other hand (which is of course statistically incomparable to the other samples due to its pre-determined 100% rate of *parasite* text occurrences), we encounter a different calibre of polemical use of *parasite* imagery altogether. All blogs start with strong assertions of *parasite*-status of immigrants, often in headlines such as "Foreign Immigrants are Parasites",[2] "Muselmanic Welfare Parasites Cost Britain £13+ BILLION A YEAR!",[3] "Britain: Muslim immigrants are the chief parasites".[4] These assertions are then followed up in the great majority (more than 80%) of cases by emphatic endorsements and reinforcements in the main text body of the blog and its further comments, which detail the *parasites'* effect in graphic detail and combine this with racist (in one case, anti-Semitic) hate speech:

> Parasitic Immigrants arrive here with their begging bowls out, to milk our hard won welfare & housing system. IDI Amin was not a nice guy but he had his country at heart, when he slung out its milking immigrants[5]

> So Whitey, do you really feel like being the butt of the joke in the country your ancestors built? [...] National humiliation from a bunch of mud parasites sent here by the JEW to destroy your genetic right to exist? *Am I making a mountain out of a molehill?* Nope. I'm highlighting the sort of stuff which will continue to flood the mainstream Jew TV propaganda machine, until we virtually cease to exist.[6]

> The irony of the situation is inescapable: their [= the immigrants'] parasitical behavior obliges governments, through taxpayers, to subsidize their adopted country's own destruction.[7]

2. http://www.stormfront.org/forum/. (last accessed 15/12/2013)

3. http://sheikyermami.com/muselmanic-welfare-parasites-cost-britain-13-billion-a-year/ (last accessed 15/12/2013)

4. http://jonjayray.wordpress.com/2007/10/03/britain-muslim-immigrants-are-the-chief-parasites/ (last accessed 15/12/2013)

5. Comment posted to http://www.weeklygripe.co.uk/a294.asp on 14/11/2012 (last accessed 15/12/2013)

6. Posted to http://expeltheparasite.com (n.d) (last accessed 15/12/2013)

7. Posted to http://answers.yahoo.com/question/index?qid=20120624051236AAds2v0, (n.d) (last accessed 15/12/2013)

Eight blogs also contain comments that are critical of the main anti-immigration thrust but these are apologetic, arguing details about exaggerated statistics, the economic benefit that a 'good' minority of immigrants bring to Britain and issues of Human Right legislation. They do not, however, tackle the issue of stigmatizing and dehumanizing imagery critically in the way the press and online fora users do. The exclusively anti-immigration comments, on the other hand, openly insult opponents and their main targets, describing them not only as criminals and scroungers but elaborating on the bio-imagery by using collocations and cognates of *parasite* terminology such as *leeches, locusts, rats, vermin, plague, germs, contamination* and denouncing them as being both metaphorically and literally *dirty*. They also include detailed analogies between the destructive effect that parasitical organisms (i.e., bio-parasites) have on their host organisms and the allegedly similar impact of immigration on their host societies.

4. Conclusions

The results of our comparison of *parasite* imagery in three media genres in the British public debate on immigration clearly show that such imagery is indeed used as part of a narrative-argumentative scenario of social groups scrounging from the nation, who supposedly deserve ethical condemnation and necessitate social and political counter-measures. The results do *not*, however, show a uniform pattern of usage; instead they are differentiated across genres and argumentative contexts. Only the "blogosphere" appears to exhibit a relatively consistent xenophobic and polemic bias insofar as the *parasite* metaphor is used together with further "disgusting and dangerous organisms" terminology to dehumanize immigrants and denounce them as not being part of the "proper" national society. However, in the online fora, and to an even greater extent in the press, such usage is explicitly criticised and ascribed to a section of the political spectrum that the respective journalists and commentators argue against, even when they employ the SCROUNGE scenario in general. *Parasite* imagery is never neutral and it also seems to be never "naïve" in the sense of non-reflective use. Whoever is employing this metaphor or its semantic "relatives" (*bloodsucker, leech*, etc.) is doing so in the knowledge of its strongly polemical, insulting, and defamatory bias. The online fora in particular show that even those who criticise its usage against immigrants often do not miss the chance to "turn the tables" by denouncing other groups as *parasites*.

This finding contributes to a growing body of evidence that, *pace* the cognitive insistence on the "unconscious", "automatic" or "non-deliberate" understanding of metaphors,[8] at least the use and interpretation of imagery in political discourse has to be considered highly deliberate. Furthermore, prominent metaphors that are deemed to be particularly offensive in the relevant community of practice, such as the xenophobic/racist use of *parasite* imagery, are usually not only employed deliberately but also reflectively, i.e. with a socio-historically informed, meta-communicative knowledge of their typical register (here, insulting and polemical hate speech) and also of their precedents in historical racist discourses (Musolff 2010, 2012, 2014). It is disingenuous to assume that the users and recipients of such imagery produce or interpret them automatically; however, it is in some cases difficult to pinpoint the degree of awareness in the users' minds. Nevertheless, *parasite* imagery is one of the clearer cases. In Britain, for instance, legal actions have been brought (in a few cases, even successfully) against its use in racist hate speech,[9] and the evidence from online fora discussed above demonstrates that it is not just "critical" journalists but also many members of the public who explicitly highlight and denounce its defamatory communicative function. Even though present-day usage of *parasite* imagery may not be as strongly associated with Nazi-jargon in Britain as it is in Germany and Austria, its closeness to racist hate speech is familiar to the online commentators (and is most probably eschewed by the majority among them for this very reason).

Still, it is important to specify as accurately as possible which particular version of *parasite* imagery should be considered as dehumanizing and potentially socially dangerous, for there are significant differences even among its xenophobic applications. In the immigration debate data, *parasite* imagery always occurs as part of the SCROUNGE scenario, and *scrounger* and *sponger* are among the synonyms that dictionaries give for *parasite* in its social meaning.[10] The cognitive approach assumes that the default metaphorization trajectory would go from a concrete source to an abstract target concept (Lakoff 1993), which in our case means that the target notion of "socio-parasites" is derived or "mapped" from the notion of 'bio-parasites' (Chilton 2005; Hawkins 2001). Curiously, the etymological and lexical history of the term *parasite* points towards a diachronic antecedence of socio- vis-à-vis bio-parasites: the latter were only gradually identified and terminologised (as characterising whole species) in the 17–18th centuries, whereas talk of individual *scrounging* socio-"parasites" antedates them by at least one hundred

8. See, for instance Gibbs 2011a; Lakoff 1993, 2008; Lakoff and Johnson 1980; for critical discussion see Gibbs 2011b, Müller 2011, Musolff 2011, Steen 2011.

9. See Musolff 2014 for detailed discussion of such prosecutions.

10. *Shorter Oxford English Dictionary*, 2002, vol. 2, 2096, *Brewer's Dictionary of Phrase and Fable*, 880.

years in English, e.g. English Renaissance dramas (William Shakespeare's and Ben Jonson's works), and by full two millennia in the languages it was borrowed from, i.e. Latin and Ancient Greek (Gullestad 2012; Serres 2007, 3–25; Zimmer 2001, 1–22). The Renaissance "parasite" was a sponging courtier or cleric or servant who 'earned' his keep not by honest work but through flattery and servility, and he was the (conceptual) descendant of a stock figure of ancient comedy, i.e. the *parasitus* (Latin) or *parasitos* (Greek) as the hanger-on of rich people (Damon 1998).

We thus have not one but two historical antecedents for *parasite* metaphors in today's usage: a) the ancient but (given the continued presence of Shakespeare's work in the British public) still comprehensible and usable figure of the lazy scrounger, a contemptible and ludicrous but ultimately only annoying figure and b) the (popular) science version of a bio-parasite, which not only damages its host by reducing its resources but can destroy it (e.g. by way of complete resource-consumption, or by injuring it or infecting it with fatal diseases). Both these versions fit the SCROUNGE scenario as identified in our corpus; so at this point we have to consider the metaphor's collocations and argumentative contexts in order to arrive at a sufficiently fine-grained analysis. In our corpus, collocations with biological terminology (*leeches* etc., see above) and explicit analogies between bio- and socio-parasites occur almost exclusively in the blogs.[11] It is these uses that can most plausibly be said to be "dehumanizing", rather than the 'simple' *scrounger/sponger* ones, which may be critical or dismissive of their referents but seem to focus on the *parasites'* alleged laziness and on resource-reduction for the host rather than on a necessarily destructive effect.

We have thus arrived at a highly differentiated result regarding the analysis of dehumanizing imagery: not only is its dehumanizing import dependent on the context of its use — which may be regarded as a pragmatic truism — but, more specifically, on its exploitation (or lack of it) of the source scenario's outcome versions. The default outcome of the bio-parasite scenario is the destruction of its host, whereas that of the (traditional) socio-parasite is damage to, but not annihilation, of the host. This conceptual-cum-argumentative difference in the use of the *parasite* metaphor coincides with its historical precedents and discourse-traditions: racist and other strongly discriminatory denunciations of alleged (socio-)parasites in history, such as those by Nazis and Stalinists, highlighted and

11. There is one online forum occurrence of a "bio-" to "socio-parasite" analogy and its argument is rather abstract: "backward looking Muslims [...] pose a serious long term danger to the cohesion of our society. [...] As such their relationship to our society is more parasitical than symbiotic" (BBC, HYS-2, 01/05/2010). By contrast, several blog comments focus on the supposedly 'funny' aspect that "all parasites are suicidal" because they destroy themselves by destroying the host, a 'conclusion' that can be found in Hitler's anti-Semitic version of the parasite metaphor in *Mein Kampf* (Hitler 1933, 334).

instrumentalized their supposedly scientifically proven destructiveness in order to justify their extermination/annihilation as a form of social hygiene/therapy. This "topos" can be traced back to the end of the 18th century, which was the earliest point that bio-parasite concepts served as source input for new analogical mappings onto society. Those who use such metaphors today may, for obvious reasons of self-exculpation, disclaim the tradition they stand in, but their conclusions from the metaphor scenarios they use speak for themselves.

References

BBC. 2010a. Have your Say: Should politicians be talking about immigration? http://www.bbc.co.uk/blogs/haveyoursay/2010/04/should_politicians_be_talking.html (last accessed 15/12/2013)

BBC. 2010b. Have your Say: How should immigration be tackled? http://www.bbc.co.uk/blogs/haveyoursay/2010/04/how_should_immigration_be_tack.html (last accessed ?????)

BBC. 2010c. Have your Say: Are immigration rules fair? http://www.bbc.co.uk/blogs/haveyoursay/2010/06/are_immigration_rules_fair.html (last accessed 15/12/2013)

Beauzamy, Brigitte. 2013. "Continuities of Fascist Discourses, Discontinuities of Extreme-Right Political Authors? Overt and Covert Antisemitism in the Contemporary French Right." In *Analysing Fascist Discourse. European Fascism in Talk and Text*, edited by Ruth Wodak, and John E. Richardson, 163–180. London: Routledge.

Böke, Karin. 1997. "Die 'Invasion' aus den 'Armenhäusern Europas'. Metaphern im Einwanderungsdiskurs.". In *Die Sprache der Migrationsdiskurse. Das Reden über die 'Ausländer' in Medien, Politik und Alltag*, edited by Matthias Jung, Martin Wengeler, and Karin Böke, 164–193. Opladen: Westdeutscher Verlag.

Bosmajian, Haig. 1983. *The Language of Oppression*. Lanham, MD: University Press of America.

Brewer's Dictionary of Phrase and Fable. 1990. Edited by Adrian Room. London: Cassell.

Cameron, Lynne, and Graham Low (eds.). 1999. *Researching and Applying Metaphor*. Cambridge: Cambridge University Press. doi:10.1017/CBO9781139524704

Charteris-Black, Jonathan. 2006. "Britain as a Container: Immigration Metaphors in the 2005 Election Campaign." *Discourse & Society* 17(5):563–581. doi:10.1177/0957926506066345

Charteris-Black, Jonathan. 2011. *Politicians and Rhetoric. The Persuasive Power of Metaphor*. Basingstoke: Palgrave-Macmillan.

Chilton, Paul. 2005. "Manipulation, Memes and Metaphors: The Case of *Mein Kampf*." In *Manipulation and Ideologies in the Twentieth Century*, edited by Louis de Saussure, and Peter Schulz, 15–43. Amsterdam/Philadelphia: John Benjamins. doi:10.1075/dapsac.17.03chi

Cienki, Alan. 2008. "The Application of Conceptual Metaphor Theory to Political Discourse: Methodological Questions and Some Possible Solution." In *Political Language and Metaphor. Interpreting and Changing the World*, edited by Terrell Carver, and Jernej Pikalo, 241–256. London: Routledge.

Cisneros, J. David. 2008. "Contaminated Communities: The Metaphor of 'Immigrant as Pollutant' in Media Representations of Immigration." *Rhetoric & Public Affairs* 11(4):569–601. doi:10.1353/rap.0.0068

Damon, Cynthia. 1998. *The Mask of the Parasite. A Pathology of Roman Patronage*. Ann Arbor, MI: University of Michigan Press.
Deignan, Alice. 1999. "Corpus-based Research into Metaphor." In *Researching and Applying Metaphor*, edited by Lynne Cameron, and Graham Low, 177–199. Cambridge: Cambridge University Press. doi:10.1017/CBO9781139524704.012
Deignan, Alice. 2005. *Metaphor and Corpus Linguistics*. Amsterdam/Philadelphia: John Benjamins. doi:10.1017/CBO9780511816802.018
Gibbs, Raymond W. 1994. *The Poetics of Mind: Figurative Thought, Language, and Understanding*. Cambridge: Cambridge University Press.
Gibbs, Raymond W. 2007. "Experimental Tests of Figurative Meaning Construction." In *Aspects of Meaning Construction*, edited by Günther Radden, Klaus-Michael Köpcke, Thomas Berg, and Peter Siemund, 19–32. Amsterdam: John Benjamins. doi:10.1075/z.136.04gib
Gibbs, Raymond W. 2011a. "Are 'Deliberate' Metaphors Really Deliberate? A Question of Human Consciousness and Action." *Metaphor and the Social World* 1(1):26–52. doi: 10.1075/msw.1.1.03gib
Gibbs, Raymond W. 2011b. "Advancing the Debate on Deliberate Metaphor". *Metaphor and the Social World* 1(1):67–69. doi:10.1075/msw.1.1.07gib
Gibbs, Raymond W., and Markus Tendahl. 2006. "Cognitive Effort and Effects in Metaphor Comprehension: Relevance Theory and Psycholinguistics." *Mind & Language* 21(3):379–403. doi:10.1111/j.1468-0017.2006.00283.x
Giora, Rachel. 2003. *On our Mind: Salience, Context, and Figurative Language*. Oxford: Oxford University Press.
Glucksberg, Sam 2001. *Understanding Figurative Language. From Metaphors to Idioms*. With a contribution by Matthew S. McGlone. Oxford: Oxford University Press.
Gullestad, Anders. 2012. "Parasite." In *Political Concepts: A Critical Lexicon*, edited by The New School for Social Research http://www.politicalconcepts.org/issue1/2012-parasite/ (accessed: 30/12/2013).
Hart, Christopher. 2010. *Critical Discourse Analysis and Cognitive Science: New Perspectives on Immigration Discourse*. Basingstoke: Palgrave Macmillan.
Hart, Christopher. 2011. "Force-interactive Patterns in Immigration Discourse: A Cognitive Linguistic Approach to CDA." *Discourse & Society* 22(3):269–286. doi: 10.1177/0957926510395440
Hawkins, Bruce. 2001. "Ideology, Metaphor and Iconographic Reference." In *Language and Ideology. Volume II: Descriptive Cognitive Approaches*, edited by René Dirven, Roslyn Frank, and Cornelia Ilie, 27–50. Amsterdam/Philadelphia: John Benjamins. doi: 10.1075/cilt.205.03haw
Hitler, Adolf. 1933. *Mein Kampf* (23rd ed.). Munich: Franz Eher Nachfolger.
Hönigsperger, Astrid. 1991. "'Das Boot ist voll' — Zur Metapher in der Politik." *Folia Linguistica* 25:229–241. doi:10.1515/flin.1991.25.1-2.229
Jung, Matthias, Thomas Niehr, and Karin Böke. 2000. *Ausländer und Migranten im Spiegel der Presse. Ein diskurshistorisches Wörterbuch zur Einwanderung seit 1945*. Opladen: Westdeutscher Verlag.
KhosraviNik, Majid. 2010. "The Representation of Refugees, Asylum Seekers and Immigrants in British Newspapers: A Critical Discourse Analysis." *Journal of Language and Politics* 9(1):1–28 doi:10.1075/jlp.9.1.01kho
KhosraviNik, Majid, Michał Krzyżanowski, and Ruth Wodak. 2012. "Dynamics of Representations in Discourse: Immigrants in the British Press." In *Migrations: Interdisciplinary Perspectives*,

edited by Michi Messer, Renée Schroeder, and Ruth Wodak, 283–295. Vienna: Springer. doi:10.1007/978-3-7091-0950-2_26

Lakoff, George. 1993. "The Contemporary Theory of Metaphor." In *Metaphor and Thought*, edited by Andrew Ortony, 202–251. Cambridge: Cambridge University Press. doi: 10.1017/CBO9781139173865.013

Lakoff, George. 2008. "The Neural Theory of Metaphor". In *The Cambridge Handbook of Metaphor and Thought*, edited by Raymond W. Gibbs, 17–38. Cambridge: Cambridge University Press. doi:10.1017/CBO9780511816802.003

Lakoff, George, and Mark Johnson. 1980. *Metaphors we Live by*. Chicago: University of Chicago Press. doi:10.7208/chicago/9780226470993.001.0001

Müller, Cornelia. 2011. "Are 'Deliberate Metaphors' Really Deliberate? A Question of Human Consciousness and Action." *Metaphor and the Social World* 1(1):61–66. doi: 10.1075/msw.1.1.06mul

Musolff, Andreas. 2004. *Metaphor and Political Discourse. Analogical Reasoning in Debates about Europe*. Basingstoke: Palgrave-Macmillan.

Musolff, Andrea. 2006. "Metaphor Scenarios in Public Discourse." *Metaphor and Symbol* 21(1):23–38. doi:10.1207/s15327868ms2101_2

Musolff, Andreas. 2010. *Metaphor, Nation and the Holocaust. The Concept of the Body Politic*. London/New York: Routledge.

Musolff, Andreas. 2011. "Migration, Media and 'Deliberate' Metaphors." *metaphorik.de* 21:7–19.

Musolff, Andreas. 2012. "Immigrants and Parasites: The History of a Bio-Social Metaphor." In *Migrations: Interdisciplinary Perspectives*, edited by Michi Messer, Renée Schroeder, and Ruth Wodak, 249–258. Vienna: Springer. doi:10.1007/978-3-7091-0950-2_22

Musolff, Andreas. 2014. "Metaphorical *Parasites* and 'Parasitic' Metaphors: Semantic Exchanges between Political and Scientific Vocabularies." *Journal of Language and Politics* 13(2):218–233 doi:10.1075/jlp.13.2.02mus

Richardson, John E., and Monica Colombo. 2013. "Continuity and Change in Anti-immigrant Discourse in Italy: An Analysis of the Visual Propaganda of the Lega Nord." *Journal of Language and Politics, Special Issue: 'Discourse and Politics about Migration in Italy'*, 12(2):180–202.

Semino, Elena. 2008. *Metaphor in Discourse*. Cambridge: Cambridge University Press.

Serres, Michel. 2007. *The Parasite (Posthumanities)*. Minneapolis, MN: University of Minnesota Press.

Shorter Oxford English Dictionary on Historical Principles (2002) edited by William R. Trumble, and Angus Stevenson. Oxford: Oxford University Press.

Steen, Gerard J. 2007. *Finding Metaphor in Grammar and Usage*. Amsterdam/Philadelphia: John Benjamins. doi:10.1075/celcr.10

Steen, Gerard J. (2011): "What does 'Really Deliberate' Really Mean? More Thoughts on Metaphor and Consciousness and Action." *Metaphor and the Social World* 1(1):53–56. doi:10.1075/msw.1.1.04ste

Wodak, Ruth. 2001. "The Discourse-Historical Approach." In *Methods of Critical Discourse Analysis*, edited by Ruth Wodak, and Michael Meyer, 63–95. London: Sage.

Wodak, Ruth. 2013. "'Calculated Ambivalence' and Holocaust Denial in Austria." In *Analysing Fascist Discourse. European Fascism in Talk and Text*, edited by Ruth Wodak, and John E. Richardson, 73–96. London: Routledge.

Zimmer, Carl. 2001. *Parasite Rex. Inside the Bizarre World of Nature's Most Dangerous Creatures*. New York: Free Press.

Zinken, Jörg. 2007. "Discourse Metaphors: The Link between Figurative Language and Habitual Analogies." *Cognitive Linguistics* 18(3):445–466. doi:10.1515/COG.2007.024

Zinken, Jörg, Iina Hellsten, and Brigitte Nerlich. 2008. "Discourse Metaphors". In *Body, Language and Mind. Vol. 2: Sociocultural Situatedness*, edited by Roslyn M. Frank, René Dirven, Tom Ziemke, and Enrique Bernárdez, 363–385. Berlin/New York: Mouton de Gruyter.

Zinken, Jörg, and Andreas Musolff. 2009. "A Discourse-Centred Perspective on Metaphorical Meaning and Understanding." In *Metaphor and Discourse*, edited by Andreas Musolff, and Jörg Zinken, 1–10. Basingstoke: Palgrave-Macmillan. doi:10.1057/9780230594647

Mobilizing against the Other

Cyberhate, refugee crisis and proximization

Monika Kopytowska, Łukasz Grabowski and Julita Woźniak
University of Łódź / University of Opole / University of Łódź

Drawing on the insights from Media Proximization Approach (MPA), the present chapter explores the dynamics of the online construction of the Other in the context of current refugee crisis and the phenomenon of hate speech within cyberspace. While content- and theme-wise, it takes under scrutiny online refugee-related discourses, on the theoretical and methodological level it presents a new approach to mediated construction of social reality based on the notion of distance and Self/Other or Us/Them dichotomy. Coached within (Cognitive) Critical Discourse Analysis, such an approach calls for an integration of corpus linguistics methods and tools. The chapter addresses the following questions: (1) How do the structural and functional features of online communication facilitate the spread of hateful and radical messages? (2) What is the perception of hate speech targeted at refugees and immigrants among Polish people (aged 18–35)? (3) What are the recurrent linguistic means, as well as the underlying cognitive and discursive mechanisms, of representing refugees as the Other? (4) How are salience and conceptualization, related to representation of the Other and proximization strategies, manifested in keywords and word co-occurrence patterns? (5) What is the interface between *othering* and *hate speech*? Some of the findings presented in this chapter are based on the analyses conducted within the European research project C.O.N.T.A.C.T., which focuses on exploration of various aspects of hate speech and hate crime in ten EU countries.

Keywords: refugee crisis, cyberspace, cyberhate, hate speech, refugees, migrants, proximization triggers

1. Introduction

The unfamiliar Other, especially when entering the in-group's geographical and cultural space, has always loomed as a threat in both physical and axiological sense. In his *Fear of Small Numbers: An Essay on the Geography of Anger*, Arjun

DOI 10.1075/bct.93.11kop

Appadurai (2006, 45) writes about "a lack of tolerance of any sort of collective stranger" tied to uncertainty resulting from blurring "the boundaries of national peoplehood" and "the inability of many states to secure national economic sovereignty in the era of globalization". Such feelings of "uncertainty and unease" become particularly evident in the case of refugee- and migrant-related issues (Esses, Medianu, and Lawson 2013, 18), when questions about refugees' motivations and intentions as well as the socio-economic consequences for the host country come to the surface. With their contradictory and polarized discourses, media additionally contribute to creating what Esses and colleagues call "crisis mentality" (ibid.), or what has frequently been referred to as "moral panics" (McLuhan 1964/1994, Cohen 1972/2002). Goode and Ben-Yehuda (1994/2009) point to "concern" and "hostility" as the main characteristics of this social phenomenon; the former means the existence of collective belief that the group or activity deemed deviant is likely to have a negative effect on the society, while the latter involves hateful attitudes towards the group in question — "folk devils" — resulting in the enhanced polarization within Us versus Them construction.

Departing from the assumption about the socially constituted and constitutive role of (media) discourse (Fairclough and Wodak 1997), in the present chapter we take under scrutiny the interface between the current refugee crisis, mediated construction of the Other and hate speech within cyberspace. The hypothesis we posit here is that the hateful discourses of online comments are encouraged by media representation of migrants and refugees (or rather by what is made salient in this representation) and enabled by the semiotic potential of cyberspace, and the key mechanism in both cases is that of *proximization*.

In the following paragraphs, we will explore how the image of refugees and immigrants is constructed by and in the media, and how it is interrelated with the social perception and legal framework concerning hate speech. While it would be a truism to say that the media representation of the Other has considerable impact on public opinion, it seems important to point out that its influence becomes even stronger when members of the audience have no direct experience (and contact with these groups) and rely in their judgements on images provided to them by TV, press, or the Internet. Such seems to be the case of the Polish data analysed in this chapter.

Poland, which similarly to other Central European and Baltic states (Hungary, Czechia, Slovakia, Lithuania, Latvia, Estonia), has vocally opposed the EU refugee quota proposal requiring the acceptance of a designated number of migrants from front-line Mediterranean countries, namely Greece and Italy, is a peculiar example of an EU state "experiencing" the refugee crisis without refugees (see Kopytowska and Grabowski, forth.). The anti-immigration sentiment has been reflected (and validated) both in the right-wing parties' rhetoric and the right-wing media, where potential refugees have been presented as a threat to national security, economy, and cultural/religious values. It is also reflected in the data collected by the Polish Public Opinion Research Center in 2015 and early 2016 showing that in April 2016, only 25 per cent of Poles thought that the country should take refugees from the Middle East and Africa (60 per cent were prepared to accept Ukrainians) (Bachman 2016). While it is our belief that religious and cultural homogeneity of the Polish society undoubtedly plays an important role in shaping collective perceptions of refugees and migrants, the anti-refugee sentiment seems to be reinforced by both defensive rhetoric of political elites and the media negative construction of the migrant crisis.

The chapter is structured in the following way. Section 2 is devoted to the notion of hate speech, together with the legal framework and current research on this phenomenon in Poland. Section 3 focuses on the media coverage of migrants and refugees, discussing dominant patterns of representation (e.g. topoi, metaphors, lexico-grammatical structures) and possible implications they might have for public perceptions. Section 4 presents the Media Proximization Approach (MPA), as a new distance-centered framework explicating the process in which media construct the salience of issues, thereby shaping collective experience, along with audience's attitudes, judgements, and emotions. The proximizing potential of cyberspace is also described here. Section 5 includes a brief overview of the current refugee crisis. In Section 6 methods, research material, tools and stages of the study are described. The final analytical part consists of two parts. In the first one, the results of an online questionnaire concerning the perception of hate speech among young people in Poland are presented and discussed. The second part presents the results of a preliminary corpus-based study of Polish online comments in response to newspaper coverage of migration crisis (*Niezalezna.pl*). An attempt is made here to demonstrate how lexical and grammatical choices act as spatio-temporal, epistemic, axiological, and emotional proximization triggers, promoting certain interpretations and perceptions and validating the anti-refugee stance.

2. Hate speech: definitions and legal framework

Despite the frequent use of the term "hate speech", there exists no definition of this phenomenon that would be universally accepted and implemented by the legislative systems of all the EU member states. The only formal definition of this concept, formulated by the Council of Europe, reads as follows:

> The term "hate speech" shall be understood as covering all forms of expression which spread, incite, promote or justify racial hatred, xenophobia, anti-Semitism

> or other forms of hatred based on intolerance, including: intolerance expressed by aggressive nationalism and ethnocentrism, discrimination and hostility against minorities, migrants and people of immigrant origin. (Council of Europe's Committee of Ministers' Recommendation 97(20); cf. Weber 2009)

Accordingly, the term "hate speech" refers to comments directed against a person or a particular group of persons.[1] Moreover, the Council of the European Union requires that each member state should

> take the measures necessary to ensure that the following intentional conduct is punishable: (a) publicly inciting to violence or hatred directed against a group of persons or a member of such a group defined by reference to race, colour, religion, descent or national or ethnic origin; (b) the commission of an act referred to in point (a) by public dissemination or distribution of tracts, pictures or other material (…) (Council Framework Decision 2008/913/JHA)

Due to the lack of uniform European laws, legislation concerning verbal expressions constituting hate speech differs within each EU member state. However, the EU countries are obliged to implement hate speech laws in accordance with international regulations such as the European Convention on Human Rights (ECHR), the International Covenant on Civil and Political Rights (ICCPR), and the International Convention on the Elimination of All Forms of Racial Discrimination (ICERD). While acknowledging the right to the freedom of expression ECHR emphasizes that it should be used "for the protection of the reputation and rights of others" (Council of Europe 1950). Similarly, ICERD and ICCPR are crucial instruments of international law delimiting the scope of free speech. While the former prohibits all and any incitement to racism (UN General Assembly 1965), the latter calls for banning "any advocacy of national, racial, or religious hatred that constitutes incitement to discrimination, hostility, or violence" (UN General Assembly 1966).

Even though Polish law does not contain any particular provision defining "hate speech", there exist a number of general anti-discriminatory laws allowing for the identification of this phenomenon.[2] They are included in the Constitution

1. In 1993, the Council of Europe established The European Commission against Racism and Intolerance (ECRI), which is an independent human rights monitoring body specializing in issues related to racism and intolerance, including hate speech (see, for example, ECRI 2015).

2. These laws also concern hate crime since the two concepts are interlinked (hate speech may encourage or accompany hate crime).

of Poland,[3] the Criminal Code of Poland,[4] and the Civil Code.[5] Additionally, provisions concerning equal treatment are set forth in the Labour Code.[6] Article 13 of the Constitution prohibits political parties and other organizations whose programmes or activities promote totalitarianism, Nazism, Fascism, Communism as well as racially motivated hatred. Other articles of the Constitution relevant in terms of penalizing hate speech are Articles 30, 32, and 35; they concern the inherent and inalienable dignity of the person, equality before the law, and the rights of national/ethnic minorities.

As far as the Polish Criminal Code is concerned, there are several articles that allow legal institutions to identify offensive language to be penalized. One of them is Article 257 of the Criminal Code, which refers to publicly insulting a group or a particular person on national, ethnic, racial, or religious grounds; also, it describes the types of activities that can be interpreted as hate speech. Article 256 prohibits promoting fascism or any other totalitarian system and inciting hatred based on national, ethnic, racial or religious grounds. More specifically, according to the said article, producing, storing and exposing materials promoting aforementioned ideas is strictly prohibited (however, this prohibition does not apply to artistic, educational, and scientific purposes). Article 119 penalizes violence or threats directed towards a group of people or a particular person on national, ethnic, racial, political, or religious grounds.

Since neither international nor national laws describe particular linguistic means allowing for the identification of hate speech, both research and legal action are not devoid of problems. As a matter of fact, hateful messages are often indirect and context-bound. Needless to say, as will be demonstrated in the following sections, cyberspace, with its potential for anonymity, interactivity, and intertextuality, becomes a fertile ground for promoting and sharing such messages, and thus increasing their visibility and impact.

3. The Constitution of the Republic of Poland as adopted by the National Assembly on 2 April 1997.

4. The Criminal Code of 6 June 1997 (Journal of Laws No. 88, item 553 with later amendments)

5. The Civil Code of 23 April 1964 (Journal of Laws No. 16, item 93, with later amendments)

6. The Labour Code of 23 December 1997 (Journal of Laws No. 21, item 94, with later amendments)

3. Media representations of migrants and refugees

Earlier research on the media portrayals of migrants and refugees invariably points to the negative representation of these social groups (see also Musolff, this volume). A study by Baker et al. (2008), combining corpus linguistics methods with the framework of Discourse Historical Approach, scrutinized a 140-million-word corpus of British press articles in terms of common categories of representation of refugees, asylum seekers, immigrants and migrants (collectively referred to as RASIM). This qualitative and quantitative analysis revealed a limited number of topics/categories and topoi, most of which conveyed a negative stance. Similarly, the most frequent migrant-related topoi in the UK press listed by Hart (2010) include: burden (the out-group needs to be supported by the in-group), character (the out-group has certain undesirable characteristics), crime (the out-group consists of criminals), culture (the out-group has different norms and values than the in-group and is unable to assimilate), danger (the out-group is dangerous), disadvantage (the out-group brings no advantages/is of no use to the in-group), disease (the out-group is dirty and carries infectious diseases), displacement (the out-group will eventually outnumber and/or dominate the in-group and will get privileged access to limited socio-economic resources, over and above the in-group), and exploitation (the out-group exploits the welfare system of the in-group) (Hart 2010, 67). Hart (ibid.) also argues that the words frequently used in the British press, connected with the concept of physical or mental threat, e.g. "damage", "danger", "threat", are prone to generate fear and evoke strongly negative emotional responses towards migrants. Likewise, the study on asylum-seekers in Australia between August 2001 and January 2002 by Klocker and Dunn (2003) demonstrated that 90% of the descriptive terms used by the federal government and 76% of the terms used by the print media to portray this group were negative, referring to asylum-seekers as illegitimate, illegal, and threatening, and presenting them as potential terrorists and criminals. Finally, Henry and Tator (2002, 111) pointed to a tendency to represent any issue dealing with immigration as a crisis, with recurring themes of "bogus refugees" taking advantage of the social benefits system, potential terrorists entering the country, and immigrants as sources of infectious diseases (see also 525).

Mahtani and Mountz (2002) argue that yet another way to evoke negative attitudes and promote anxiety and panic is the use of metaphors conceptualising immigration as an invasion and as flooding the country. Musolff (2012, 2014, 2015, also this volume), in turn, discusses the role of "parasite metaphor" in the construction of such negative portrayal of migrants. In their analysis covering both verbal and visual aspects of anti-immigration rhetoric and focused on the discourse of the Italian extreme right party Lega Nord (The Northern League),

Richardson and Colombo (2013) also mention the economy- and welfare-related problems among four dominant arguments used against migrants: a) immigrants are a threat to ethno-national identity; b) immigrants are a major cause of criminality and other kinds of social insecurity; c) immigrants are a cause of unemployment; d) and immigrants are abusers of the generosity of the welfare states of Western democracies. As argued by numerous authors, such patterns of representation have the potential to reinforce the image of the primitive Other (Bleiker et al. 2013) as diseased, uneducated and unable to assimilate (Wright 2000).

Maskaliūnaitė (2015, 98) puts forward a claim that the current refugee crisis "worked to entrench existing stereotypes, to rekindle nationalist and populist rhetoric and to increase the undercurrent of Euroscepticism". Adopting Huysmans' (2006) securitization approach, she examines discourse and institutional practices related to current migration crisis in Lithuania demonstrating that migration emerged primarily as a security issue. Importantly, terrorism and links to ISIS are only one aspect of the security-related threat. More often, as argued by Maskaliūnaitė (2015), securitization reflects cultural and identity fears. The concept of "societal security", developed by the Copenhagen school, can be of use here (Buzan et al. 1998). According to Buzan et al. (1998), societal insecurities stem from whatever is perceived as a threat to collective identities and the survival of a community as a cohesive unit. Migrants and refugees — the Other — inevitably constitute such a threat. Coming from a predominantly Muslim background, they are likely to bring in beliefs and traditions incompatible with the European Christian worldview. Likewise, in their analysis of late 2015 media debates in Latvia, Lulle and Ungure (2015) speak of emerging discourses of fear on the one hand and safety and security on the other. In this respect typical Muslim-related stereotypes come to the fore bringing into public discourse a whole range of issues concerning civil liberties, human rights, religion and, more importantly, security and terrorist threat (Kopytowska 2010a, 2010b, Poole 2002, Richardson 2004, Poole and Richardson 2006). The press thus eagerly reports on 'no-go areas' created in the British or Swedish towns, the introduction of Sharia law, or cases of violence against women. At the same time, however, safety and security is imagined through certain discursive representations of a desired refugee: family, children, real political refugee (not an economic migrant), who will work hard to prove his or her worth (Lulle and Ungure 2015, 83). Economic security-wise, migrants are seen as competitors for the scarce (welfare) resources. The image of a migrant is that of a lazy person, looking for welfare benefits in a European country, and prone to have a large family (Lulle and Ungure 2015, 77).

The results of an experimental study conducted by Esses, Medianu, and Lawson (2013) suggest that the uncertainty surrounding immigration, coupled with media tendency to focus on negative rather than positive news stories, can lead to extreme negative reactions to immigrants and refugees. Through a series of experiments, they have demonstrated that there exists a cause-and-effect relation between such negative media portrayals of immigrants and refugees and the dehumanization of these groups, which may serve to reduce uncertainty among the members of the host population, particularly those with no direct experience with migrants, by alerting them to potential physical, economic, and cultural threats and providing answers as to how immigrants and refugees should be viewed and treated (ibid. 522). In a similar vein, in our study, we will attempt to identify the recurrent linguistic means, as well as the underlying cognitive and discursive mechanisms, of representing refugees as the Other in the press articles and Internet users' comments under scrutiny. We will demonstrate how, by appealing to previous knowledge, existing stereotypes and values, by using individual cases as premises for generalization, both journalists and commenters evoke negative feelings towards refugees, predominantly fear and disgust, thus possibly legitimizing verbal and physical aggression directed at them.

4. The Self and the Other in cyberspace: the Media Proximization Approach (MPA)

The Media Proximization Approach developed by Kopytowska (2013, 2014, 2015a, 2015b, 2015c) is based on the assumption that mediated experience, being a constitutive part of mediated construction of social reality, is formed within the process of manipulation of the perceived distance between the Self and the surrounding reality with its various elements (other individuals and groups, events, phenomena, etc.). The idea comes from Chilton's Discourse Space Theory (DST) (2004, 2005; Deictic Space Theory in 2014), which explains how people position various entities (people, events, ideological constructions, etc.) in relation to themselves (the Self — I or we), being in the deictic centre. While this process has its discursive manifestations, it is cognitive by nature and related to the cognitive linguistics notion of "conceptualization", defined by Langacker (1990, 18) as "the cognitive activity constituting our apprehension of the world". The perception of time and space are key here as they are, as Langacker (1987, 147–154) puts it, "basic domains", i.e. primitive representational fields. Chilton also explains how individuals, using background assumptions and indexical cues, position various entities along three intersecting axes within DS — time, space and modality. The latter dimension involves both notions of truth and deonticity. In further developments of the theory, Hart (2010) and Cap (2006, 2008, 2010, 2013), who adds the axiological dimension in his STA model, demonstrate how the perception of distance from the Self can be skilfully manipulated in political discourse to legitimize the actions to be taken by political actors. The framework of MPA presented here, however, goes far beyond legitimizing function suggested by Cap (2013); it is inherent in the process of mediated construction of social reality (Kopytowska 2015c) and enabled by the semiotic potential of various media.

The Self, as posited by philosophical, anthropological, and psychological theories, has a natural tendency to position itself vis-à-vis Others within the environment and to group or classify surrounding entities as spatially and thus epistemically and axiologically close/distant (similar/different). Indeed, according to Urry (2002), all interactions can be understood as complex combinations of proximity and distance, or absence and presence, with the latter being the default choice (see also Boden and Molotch's (1994, 258, 277) concept of "compulsion of proximity"). The appeal and, consequently, the power of the media lie to a large extent in their potential to co-construct and manipulate this distance, or rather its perception. Whether it is about news discourse or other forms of mediated communication (e.g. blogging and other social media discourse), entities from the real (objective) world (events, groups, individuals, phenomena, both abstract and material) are selected and brought closer to the media users, thus influencing their cognitive-affective involvement and, as a result, perceptions, judgements and actions. Thanks to its semiotic affordances, media space (including cyberspace), in its various forms and genres, enables "mediated experience" defined by Giddens as "the involvement of spatially/temporally distant influences with human sensory experience" (1991, 243) or "the intrusion of distant events into everyday consciousness" (1991, 189). Accordingly, in the words of Thompson, media users "become space-time travellers who are involved in negotiating between different space-time frameworks and relating their mediated experience of other times and places back to the context of their everyday lives" (1995, 94).

What can be seen here is that time and space are key, or rather basic dimensions of distance to be bridged in the case of media proximization process: the entities accessed or individuals contacted are "located" out there in the world, beyond the audience's immediate reach. The epistemic distance results from the fact that the audience is to various degrees unfamiliar with the events and phenomena presented to them; it is thus related with media users' experience-based cognitive schema of interpretation and gains particular prominence in the case of news about distant and/or unfamiliar places, cultures, groups or events. The axiological distance is contingent on differences in cultural values, beliefs and practices and often involves the opposition of Us versus Them, or Us versus the Other. As argued by Berger and Luckmann (1966/1991, 111), "knowledge precedes values in legitimation of institutions". Hence, we believe that the axiological dimension of distance is, to a large extent, contingent on the epistemic one; the unfamiliar in most cases receives negative valuation as it is perceived as a potential threat to the status quo. These two types of distance can be linked to Hester's (1973) concept of "cultural affinity" and Shoemaker et al.'s (1991) notion of "ethnic similarity". In fact, viewers or readers will understand an event better if they are able to "incorporate" it into their "mental map", that is culturally determined knowledge about the structure of reality (Hall et al. 1978). In order to proximize such an event or phenomenon epistemically, journalists often refer to the already existing scenarios of representation, ideological patterns and cultural stereotypes (which they assume the audience to be familiar with). The consequences of this fact are twofold: firstly, events compatible with such "schemata of interpretation" or "mental scripts" are more likely to be included in the news (Schank and Abelson 1977), and secondly, new events and phenomena will often be simplified, re-contextualized and interpreted in terms of the already familiar ones.

This can explain the perpetuation of certain ideologies and stereotypes, for example the Orientalist division into the West and the rest, which in this light turns out to be the result of not only the conscious and manipulatory endeavours of political elites, but also of professionally-motivated choices (related to journalistic ethics/culture and news/media discourse conceptualized as a process; see Kopytowska 2015b). Finally, journalistic work also concerns emotional distance. Increasing the emotional involvement of media users seems to be one of the ways of making selected aspects of objective reality more salient than others, and, at the same time, a factor enhancing persuasiveness of media messages. As a matter of fact, emotions form an integral part of news values such as "negativity" and "superlativeness". Their discursive manifestations include, for example, negatively charged words, hyperboles and quantity expressions, comparison and contrast, etc. Likewise, presenting events from the perspective of individual experience (value of "personalization"), which at the level of discourse brings forth personal narratives, has a highly proximizing function.

The in-group vs. out-group representation gains particular prominence in times of conflict and crisis with their various dimensions (political, ethnic, cultural, religious, etc.). Defining the Other allows for the (re)definition of the Self and for creating clusters of similar values and norms with an inclusive subject "we". This, in turn, "functions to promote straightforward feelings of identification, empathy or disapproval" (Fowler 1991, 15). The dynamics of this process is captured by van Dijk's "ideological square" (1998, 33), set to present "us" in a favourable light and "them" unfavourably, and consisting in emphasizing "our" good properties/actions, while highlighting "their" bad properties/actions. According to Kopytowska (2015b, 317–318), cognitive-discursive operations within the domain of axiology can be characterized by three functions:

1. establishing axiological status: "our" values/norms;
2. delineating axiological conflict: incompatibility of "our" values/norms with "their" values/norms;
3. conveying axiological urgency: responding to a threat posed (often by "their" actions) to "our" values/norms and accepting moral responsibility to act;

The demonization of the Other can be regarded as an instance of what Chilton (2004, 47) calls delegitimization, involving "acts of negative other presentation, acts of blaming, scape-goating, marginalizing, excluding, attacking the moral character of some individual or group, attacking the communicative cooperation of the other, attacking the rationality and sanity of the other." In its most extreme form, this strategy consists in denying the humanness of the other (ibid.). Although Charteris-Black (2004, 21, 2005, 15) uses the term "depersonification" while referring to the act of concealing the humanity of the Other, we will opt here for a more encompassing term, namely "dehumanization". It refers to a psychological process whereby opponents regard each other as less than human, and thus psychologically distant, expendable, and not deserving humane treatment, basic human rights and moral consideration (Opotow 1995, 347). Portraying the Other as a sub-human makes it possible to legitimize increased violence or justify the violation of human rights. In some cases, when he or she is perceived as a threat to our well-being or values, dehumanization makes violation of generally accepted norms of behaviour reasonable, or even necessary (Deutsch 2000, 51). Animal metaphors, conceptualizing the Other in terms of animal features and behaviour act here as a powerful epistemic, axiological and emotional proximization trigger. Knowledge-wise they allow for a complex cognitive mapping entailing value and moral judgements. As cases of genocide rhetoric have shown, labelling the victims as animals not only dehumanized the labelled, but also desensitized the labellers. During the genocide of the Hereros (1904–1908) the Germans in South West Africa referred to the natives as "baboons." It seemed reasonable to destroy these "wild animals" to protect peaceful, civilized white people from future attacks (Bridgman and Worley 2004, 36). At the time of the Holocaust, the Nazis redefined Jews as "bacilli," "parasites," "vermin," "lice," or "demons," while in the camps, the verb used to describe the male inmates eating was "fressen," the word for animals eating (Nagengast 2002, 339). In Cambodia, from 1975 to 1979, the West-educated intellectuals were portrayed as "microbes" by Pol Pot, while in Rwanda, in 1994, the Tutsis were referred to as "cockroaches" and "snakes."

As already mentioned in the previous section, the results of an experimental study by Esses, Medianu, and Lawson (2013) revealed that dehumanization of migrants and refugees also translates into negative and hostile attitudes towards these groups. Bandura et al. 1975, in turn, demonstrated that as personal responsibility becomes more diffused in a group, people tend to dehumanize others and become more aggressive towards them. This finding has important implications for messages of hate within cyberspace. Anonymity (with its both psychological and legal consequences) is one of the key factors behind the production and spread of hateful messages. In his study of online comments, Santana (2014) argued that anonymity encourages incivility of Internet users. Another study, exploring the impact of accountability on the complexity of the thinking process, showed that people not held immediately accountable for their words (which is the case with anonymous commenters) are more likely to rely on mental shortcuts and simplistic judgements (Tetlock 1983).

The proximizing potential of the cyberspace is not without impact here either. As demonstrated by Kopytowska (2013), interactivity and non-linearity play a key role as regards spatial and temporal proximization. The user-reader has an opportunity to (a) select from among the links offered and (b) produce content in the form of comments. In the former case, they can be, at any time, shifted automatically to another discourse space, while in the latter they can incorporate their discourse spaces into the text of comments. This spatial and temporal proximization correlates with the axiological one, as the hyperlinks within the article or the news site "transport" the reader to other places within the cyberspace, which are related in terms of values, opinions and beliefs. Indeed, as mentioned in the introduction to this volume, by removing the boundaries of time and space and allowing dispersed individuals with similar (often radical) views to connect, online fora, Facebook and blogs enable the functioning of "hate speech platforms". What is more, explicit manifestations of hate, supported and further inflamed by other Internet users, often result in the emergence of "discursive spiral of hate".

5. Refugee crisis in Europe: background and recent developments

Even though Europe is no stranger to migration, the years 2015 and 2016 saw an unprecedented influx of refugees and migrants, exceeding considerably the World War II-induced displacement (Alfred 2015). Only in 2015 over 1 million people reached the Old Continent, triggering what has been labelled interchangeably as refugee or migrant crisis (UNHCR 2015a, 2015b). They prevailingly came from Muslim-majority countries of the Middle East, North and Sub-Saharan Africa as well as Western Balkans, and travelled either across the Mediterranean Sea or overland through Southeast Europe. According to the reports of the United Nations High Commissioner for Refugees (UNHCR), most migrants who arrived in the EU between January 2015 and March 2016 were Syrian (46,7%),[7] Afghan (20,9%) and Iraqi (9,4%) (UNHCR 2016a).

While the reasons behind migration movements are complex and related to on-going conflicts and post-natural disaster conditions in several African and Asian countries, the main causes of the current crisis are the Syrian Civil War along with wars in Afghanistan, Iraq, Eritrea, Somalia, and Darfur (Sudan). Most migrants and refugees choose to enter the EU by sea, heading for one of the Greek islands (Chios, Kos, Lesbos and others) or the Italian island of Lampedusa.[8] Upon arrival in Southern Europe, however, they continue their journey to reach one of the northern European countries, in particular Germany, Great Britain or Sweden.

Since April 2015, the EU has taken several measures to solve the refugee crisis. The European Commission proposed compulsory immigrant quotas, asking the EU member states to relocate refugees and in this way alleviate the burden on countries with external EU borders. However, several states, including the Visegrád Group countries (Poland, Hungary, Czech Republic and Slovakia), rejected this proposal and expressed disagreement with the EU forcing such a solution regardless of a particular country's national interests. Other steps taken by the EU included devising procedures to fight migrant smuggling networks and increasing border patrol operations in the Mediterranean Sea. Additionally, some countries within the Schengen Area reintroduced border controls, and others (e.g. Austria and Hungary) decided to build a fence along their borders to prevent further migrants' arrivals.[9]

The mass influx of entrants into Europe revealed the weakness of the EU immigrant/refugee policy and undermined the European solidarity. Also, media reports on violent assaults on women in Germany in January 2016 resulted in a wave of anti-immigrant protests across Europe, giving a clear message that refugees should not be treated as a homogenous group and entitled to unconditional help; instead, both their identity and motives for migration should be thoroughly scrutinized. This observation provided motivation to undertake a study like this one, that is focusing on the perception as well as discursive representation of refugees and immigrants in the selected Polish press articles and Internet users' comments. In what follows, more details regarding the research material and methodology employed in this study are presented .

7. In November 2015 the total number of Syrians' asylum applications amounted to 813,599 (57% of them were lodged in Germany and Serbia) (UNHCR 2016b)

8. According to the International Organization for Migration the total number of immigrants or refugees who lost their lives in the Mediterranean and Aegean Sea in 2015 is estimated at 3,692 (over 400 more than in 2014) (IOM 2015).

9. For details see "Ten point action plan on migration" that was proposed at a joint meeting of Foreign and Interior Ministers in Luxembourg 20 April 2015 (European Commission 2015).

6. Methods, research material, tools and stages of the study

In this study, we will switch between quantitative and qualitative research methods in order to analyze the perception of hate speech and the image of refugees and immigrants, constructed in the Internet users' comments following press articles about refugees in Europe, in terms of proximization strategies and the resulting salience of aspects and problems related to this particular group of people. To that aim, we conducted a questionnaire study followed by a preliminary corpus linguistic study, which are described in greater detail in the following sub-sections.

6.1 A questionnaire study

The questionnaire discussed here was conducted within the Polish component of the C.O.N.T.A.C.T project (*Creating an Online Network, Monitoring Team and Phone App to Counter Hate Crime Tactics*), the European Union supported research that focuses on hate speech and hate crime of a racist, xenophobic, homophobic or trans-phobic nature. The aim of the survey was to explore the perception of hate speech among young people from Poland aged 18–35, most of them university students. Prepared using Google Forms, the survey was administered online in November and December 2016 and it provided both quantitative measurements and qualitative language-based data. More specifically, the online questionnaire consisted of seven Likert-scale, categorical and open questions (with categorical questions often supplemented with open questions).

In Question 1, the participants were asked to assess on a Likert scale (*acceptable, somewhat acceptable, less acceptable, not acceptable*) the degree of acceptability of six examples of comments published on online fora. The examples reflecting negative, neutral or positive attitude towards refugees and LGBT groups, respectively, were randomly chosen from the corpus of *Youtube* comments collected as part of C.O.N.T.A.C.T qualitative research. The participants were also asked a categorical question (*Yes, No, Don't know*) whether the six examples would have been assessed differently if they had been written in private contexts online (e.g. private emails, private chat, private Facebook pages), and if they answered *Yes*, they were asked if the comments would have in their opinion been *More acceptable* or *Less acceptable*. Next, the participants were asked a categorical question (*Yes-often, Yes-rarely, No, Don't know*) concerning whether they had ever been a target of insults, threats on the grounds of nationality, skin colour, ethnic origin, religion, gender, sexual orientation or other. As regards the "other" category, the participants were asked an open question to provide a particular reason. If their answer was *yes*, then they were asked to mark one or more categories from the list related to where they had been subjected to threats or insults, that is, at work, at school, in the street, on public transport, online, in relation to sports or other. In the next question, the participants were asked whether they had ever witnessed anyone being a target of insults or threats (*Yes-often, Yes-rarely, No, Don't know*) on the grounds of nationality, skin colour, ethnic origin, religion, gender, sexual orientation or other. As regards the "other" category, the participants were again asked an open question to provide a particular reason. In the same vein, they were further asked where they had witnessed such incidents. In Question Four, the participants were first asked whether they would ever report insults or threats directed at them because of their nationality, skin colour, ethnicity, religion, gender or sexual orientation (*Yes, No, Don't know*). If their answer was *No* or *Don't know*, they were asked to choose one of the seven reasons from the list or provide a descriptive answer in the category *Other*. In the same way, in Question Five they were asked if they would report being a witness to someone being insulted or threatened because of their nationality, skin colour, ethnic origin, religion, gender or sexual orientation. Question Six referred to whether the participants had ever heard of the key notion from the perspective of this study, that is *Hate Speech*. As regards Question Seven, the participants were presented with four definitions of hate speech and they were asked to indicate the extent to whether they agree or disagree with each of them (*Strongly agree, Agree, Somewhat agree, Don't know, Somewhat disagree, Disagree, Strongly disagree*). Additionally, there were asked for an opinion whether there should be any laws against each type of hate speech (*Yes, No, Don't know*). Finally, the respondents were asked to anonymously provide background information related to age, gender, religion, nationality, sexual orientation and education using the categories provided in the relevant lists.

6.2 A corpus linguistic study

Apart from presenting and discussing the results of a questionnaire study, we also used both quantitative and qualitative research methods offered by Critical Discourse Analysis and corpus linguistics.[10] In short, we believe that corpus linguistics, in particular when employed in conjunction with qualitative approaches, is a valuable tool for discourse analysis because it enables one to identify recurrent linguistic patterns necessary to substantiate qualitative insights as well as to arrive at reliable generalizations of the effects of making various linguistic choices (Stubbs 1997, 107,111; see also O'Keeffe 2006, 51, 158, see also Baker 2006, Baker et al. 2008, Love and Baker, this volume).[11] Because we treat corpus linguistics

10. According to McEnery and Wilson (1996, 1), corpus linguistics can be described as "the study of language based on examples of 'real life' language use".

11. Corpus linguistics has been used by a growing number of media researchers, mostly in corpus-based analyses of the press language (e.g. Baker et al. 2008, Gabrielatos and Baker 2008, Kopytowska 2009, 2015a, 2015b).

primarily as a methodology for data analysis rather than as a distinct approach to study language, this study can be described as a corpus-based rather than a corpus-driven one (using annotated corpora, pre-selecting search words, pre-selecting syntactic patterns in which they occur, etc.)[12]

More specifically, we focused on keywords and word co-occurrence patterns, which can provide an insight into the lexical exponents of hate speech and proximization triggers in the process of othering. In corpus linguistics, keywords are described as words that occur with outstanding frequency in a text or collection of texts as compared with the reference corpus (Scott 2001). Providing specific clues as to the topics or themes broached upon in a particular text or corpus, which can be referred to as "aboutness" (Phillips 1989, cited in Scott 2001, 110), they become "an essential feature for making general claims about the discourse" (Teubert 2005, 5) and can serve as a starting point for identifying patterns within discursive representation. It is our assumption that this discursive representation (linguistic view)[13] reflects the standpoint of editors, journalists, and readers of *Niezalezna.pl*, their judgments and evaluations of the refugee crisis, but at the same time is likely to be constitutive for the public perception of the crisis.

In this preliminary study, we used Sketchengine (Kilgarriff et al. 2014), a computer program custom-designed for text analysis so that the keywords were revealed by comparing the corpus of the Internet users' comments following press articles about immigrants and refugees in Europe published by *Niezalezna.pl*, a Polish right-wing online news portal (henceforth 'CNPL') with the corpus of the press articles published by *Niezalezna.pl* only (henceforth 'NPL). More specifically, the keywords were generated using the Simple math[14] method proposed by Kilgarriff (2009). This will enable us to identify the main themes or topics within the Internet users' discourse in response to press articles about refugees published by *Niezalezna.pl*.

12. The distinction between a corpus-based and corpus-driven approach to study linguistic data is discussed in greater detail by Tognini-Bonelli (2001), among others.

13. The same situation in the world can be conceptualized in multiple ways (cognitive linguistic notion of *conceptualization*, Langacker (1990, 18) which is also captured in the theoretical notion of "a linguistic view of the world" (*językowy obraz świata*), defined by Bartmiński (2010, 156) as a collection of judgments and evaluations of the people, artifacts, events or phenomena making up a subjective interpretation of the world recorded in language. Importantly, since "[m]ost concepts presuppose other concepts and cannot be adequately defined except by reference to them, be it implicit or explicit (Langacker 1987, 147)", linguistic expressions will always function in a specific conceptual environment within which they will enable access to stored knowledge and experience, determining in this way further conceptualizations. See, for example, Grabowski (2014) for a corpus-based analysis of "a linguistic view" of Europe within the British National Corpus.

14. https://www.sketchengine.co.uk/documentation/simple-maths/

In the next stage, to explore word co-occurrence patterns, we also used SketchEngine (Kilgarriff et al. 2014) to identify and further describe the so-called word sketches, that is, lexical profiles featuring the most important lexical and grammatical relations of the keywords selected using several dimensions of proximization (see Section 4), that is spatio-temporal, axiological, epistemic and emotional (Kopytowska 2013).

When compiling our study corpora,[15] we extracted Internet users' comments submitted in response to the press articles (95 items) about immigrants and refugees published by *Niezalezna.pl* in the years 2015–2016, that is at the time when the refugee crisis in Europe reached its peak and was widely discussed by Polish mass media. As a reference corpus, we used the press articles published by *Niezalezna.pl* only. While compiling the reference corpus, we used an in-built search engine on the *Niezalezna.pl* website in order to identify — by keying in the search word *uchodźcy* 'refugees' — and further retrieve relevant articles on refugees published in the years 2015–2016. Then we used the Compile Corpora facility of the SketchEngine software (Kilgarriff et al. 2014) to automatically compile the corpus using the provided links. Finally, both corpora (of online comments and press articles) under scrutiny were tagged and parsed using Sketch Grammar for Polish developed on the basis of the tagset of the IPI PAN Corpus of Polish, which is implemented into the SketchEngine (Kilgarriff et al. 2014) software. More detailed information regarding the corpora used in this study is presented in Table 1.

Table 1. Study corpora in terms of their size

Genre	Corpus source	Corpus size in word tokens
Online comments	*Niezalezna.pl* (CNPL)	215,848
Press articles	*Niezalezna.pl* (NPL)	31,229

7. Empirical part: results

In what follows, we will first present the results of a questionnaire study followed by the results of a preliminary corpus linguistic study. Afterwards, we will present conclusions, including suggestions on how this research can be pursued further in the future.

15. The corpora used in this study were compiled, using texts freely available online, for non-commercial personal research in accordance with the fair use doctrine specified in the Polish copyright law.

7.1 Results of a questionnaire study

The survey was completed by 457 respondents, including 106 men, 350 women and 1 person of unspecified gender. The majority of the respondents (59.1%) were aged 18–23, 27.1% were aged 24–29 and 19.3% were aged 30–35. As far as religion is concerned, the largest group did not declare any religious affiliation (35.4%), followed by Catholicism (30.9%), other (4.4%), Orthodox and Protestant (1.3%), Judaism (0.4%) and Buddhism (0.4%). While an overwhelming majority (96.1%) of the respondents were Poles, 3.3% of the study participants declared a mixed nationality and 0.7% declared other nationality. As for the sexual orientation, an overwhelming majority were heterosexuals (87.1%), followed by LGBT (10.5%) and other sexual orientation (2.4%). Finally, 54.9% of the respondents declared to have higher education, 44.9% declared secondary education and 1 person (0.2%) declared primary education.

In Question 1, the participants were asked to assess, on a Likert scale (*acceptable, somewhat acceptable, less acceptable, not acceptable*), the degree of acceptability of six examples of the following comments published on online fora. The results of the respondents' assessments are presented in square brackets right next to the English glosses of the original Polish-language comments.

(1) W ramach "Polskiej goscinnosci", kazdemu ciapatemu i asfaltowemu smieciowi kulka 9mm miedzy oczy… Moze wtedy to "ludzkie" GOWNO zacznie trybic, ze nikt tu nie chce pierdolonych negatywow i pustynnych czarnuchow w Europie/Polsce.
'As a reflection of "Polish hospitality" each Paki and Nigger trash should get a 9mm bullet in between the eyes. Perhaps then this 'human' SHIT will understand that nobody here wants these fucking desert blacks in Europe/Poland' [*Acceptable — 1.8%, Somewhat acceptable — 1.3%, Less acceptable — 7.7%, Not acceptable — 89.3%*]

(2) Dla tych "ludzi" [uchodźców] nie ma miejsca w naszym społeczeństwie. Czują się bezkarni, mają za nic wartości innych narodów.
'For these "people" (refugees) there is no place in our society. They act with impunity and completely ignore the values of other nations' [*Acceptable — 11.6%, Somewhat acceptable — 24.9%, Less acceptable — 31.5%, Not acceptable — 31.9%*]

(3) Uchodźcom musimy pomóc — to nasz zasrany obowiązek. Kto by to nie był, drugiemu zawsze winni jesteśmy serdeczność i szacunek. I to nie ważne czy chrześcijanin, muzułmanin, buddysta albo nie ważne czy to człowiek, krowa czy kura (chyba, że jest naszym wrogiem).

'We have to help refugees — this is our fucking duty. Whoever it is, we owe them cordiality and respect. And it makes no difference whether it is a Christian, a Muslim, a Buddhist or whether it is a human, a cow or a hen (unless it is our enemy).' [*Acceptable — 14.7%, Somewhat acceptable — 50.8%, Less acceptable — 27.6%, Not acceptable — 7%*]

(4) Nie rozumiem czemu ktoś ma jakieś ALE do geja. To jest taki sam człowiek jak wszyscy po prostu kocha inaczej i niech taka osoba co hejtuje geji niech sie postawi na jego miejscu.
'I don't understand why somebody should have any 'BUT'S' about gays. They are the same people as everybody else, it's just that they love in a different way, and a person who writes hateful comments about gays should put him- or herself in their position' [*Acceptable — 48.1%, Somewhat acceptable — 38.5%, Less acceptable — 10.1%, Not acceptable — 3.3%*]

(5) TYLKO CHŁOPAK I DZIEWCZYNA TO NORMALNA POLSKA RODZINA!!!
'Only a boy and a girl are a normal Polish family!!!' [*Acceptable — 14%, Somewhat acceptable — 23%, Less acceptable — 25.2%, Not acceptable — 37.9%*]

(6) Choroba nazywana homoseksualizmem rozprzestrzenia sie jak wirus, z kim sie zadajesz tym sie stajesz, to niemoralne i wbrew woli boskiej i prawom natury, dewiacja i szalenstwo powoli staja sie norma OHYDA TFU
'A disease called homosexuality spreads like a virus, you become the one you interact with, it's immoral and against God's will and nature's laws, deviations and madness are gradually becoming the norm. That's ATROCIOUS. PHOOEY' [*Acceptable — 4.8%, Somewhat acceptable — 9.8%, Less acceptable — 21.7%, Not acceptable — 63.7%*]

As far as refugees are concerned it can be seen that while only 3.1 % accept explicit incitement to physical violence (shooting) and dehumanization of this group ('shit'), the rate of comment's acceptance increases to 36.5 % when the lack of moral values is given as the reason for refusing to treat refugees as an integral part of the Polish society. A similar number of respondents, namely 34.6 %, do not accept the need to help refugees and treat them as equal and with respect irrespective of religion. Interestingly, 86.6 % of respondents are willing to accept the same argument concerning an equal status in relation to the LGBT group. However, at the same time, 37 % accept the statement that a "normal" Polish family consists of a man and a woman, and 14.6 % agree with expression of disgust at homosexuality conceptualized as disease, deviance and immoral behaviour. What can be seen in this particular group of respondents is that while explicitly offensive dehumanizing language is less likely to be accepted, polarizing arguments related to moral standards and value systems have a higher chance of receiving a positive evaluation.

Next, the participants were asked whether the six aforementioned examples would be assessed differently if they had been written in private contexts online (e.g. private emails, private chat, private Facebook pages): 29.5% replied *Yes*, 57.3% replied *No*, and 13.1% — *Don't know*. The fact that the majority of respondents did not see any difference here might reflect the phenomenon of blurring the boundaries between private and public modes of communicating within cyberspace. Those (61.4%) who answered *Yes* claimed that private context would render the comments more acceptable. The finding thus shows that respondents' sensitivity decreases in private contexts of language use.

In Question 2, the participants were asked a categorical question (*Yes-often, Yes-rarely, No, Don't know*) concerning whether they had ever been a target of insults, threats on the grounds of nationality, skin colour, ethnic origin, religion, gender, sexual orientation or other. The results are summarized in Table 2.

Table 2. Respondents' answers: being a target of insults or threats on various grounds

	Yes-often	*Yes-rarely*	*No*	*Don't know*
Nationality	2%	14.4%	81.6%	2%
Skin colour	0.9%	3.1%	95.4%	0.7%
Ethnic origin	0.9%	6.3%	91.9%	0.9%
Religion	5%	21%	73.1%	0.9%
Gender	6.6%	30.4%	60.6%	2.4%
Sexual orientation	3.1%	5.9%	90.4%	0.7%

As regards the Other category, the participants mentioned the whole variety of factors, such as appearance, political views and affiliations, weight, age difference in peer group, clothes, family problems, hair length, defending others against hate speech, promoting multi-culturalism, belonging to a subculture, place of residence, disability, education, early pregnancy, social democratic views (being leftist), being pro-refugee, provenance from a small town or village, provenance from a poor less affluent family, musical preferences, being a feminist, achieving good standards at a university, sexual identity, supporting a particular sport club. When asked to mark one or more categories where the respondents were subjected to threats or insults, the most frequently selected items were "at school" (59.3%), "online" (46.3%), "in the street" (41.1%), "on public transport" (23.3%), "at work" (23.3%) and "in relation to sports" (14.1%). The results show that gender and religion are the most frequent causes of threats and insults, with school and cyberspace being spaces where such attacks most often take place. Needless to say, online incivility is of particular relevance to our study.

In Question 3, the participants were asked whether they had ever witnessed anyone being a target of insults or threats on the grounds of nationality, skin colour, ethnic origin, religion, gender, sexual orientation or other. The results are summarized in Table 3.

Table 3. Respondents' answers: witnessing anyone being a target of insults or threats on various grounds

	Yes-often	*Yes-rarely*	*No*	*Don't know*
Nationality	23.4%	38.9%	37%	0.7%
Skin colour	24.7%	40.9%	33.7%	0.7%
Ethnic origin	21%	32.2%	44.2%	2.6%
Religion	27.1%	38.7%	32.8%	1.3%
Gender	17.1%	34.4%	47%	1.5%
Sexual orientation	34.6%	37%	27.1%	1.3%

As regards the Other category, the participants were again asked an open question to provide the particular reason; the most frequently selected ones include political views, physical appearance, weight, personality traits, behaviour, homelessness, alcoholism, poor financial status, begging, personal views and values and no reason at all. In the same vein, such incidents were most often witnessed "online" (83.4%), "in the street" (71.9%), "at school" (57.9%), "on public transport" (55.6%), "at work" (25.2%) and "in relation to sports" (24.7%). When it comes to witnessing insults directed at others, the results concerning different motivations are rather comparable, with gender being the slightly less frequent cause. Online discourse, however, ranks first as a space within which verbal attacks on others can be witnessed.

In Question Four, the participants were first asked whether they would ever report insults or threats directed at them because of their nationality, skin colour, ethnicity, religion, gender or sexual orientation. Here, most respondents (48.5%) answered *Don't know*, 26.8% answered *No* and only 24.8% were in favour of reporting such incidents to the authorities. Those respondents who answered *No* or *Don't know* provided the following most common reasons for not doing so: *I do not think that the Police or authorities would do anything* (78.5%), *I would not know how to report it* (34.7%), *I do not think it is serious enough to report it* (25.5%), *It would be too much trouble to report it* (43%), *I would feel ashamed, embarrassed or uncomfortable* (22.6%), *I would be worried about reprisals* (16.9%), *The incident is too common an occurrence to report it* (15.2%). The results show that not much action is likely to be taken in the case of such incidents, mostly due to the lack of trust in the effectiveness of law enforcement bodies, lack of familiarity with the procedures of reporting and the perceived complexity of such procedures. Importantly, a considerable number of respondents do not consider verbal aggression to be an issue deserving serious attention.

In Question Five, the respondents were asked if they would report being a witness of someone being insulted or threatened because of their nationality, skin colour, ethnic origin, religion, gender or sexual orientation. The results revealed that the majority of the respondents (51.4%) answered *Don't know*, 19.3% answered *No* and 29.3% were in favour of reporting to the authorities being a witness of such incidents. Those respondents who answered *No* or *Don't know* provided the following most common reasons for ignoring the problem: *I do not think that the Police or authorities would do anything* (67.9%), *I would not know how to report it* (33.9%), *It would be too much trouble to report it* (31.2%), *I would be worried about reprisals* (23.7%), *I would feel ashamed, embarrassed or uncomfortable* (22.6%), *I think it is not my problem* (21.3%), *I do not think it is serious enough to report it* (14.1%), *The incident is too common an occurrence to report it* (9.6%). As it was the case with the previous question, the main reason behind the possible inaction of the majority of respondents seems to be the perceived ineffectiveness of law-enforcement authorities, not knowing the procedures related to reporting such cases or considering such a process too complicated.

Question Six referred to whether the participants had ever heard of the notion of *Hate Speech*. Here, 84.5% answered *Yes*, 9.2% answered *No* and 6.3% claimed that that they have no recollection of that. The results then demonstrate that the concept of "hate speech" as such is well known among young Polish people.

Finally, in Question Seven, the participants were presented with four definitions of hate speech and they were asked to indicate the extent to which they agree or disagree with each of them. The results are presented right next to the English glosses of the Polish-language definitions.

(1) Mowa nienawiści oznacza wypowiadanie negatywnych, opartych na uprzedzeniach komentarzy na temat ludzi z powodu ich rasy lub narodowości lub pochodzenia etnicznego lub religii lub płci lub orientacji seksualnej 'Hate speech means making negative prejudiced remarks about people because of their race or nationality or ethnic origins or religion or gender or sexual orientation' [*Strongly agree — 33.9%, Agree- 36.8%, Somewhat agree — 18.2%, Don't know — 4.6%, Somewhat disagree — 2%, Disagree — 2.4%, Strongly disagree — 2.2%*].

(2) Mowa nienawiści oznacza obrażanie kogoś ze względu na rasę, narodowość lub pochodzenie etniczne lub religię lub płeć lub orientację seksualną

'Hate speech means insulting someone because of their race or nationality or ethnic origin or religion or gender or sexual orientation'[*Strongly agree — 34.6%, Agree — 43.8%, Somewhat agree — 14.2%, Don't know — 3.5%, Somewhat disagree — 1.1%, Disagree — 1.1%, Strongly disagree — 1.8%*].

(3) Mowa nienawiści oznacza grożenie komuś ze względu na rasę, narodowość lub pochodzenie etniczne lub religię lub płeć lub orientację seksualną
'Hate speech means threatening someone because of their race or nationality or ethnic origin or religion or gender or sexual orientation' [*Strongly agree — 40.5%, Agree — 35.4%, Somewhat agree — 13.3%, Don't know — 6.3%, Somewhat disagree — 2%, Disagree — 0.9%, Strongly disagree — 1.5%*]

(4) Mowa nienawiści oznacza nakłanianie innych do przemocy lub okazywania nienawiści wobec ludzi ze względu na rasę, narodowość lub pochodzenie etniczne lub religię lub płeć lub orientację seksualną
'Hate speech means encouraging other people to be violent towards or show hatred towards people because of their race or nationality or ethnicity or religion or gender or sexual orientation' [*Strongly agree — 39.6%, Agree — 28.4%, Somewhat agree — 16.4%, Don't know — 9.4%, Somewhat disagree — 3.3%, Disagree — 1.5%, Strongly disagree — 1.3%*]

As demonstrated by the results (Table 4), the majority of respondents would agree with defining hate speech as making negative prejudiced remarks about people, offending and threatening them on the grounds of nationality, ethnicity, religion, gender or sexual orientation as well as inciting others to such acts. What is more, in response to the answer whether there should be any laws against these types of hate speech, most of the respondents were in favour of that idea. Yet, slight differences can be observed when it comes to approval of penalizing particular types of hate speech, which is the highest for threats, followed by incitement to violence, insults and negative comments respectively. When it comes to the percentage of respondents who answered *No* to penalizing various types of hate speech, it was the highest for negative comments, slightly lower for insults and then decreased by half for incitement to violence, being the lowest for threats. This shows that negative prejudiced comments and insults posted online are less likely to be perceived as something that requires legal regulations.

Table 4. Respondents' opinion on whether there should be laws against different types of hate speech

	Definition 1	Definition 2	Definition 3	Definition 4
Yes	71.3%	77.5%	89.1%	85.8%
No	13.3%	8.8%	2.8%	4.2%
Don't know	15.3%	13.8%	8.1%	10.1%

7.2 Corpus linguistic study: results and discussion

Using SketchEngine software (Kilgarriff et al. 2014), we identified keywords in the corpus of the Internet users' online comments as compared with the *Niezalezna.pl* (NPL) corpus used for reference purposes. More specifically, the keywords were identified by using the Simple math[16] method proposed by Kilgarriff (2009) and focusing on rare words with the minimum frequency of 5 in the study corpus (CNPL). For the sake of clarity, we decided to filter out function words and proper names from the list of keywords. At the same time, we decided to retain keywords with spelling errors. The reason for that is that Polish internet users often use English keyboard settings when writing their comments, which results in the omission of Polish diacritics and subsequent failure to conform to orthographic and spelling norms of standard Polish. Finally, we did not convert capital letters to small letters. The top-25 keywords in the CNPL corpus, supplemented with frequency information (raw and normalized per million words, in short 'pmw'), are presented in Table 5.

As in the present study, we focus on anti-refugee discourse, we first compared, in terms of selected lexical and grammatical contexts, the nouns *uchodźca*, *uchodzcy* and *uchodzcow* 'refugee/refugees' as used in the press articles (NPL) and the online comments following them (CNPL) respectively. The first one (*uchodźca*) is a distinct lemma (noun), while the remaining ones (*uchodzcow, uchodzcy*), ranked 1st and 5th on the keyword list in the CNPL corpus, are two inflectional forms of the said noun used in the genitive case plural and nominative case plural respectively. Because the two inflectional forms are used with spelling errors (the lack of Polish diacritics), they have not been lemmatized.[17] Also, two negatively charged nouns, if used with reference to people, are conspicuous in the keyword list, namely *dzicz* 'savages' and *bydło* 'beasts' (ranked 8th and 23rd respectively). As we hypothesize that these nouns may constitute important exponents of hate speech, they were also analyzed in greater detail in their larger lexical and grammatical contexts, as attested in the CNPL corpus. In the analysis, we focused on the top 10 collocates (or fewer, depending on data availability) as computed by the software using a modified logDice score (Rychlý 2008), with later modifications. Needless to say, collocations, or combinations of words that frequently occur together (e.g. *heavy traffic, slanted eyes, decline an offer*), are identified statistically by corpus linguists who aim to establish whether words occur together in texts

16. https://www.sketchengine.co.uk/documentation/simple-maths/

17. Likewise, those collocates of the keywords, which are written with spelling errors, have not been lemmatized throughout the analyses. That is why one may occassionally notice problems with concord or agreement.

Table 5. The top-25 keywords in the CNPL corpus

No.	Keyword	Frequency	Frequency pmw
1.	***uchodzcow***	73	253
2.	*powinien*	73	253
3.	*inaczej*	63	218
4.	*masz*	62	214
5.	***uchodzcy***	52	180
6.	*lewactwo*	49	169
7.	*demokracji*	49	169
8.	***dzicz***	48	166
9.	*nalezy*	43	148
10.	*dać*	42	145
11.	*unii*	41	142
12.	*dobrze*	41	142
13.	*socjal*	38	131
14.	*demokracja*	36	124
15.	*gości*	35	121
16.	*wiary*	33	114
17.	*żaden*	31	107
18.	*rządzi*	31	107
19.	*Boga*	31	107
20.	*żyć*	30	104
21.	*najlepiej*	30	104
22.	*moga*	30	104
23.	***bydło***	30	104
24.	*zycia*	29	100
25.	*emigranci*	28	97

systematically or by chance. In the tables presented below, the words co-occurring with the keywords are sorted according to logDice score, yet for the sake of clarity we also provide frequency information. As our aim was to conduct a maximally comprehensive description of the lexical means contributing to the discursive representation of refugees, we did not decide to filter out those collocates that occur in the study corpora only once; however, since some of them may be considered idiosyncratic, we did not resort to making any far-fetched conclusions based on the use of those low-frequency keywords.

Table 6. Adjectival modifiers + *uchodźca / uchodzcy / uchodzcow*

uchodźca 'refugee' in *NPL*		*uchodźca* 'refugee' in *CNPL*		*uchodzcy* 'refugees' in *CNPL*		*uchodzcow* 'refugees' in *CNPL*	
Collocate	Freq.	Collocate	Freq.	Collocate	Freq.	Collocate	Freq.
syryjski	8	*tzw.*	11	*zadni*	3	*ukrainskich*	1
islamski	4	*żaden*	14	*wszyscy*	1	*bialych*	1
tzw.	2	*wojenny*	6	*przybyły*	1	*mlodych*	1
afgański	2	*biedny*	5	*kochany*	1	*muzulmanskich*	1
arabski	2	*islamski*	6	*wojenny*	2	*tzw.*	2
		jeden	7	*jeden*	2	*biedny*	1
		który	5	*który*	1	*muzułmański*	1
		wszystek	5	*ten*	4	*wszystek*	1
		zmęczony	2			*ten*	3
		afrykański	2				

First, we compared the nouns *uchodźca*, *uchodzcy* and *uchodzcow* ('refugee/refugees') (Table 6) in terms of their adjectival modifiers. Interestingly, the results revealed that in most cases when the term "refugee" appears in the articles it is used in inverted commas to undermine the person's legal (and social) status. A similar effect is achieved by using the word *tzw.* 'so-called' (1):

(1) Grupa tzw. „uchodźców" zaczęła zaczepiać tam młoda kobietę. [Niezalezna.pl, 07/02/2016]
'A group of the so-called „refugees" began to bother a young woman there.'

The same attitude is adopted in the comments, where the collocates "so-called refugees" or "pseudo-refugees" are used to undermine the status of this group (2). If we look at it from the perspective of Searle's (1995) status functions and deontic powers, the "so-called" status has two serious implications. Firstly, not being "real" refugees these people are not trustworthy; secondly, they are not entitled to expect help and European solidarity. We can see, however, that readers-commenters go one step further than journalists as they assign a new status to migrants, using such constructions as *To nie są żadni uchodźcy, tylko...* ('These are no refugees, but...') or *To nie są żadni uchodźcy, to są ...* ('These are no refugees, these are...'), where the term "refugees" is juxtaposed with "terrorists" or "criminals". Alternatively, they are referred to as "Islamic invaders" or "savages", either intending to destroy Europe or sent to do so. Interestingly, as we can see in example (7) conclusions as to their status are sometimes drawn on the basis of their physical appearance as presented in photos and videos provided by the site.

(2) Nie chcemy pseudo uchodźców islamskich
'We don't want Islamic pseudo refugees'

(3) Zamachowcy z Brukseli to "uchodźcy". Ilu jeszcze terrorystów wpuszczono do Europy?
'Bombers from Brussels are "refugees". How many terrorists were admitted to Europe?'

(4) to nie sa zadni uchodzcy lecz nasylana na Europe dzicz
'these are not refugees but savages sent to Europe'

(5) To nie są żadni uchodźcy ! To zwyczajni bandyci i terroryści!
'these are not refugees ! These are regular bandits and terrorists!'

(6) Bandziory wypuszczone z więzień w Iraku, Afganistanie i państw północno-afrykańskich nie są żadnymi uchodźcami tylko arabskimi kryminalistami
'Goons released from prisons in Iraq, Afghanistan and North African countries are not refugees but Arab criminals'

(7) tak nie wyglądają uchodźcy wojenni! Tak wyglądają islamscy najeźdźcy!
'this is not what war refugees look like! This is what Islamic invaders look like'

To negate their war refugee status, the concept of "social parasite" is also employed by commenters (for parasite metaphors see Musolff, this volume). Migrants are thus conceptualized as "ten-lined potato beetle" preying on the host country's population. References are even made to past events, a countrywide action in Poland in the 1950s to eliminate this pest (temporal and epistemic proximization).

(8) Takie zachowanie najeźdźców tyko potwierdza, że nie są uchodźcami wojennymi a jedynie pasożytami społecznymi, żerującymi na danym państwie, do którego się dostaną. Przypominają stonkę ziemniaczaną. Walka ze stonką była ciężka i uciążliwa od 1952 roku…
'Such behaviour of invaders only confirms that they are not war refugees but social parasites only, preying on the country to which they get. They resemble Colorado potato beetle. The fight against the Colorado potato beetle was heavy and cumbersome since 1952 …'

An important spatio-temporally proximizing function of deictic "these" used as a modifier should also be mentioned here. The phrase "these refugees" makes the group present "here and now" and evokes an image of someone pointing at this group with contempt. Judgements about their evil intentions, which are a priori attributed to them, are made, as well as predictions about their behaviour in the near future.

(9) trzeba takich tępić bo to są nieroby,złodzieje, kombinatorzy, gwałciciele, zbrodniarze, bandyci !! Ci uchodzcy,nie szukają żadnego schronienia,tylko chcą się rozsiać po całej UE,to jest ich przeznaczenie i cel aby zniszczyć całą UE !!
'you have to combat them because they are spivs, thieves, swindlers, rapists, criminals, bandits !! These refugees do not seek any shelter, they want to spread across the EU, it is their destiny and purpose to destroy the whole of the EU !!'

(10) Ci uchodzcy w tym roku zaczna na dobre rozrabiac, to jest banda nie wyksztalconych oprychow nie przydatnych do niczego, ktorzy beda zyc tylko z pomocy socjalnej i z bandyctwa.
'This year these refugees will start, for good, to brawl, this is a bunch of uneducated thugs not useful for anything, who will live on social benefits and robbery.'

In *Niezalezna.pl* articles, all occurrences of "Islamic refugees" are linked to negative, morally unacceptable actions (axiological proximization) and a possible threat to the host population (11, 12, 13, 14). They are presented as having no respect for human life in general and women in particular (frequent mentions of attacks directed at European women). Additionally, they are linked to terrorist activities. The collocate "Arab refugees" is used in a similar context, while "Afghan refugees" is further modified by a negatively-charged adjective associated with the concept of violence, e.g.:

(11) W Finlandii aresztowano islamskich uchodźców. W Iraku mordowali strzałem w tył głowy. [Niezalezna.pl, 12/12/2015]
'In Finland, Muslim refugees were arrested. In Iraq, they killed with shot in the head.'

(12) Napady islamskich uchodźców na kobiety trwały w Niemczech już od miesięcy, lecz były skutecznie skrywane przed opinią publiczną. [Niezalezna.pl, 13/01/2016]
'Attacks by Islamic refugees on women in Germany lasted for months, but they were effectively concealed from the public.'

(13) Arabscy uchodźcy podejrzewani są o dokonanie przynajmniej 11 morderstw w ramach działań terrorystycznych. [Niezalezna.pl, 12/12/2015]
'Arab refugees are suspected of perpetrating at least 11 murders in the context of terrorist activities'

(14) Został zaczepiony przez dwóch agresywnych afgańskich uchodźców. [Niezalezna.pl, 30/07/2016] 'He was accosted by two aggressive Afghan refugees.'

In the comments following the articles from which the above examples are extracted, the collocate "Islamic refugees" is often replaced with "Islamic immigrants", "Islamic savages", and "Islamic beasts". One of the commenters makes a reference to Hitler, thus implying a possible way of dealing with the "problem" (15). The structure "Imagine that now…", followed by verbs in present tense, acts as a strong proximization trigger — the possible scenario can be visualized as happening right now in front of readers' eyes (spatiotemporal dimension), and based on audience's knowledge of history is likely to evoke particular associations, judgements and emotions (epistemic, axiological, and emotional dimension).

(15) Proszę sobie wyobrazić, że teraz na trybunę wchodzi nowy Adolf i krzyczy ze zrobi z islamskimi uchodźcami porządek.
'Imagine that now a new Adolf enters a grandstand and shouts that he will put things in order with Islamic refugees.'

Speculations about a possible (and desirable) appearance of "new Adolf" are also made by other commenters. It seems worth mentioning at this point that the most frequent historical references with epistemically and axiologically proximizing function are those concerning John III Sobieski, a Polish king credited with turning back the last great wave of Muslim expansion in Europe because of his victory against the Turks in the battle of Vienna in 1683. His actions are given as an example of patriotic spirit and something to be cherished and continued. From this perspective, letting in refugees, who are Muslims, will be a crime and lack of respect for national history and values, as we read in (19).

(16) i usilnie namawiam rodaków do bezwzgledności ! Po co Jan III Sobieski ich pogonił, tak sobie a my mamy to w d…e ?
'and I strongly urge my compatriots to be ruthless! Why John III Sobieski chased them away, for nothing and we don't give a f…k?'

(17) Tolerancja dla islamu ? TAK ! TAKA JAK JAN III SOBIESKI MIAŁ :)
'Tolerance for Islam ? YES! SUCH TOLERANCE AS SHOWN BY JOHN III SOBIESKI :)'

(18) już Jan III Sobieski pokazał jak trzeba nawracać islamistów pod Wiedniem
'John III Sobieski showed how to convert Muslims at [the Battle of] Vienna'

(19) Jeśli ktoś wpuści do Polski muzułmanów popełni zbrodnię, zaprzeczy pamięci morza krwi, którą przelali nasi Dziadowie walcząc a właściwie broniąc Europy przed islamizacją. wg standardów dzisiejszej poprawności politycznej Jan III Sobieski był nietolerancyjnym nazistą.

> 'If someone admits Muslims to Poland, he/she will commit a crime, deny the memory of the sea of blood shed by our grandfathers fighting, actually — defending, Europe from Islamization. according to the standards of today's political correctness, John III Sobieski was intolerant Nazi.'

While appeals to the national pride, identity and history seem to be one way of motivating people to act against refugees, another strategy is evoking fear and anger by describing their actions. Accordingly, we decided to examine verbs following nouns "refugee/refugees" in the subject position to see how the agency of this group is constructed (Table 7).

Table 7. *Uchodźca* in the subject position + verb

uchodźca 'refugee' in *NPL*		*uchodźca* 'refugee' in *CNPL*		*uchodzcy* 'refugee' in *CNPL*		*uchodzcow*[17] 'refugee' in *CNPL*	
Collocate	Freq.	Collocate	Freq.	Collocate	Freq.	Collocate	Freq.
mieć	9	*zaatakować*	*3*	*przedchodzą*	1		
trafić	4	*trafić*	*3*	*potrzebuja*	1		
otrzymywać	3	*mieć*	*4*	*lecieć*	1		
kosztować	3			*iść*	1		
pochodzić	3						
zaatakować	3						
przyjechać	3						
napaść	2						
zabić	2						
zgwałcić	2						
podpalić	2						

In addition to spatially proximizing motion verbs (e.g., *przyjechać* 'arrive', *trafić* 'land/end up') used by *Niezalezna.pl*, the website also mentions criminal and violent actions undertaken by refugees (*zaatakować* 'attack', *napaść* 'assault', *zgwałcić* 'rape', *podpalić* 'set on fire', *zabić* 'kill'). The role of a victim is not without importance here as far as axiological and emotional proximization is concerned. In most cases, the victim of refugees' criminal acts is either a woman or a child — their inscribed vulnerability emphasizes the immorality of the attack, which is more likely to evoke negative emotional reactions, including anger and need for revenge, in the audience. Another strong emotional trigger is a reference to Polish people as victims of violent acts (21, 23, 24, 25). Due to cultural affinity, the threat becomes

18. Since the word *uchodzcow* is used in the genitive case plural, it cannot function as a subject of the sentence in Polish.

more tangible and imminent. It is also likely to evoke stronger in-group–out-group tensions and, eventually, hostility. A critical point is reached when a victim, killed with a machete, turns out to be a woman, who is not only Polish but also pregnant (21). Yet another example of a person fit for a perfect victim status is a Polish homeless man set on fire while asleep (25).

(19) 23-letni islamski uchodźca napadł na 10-letnią uczennicę. [Niezalezna.pl, 13/01/2016] '23-year-old Muslim refugee attacked a 10-year-old student.'

(20) Kolejny dramat w Niemczech — syryjski uchodźca zabił maczetą kobietę. [Niezalezna.pl, 26/07/2016] 'Another drama in Germany — a Syrian refugee killed a woman with a machete.'

(21) Ofiarą syryjskiego uchodźcy z maczetą była młoda Polka w ciąży. [Niezalezna.pl, 24/07/2016]
'A victim of a Syrian refugee with a machete was a young Polish pregnant woman.'

(22) Uchodźcy zgwałcili tłumaczkę telewizyjnej ekipy w Calais. W Dżungli to nic nadzwyczajnego. [Niezalezna.pl, 18/10/2016]
'Refugees raped an interpreter of a television crew in Calais. It is anything but extraordinary in The Jungle.'

(23) Afgańscy uchodźcy napadli na polską parę. Bili także kobietę z dzieckiem. [Niezalezna.pl, 30/07/2016]
'Afghan refugees attacked a Polish couple. They beat the woman and her child.'

(24) Uchodźcy zaatakowali Polaka. Przy granicy polsko-niemieckiej doszło do tragedii. W niemieckiej części Zgorzelca dwóch imigrantów z Syrii napadło na Polaka. 21 i 18-latek w centrum handlowym za pomocą sygnetu do podcinania gardła zranili Polaka. [Niezalezna.pl, 21/05/2016]
'Refugees attacked a Pole. At the German-Polish border a tragedy unfolded. In the German part of Zgorzelec, two immigrants from Syria attacked the Pole. Using a signet designed to undercut the throat, 21- and 18-year-old hurt the Pole at the mall.'

(25) Uchodźcy podpalili Polaka. Grupa siedmiu młodych uchodźców w Boże Narodzenie podpaliła bezdomnego mężczyznę — Polaka, który spał na stacji metra w Berlinie. [Niezalezna.pl, 28/12/2016]
'Refugees set fire to a Pole. During Christmas, a group of seven young refugees set fire to a homeless man — a Pole, who was sleeping in an underground station in Berlin.'

The responses of commenters to, for example, the death of the Polish woman, are more emotionally-charged, both in terms of aggression directed to the refugee and empathy for the victim. We have a contrast between the woman, "our Compatriot" (the capital letter indicating respect), who went abroad to earn a living for her children (positive moral evaluation of her actions), and "a Muslim beast" or "some Islamic barbarian", who, as the terms suggest, is sub-human.

(26) Muzułmańskie bydle zaszlachtowało naszą Rodaczkę.
'A Muslim beast slaughtered our compatriot'

(27) Kobieta pojechała za granicę, żeby zapewnić byt swoim dzieciom, a jakiś islamski barbarzyńca zabił ją maczetą.
'The woman went abroad to ensure survival of her children, and some Islamic barbarian killed her with a machete.'

Since dehumanizing metaphors play an important role in the comments because of their frequency-related salience and axiologically- and emotionally-proximizing potential, we decided to focus on two negatively-charged keywords in the CNPL, namely *dzicz* 'savages' and *bydło* 'beasts' (Table 8). As mentioned earlier, the words co-occurring with the two keywords are sorted according to logDice score, yet for the sake of clarity we also provide frequency information.

Table 8. Adjectival modifiers of the nouns *dzicz* and *bydło* in the CNPL

dzicz* 'savages' in *CNPL		***bydło* 'beasts' in *CNPL***	
Collocate	**Freq.**	**Collocate**	**Freq.**
barbarzynska	2	*To*	6
muzulmanska	2	*islamski*	6
prymitywny	2	*pozaeuropejski*	1
islamski	6	*pustołbe*	1
ten	17	*muslimskie*	1

Dehumanizing refugees by conceptualizing them as "savages" and "beasts" has, as mentioned in Section 4, two important consequences. Firstly, being lower than human, they have no respect for "human" values. Secondly, they do not deserve to be treated in the humane way. The emphasis is thus placed on their aggressive behaviour, animal instinct, and murderous desires. These are used (as in 29) as a pretext to legitimize actions against members of this group, ranging from chasing them away to killing. To proximize the threat they constitute temporally, present tense is used as in (28). Hence, as the threat is presented as imminent, there appears an urgency to act, manifested in exclamations and imperatives expressing commands.

(28) dzicz islamska atakuje
'Islamic savages are attacking us'

(29) A to bydło islamskie. Dlaczego nikt do tego czegoś nie strzela?
'Such Islamic beasts. Why isn't anyone shooting at them?'

(30) POGONIĆ TO MUSLIMSKIE BYDŁO ! Co to wogólle za czasy by do każdego kraju w Europie wjeżdżało co chciało
'CHASE AWAY THESE MUSLIM BEASTS' What times are we living in — anything may enter any country in Europe'

While as expected adjectives describing religious affiliation are used as collocates of both, the word "savages" is further modified by "primitive" and "barbarian", while the word "beasts" by "empty-headed". An opposition is constructed between a Christian, European, civilized world and the world of the primitive Other. Having no intelligence and morality, this Other has no respect for "our" values and since reasoning with him or her is out of the question the only way to protect our values is to use force.

(31) To jest barbarzynska dzicz, dla ktorej tolerancja i demokracja sa oznakami slabosci.
'They are barbaric beasts, for which tolerance and democracy are the signs of weakness.'

(32) Dzicz muzulmanska precz z Europy.
'Muslim beasts go away from Europe.'

The threat is also presented as being of financial nature and spatiotemporally proximized by the use of water metaphors in the form of such verbs as "flood", "stream into", "pour into" further de-individualising these people but also implying unpredictability and lack of control. Another strategy is evoking the feeling of disgust. Not only is the Other primitive, but also stinky.

(33) Bydło islamskie wleje się do nas i będziemy ich utrzymywać.
'Muslim beasts will pour into us and we will financially support them'

(34) To jest skandal, żeby za pieniądze podatników utrzymywać w cywilizowanym świecie tą prymitywną dzicz !
'It is outrageous that in the civilized world these primitive beasts is financially supported with taxpayers' money'

(35) A może warto się pozbyć tego co zasmradza ulice Warszawy. Skąd ta dzicz islamska się tu wzięła? Nie mam zamiaru jako Polska płacić na ich socjal i mieszkanie.

> 'Maybe we should get rid of what contaminates the streets of Warsaw. Where have these Islamic beasts come from? As a Pole, I'm not going to pay for their social benefits and housing.'

9. Conclusions

In our study of hateful discourses, we wanted to explore the interface between hate speech (and the perception of this phenomenon), online communication, and discursive construction of the Other. The current socio-political context, in particular refugee crisis, coupled with growing nationalism and xenophobia throughout Europe, was a motivation to look at refugees and immigrants as the Other. As a matter of fact, since ethnicity and religion have always been the key criteria in self-identification and in-group vs. out-group polarization, migrants with a predominantly Middle Eastern provenance and Muslim faith can be regarded as an "ideal" Other, notably in ethnically and religiously homogenous societies, such as, for example, Polish.

The hypothesis we put forward at the beginning of this chapter was that the hateful discourses of online comments are encouraged by media representation of migrants and refugees (or rather by what is made salient in this representation) and enabled by the semiotic potential of cyberspace, and the key mechanism in both cases is that of *proximization*. To validate this hypothesis we analysed and compared a corpus of articles from the conservative online news portal *Niezalezna.pl* with a corpus including online comments following these articles. We focused on keywords and word co-occurrence patterns in both corpora; the former, because, as stipulated in the previous sections, they act as proximization triggers making certain aspects of discursively represented events or groups more salient; the latter, as they allowed us to examine patterns of representation of groups in question in terms of naming and reference, as well as agency. The results show that negative aspects of representation present in the articles are adopted and further developed by the commenters. Due to journalistic standards, an explicitly hateful discourse was not used in the articles. For example, dehumanizing metaphors of "savages" and "beasts" could only be found in the comments. However, with their negative representation built on undermining the real status of refugees and constructing them as a threat (by attributing aggressive and harmful actions to them), the articles provide powerful epistemic, axiological, and emotional triggers for contempt and aggression in ensuing comments. It should be mentioned at this point that negativity in the articles is only partially the result of the news portal's conservative (and anti-refugee) stance. Rather, it should be linked to proximization mechanism inherent in news discourse as such. In order to reduce the epistemic, axiological and emotional distance, journalists will rely on stereotypical representations and opt for personalised tragedies and conflict of moral values resulting in Us vs. Them polarization. There are also biological and psychological reasons behind it, namely "people's innate interest in two types of information: (1) people, ideas, or events that are deviant (either positive or negative); and (2) people, ideas, or events that have significance to the society" (Shoemaker and Cohen 2006, 3). In this light, the media construction of threat and presenting it as imminent and relevant to the society is indeed self-explanatory. Provided with such triggers and alerted to the threat, the Internet users, subject to less editorial control, may further construe the Other as an enemy to be debased, dehumanized, and, ultimately, annihilated. Since, as mentioned at the beginning of this volume, cyberspace, with its interactive and intertextual potential, allows groups and individuals with similar (often radical) ideas to connect, a "spiral of hate" can be generated by subsequent comments.[19] Furthermore, as shown by the results of our survey concerning public perception of hate speech, there exists considerable social acceptance of verbal abuse and aggression in online communication; also, the survey results revealed that the instances of hate speech are rarely reported to the police mostly due to perceived ineffectiveness of law enforcement agencies. From that it follows that more interdisciplinary research is required in the future to explore the links between legal instruments, law enforcement and social acceptance of hate speech in online and offline modes of communication, both private and public.

Acknowledgements

This study is part of the research project C.O.N.T.A.C.T. *Creating On-line Network, Monitoring Team and Phone App to Counter Hate Crime Tactics* 2015–2017 (www.reportinghate.eu), co-financed by the EU Commission (grant no. JUST/2014/RRAC/AG/HATE/6706).

19. The degree to which a given forum is moderated is not without influence here. The Rules and Regulations of the forum we analysed stipulate: "On the forum of Niezalezna.pl, we publish opinions of users of our website. All posts are subject to moderation. We shall remove all and any posts that contain punishable threats and any provocations targeted at Niezalezna.pl. We do not publish vulgar posts, and we fight against trolling". As our analysis demonstrated, despite these provisions, both offensive comments targeted at refugees and incitement to violence could be found in the data we examined. Still, it should be emphasized that the amount of hate speech found there cannot compare with the number and quality of hateful comments identified within *Youtube* corpus, which was also collected and analyzed within the C.O.N.T.A.C.T. project.

References

Alfred, Charlotte. 12 September, 2015. "What history can teach us about the worst refugee crisis since WWII". *Hu ngtonpost.com.au.* Available at: http:// www.huffingtonpost.com.au/entry/alexander-betts-refugees-wwii_55f30f7ce4b077ca094edae c?section=australia&adsSite Override=au. [Accessed 15 September 2016].

Appadurai, Arjun. 2006. *Fear of Small Numbers: An Essay on the Geography of Anger.* Durham: Duke University Press.

Bachman, Bart. 16 June 2016. "Diminishing solidarity: Polish Attitudes toward the European migration and refugee crisis". *The Online Journal of the Migration Policy Institute.* Available at: http://www.migrationpolicy.org/article/diminishing-solidarity-polish-attitudes-toward-european-migration-and-refugee-crisis. [Accessed 25 September 2016].

Baker, Paul. 2006. *Using Corpora for Discourse Analysis.* London: Continuum.

Baker, Paul. 2016. "The shapes of collocation". *International Journal of Corpus Linguistics* 21(2): 139–164.

Baker, Paul, Costas Gabrielatos, Majid Khosravinik, Michał Krzyzanowski, Tony McEnery, and Ruth Wodak. 2008. "A useful methodological synergy? Combining critical discourse analysis and corpus linguistics to examine discourses of refugees and asylum seekers in the UK press". *Discourse & Society* 19(3): 273–305.

Bandura Albert, Bill Underwood, and Michael E Fromson. 1975. "Disinhibition of aggression through diffusion of responsibility and dehumanization of victims". *Journal of Research in Personality* 9(4): 253–269.

Bartmiński, Jerzy. 2010. "Pojęcie językowego obrazu świata i sposoby jego operacjonalizacji". In: *Jaka antropologia literatury jest dzisiaj możliwa,* edited by Przemysaw Czapliński, Anna Legeżyńska, and Marcin Telicki, 155–178. Poznań: Poznańskie Studia Polonistyczne.

Berger, Peter, and Thomas Luckmann. 1966/1991. *The social construction of reality. A treatise in the sociology of knowledge.* London: Penguin Books.

Bleiker, Roland, David Campbell, Emma Hutchison, and Xzarina Nicholson. 2013. "The visual dehumanization of refugees". *Australian Journal of Political Science* 48(4): 398–416.

Boden, Deirdre, and Harvey L. Molotch. 1994. "The compulsion of proximity". In *NowHere: Space, time, and modernity,* edited by Roger Friedland, and Deirdre Boden, 257–286. Berkeley: University of California Press.

Bridgman, Jon, and Leslie J. Worley. 2004. "Genocide of the Hereros". In *Century of Genocide: Critical Essays and Eyewitness Accounts,* edited by Samuel Totten, William S. Parsons, and Israel W. Charny, 15–51. New York: Routledge.

Buzan, Bary, Ole Wæver, and Jaap de Wilde. 1998. *Security: A New Framework for Analysis.* Boulder, London: Rienner.

Cap, Piotr. 2006. *Legitimization in Political Discourse: a Cross-Disciplinary Perspective on the Modern US War Rhetoric.* Newcastle: Cambridge Scholars Press.

Cap, Piotr. 2008. "Towards the proximization model of the analysis of legitimization in political discourse". *Journal of Pragmatics* 40: 17–41.

Cap, Piotr. 2010. "Axiological aspects of proximization". *Journal of Pragmatics* 42: 392–407.

Cap, Piotr. 2013. *Proximization: the Pragmatics of Symbolic Distance Crossing.* Amsterdam: Benjamins.

Charteris-Black, Jonathan. 2005. *Politicians and Rhetoric. The Persuasive Power of Metaphor.* New York: Palgrave Macmilan.

Charteris-Black, Jonathan. 2004. *Corpus Approaches to Critical Metaphor Analysis.* Basingstoke: Palgrave Macmillan.
Chilton, Paul. 2004. *Analysing Political Discourse: Theory and Practice.* London: Routledge.
Chilton, Paul. 2005. "Discourse Space Theory: geometry, brain and shifting viewpoints". *Annual Review of Cognitive Linguistics* 3: 78–116.
Chilton, Paul. 2014. *Language, Space and Mind: the Conceptual Geometry of Linguistic Meaning.* Cambridge: Cambridge University Press.
Cohen, Stanley. 1972/2002. *Folk Devils and Moral Panics: The Creation of the Mods and Rockers.* London: Routledge.
Deutsch, Morton. 2000. "Justice and Conflict". In *The Handbook of Conflict Resolution,* edited by Morton Deutsch, and Peter T. Coleman, 41–64. San Francisco: Jossey-Bass.
Esses, Victoria, Stelian Medianu, and Andreas Lawson. 2013. "Uncertainty, Threat, and the Role of the Media in Promoting the Dehumanization of Immigrants and Refugees". *Journal of Social Issues* 69(3): 518–536.
Fairclough, Norman, and Ruth Wodak. 1997. "Critical discourse analysis". In *Discourse as social interaction,* edited by Teun A. van Dijk, 14–31. London: Sage.
Fowler, Roger. 1991. *Language in the news: discourse and ideology in the press.* London: Routledge.
Gabrielatos, Costas, and Paul Baker. 2008. "Fleeing, Sneaking, Flooding: A Corpus Analysis of Discursive Constructions of Refugees and Asylum Seekers in the UK Press 1996–2005". *Journal of English Linguistics* 36(1): 5–38.
Giddens, Anthony. 1991. *Modernity and Self-Identity: Self and Society in the Late Modern Age.* Stanford, CA: Stanford University Press.
Goode, Erich, and Ben-Yehuda, Nachman. 1994/2009. *Moral Panics: The Social Construction of Deviance* (2nd ed.). Oxford: Blackwell.
Grabowski, Łukasz. 2014. "Obraz Europy w Brytyjskim Korpusie Narodowym". In *Wartości w językowo-kulturowym obrazie świata Słowian i ich sąsiadów II,* edited by Jerzy Bartmiński, Stanisława Niebrzegowska-Bartmińska, and Iwona Bielińska-Gardziel, 163–183. Lublin: Wydawnictwo UMCS.
Hall, Stuart, Chas Critcher, Tony Jefferson, John Clarke, and Bryan Roberts. 1978. *Policing the Crisis: Mugging, the State and Law and Order.* London, UK: Macmillan.
Hart, Christopher. 2010. *Critical Discourse Analysis and Cognitive Science: New Perspectives on Immigration Discourse.* Basingstoke: Palgrave.
Harvey, David. 1990. *The Condition of Postmodernity: an Enquiry into the Origins of Cultural Change.* Cambridge, MA: Blackwell.
Henry, Frances, and Carol Tator. 2002. *Discourses of Domination: Racial Bias in the Canadian English-Language Press.* Toronto: University of Toronto Press.
Hester, Al. 1973. Theoretical considerations in predicting volume and direction of international information flow. *International Communication Gazette* 19: 239–247.
Huysmans, Jef. 2006. *The Politics of Insecurity. Fear, Migration and Asylum in the EU.* London and New York: Routledge.
IOM. 2015. "Irregular Migrant, Refugee Arrivals in Europe Top One Million in 2015: IOM", 22 December 2015. Retrieved from: https://www.iom.int/news/irregular-migrant-refugee-arrivals-europe-top-one-million-2015-iom. [Accessed 15 January 2017].
Kilgarriff, Adam. 2009. "Simple maths for keywords". In *Proceedings of Corpus Linguistics Conference CL2009.* University of Liverpool, UK, July 2009, edited by Michaela Mahlberg, Victorina González-Díaz, and Catherine Smith, Available at: https://www.sketchengine.co.uk/wp-content/uploads/2015/04/2009-Simple-maths-for-keywords.pdf

Kilgarriff, Adam, Vit Baisa, Jan Bušta, Milos Jakubícek, Vojtech Kovář, Jan Michelfeit, Pavel Rychlý, and Vit Suchomel. 2014. "The Sketch Engine: ten years on". *Lexicography* 1(1): 7–36. doi: 10.1007/s40607-014-0009-9

Klocker, Natascha, and Kevin Dunn. 2003. "Who's driving the asylum debate?: Newspaper and government representations of asylum seekers". *Media International Australia, Incorporating Culture & Policy* 109: 71–92.

Kopytowska, Monika. 2009. "Corpus linguistics and an eclectic approach to the study of news — the mechanism of framing". In *Studies in Cognitive Corpus Linguistics*, edited by Barbara Lewandowska-Tomaszczyk, and Katarzyna Dziwirek, 83–109. Frankfurt am Main: Peter Lang.

Kopytowska, Monika. 2010a. "Unveiling the Other — the pragmatics of Infosuasion". *Łódź Papers in Pragmatics* 6(2): 249–282.

Kopytowska, Monika. 2010b. "Mass-mediated multiculturalism and identity –representations of Muslims in the British press". In *Intercultural Europe: Arenas of Difference, Communication, and Mediation,* edited by Hanna Pułaczewska, 181–193. Stuttgart: Ibidem.

Kopytowska, Monika. 2013. "Blogging as the mediatization of politics and a new form of social interaction". In *Analyzing Genres in Political Communication*, edited by Piotr Cap, and Urszula Okulska, 379–421. Amsterdam: Benjamins.

Kopytowska, Monika. 2014. "Pictures in our heads: crisis, conflict, and drama". In *Why Discourse Matters: Negotiating Identity in the Mediatized World*, edited by Yusuf Kalyango, and Monika Kopytowska, 89–109. New York: Peter Lang.

Kopytowska, Monika. 2015a. "Ideology of 'here and now'. Mediating distance in television news". *Critical Discourse Studies* 12(3): 347–365.

Kopytowska, Monika. 2015b. "Covering conflict: between universality and cultural specificity in news discourse genre and journalistic style". *International Review of Pragmatics* (Special Issue on *Communicative styles and genres: between universality and culture-specificity*) 7. 308–339.

Kopytowska, Monika. 2015c. "Mediating identity, ideology and values in the public sphere: towards a new model of (constructed) social reality". *Łódź Papers in Pragmatics* 11(2): 133–156.

Kopytowska, Monika, and Grabowski Łukasz (2017). European security under threat: mediating the crisis and constructing the Other. In *National Identity and Europe in Times of Crisis Subtitle: Doing and Undoing Europe*, edited by Christian Karner, and Monika Kopytowska, 83–112. Bingley: Emerald Publishing.

Langacker, Ronald W. 1987. *Foundations of Cognitive Grammar. Theoretical Prerequisites.* Stanford: Stanford University Press.

Langacker, Ronald W. 1990. *Concept, image and symbol. The Cognitive Basis of Grammar*. Berlin: Mouton de Gruyter.

Lulle, Aija, and Elza Ungure. 2015. "Asylum seekers crisis in Europe 2015: Debating spaces of fear and security in Latvia". *Journal on Baltic Security* 1(2): 62–95.

Mahtani, Minelle, and Alison Mountz. 2002. "Immigration to British Columbia: Media Representation and Public Opinion". *Research on Immigration and Integration in the Metropolis Working Paper Series,* No. 02-15. [Accessed 15 January 2017]. Accessed at: http://mbc.metropolis.net/assets/uploads/files/wp/2002/WP02-15.pdf

Maskaliūnaitė, Asta. 2015. "Discursive and institutional management of refugees and their crisis in Lithuania". *Journal on Baltic Security* 1(2): 96–124.

McEnery, Tony, and Andrew Wilson. 1996. *Corpus Linguistics*. Edinburgh: University Press.

McLuhan, Marshall. 1994. *Understanding Media: the Extensions of Man*. Cambridge, Massachusetts: MIT Press.

Musolff, Andreas. 2012. "Immigrants and Parasites: The History of a Bio-Social Metaphor." In *Migrations: Interdisciplinary Perspectives,* edited by Michi Messer, Renée Schroeder, and Ruth Wodak, 249–258. Vienna: Springer.

Musolff, Andreas. 2014. "Metaphorical *parasites* and 'parasitic' metaphors: Semantic exchanges between political and scientific vocabularies." *Journal of Language and Politics* 13(2): 218–233

Musolff, Andreas. 2015. "Dehumanizing metaphors in UK immigrant debates in press and online media". *Journal of Language Aggression and Conflict* 3(1): 41–56.

Nagengast, Carole. 2002. "Inoculations of Evil in the U.S.-Mexican Border Region: Reflections on the Genocidal Potential of Symbolic Violence." In *Annihilating Difference: The Anthropology of Genocide,* edited by Alexander Laba Hinton, 325–347. Berkeley and Los Angeles: University of California Press.

O'Keeffe, Anne. 2006. *Investigating Media Discourse*. New York: Routledge.

Opotow, Susan. 1995. "Drawing the line: Social categorization, moral exclusion, and the scope of justice". In *Conflict, Cooperation, and Justice*, edited by Barbera. B. Bunker, and Jeffrey. Z. Rubin, 347–369. San Francisco: Jossey-Bass.

Phillips, Martin. 1989. *Lexical Structure of Text. Discourse Analysis Monographs 12*. Birmingham: University of Birmingham.

Poole, Elizabeth. 2002. *Reporting Islam. Media Representations of British Muslims*. London: IB Tauris.

Poole, Elizabeth, and John E. Richardson. 2006. *Muslims and the News Media*. London: IB Tauris.

Richardson, John. E. 2004. *(Mis)Representing Islam. The Racism and Rhetoric of British Broadsheet Newspapers*. Amsterdam: John Benjamins.

Richardson, John E., and Monica Colombo. 2013. "Continuity and change in anti-immigrant discourse in Italy: An analysis of the visual propaganda of the Lega Nord". *Journal of Language and Politics12*(2): 180–202.

Rychlý, Pavel. 2008. "A lexicographer-friendly association score". In *Proceedings of Recent Advances in Slavonic Natural Language Processing*, RASLAN, 6–9.

Santana, Arthur D. 2014. "Virtuous or Vitriolic". *Journalism Practice* 8 (1): 18–33.

Schank, Roger, and Robert Abelson. 1977. *Scripts, Plans, Goals, and Understanding*. Hillsdale: Erlbaum.

Scott, Mike. 2001. "Mapping key words to *problem* and *solution*". In *Patterns of Text: In Honour of Michael Hoey*, edited by Michael Hoey, Mike Scott Geoff Thompson, 109–127. Amsterdam: John Benjamins.

Searle, John. 1995. *The Construction of Social Reality*. London: The Penguin.

Shoemaker, Pamela, Lucig Danielian and Nancy Brendlinger. 1991. "Deviant acts, risky business and US interests: The newsworthiness of world events". *Journalism & Mass Communication Quarterly*, 68(4): 781–795.

Shoemaker, Pamela, and Akiba Cohen. 2006. "Introduction". In *News around the World: Content, Practitioners, and the Public*, edited by Pamela Shoemaker, and Akiba Cohen, 3-6. New York: Routledge.

Stubbs, Michael. 1997. "Whorf 's Children: Critical comments on Critical Discourse Analysis (CDA)". In *Evolving Models of Language,* edited by Ann Ryan, and Alison Wray, 110–116. Clevedon: BAAL in association with Multilingual Matters.

Tetlock, Philip E. 1983. "Accountability and judgment processes in a personality prediction task." *Journal of Personality and Social Psychology* 45(1): 74–83.
Teubert, Wolfgang. 2005. "My version of corpus linguistics". *International Journal of Corpus Linguistics* 10(1): 1–13.
Thompson, John B. 1995. *The Media and Modernity*. Cambridge: Polity Press.
Tognini-Bonelli, Elena. 2001. *Corpus Linguistics at Work*. Amsterdam: John Benjamins.
UNHCR. 2015a. "Over one million sea arrivals reach Europe in 2015". Available at: http://www.unhcr.org/5683d0b56.html. [Accessed 15 December 2016].
UNHCR. 2015b. "Mediterranean Sea arrivals 2015. Data by location, country of arrival, demographic and country of origin". Available at: http://data.unhcr.org/mediterranean/download. php?id 490. [Accessed 15 December 2016].
UNHCR. 2016a. *The UN Refugee Agency webpage:* "Monthly Arrivals by Nationality to Greece, Italy and Spain". *Refugees/Migrants Emergency Response — Mediterranean. 31 March 2016.* Retrieved from: http://data.unhcr.org/mediterranean/documents.php?page=1&view=grid &Type%5B%5D=3&Search=%23monthly%23. [Accessed 1 February 2017].
UNHCR. 2016b. "Syria Regional Refugee Response". From Apr 2011 to Oct 2016. Retrieved from: http://data.unhcr.org/syrianrefugees/asylum.php. [Accessed 1 February 2017].
Urry, John. 2002. "Mobility and proximity". *Sociology* 36(2); 255–274.
Van Dijk, Teun A. 1998. "Opinions and Ideologies in the Press". In *Approaches to Media Discourse*, edited by Alan Bell, and Peter Garrett, 21–63. Oxford: Blackwell Publishers:
Weber, Anne. 2009. *Manual on hate speech, Council of Europe Publishing*. Retrieved from: https://www.coe.int/t/dghl/standardsetting/hrpolicy/Publications/Hate_Speech_EN.pdf. [Accessed 1 February 2017].
Wright, Terence. 2000. *Refugees on Screen*. Oxford, UK: Refugee Studies Centre.

Legal references

Council of Europe. 1950. "European Convention on Human Rights", 04 November 1950. Retrieved from: http://www.echr.coe.int/Documents/Convention_ENG.pdf. [Accessed 1 February 2017].
Council of Europe. 1997. Council of Europe Committee of Ministers Recommendation No. R (97) 20 of the Committee of Ministers to Member States on "Hate speech", 30 October 1997, Retrieved from: https://rm.coe.int/CoERMPublicCommonSearchServices/DisplayDCTM Content?documentId=0900001680505d5b. [Accessed 1 February 2017].
Council of the European Union. 2008. "Council Framework Decision 2008/913/JHA of 28 November 2008 on combating certain forms and expressions of racism and xenophobia by means of criminal law". Retrieved from: http://eur-lex.europa.eu/LexUriServ/LexUriServ. do?uri=OJ:L:2008:328:0055:0058:en:PDF,. [Accessed 1 February 2017].
ECRI. 2015 "ECRI Report on Poland (fifth monitoring cycle), European Commission against Racism and Intolerance", 20 March 2015. Retrieved from: https://www.coe.int/t/dghl/monitoring/ecri/Country-by-country/Poland/POL-CbC-V-2015-20-ENG.pdf. [Accessed 1 February 2017].
European Commission. 2015. "Press release of Joint Foreign and Home Affairs Council: Ten point action plan on migration". *Press Release Database*. Retrieved from: http://europa.eu/rapid/press-release_IP-15-4813_en.htm. [Accessed 1 February 2017].

The Constitution of The Republic of Poland as adopted by the National Assembly on 2nd April 1997, Retrieved from: http://www.sejm.gov.pl/prawo/konst/angielski/kon1.htm. [Accessed 1 February 2017].

UNHCR. 1967. Convention and Protocol relating to the Status of Refugees, *Geneva, Switzerland: Office of the United Nations High Commissioner for Refugees (UNHCR), Communications and Public Information Service, 1967* Retrieved from: http://www.unhcr.org/protect/PROTECTION/3b66c2aa10.pdf. [Accessed 1 February 2017].

United Nations General Assembly. 1965. General Assembly resolution 2106 (XX) of 21 December 1965, „International Convention on the Elimination of All Forms of Racial Discrimination (ICERD)". Retrieved from: http://www.ohchr.org/EN/ProfessionalInterest/Pages/CERD.aspx. [Accessed 1 February 2017].

United Nations General Assembly. 1966. General Assembly resolution 2200A (XXI) of 16 December 1966, „International Covenant on Civil and Political Rights (ICCPR)". Retrieved from: http://www.ohchr.org/Documents/ProfessionalInterest/ccpr.pdf. [Accessed 1 February 2017].

The Civil Code of 23rd April 1964 (Journal of Laws No. 16, item 93, with later amendments) Retrieved from: https://supertrans2014.files.wordpress.com/2014/06/the-civil-code.pdf. [Accessed 1 February 2017].

The Criminal Code of 6th of June 1997 (Journal of Laws No. 88, item 553 with later amendments) Retrieved from: https://www.imolin.org/doc/amlid/Poland_Penal_Code1.pdf. [Accessed 1 February 2017].

The Labour Code of 23rd December 1997 (Journal of Laws No. 21, item 94, with later amendments) Retrieved from: http://www.ilo.org/dyn/natlex/natlex4.listResults?p_lang=en&p_country=POL&p_classification=01.02. [Accessed 1 February 2017].

The hate that dare not speak its name?

Robbie Love and Paul Baker
Lancaster University

This chapter uses corpus-based methods to explore how British Parliamentary arguments against LGBT equality have changed in response to decreasing social acceptability of discriminatory language against minority groups. A comparison of the language of opposition to the equalisation of the age of consent for anal sex (1998–2000) is made to the oppositional language in debates to allow same-sex marriage (2013). Keyword, collocation and concordance analyses were used to identify differences in overall argumentation strategies, assessing the extent to which previously *explicit* homophobic speech (e.g. homosexuality as *unnatural*) has been replaced by more indirect strategies (e.g. less use of personalised argumentation via the pronoun *I*). We argue that while homophobic language appears to be on the decrease in such contexts, there is a mismatch between words and acts, requiring analysts to acknowledge the presence of more subtle indications of homophobic discourse in the future.

Keywords: homophobia, parliament, debate, corpus, keywords

1. Introduction

In 1894, Oscar Wilde's lover Lord Alfred "Boysey" Douglas published the poem "Two Loves", which referred to homosexuality as "the love that dare not speak its name". The poem was mentioned at one of Wilde's trials for "gross indecency" after which he was imprisoned for two years. Along with Wilde's incarceration, the poem indicates how during Victorian times, homosexuality in Britain was seen as a criminal offence. Such thinking continued for much of the twentieth century, with medical discourses viewing it as a sickness, newspapers linking it to shame, scandal, deviancy, paedophilia and communism, while religious discourse widely held it to be a sin. However, gradually at first, people began to speak up on behalf of the love that dare not speak its name: homosexuality was decriminalised to an extent in 1967 and despite a backlash in 1988 which forbade its "promotion" by

DOI 10.1075/bct.93.03lov

education authorities, since the 21st century much of the earlier discriminatory legalisation has been overturned.

This chapter is concerned with the language around the legal processes involved in two (successful) attempts to award equality to gay men and women in the UK. The first took place in a series of political debates between 1998–2000 which resulted in equalising the age of consent for sexual intercourse for gay men at 16 (it had previously been 18 while the age of consent for heterosexual people was 16). The second set of debates occurred in 2013 and involved allowing same-sex partnerships to be legally recognised as marriages (an earlier Bill had defined such relationships as civil partnerships since 2005, but this was felt to be a compromise by some people).

The sets of debates occurred in both the lower (House of Commons) and upper (House of Lords) chambers of the British government, and had several readings each. In the case of the age of consent (AOC) debate, the Lords rejected the proposed Bill three times, causing the lower house to use the Parliament Act to pass the Bill.[1] The same-sex marriage (SSM) Bill was twice rejected by the Lords but passed on its third reading.

These two sets of debates are a rich source of data for the analysis of discourse and argumentation around homosexuality and equality. While public attitudes have become more liberal towards homosexuality,[2] in both debates a substantial number of Members of Parliament and Lords voted against equality, being willing to go "on-record" about their decision, and sometimes speaking at length about why they wished to do so. Considering the shift in public opinion it is pertinent to consider whether and how anti-equality speakers differed over the two time periods in the ways they constructed their anti-equality arguments and attendant representations of gay people.

This chapter examines the extent and ways in which such arguments and representations differ between the two sets of debates. We aim to assess the extent to which previously *explicit* homophobic speech (e.g. constructions of homosexuality as *unnatural*) has undergone replacement with *implicit* or indirect homophobia (i.e. by accessing discourses that are harder to interpret as homophobic on the surface level, but, are nonetheless, very clear in their opposition to LGBT equality). Just as Mills (1998, 247–8) points to more subtle and indirect manifestations of sexist discourse, we aim to show how homophobic discourse "responds" to pressure by transforming its nature. Such discourse can be more difficult to

1. Since 1949 only four Acts have been passed by the government without consent of the Lords.

2. In 1983 62% of people believed sexual relations between two adults of the same sex was almost always or mostly wrong, while this figure was 28% in 2012 (British Social Attitudes Survey 2013 Edition Report).

identify and challenge, however, requiring a more in-depth and critical form of analysis.

We use a range of approaches from corpus linguistics in order to examine and compare the anti-equality speech from the two sets of debates. Corpus approaches are well-placed to handle large amounts of data. As discussed in Baker (2006, 10–7) such approaches can reduce researcher bias, act as a form of triangulation and aid the identification of minority positions. We have combined corpus-driven and corpus-based methods (Tognini-Bonelli 2001), the former involving using statistical tests to identify words with comparatively high frequencies in texts, while the latter involves the analysis of a pre-selected set of terms that are felt to be relevant "sites" for discussion of argumentation and representation (in this case words directly relating to homosexual identity and homophobia).

After positioning this research in relation to other relevant studies, we discuss how we built and analysed our corpora. This is followed by four results sections after which we conclude with a section which summarises and reflects on the study.

2. Literature review

In this section we focus on a small number of key studies that have examined negative representations of gay people via the use of language. Many studies have identified how gay identities are problematized: for example, Kitzinger (2005) used techniques from Conversation Analysis to show how people oriented to references to sexual orientation (either heterosexual or gay) during spoken interactions. In the transcripts she examined, heterosexuality was a taken-for-granted disclosure and did not result in any marked orientation from listeners. On the other hand, during one conversation disclosure of a gay identity became the focus of the conversation while in another it acted as a conversation killer.

The genre of newspaper discourse is perhaps one of the largest areas of analysis of homophobia. For example, Henley et al. (2002) in their study of stories about violent attacks found that the *Washington Post* used fewer, and less specific nominals when referring to anti-gay violence than to violence against heterosexual people. Chirrey (2003) studied a series of newspaper articles regarding the public "coming out" of a pop star, noting how a liberal newspaper used the verb *disclosed* to frame the act in a relatively neutral non-judgemental way, while tabloids used more sensational language such as *admits*, *frank admission*, *secret* and *in hiding*. Morrish (2002) has noted how broadsheet newspapers have used coded references to negatively represent gay men, indicating that coverage of the government minister Peter Mandelson included references to homosexual acts e.g. "What Peter Mandelson did was the political equivalent of bare-backing", while he was described as camp, hedonistic and narcissistic. Further to that, Baker's (2005) corpus-based study of two newspapers indicated a number of frequently cited discourse prosodies around the words *gay* and *homosexual*, including representations of homosexuality as a behaviour rather than an identity, gay relationships as transient, and gay men as promiscuous, involved in crime, shameless or shameful, politically militant, and proselytising children.

Baker (2005) also used corpus-driven techniques to examine the Age of Consent debate, focussing only on the House of Lords but comparing the argumentation of those who were for vs. those who were against equalisation. Using a procedure called a keyword analysis (described in the following section) he found that those who argued for equalisation were more likely to construct gay people in terms of their identity rather than their behaviour, and argue that it was wrong to criminalise 16 and 17 year olds for having consensual sex. Also (perhaps strategically), they made reference to the fact that the UK would be forced to pass legislation eventually due to the European Convention of Human Rights. Those who argued against equalisation made more use of historic legal terminology like *gross indecency* as well as indicating concern for the health and reputations of boys while claiming that the Bill was not needed because the age of consent for anal sex was already equal for boys and girls at 18. They also expressed concern that equality would be the "thin end of the wedge", leading to demands for further changes to the law (a point which is discussed in more detail in our analysis).

Following Baker (2005), Bachmann (2011) examined transcripts of UK parliamentary debates over the Civil Partnership Act which took place in 2004. Having identified five different standpoints regarding the Act, it was less easy to split the corpus into "for" and "against" camps so instead Bachmann compared the debates as a whole to a 4 million word reference corpus of general English. His analysis of the debate keywords led him to identify discourses of same-sex relationships as being fundamentally different to or the same as opposite-sex ones, or as one type of many relationships that were seen as disadvantaged in British society (along with unmarried heterosexual couples or cohabiting spinsters). Another dichotomy involved arguments that same-sex relationships would be detrimental to society if legally recognised, while others viewed them as beneficial to society. Finally, Bachman also found evidence of the "thin end of the wedge" discourse mentioned above.

Our study differs from Baker (2005) and Bachmann (2011) in that, in keeping with our research question, we are only examining the speech of people who voted against changes to the law. Such people wanted to maintain the status quo which arguably disadvantaged gay people. Our focus in this chapter is on how speakers who voted to keep the status quo have altered their language use when the two debates are compared. The following section describes our data, analysis tool and procedures used.

3. Method

3.1 Data

The data used in this analysis come from a selection of House of Commons and House of Lords debates from the late 1990s/early 2000s and from the year 2013. The former set concerns the Sexual Offences (Amendment) Bill, and the latter set the Marriage (Same Sex Couples) Bill. Selecting only the language of those in opposition to these Bills, and making this data available for comparative corpus-based analysis, required a manual process of removing everything that was not relevant to this study. Firstly, we retrieved electronic transcripts of all of the debates from the government Hansard documents, located online.[3] These then had to be "cleaned" to exclude "parts of the transcript which did not directly refer to speech" (Bachmann 2011, 84), including:

- time stamps (e.g. "3.16 pm"),
- date and column stamps (e.g. "15 July 2013 : Column 534"),
- non-linguistic descriptions (e.g. "Stephen McCabe (Birmingham, Selly Oak, Labour) rose"), and
- meta-discussion of general procedural matters (e.g. "That the Bill be now read the Third time").

We then annotated the transcripts according to the stance of each speaker, in order to isolate the speech of those in opposition to the Bill being discussed. In most cases, this was done by matching the names of the speakers on the transcripts to lists of how they actually voted immediately after the debates (see Baker 2005). In debates that were not resolved by a vote (for example the Third Reading of the Marriage (Same Sex Couples) Bill in the House of Lords), the stance of the speaker was obtained by a manual, qualitative analysis of the content of the individual speeches.

Once each contribution to the debates was identified for the stance of each speaker, we removed all speech by those who did not vote (the Speaker, Deputy Speaker(s) and those who abstained) as well as those who voted in favour of the Bills (or otherwise indicated their support for the Bill in instances where there was no vote). For example, the following by the Speaker of the House of Commons was omitted:

> There is a four-minute limit on Back-Bench speeches, and 71 Members want to speak. (John Bercow, Speaker, 5 February 2013)

3. www.parliament.uk/business/publications/hansard/

We then removed all prefacing names (e.g. "Maria Miller (Basingstoke, Conservative)", see Baker 2006, 128) in both corpora, leaving only the speech of those who voted against the Bills. Despite removing everything that did not

Table 1. Debates in the Age of Consent and Same-Sex Marriage corpora.

	Topic	Date	Length in tokens
Age of Consent (AOC) corpus (1998–2000) [a]			
House of Commons	1st attempt: Second Reading[b]	22nd June 1998	6,673
	2nd attempt: Second Reading[c]	25th January 1999	13,950
	2nd attempt: consideration of clause 1	10th February 1999	14,224
	2nd attempt: Third Reading	1st March 1999	5,102
	3rd attempt: Second Reading	10th February 2000	12,094
House of Lords	1st attempt: rejection	22nd July 1998	12,063
	2nd attempt: Second Reading (rejection)	13th April 1999	28,156
	3rd attempt: Second Reading (rejection)	11th April 2000	18,449
	3rd attempt: Resolution to Committee[d]	13th November 2000	13,331
TOTAL			124,042
Same-Sex Marriage (SSM) corpus (2013)[e]			
House of Commons	Second Reading	5th February 2013	22,331
	Third Reading	21st May 2013	2,750
House of Lords	Second Reading	3rd–4th June 2013	37,539
	Third Reading	15th July 2013	1,363
TOTAL			63,983

[a] In the collection of both the AOC and SSM corpus, the First Readings in both Houses of Commons and Lords were omitted because they contained no debate and therefore no oppositional speech. Second Readings are treated as the first opportunity for a proposed change to legislation to be debated in the Houses.

[b] The first attempt to introduce this legislation was the insertion of a clause into the Crime and Disorder Bill. This was blocked by the Lords (22nd July 1998). See Public Whip: http://www.publicwhip.org.uk/division.php?date=1998-06-22&number=311

[c] The second attempt was debated and amended in the Commons three times (25th January, 10th February, 1st March 1999) before being blocked again by the Lords (13th April 1999).

[d] After the 3rd attempt was blocked again by the Lords, the Parliament Act was used to pass the Bill. See http://www.legislation.gov.uk/ukpga/2000/44/notes/division/9

[e] This Bill passed through to legislation on its first attempt; therefore there were fewer debates about this issue than AOC.

directly represent oppositional speech, we did keep original copies of the transcripts in order to search for entire quotes (and the identities of the debaters who spoke them) to use as examples in this chapter.

The resulting corpus of oppositional language against both Bills contains a total of 188,025 tokens, which we deemed large enough to require corpus-driven and corpus-based techniques of analysis. This is split between the *Age of Consent corpus (AOC corpus)* (124,042 tokens) and the *Same-Sex Marriage corpus (SSM corpus)* (63,983 tokens). The difference in size between these two corpora (the AOC corpus contains almost twice as many tokens as the SSM corpus) is important to consider due to the comparative nature of this diachronic analysis. To account for this, we worked to ensure that all quantitative comparisons between the AOC and SSM corpora were calculated relative to the total size of each of the corpora.

The corpora of oppositional language used in this analysis, the debates they were collected from, and their size, are detailed in Table 1.

3.2 Tools and procedures

The two corpora, saved as separate .txt files, were uploaded to the corpus analysis tool AntConc (Anthony 2011) for the subsequent corpus-driven and corpus-based analysis. This is a freely available piece of software that allows, among other features, the automatic generation of concordances, collocations and keywords, each of which were necessitated by our analysis.

Our initial approach is corpus-driven in that we have used keywords as a way of identifying salient lexical items in the debates, which can act as signposts to discourses. Keywords are words which occur frequently in one corpus when compared against a second corpus and are identified via statistical tests which take into account both word frequency and the overall sizes of both corpora (Baker 2006, 125). We have used AntConc's default settings which carry out log-likelihood tests for keyness. Keywords are analysed via concordance analyses which involve viewing all the citations of a particular word in a corpus within its immediate context.

Following the keyword analysis, we have supplemented our approach with a corpus-based focus by examining a number of words that were chosen by us because they directly relate to homosexuality. These words are analysed by comparing their frequencies within the two debates and then by studying their collocates. Collocates are words which occur next to or near each other, either frequently and/or more often than would be expected if all the words in a text were randomly ordered. Again, we use AntConc's default method of calculating collocation, the mutual information test, which measures strength of collocation (rather than certainty) and gives a score for each pair of words under consideration. Hunston

(2002, 71) notes that any score of 3 or above "can be taken to be significant". As with the keyword analyses, collocates are subjected to concordance analyses in order to identify why they occur together.

We argue that such a combination of analytical foci (keywords plus a predetermined list of relevant terms) will result in a more thorough analysis, enabling us both to focus on the terminology we hypothesised to be of relevance to the construction of gay identity, as well as to identify areas of interest that we may not have otherwise considered.

4. Analysis

4.1 Keywords

Our analysis begins with a corpus-driven approach, deriving keyword lists in order to identify the most salient lexical differences between the two debates. Table 2 indicates the strongest 40 keywords for both corpora when the relative word frequencies in each were compared against the other (using the log-likelihood measure). The table is ordered via keyness score. With many keywords to choose from, we focus below on the analysis of those which reveal something about representations of homosexuality or/and the ways in which anti-equality arguments were presented by speakers.

Table 2. Keywords from a comparison of the Age of Consent and Same Sex Marriage debates.

Rank	AOC keywords	Freq. AOC	Freq. SSM	SSM keywords	Freq. AOC	Freq. SSM
1	age	685	14	marriage	39	664
2	young	484	10	civil	4	136
3	consent	361	9	same	99	267
4	homosexual	387	30	partnerships	2	96
5	boys	130	0	institution	3	74
6	girls	140	0	couples	21	100
7	anal	122	0	union	7	54
8	Member[a]	221	18	woman	18	92
9	year	185	13	Bill	581[b]	556
10	men	195	18	Marriage	0	44
11	intercourse	118	4	married	9	60
12	activity	86	0	Dear	0	38

Table 2. (*continued*)

Rank	AOC keywords	Freq. AOC	Freq. SSM	SSM keywords	Freq. AOC	Freq. SSM
13	he	409	85	faith	7	55
14	buggery	81	0	sex	199	240
15	AIDS	77	0	traditional	9	57
16	olds	71	0	partnership	1	39
17	I	2786	1101	this	736	613
18	Young	69	0	change	64	116
19	health	77	1	love	14	59
20	But	140	13	commitment	12	56
21	abuse	117	8	church	0	31
22	acts	79	2	legislation	60	109
23	lowering	61	0	definition	10	51
24	report	84	3	marriages	11	52
25	people	663	200	meaning	6	42
26	older	74	2	religious	22	64
27	trust	90	5	and	2667	1740
28	homosexuality	108	9	consultation	7	41
29	hon	441	118	has	459	393
30	advice	75	3	consummation	0	23
31	boy	59	1	redefinition	0	21
32	protection	161	25	process	10	34
33	clause	70	3	state	20	52
34	moral	70	3	create	5	31
35	adults	54	1	society	91	116
36	HIV	44	0	Church	28	58
37	under	159	27	been	361	304
38	medical	58	2	redefine	0	38
39	old	82	7	man	84	106
40	vulnerable	55	2	forced	3	25

[a] By default AntConc treats initial capital words separately from lower-case words when calculating keywords. We have retained this feature as it was useful for distinguishing surnames of politicians who were mentioned in the debate e.g. *Young* and *Dear*.

[b] Despite that the word *Bill* is more frequent in the AOC debate it is actually a SSM debate keyword due to the fact that the AOC debate contains much more text than the SSM debate, so proportionally, it is still more frequent in the SSM debate. The same applies for the keywords *this*, *and*, *has* and *been*.

To a large extent, the top keywords reflect specific aspects of changes to the law. The AOC debate was concerned with allowing males aged 16 and 17 to engage in same-sex sexual behaviour. It is not surprising to see AOC keywords like *lowering, age* and *consent* then. Although potentially this could have included a range of different sexual behaviours, it is notable to see keywords like *anal, intercourse, buggery* and *activity* in the AOC corpus. The first three indicate the emphasis on anal sex in the debate. Anal sex/intercourse is characterised as a *practice* (5 times), associated with *dangers* (6 times) and even an indulgence (the word *indulge* occurs 16 times in the corpus and always refers to anal sex):

> There is not such a product as a safe condom for those who indulge in **anal** sex.
> (Baroness Seccombe, 13 November 2000)

Buggery is variously described as "an unnatural, unsanitary, and dangerous act", "pathological", "the abominable crime", and a "dangerous practice", while it is also equated with *sodomy*. The word *buggery* also occurs seven times with the verb lemma COMMIT as in "buggery committed on a girl aged over 18" or "heterosexuals can commit sexual acts at 16 but must wait until they are 18 to commit buggery." Collectively, homosexuality or sexual acts associated with it are referred to as *unnatural* 38 times in the AOC corpus (the word *unnatural* never occurs in the SSM corpus).

AOC keywords like *AIDS* and *health* acted tangentially, as a way of discussing health risks associated with this practice.

> as time passes we learn more and more about the frightening **health** risks of anal intercourse and the widespread abuse to which young people are subjected.
> (Lord Davies of Coity, 13 November 2000)

> Both teenage boys and girls will now be exposed to all the risks of anal intercourse; they will be far more likely to run the risk of **AIDS**.
> (Baroness Young, 13 April 1999)

As indicated in Baker (2005, 51), there were many references to *girls* in the AOC debate as those against equalisation argued that the change to the law would affect girls as well as boys (which could be interpreted as a way of legitimating against accusations of homophobia) but also that girls were seen as more mature than boys, so boys were particularly at risk.

> There is no doubt that **girls** mature much earlier than boys. Boys very often are only just coming to terms with their sexuality at 16. Consequently, I accept that there is more of a case for the age of consent for **girls** to be lower than for boys.
> (Baroness Seccombe, 13 April 1999)

Similarly, the keyword *boy* is used to argue that there is gender difference between boys and girls:

> …there is a great difference between a young girl of 16 and a young **boy** of 16. If a young girl of 16 is seduced, it may do her a great deal of harm. If a young man of 16 is seduced, he may be turned into a rent **boy**, possibly ruining him for life.
> (The Earl of Longford, 13 November 2000)

> if I were the parent of a **boy** who had been seduced by some middle-aged gentleman, I should feel that his life had been taken a long way towards ultimate ruin. It would not be quite certain, but the chances are that if he was installed in life as a homosexual, he would never marry. He would probably in the end become promiscuous. A lonely old homosexual is one of the most pathetic sights that I know.
> (The Earl of Longford, 13 April 1999)

A related AOC keyword is *protection*, also used as part of the argument that young people (especially boys) require protection from older men.

> It is in my view wrong — I stand by that position — that a young person of 16 should be free in law to embark on a course of action that might lead to a life style that would separate him, perhaps permanently, from the mainstream life of marriage and family. In particular, I believe that such a person needs **protection** from older men. (Miss Widdecombe, 10 February 2000)

Similarly, boys are also characterised with the keyword *vulnerable*.

> I am convinced that to allow the age of consent to be lowered to 16 could be seen as a form of cruelty as legally it could expose **vulnerable** adolescent boys to predatory older or indeed younger men. (Baroness Seccombe, 13 April 1999)

The AOC debate is also characterised by moral arguments, with the keyword *moral* appearing 70 times. Debaters make reference to moral principles and the idea that there is no moral equivalence between heterosexual and homosexual relationships. Homosexuality is viewed as a violation of a moral code, and it is argued that there is a moral case against homosexuality. In the SSM debate, *moral* only occurs three times and is used less explicitly to refer to homosexuality e.g. it is argued that "our country has lost its moral compass", while the Bill is described as a "moral mess" and a "moral minefield".

One "unexpected" keyword in the AOC debate is the pronoun *I*, which occurs 2786 times in that debate. This word can potentially occur in many contexts but verb collocates of *I* (occurring over 10 times and having an MI score of above 3) are *agree, believe, conclude, hope, intend, oppose, quote, regret, remember, remind, repeat, think, say, suggest, support, suppose, suspect, understand, welcome* and *wonder* which concordance analyses identified as being generally used to indicate cognitive stance or to mark arguments. An analysis of 100 random AOC concordance lines revealed that in all cases the word *I* was used to refer to the speaker rather than the speaker quoting someone else (the same result was found for the SSM corpus).

The word *I* is notable because it occurred as a keyword in another UK parliamentary debate (Baker 2006, 126) involving banning fox hunting, which took place in 2002–3. MPs who wanted to ban hunting used *I* much more than those who wanted to keep hunting (to the extent that *I* was the third strongest keyword used by anti-hunting MPs). The anti-hunting stance had more public support during the debate, with an IPSOS Mori poll of 1000 people in 2003 finding that 69% of respondents thought fox hunting should be illegal, 28% thought it should be legal and 3% were undecided.[4] The bill to ban fox hunting was eventually enforced from 2005.

Looking at the contexts of *I* across these parliamentary debates, one way the word could be interpreted is in directly associating the speaker with the argument; the word *I* could be seen as personalising an argument. Therefore, one conclusion could be that the more frequent use of *I* in the AOC debate indicates that the anti-equality speakers were more confident about indicating ownership of their positions than those in the SSM debate. The reduction of *I* thus represents a subtle shift in discourse style.

Let us turn to the keywords for the SSM debate. As with the AOC debate, most of these keywords represent what the Bill was actually about — a change to the law to allow gay partnerships to be recognised as marriages, updating earlier legislation which called such relationships civil partnerships. Therefore, it is not surprising to see keywords like *marriage*, *civil*, *partnerships*, *couples*, *union*, *married* and *partnership*. The keyword *sex* is somewhat surprising although in fact this word never refers to sex as an act but instead is used in contexts like *same-sex couples* or *opposite-sex marriage*.

One less expected keyword is *consultation*, occurring 41 times. This word refers to the government's consultation on changing the law, where members of the public were invited to submit their opinions regarding the change. A report published in 2012 indicated that 228,000 opinions had been received, along with 19 petitions, the largest ever response to a consultation of this nature. The report concluded that "the majority of responses to the consultation (not including petitions) supported opening up marriage to same-sex couples." (HM Government 2012, 6).

How was *consultation* used by the anti-equality debaters in the SSM corpus? Scrutiny of concordance lines reveals that it was criticised in general terms:

4. http://www.ipsos-mori.com/researchpublications/researcharchive/796/Most-Say-Hunting-Should-Not-Be-Legal.aspx

> I believe that this Bill is wrong and that the **consultation** process was a complete sham. (Gerald Howarth, 5 February 2013)

> Regardless of our views on same-sex marriage, I think that we would all agree that the **consultation** on the introduction of same-sex marriage has been seriously deficient. (Lord Browne of Belmont, 3 June 2013)

More specific criticisms were aimed at the consultation, including the accusation that it avoided certain groups, that it focussed on how to change the law and not whether the law should be changed (so it was "rigged"), and that the pro-equality comments were of "dubious origin" while those which were against equality were all from "uniquely identified individuals".

Thus, one aspect of the criticism of the SSM Bill was to do with the procedure rather than the content of the Bill. This was also noted through examination of the keyword *process* which was a collocate of *consultation*. There were references to a flawed process, abuse of process, doubts about the process, and the Bill being without proper process.

> There seems to be, if not general agreement, certainly some agreement that the Bill is in a mess, ill thought through and without proper **process** or popular mandate. (Lord Dear, 4 June 2013)

As suggested above, another procedural criticism of the SSM Bill was that the government had no mandate to introduce the Bill, with *mandate* occurring in the SSM corpus 29 times. Another criticism was that the Bill was trying to redefine the concept of marriage (via keywords like *redefine*, *redefinition*, *meaning*, *definition* and *change*).

> It is not possible to **redefine** marriage. Marriage is the union between a man and a woman. It has been that historically and it remains so. (Sir Roger Gale, 5 February 2013)

A final SSM keyword worth referring to is *religious*, along with related keywords *faith* and *church*. While the AOC debaters referred more to moral arguments, in the SSM debate, there is more mention of religion, and it is particularly argued that the Bill contravenes religious freedoms and churches will ultimately be *forced* (another keyword) to perform same sex marriages.

> It will be impossible to guarantee that **religious** freedom will not be compromised. (Graham Brady, 5 February 2013)

> If the Government really respected the **faith** community, as they say they do, then this Bill would not be here today. (Lord Mawhinney, 3 June 2013)

> Does he share my view that the reason the Government have had to put quadruple locks into the Bill to make sure that no **Church** will be **forced** into performing single-sex marriages is because they are worried that the locks will be broken, that cases will be taken to the Strasbourg Court and that Churches will then be forced to perform single-sex marriages against their will?
>
> (Neil Parish, 5 February 2013)

To conclude this section, one way that the anti-equality debate around the two Bills differs is in the type of arguments that are presented. The anti-equality debaters in the AOC debate use moral arguments which are linked to the protection of children (especially young boys who are constructed as more at risk than girls) from the dangers of disease and predatory older men. Homosexuality is strongly linked to crime and danger. On the other hand, the SSM marriage debate focuses more on matters of procedure (there was no mandate, the consultation was flawed), that marriage has always meant the same thing and cannot be redefined, and that the Bill is an attack on religious freedom.

We now move on to the corpus-based forms of analysis, which are centred around frequencies and collocates of a small set of preselected words which relate specifically to homosexuality and homophobia.

4.2 Gay* and homosexual*

To tap into the ways that discourses and argumentation strategies around homosexuality and equality have changed between the two sets of debates, we next compared the forms of the lemmas *gay** and *homosexual** (the * symbol acts as a wildcard for any series of letters, ostensibly meaning that we searched on all forms that contain these words as the "head", including *gays, homosexuality* etc.). Intuitively, it seems appropriate to consider these terms, not only because they were also addressed by Baker (2005) and Bachmann (2011), but because these concepts are salient to the topics of both sets of debates and therefore act as good points of comparison between the two. In Table 3, log-likelihood comparisons[5] of the frequency of these terms (relative to the total number of tokens in the corpora) reveal a statistically significant ($p < 0.0001$) difference in the occurrence of *homosexual** between the AOC corpus and the SSM corpus, whereas the relative frequency of *gay** has remained almost unchanged.

5. Using an online log-likelihood calculator (UCREL 2013).

Table 3. Frequency of *gay** and *homosexual**.

	AOC corpus (1998–2000)		SSM corpus (2013)			
	raw	%	raw	%	% change	LL of change between whole corpora
gay*	110	0.09	65	0.10	+0.01	0.75
homosexual*	604	0.49	52	0.08	−0.41	251.18**

** = $p < 0.0001$

Figure 1 shows the difference between the two sets of debates more clearly.

Even without considering the uses of these forms in the contexts of the debates, the figure indicates a radical decline in preference for the use of *homosexual** between the AOC and SSM anti-equality language. *Homosexual** has declined to the extent that, despite barely increasing in relative frequency, *gay** is the more frequent term in the SSM corpus. What is it about the contexts in which these terms were spoken that lends evidence to a shift in anti-equality argumentation? A qualitative disambiguation of these words helps us to interpret the nature of this shift in preference (Tables 4 and 5).

In the AOC corpus, the lemma *homosexual** is realised by all 7 forms listed in Table 4. *Gay** is realised by all 4 forms in Table 5 (which contains no statistically significant differences). The noun form *homosexualism,* which occurs 5 times in the AOC corpus, characterises homosexuality as an illness that is "lifelong" and yet potentially curable.

> Of course I have seen people recover from **homosexualism**. A boy at Eton assaulted my elder brother in the bath there and was later expelled for repeating the offence on another boy. Later he became a pillar of county society and captained the county cricket team. (The Earl of Longford, 13 April 1999)

> First, I regard **homosexualism**, certainly lifelong **homosexualism**, as a sad disorder and handicap. (The Earl of Longford, 13 November 2000)

Homosexually (occurring 4 times) is used to distinguish homosexual and heterosexual people in terms of how they are "inclined" to behave sexually, while the adjective *homosexualist* occurs once, constructing gay people as a dangerous group attempting to convert others to homosexuality.

> There is another motive, however. There is a **homosexualist** agenda. The homosexual community, by its nature, is sterile, and it can survive and grow only by proselytising. (Mr. Swayne, 1 March 1999)

A notable feature of the observed decline in the frequency of *homosexual** in the SSM corpus is that these 3 low frequency variants do not occur in the 2013 data. Likewise, for *gay** there has been the elimination of "nouning" forms *gayness* and

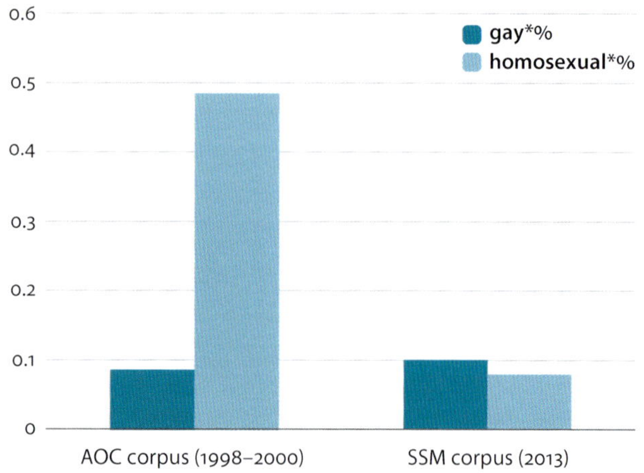

Figure 1. Relative frequency comparison of *homosexual** and *gay** between the two debate corpora.

Table 4. Frequencies of the disambiguated forms of lemma *homosexual**.

		AOC corpus (1998–2000)		SSM corpus (2013)			
		raw	%	Raw	%	% change	LL of change between whole corpora
adjective	homosexual	377	0.30	29	0.05	−0.26	167.21**
noun	homosexuality	116	0.09	9	0.01	−0.08	51.21**
noun	homosexuals	89	0.07	13	0.02	−0.05	24.24**
noun	homosexual	12	0.01	1	0.00	−0.01	5.09*
noun	homosexualism	5	0.00	0	0.00	0.00	4.16*
adverb	homosexually	4	0.00	0	0.00	0.00	3.33
adjective	homosexualist	1	0.00	0	0.00	0.00	0.83

* = $p < 0.05$; ** = $p < 0.0001$

singular *gay*. Marshall (2004, 8) describes the use of *gay* as a noun as "central to the process of adverse discrimination" by "defining people by a single element of who they are". One *could* argue that these changes relate simply to the difference in the legislative changes being debated in the two corpora. However, as shown, several of these forms are used not to discuss the age of consent but, in several cases, to make discriminatory and homophobic statements about the nature of homosexuality. These are, in a sense, and at least within the context of these debates, "homophobic words", used to express distaste for homosexuality.

What remains are the forms that are present in both corpora. In the SSM data, *homosexual** is realised only by *homosexual* (adjective), *homosexuality*,

Table 5. Frequencies of the disambiguated forms of lemma *gay**.

		AOC corpus (1998–2000)		SSM corpus (2013)			
		raw	%	raw	%	% change	LL of change between whole corpora
adjective	gay	101	0.08	61	0.10	0.01	0.93
noun	gays	6	0.00	4	0.01	0.00	0.15
noun	gayness	2	0.00	0	0.00	0.00	1.66
noun	gay	1	0.00	0	0.00	0.00	0.83

homosexuals, and *homosexual* (noun). *Gay** is realised by *gay* (adjective) and *gays.* Perhaps unsurprisingly, the most common forms of both lemmas, in both corpora, are the adjectives *homosexual* and *gay.* The adjective *homosexual* has decreased in frequency significantly, whereas the proportion of *gay* as an adjective has increased slightly. It is worth considering the types of nouns that these adjectives modify in the debates. What, exactly, is described as *gay* or *homosexual,* and (how) has this changed over time? Based on Bachmann (2011, 91), we categorised *gay* and *homosexual* according to whether they describe the *identity* of one or more human referents, or some sort of related behaviour with no direct human referent. Examples of *identities* include *community, couple, men, people,* and *women* while examples of *behaviours* include *act, activity, desire, intercourse, lifestyle, marriage, relationship, sex,* and *suffering.* Table 6 shows the proportion of nouns modified by *gay* or *homosexual* in terms of their qualitative classification as either *identity* or *behaviour.*

Table 6. Combined frequencies of *homosexual* and *gay* used as adjectives to signal *identity* and *behaviour.*

	AOC corpus (1998–2000)		SSM corpus (2013)			
	raw	%	raw	%	% change	LL of change between whole corpora
homosexual/gay as identity	169	0.14	49	0.08	−0.06	13.90*
homosexual/gay as behaviour	309	0.25	41	0.06	−0.19	92.62**

* = $p < 0.001$; ** = $p < 0.0001$

In the AOC corpus, homosexuality is associated with behaviour almost twice as much as it is viewed as an identity. However, in the SSM corpus the view of homosexuality as a behaviour has diminished, becoming less frequent than the "identity" representation. This indicates a shift in understanding of homosexuality,

Table 7. All nouns modified by *homosexual* categorised as *behaviours* in the AOC and SSM corpora. Those in bold occur in both lists.

Behaviours described as *homosexual* in the AOC corpus (bold are shared with SSM):	*act, activity, activities, acts, age, attitudes, behaviour, case, conduct, consent, debates, desires, disease, disposition,* ***equality,*** *experience, experiences, gene, gross indecency, intercourse, issue, leanings,* ***lifestyle(s),*** *literature,* ***lobby, marriage,*** *object, offences, organisations, orgy, orientation, partnerships, persuasion, phase, practice, propaganda, relations, relationship, relationships, sex, sex outside marriage, sexual activities, side, stance, sub-culture, tendencies, vote, way of life*
Behaviours described as *homosexual* in the SSM corpus (bold are shared with AOC):	*civil partnership,* ***equality, lobby, marriage, lifestyles,*** *rights, suffering, union, wish*

even within people who voted against equalisation of laws. Furthermore, looking at concordance lines which feature *homosexual* as a behaviour, it seems that a reduction of range of behaviours in use has co-occurred with a drastic change in the nature of such behaviours (Table 7).

As anticipated, some of the nouns that are no longer described as *homosexual* in the SSM corpus include concepts specific to the topic of the AOC debate (*age, consent, intercourse, orgy, sex,* and *sexual activities*). However, some of the other nouns imply that homosexuality is bad or problematic (*conduct, disease, issue, gross indecency, offence, propaganda*) or some kind of optional or temporary phenomenon (*attitudes, behaviour, desires, experience, leanings, persuasion, phase, stance, tendencies, way of life*), and do not necessarily relate directly to the topic of the age of consent. Since such "homosexual behaviours" are not discussed by the SSM opposition debaters, we argue, then, that their absence in the SSM debate (along with the "homophobic words" above) is not topic-specific but indicative of societal change. Similar uses of such forms in the 2013 Same-Sex Marriage debates would likely be interpreted as explicit realisations of homophobic discourse, and viewed as no longer acceptable in Parliamentary debate. We argue that anti-equality language has eliminated such controversial forms "in response" to societal pressure to no longer be viewed as holding homophobic views.

4.3 Collocates

In this section we take a closer look at the contexts within which the lemmas *homosexual** and *gay** occur, by focussing on their *collocates*. Specifically, we consider how the collocates of these lemmas have changed between the AOC and SSM debates. As described in the Method, collocates are calculated by Mutual Information score, which measures the strength of the "collocational bond" between words (Mautner 2007, 57). We calculate collocates within a range of four words to the left and four words to the right of the nodes *homosexual** and *gay**, and exclude pairs with a combined raw frequency of lower than 5. The top 10 most significant collocates of *homosexual** in the AOC and SSM corpora are shown in Table 8 and those of *gay** in Table 9.

In the AOC debate data, *homosexual** tends to co-occur with words related to sexual behaviour (*acts, consenting, homosexualism, activity*), which seems to correspond with such uses as described in the previous section.

Table 8. The top 10 collocates of *homosexual** in the AOC and SSM corpora.

	AOC corpus (1998–2000)	Freq. as collocate	MI	SSM corpus (2013)	Freq. as collocate	MI
1	adoption	5	7.83885	rights	5	8.49807
2	acts	46	7.54406	people	7	7.42711
3	heterosexuality	8	7.41739	about	6	7.02202
4	heterosexuals	10	7.32428	was	5	6.44088
5	marriages	5	7.18678	marriage	9	6.05849
6	lobby	9	7.17228	are	5	5.85762
7	consenting	6	7.10189	and	20	5.82066
8	heterosexual	46	7.07966	a	13	5.53883
9	homosexualism	7	7.00235	not	7	5.49921
10	activity	34	6.98548	of	19	5.41878

Table 9. The top 10 collocates of *gay** in the AOC and SSM corpora.

	AOC corpus (1998–2000)	Freq.	MI	SSM corpus (2013)	Freq.	MI
1	clubs	5	10.26226	community	9	8.39588
2	lesbian	5	9.58419	said	6	5.5959
3	community	13	8.79277	would	6	5.15884
4	rights	7	7.4549	marriage	22	5.1177
5	gay	114	7.30449	gay	63	5.10257
6	men	9	5.82485	people	6	4.97442
7	against	6	5.62805	who	7	4.81276
8	young	19	5.59132	or	6	4.61265
9	people	25	5.53325	The	5	4.07447
10	sex	7	5.43299	in	14	3.65208

> If, on the other hand, the origins of homosexuality are more complex, we may be right to see **homosexual activity** and acts of buggery as pathological.
>
> (Lord Ashbourne, 13 April 1999)

In contrast, the word *activity*, and therefore the phrase *homosexual activity*, does not occur at all in the SSM corpus. This is likely to be related to the topic of the debates; however the presence of collocate *marriages* in the AOC list, despite the debate being about age of consent, suggests further that the language of the debaters is not necessarily contained within the particular topic of the Bill in question. The use of the collocate *marriages* expresses a fear that if one piece of equality is granted to LGBT people (equal age of consent), then other, apparently worse changes (same-sex marriage) will be demanded next:

> ...those who support the reduction of the age of consent would lay themselves open to the argument...that there should be equality in everything else. Should there be equality in pensions? Should there be equality in terms of marriage, so that there could be **homosexual marriages**? That will be the next thing.
>
> (Gerald Howarth, 10 February 1999)

Similarly, despite the topic of the debate being age of consent, the top collocate of *homosexual** in the AOC debate data is *adoption*. All of these refer to adoption (of children) "by homosexual couples", of which the debaters appear to strongly disapprove. Discussion of adoption is used to place the equalisation of age of consent within a category of other gay rights issues (including marriage) which are construed as even less desirable.

> Does he recall the letter that he wrote to me over the summer in which he gave a firm and clear statement of Government policy — that there would be no reduction in the age of consent to 14 for homosexual acts in our country, that no legalisation of homosexual marriages would be proposed by the Government, and that there would be no legal adoption of children by homosexual couples?
>
> (Stuart Bell, 25 January 1999)

The collocates in the AOC debate also indicate that *homosexual** is often compared to the concept of heterosexuality (*heterosexuality, heterosexuals, heterosexual*). These are used in similar ways, mostly to reinforce a difference between the sexual activities of heterosexual and homosexual people. Of the 38 comparisons made between homosexual and heterosexual sex, 25 (65.8%) state explicitly that there is not or should not be equality between the two.

> Those who support the amendment say that they demand equality before the law for homosexual acts. But there is no equality between **heterosexual** and **homosexual** behaviour. One is the natural order of things; the other is not. Indeed, if nature had intended otherwise, it would undoubtedly have constructed the human body differently. (Lord Stoddard of Swindon, 22 June 1998)

> But, in terms of sexual activity, boys and girls, and **homosexuals** and **heterosexuals** are not equal. That is the whole point. They are different. To treat them as though they were equal is, I believe, to open a door to changes further down the line which could be highly undesirable. (Lord Habgood, 22 July 1998)

These sorts of coordination appear to characterise homosexual people as identifiably different to heterosexual people, and this is realised mostly through descriptions of the differences between their sexual behaviours.

Turning to the SSM collocates of *homosexual**, it is clear that the situation has changed with regards to the use of this lemma. Perhaps surprisingly, there is a strong emergence of grammatical words (*was, are, and, a, not, of*) that now frequently co-occur with the node. However, this may relate to the smaller size of the SSM corpus, or perhaps the low frequency (52) of *homosexual** in the SSM corpus. The collocate *are* is brought to our attention: the one occurrence of the phrase *homosexuals are* is shown below:

> This Bill ignores a fact well understood for centuries: marriage is not about just love. Of course, **homosexuals are** often very delightful, artistic and loving people. No one doubts that for one single moment. However, marriage is not about just love. It is about a man and a woman, themselves created to produce children, producing children. (Baroness Knight, 3 June 2013)

In contrast to the oppositional collocates of the AOC debate, Baroness Knight appears to *compliment* gay people (by characterising them as "delightful", "artistic" and "loving") while expressing her defence of opposite-sex marriage. This type of argument poses gay people as able in almost every way (including emotionally) to maintain marriage, but excluded because they do not qualify physically to carry out what is construed as the defining purpose of marriage (to reproduce biologically). This signals a departure from the fearful expressions of opposition to same-sex marriage in the AOC corpus, but at the same time very much speaks of homosexual couples in a different way to heterosexual couples. Baroness Knight's comment also articulates a somewhat narrow stereotype of gay people as associated with the arts, while the term *delightful* could be interpreted as patronising.

Moving on, we want to consider the collocate *not* and what it is used to negate. It seems that *not* is used to describe how some features of opposite-sex marriage (rules surrounding *adultery* and *consummation*) would not be able to apply to same-sex marriage in the new Bill. Therefore, same-sex marriage is construed as not a way of creating equality for same-sex couples but a way of creating discrimination against opposite-sex couples.

> I understand that there is no definition of how a same-sex marriage would be consummated, or of what would be regarded as adultery in a same-sex marriage. Therefore, a heterosexual marriage would stand liable to annulment because of non-consummation but a **homosexual** marriage would **not**. Similarly, a heterosexual husband or wife might be found to have committed adultery, whereas a **homosexual** could **not** be found to have committed adultery. That is real discrimination. (Lord Tebbit, 3 June 2013)

It appears that oppositional language has shifted its focus away from explicit negative discrimination against LGBT people. This has been replaced by considerations of the effect on the majority. In the SSM data, there is a fear expressed that, by creating equality for a minority, discrimination will be created for the majority.

Looking at the collocates of *gay**, several of the AOC debate collocates appear to collectivise gay people in some way (*clubs, community, men, people,* and *lesbian*, from the phrase "gay and/or lesbian", occurring 5 times). Three out of the 5 hits for the collocate *clubs* occur within the same sentence.

> However, in the gay community sexuality seems to matter almost totally. There are **gay clubs**, **gay** bars, the **gay** press, gay this and gay that, and it is not healthy. (Jamie Cann, 25 January 1999)

This is because each of the instances of *gay* occurs within 4 words either side of *clubs*. In the AOC debate gay clubs are negatively implied to be "not healthy" in the case above, while they are described as "less desirable surroundings" and linked to "God knows what" in other speeches. The use of vague terms like "gay this and gay that" and "God knows what" imbue homosexuality with a sense of the unknown, helping to make it appear unspeakably strange and worrying.

The collocate *men* appears to co-occur with *gay** in discussions around research on HIV, AIDS and sexual health (7 times, 77.8%), whereby gay men, particularly *young* gay men, are construed as the carriers of a dangerous disease. Some debaters present research as evidence of "the prevalence of HIV among gay men" (Julian Lewis, 25th January 1999), a point echoed in the example below:

> People need not listen to me, but they should listen to the Terence Higgins Trust, a body trusted by the homosexual lobby, which says that one in five **gay men** in London is HIV positive. (Mr Leigh, 25 January 1999)

Another way that the AOC debaters characterise gay people is to use the collocate *community*, which is also a collocate of *gay** in the SSM corpus. Their use in the two sets of debates, however, is indicative of yet another change in argumentation structure. In the AOC data, the *gay community* is characterised as the victim of *prejudice, hostility,* and *antagonism* (by people other than the debaters); but it is also described as being inherently involved with promiscuous sexual behaviour because it is "an overt community defined by gayness" (The Lord Bishop of Bath and Wells, 13th April 1999). There is also evidence of what appears to be tautological double-marking of sexuality adjectives:

> I hope that although many of us may disagree with the Government's proposal, we shall not be regarded as antagonistic to the homosexual **gay community**, because that is not our intention. (Sir Normal Fowler, 10 February 1999)

This contrasts with a very different characterisation in the SSM data. Here, the *gay community* is most often (6 times, 66.7%) described as, contrary to popular opinion, viewing same-sex marriage as unnecessary. Debaters take it upon themselves to speak on behalf of the *gay community* by expressing their satisfaction with the current levels of equality.

> Where has all this come from? The impetus for redefining the meaning of marriage is not largely from the **gay community**, many of whom are perfectly happy with civil partnership as crafted a few years ago. (Lord Flight, 3 June 2013)

> Many MPs were quick to praise the civil partnerships legislation as being everything that the **gay community** wanted — that it created the equality for which they had fought for so long. (Robert Flello, 5 February 2013)

> The Labour MP Ben Bradshaw, who was the first Cabinet Minister to enter into a civil partnership, has openly criticised the idea of gay marriage, saying that the move to smash centuries of church teaching is "pure politics" and not wanted by the **gay community**, which has already won equality through civil partnerships. (Lord Singh of Wimbledon, 3 June 2013)

Surprisingly, one instance of *gay community* is preceded by the plural possessive pronoun *our*, implying a form of shared ownership.

> The equality that it purports to seek is a cheapened version of spurious uniformity in glaring defiance of reality. Our **gay community**, talented and caring, deserves better and can have it. (Lord Quirk, 3 June 2013)

Similar to Baroness Knight, Quirk employs a strategy of overtly marking gay people by their (apparently unique) positive attributes while expressing his opposition to same-sex marriage. In this case, he criticises the "linguistic acrobatics" of the bill and claims that it is badly written; therefore requiring a "root-and-branch rethink".

People, the only other collocate shared with the AOC debate, is also used differently in the SSM data. Here, *gay* is listed with *lesbian* (3 times) and once with "gender-transmuted" to describe different kinds of *people*.

> My Lords, we have just had a telling and detailed explanation of the road that we have travelled in getting equality for lesbian, **gay** and gender-transmuted **people**. (The Duke of Montrose, 4 June 2013)

This use could be interpreted as discriminatory against transgendered people, as it brings about connotations of *mutation*. It appears to be particularly rare — a Google search for the term "gender-transmuted" retrieves only 19 results; 6 of which refer to its single use in this debate.

To conclude this section, we have shown that the contexts in which the concept of *homosexuality* is used have changed in several ways between the AOC and SSM debates. The contexts of *homosexual** originally comprised of negative constructions of sexual activity and reiterations of the differences between homosexuality and heterosexuality. In the SSM debates, these have been replaced by arguments that attempt to portray LGBT people in a positive light, as well as shifting the focus from the minority under consideration to the effects on the wider heterosexual society. The use of *gay** has changed from concerns over health to the collectivisation of an LGBT community that is described as not actually wanting gay marriage and requires to be spoken for by the debaters themselves. In general, there does appear to have been a movement away from characterisations of homosexuality that could be interpreted as explicitly homophobic; however, some of the discriminatory arguments that remain contain complimenting strategies which appear intended to diminish the perception of discrimination and could thus be viewed as insincere.

4.4 Terms relating to homophobia

In this section, we examine terms specifically relating to homophobia in order to focus on how anti-equality debaters addressed accusations that their position might be seen as homophobic. Table 10 shows the frequencies of these words across the two debates. Apart from *prejudice** and *intoleran** these terms are proportionally higher in the anti-equality speech in the SSM corpus, suggesting that such speakers felt required to comment more on issues surrounding homophobia, prejudice and discrimination in the later debate.

Table 10. Frequencies of terms relating to homophobia and prejudice.

	Freq. AOC	% AOC	Freq. SSM	% SSM	% change	LL of change between corpora
homophob*	20	0.02	32	0.05	+0.03	16.33*
bigot*	13	0.01	25	0.04	+0.03	15.89*
intoleran*	10	0.01	9	0.01	0	1.44
prejudice*	24	0.02	9	0.01	−0.01	0.70
discriminat*	60	0.05	41	0.06	+0.01	1.89
Total	127	0.10	116	0.18	+0.08	19.37*

* $p < 0.0001$

In the AOC debate, there are four occurrences of anti-equality voters referring to *homophobic ranting(s)* by other debators, suggesting dissent (at least on style and argument type) within the anti-equality camp.

Other AOC debators argue that their opposition to the Bill does not make them homophobic.

> I am not **homophobic** in any way. I do not dislike or hate people of a different sexual orientation from the normal, so long as they are adult and know what they are doing. It is not a question of **homophobia**; it is a question of people having a differing view. (Lord Stoddart of Swindon, July 22 1998)

> I am a practising Christian. Christians are not **homophobic** — along with most genuine religions — but we are against homosexual practices. That is our genuine belief. (Lord Stallard, 13 April 1999)

One speaker is critical of the concept of homophobia:

> "**Homophobe**" must be one of the most contrived words to have entered our language recently. (Mr Robathan, 25 January 1999)

In the SSM debate, anti-equality debaters tend to mount a defence of their stance which goes beyond arguing that they are not homophobic for various reasons. Instead, they express concern that they or people who hold similar views to them will be attacked for perceived homophobia.

> It is intolerable, however, that as soon as Members of Parliament put their heads above the parapet and speak to the media, they are called a homophobe, a Nazi — I have been called that a **bigot**, and many other expletives that I would not dare to read out. I have been told to be ashamed of myself, and to die: I have received specific death threats relating to my travel plans. I have been told that I am a disgrace, and that I have no right to express my opinion on this subject. My children have been told that their dad is a **bigot** and a **homophobe**.
> (Mr Burrowes, 5 February 2013)

> Ordinary people with deep feelings about the sanctity of marriage will also be demonised as **homophobic** and will be very lucky if they do not finish up accused of hate crime. (Lord Waddington, 3 June 2013)

> I never imagined that I would be put in a position where I have, by virtue of standing up for marriage, been characterised variously as a **homophobic bigot**, a religious nutter, a product of the dark ages, or, as I see in this weekend's press, on the brink of making a tragic mistake that I will have many years to regret.
> (John Glen, 5 February 2013)

Thus, the anti-equality SSM debaters engage in re-appropriation of an oppositional argument, representing themselves as the true victims, who are threatened and bullied for simply stating their opinions.

5. Conclusion

The AOC debate contains more openly homophobic discourse than the SSM debate, framing gay sex as criminal and dangerous, implying that older gay men are sexual predators, and they can transmit "homosexualism" to boys, ruining them for life by making them promiscuous. Homosexuality is framed as temporary and optional, as well as unnatural and immoral. Links are often made between the perceived promiscuous sexual lifestyle of gay men and the proliferation of dangerous sexually transmitted diseases. There is maintenance of a distinction between both the sexual activities and (therefore) the prescribed rights of gay people and heterosexual people. As a result, the language of opposition to equalising the age of consent (accurately, in fact) expresses fear that allowing one piece of equality for LGBT people will pave the way for further changes for gay people in the future, including "homosexual marriages". However, even in the AOC debate, there are signs that some participants wish to distance themselves from other speakers, referring to the speech of some of their peers as "homophobic rantings", and using a "strategic" equality argument which claims that the status quo is good because it equally protects boys and girls from anal sex (although this is somewhat diminished by the other argument that boys are different from girls).

On the other hand, the SSM debaters are much more cautious in condemnation of homosexuality. A radical decline in the use of *homosexual* corresponds with the elimination of the controversial terms (e.g. *homosexualism*) found in the older debates. Furthermore, *gay* and *homosexual* are much less likely to be associated with *behaviours* and more likely to describe the *identities* of the people concerned. The behaviours that do persist no longer refer to sexual activities or the apparently transient nature of homosexuality. The less frequent use of the use of *I* in the SSM debates (in relation to the AOC debaters) is perhaps indicative of a reluctance among SSM "no" debaters to personally identify with their positions. And argumentation has changed in several ways: there are criticisms of procedure, rather than making attacks on gay people there is an attempt to mitigate opposition by *complimenting* gay people (as "artistic" or "talented"), as well as a focus not on the benefits of the legislation but on the apparently discriminatory effects on heterosexuals and religious people. Even gay people themselves are described as not wanting the change. And, perhaps ironically, the debaters appropriate the discourse of gay liberation by positioning themselves as victims of intolerance, complaining that they have been attacked for their stance.

Overall, what differentiates the same-sex marriage opposition from the previous data is that the debaters of 2013 realise their oppositional stance in almost any way other than one that is *explicitly* homophobic. Since society has changed to the extent that it is no longer acceptable to be seen to publically discriminate against social minority groups, the debates were a chance for those who oppose same-sex marriage to refute accusations that simply voting against LGBT equality is a homophobic act in and of itself. And though, on the surface, they appear to have done just that through careful avoidance of explicit homophobic language, we believe that at least in some cases there now exists *a hate that dare not speak its name*. The *act* of voting against equality for gay people could be interpreted as homophobic, although in the SSM debate it is less easy to level that accusation at the *discourse* of the people who voted that way. The analysis drives home a key point about discourse analysis — that the linguistic analysis must always be considered alongside social context. Knowing that the speakers in the SSM debate voted against gay marriage, and that public attitudes towards homosexuality had altered enables a fuller interpretation and explanation of their language.

This chapter has indicated numerous strategies that may be transferable to other contexts where people hold negative attitudes about a social group that they are reluctant to own up to. We would hope that by outlining such strategies, these more subtle discourses are easier to identify and challenge. We acknowledge a potential limitation of this study in that as Sunderland (2004) notes "discourse identification is...always *interpretive*" (p. 3, cited in Bachmann 2011, 81). Because of this, Bachmann (2011, 81) acknowledges that his "perspective as a gay man...plays a significant role" in his interpretation of discourses. Therefore our own perspectives as gay men may be said to bias our analysis; however, like Bachmann (2011, 81), we aimed to ensure that the discourses we identified are "recognisable to other language users" and were based upon frequent and salient patterns found via corpus analysis tools rather than simply picking stretches of text that we thought were interesting.

Future research projects could examine similar debates around LGBT equality as they occur in other countries, in order to identify additional strategies or to indicate commonalities. We are also mindful that the process of obtaining equality for minority groups should never be taken for granted. As indicated by recent events in countries like Russia and Uganda, moves towards equality can be reversed under certain circumstances. And as this chapter has shown, homophobic acts and attitudes are not necessarily always reflected by equally strong accompanying discourses. Vigilance, rather than complacency is recommended, to ensure that such hard-won rights remain in existence.

Acknowledgement

The research presented in this chapter was supported by the ESRC Centre for Corpus Approaches to Social Science, ESRC grant reference ES/K002155/1

References

Anthony, Laurence. 2011. *AntConc* (Version 3.2.4w) [Computer Software]. Tokyo, Japan: Waseda University. Available from http://www.antlab.sci.waseda.ac.jp/

Bachmann, Ingo. 2011. "Civil Partnership — 'Gay Marriage in all but Name': A Corpus-Driven Analysis of Discourses of Same-Sex Relationships in the UK Parliament." *Corpora* 6(1):77–105. doi:10.3366/cor.2011.0005

Baker, Paul. 2005. *Public Discourses of Gay Men*. London: Routledge.

Baker, Paul. 2006. *Using Corpora for Discourse Analysis*. London: Continuum.

Baker, Paul. 2013. "From *Gay Language* to *Normative Discourse:* A Diachronic Corpus Analysis of Lavender Linguistics Conference Abstracts 1994–2012." *Journal of Language and Sexuality* 2(2):179–205. doi:10.1075/jls.2.2.01bak

Chirrey, Deborah 2003. "'I hereby Come out': What Sort of Speech Act is Coming out?" *Journal of Sociolinguistics* 7(1):24–37. doi:10.1111/1467-9481.00209

Henley, Nancy M., Michelle. D. Miller, Jo Anne Beazley, Diane N. Nguyen, Dana Kaminsky, and Robert Sanders. 2002. "Frequency and Specificity of Referents to Violence in News Reports of Anti-gay Attacks." *Discourse and Society* 13:75–104. doi:10.1177/0957926502013001004

HM Government. 2012. *Equal Marriage: The Government's Response.*

Hunston, Susan. 2002. *Corpora in Applied Linguistics*. Cambridge: Cambridge University Press. doi:10.1017/CBO9781139524773

Kitzinger, Celia. 2005. "'Speaking as a Heterosexual': (How) does Sexuality Matter for Talk-in-interaction?" *Research on Language and Social Interaction* 38(3):221–65. doi: 10.1207/s15327973rlsi3803_2

Marshall, Sue. 2004. *Difference and Discrimination in Psychotherapy and Counselling*. London: Sage.

Mautner, Gerlinde. 2007. "Mining large Corpora for Social Information: The Case of the Elderly." *Language and Society* 36:51–72. doi:10.1017/S0047404507070030

Mautner, Gerlinde. 2009. "Corpora and Critical Discourse Analysis." In *Contemporary Corpus Linguistics*, edited by Paul Baker, 32–46. London: Continuum.

Mills, Sara. 1998. "Post-feminist Text Analysis." *Language and Literature* 7(3):235–53. doi: 10.1177/096394709800700304

Morrish, Liz. 2002. "'That's so Typical of Peter — As soon as there's a Cock-up he Tries to Sit on it.': British Broadsheet Press versus Peter Mandleson 1996–2001." Paper given at the 9th Annual American University Conference on Lavender Languages and Linguistics.

Pink News. 2013. [Online] *Baroness Knight: Parliament Can't Help Blind People See, so Can't Help 'Artistic' Gays Get Married.* Available at: http://www.pinknews.co.uk/2013/06/03/baroness-knight-parliament-cant-help-blind-people-see-so-cant-help-artistic-gays-get-married/. [Accessed 02 September 2013].

Sunderland, Jane. 2004. *Gendered Discourses*. Houndmills: Palgrave Macmillan.

Toginini-Bonelli, Elena. 2001. *Corpus Linguistics at Work*. Amsterdam/Philadelphia: John Benjamins. doi:10.1162/coli.2002.28.4.583a

UCREL 2013. [Online]. *How to Calculate Log-likelihood*. Available at http://ucrel.lancs.ac.uk/llwizard.html. [Accessed 13 August 2013].

UK Parliament. 2013. [Online] *House of Commons: Tuesday 5 February 2013*. Available at: http://www.publications.parliament.uk/pa/cm201213/cmhansrd/cm130205/debtext/130205-0004.htm#13020569000004. [Accessed 22 March 2013].

The paranoid style in politics

Ideological underpinnings of the discourse of Second Amendment absolutism

Adam Hodges
Carnegie Mellon University

In American politics, the National Rifle Association (NRA) has asserted itself as a leading voice in the gun rights movement. The strident rhetoric emanating from the NRA leadership impacts the development of a broader discourse in American public life over gun rights — a *discourse of Second Amendment absolutism* — that articulates a set of assumptions and explanations in defense of an absolutist stance against gun regulation in any form. This chapter examines the ideologies that underlie this absolutist discourse and the identities those ideologies help to construct. In particular, the absolutist discourse is analyzed through the lens of what historian Richard Hofstadter termed "the paranoid style in American politics." The aim is to isolate and expose the extremist elements of this discourse, which polarize political debate and hinder the democratic process.

Keywords: gun rights movement, ideology, National Rifle Association, paranoid style, Second Amendment absolutism

> *"Go ahead, write about our paranoia, as if we should just close our eyes and buy some candles and duct tape and extra water."*
> Wayne LaPierre, NRA Executive Vice-President
> (2012 NRA Annual Meeting)

1. Introduction

The debate in American society over what limits should be placed on the sale, ownership, and use of firearms represents a longstanding and contentious political issue that takes on heightened concern with each new mass shooting. As part of the larger gun rights movement in the United States, the National Rifle Association (NRA) has asserted itself as a leading voice of resistance against gun

DOI 10.1075/bct.93.04hod

regulations. Although more radical gun rights groups exist in the American political landscape, the NRA is the most powerful and institutionalized with a lobbying arm that has come to exert enormous influence on legislative action and electoral politics. Yet the NRA is more than a special interest lobbying group. As Melzer (2009) argues, it is best characterized as a social movement organization, engaging in various forms of consciousness raising that range from local rallies and protests to its annual national membership meetings. As a result, the NRA's reach impacts the development of a broader discourse in American public life over gun rights — a *discourse of Second Amendment absolutism* — that articulates a set of assumptions and explanations in defense of an absolutist stance against gun regulation in any form.

The Second Amendment to the US Constitution concerns itself with the right to own and use firearms. In full, the Amendment reads: "A well regulated Militia, being necessary to the security of a free State, the right of the people to keep and bear Arms, shall not be infringed." As with any Constitutional issue, much legal debate exists over how to interpret the meaning of the Amendment and its implications for the issue of gun rights and regulations in the twenty-first century. To date, the US Supreme Court has affirmed the right for individual US citizens to own and use firearms while allowing for some restrictions to be put in place on those rights through government regulations. Second Amendment absolutists nevertheless argue that the amendment enshrines a natural or God-given right for individuals to own firearms without restriction. They view any governmental actions to regulate firearms as unconstitutional and view even limited gun control measures as a first step down a slippery slope toward the complete abolishment of gun rights. The NRA's discourse of Second Amendment absolutism is conveyed through strident rhetoric that positions even moderate proposals as part and parcel of an agenda that will lead to government confiscation of guns from all law-abiding citizens.

In this chapter, I examine the ideologies that underlie this discourse of Second Amendment absolutism and the identities those ideologies help to construct. In particular, I analyze the absolutist discourse through the lens of what historian Richard Hofstadter (2008[1965], 3) terms "the paranoid style in American politics," a rhetorical style with "qualities of heated exaggeration, suspiciousness, and conspiratorial fantasy." As Hofstadter suggests, a distorted style of rhetoric may signal a "distorted judgment" and an underlying "political pathology." Although he does not fully unpack this metaphor, I suggest that what is pathological about the paranoid style in politics is that it poisons the type of healthy, robust, and reasoned debate that is vital to the political process. As Hofstadter (2008, 31) explains, those practicing the paranoid style do not "see social conflict as something to be mediated and comprised, in the manner of the working politician." Rather, the political struggle in which they are engaged is seen to be "totally irreconcilable, and thus by nature not susceptible to the normal political processes of bargain and compromise" (Hofstadter 2008, 39). Where the paranoid style dominates debate, deliberative democracy suffers. Isolating and examining the elements of the paranoid style in the discourse of Second Amendment absolutism therefore opens up for inspection the elements of an extremist discourse that may hinder the democratic process.

The corpus of discourse data examined for the analysis consists of speeches delivered by the NRA's Executive Vice-President, Wayne LaPierre, during the organization's annual membership meetings over the past decade with emphasis on his most recent speech in 2013. LaPierre's tenure as the NRA's top leader (a post he has held since 1991) has helped institute a more strident rhetorical style as part of its ongoing consciousness raising efforts (Melzer 2009, 91). LaPierre's remarks therefore provide a well thought out and clearly articulated perspective that is representative of the discourse of Second Amendment absolutism promulgated by the organization. In examining the data, I worked with written transcripts available on the NRA's website and videos available on the NRA's YouTube channel.

The approach I take draws from the concern in critical discourse analysis with the ideological underpinnings of discourse (e.g. Fairclough 1989, 1992, 1995; van Dijk 1998) and the conception of discourse forwarded by philosopher Michel Foucault (1972, inter alia). In the Foucauldian perspective, a discourse encompasses the way language is used to both represent and constitute knowledge about a particular topic during a particular historical moment. A discourse therefore provides a powerful set of assumptions, explanations, and expectations that gives meaning to an issue (such as gun control) and constrains the way it can be reasoned about. In this way, a discourse draws boundaries around a domain of knowledge, constraining and governing discussion. As a result, speaking outside the discourse can be seen as heretical, making it difficult for alternative views and perspectives to be entertained. This is because to step outside of a discourse — such as the discourse of Second Amendment absolutism — is to step outside the ideological system in which certain social relations and cultural understandings are made possible, meaningful, and logical. Therefore, in viewing the discourse of Second Amendment absolutism as a discourse in the Foucauldian sense of the term, I wish to underscore its role as a guiding narrative or myth (Barthes 1957) that governs absolutist thinking on the Second Amendment.

Central to the discourse is the construction of a clearly delineated, invidious dichotomy between an in-group defined as "freedom fighters" struggling to save the Second Amendment from an out-group defined as an "elite ruling class" that is said to be the "enemy of freedom." These identities are stitched together out of different ideological strands to form a cohesive fabric of meaning within the discourse. In analyzing the Us versus Them binary, I therefore focus on the ideological systems that come together to support the discourse of Second Amendment absolutism. Rather than a single ideology, the discourse draws from multiple, intersecting cultural and political ideologies.

Ideologies are not simply individual beliefs or isolated ideas. Rather, an ideology is a shared system of ideas and beliefs that guide representations of the world for a social group. The concept of ideology can be viewed as encompassing both sociocultural and cognitive dimensions (van Dijk 1998). In discussing ideology as a cultural system, Geertz (1973, 207) defines "ideologies as systems of interacting symbols, as patterns of interworking meanings." Hall (1996, 26) defines ideology as "the mental frameworks — the languages, the concepts, categories, imagery of thought, and the systems of representation — which different classes and social groups deploy in order to make sense of, figure out and render intelligible the way society works." Common to any definition of ideology is its group component — that is to say, ideologies are "not individual, idealistic constructs, but the social constructs shared by a group" (van Dijk 1998, 9). Ideologies are "socially situated and collectively shared" (Thompson 1990, 51). These shared frameworks of meaning provide the basis for articulating the image of the world found in the discourse of Second Amendment absolutism. The aim of the analysis is therefore to identify these ideological influences and expose their assumptions as the partial and interested positions that they are, rather than allowing them to pass unnoticed as taken-for-granted assumptions or naturalized facts.

Before delving into the analysis, I provide a brief overview of the NRA and discuss in more detail Hofstadter's (2008) concept of the paranoid style in politics. The analysis then focuses on the discursively constructed image of the NRA as the defender of individual liberty against an oppressive government controlled by an elite vanguard determined to stifle the freedom of ordinary citizens. Through the analysis, I seek to illuminate the ideological influences that contribute to the discourse of Second Amendment absolutism, which provides a Manichean vision of the world that works to foreclose reasonable debate on the topic of gun rights and regulations.

2. The evolution of today's NRA

Since its founding in 1871, the National Rifle Association has undergone an evolution from an organization of soldiers to sportsmen to lobbyists. The original impetus for the organization centered on a desire to improve marksmanship among American soldiers. Two veterans of the Civil War, George Wood Wingate and William Conant Church, were concerned with the poor shooting skills of Union troops during the war and the ineffectiveness of the National Guard in addressing the issue after the war. So they set out to create a private organization modeled on the National Rifle Association of Great Britain, which was begun in 1859 by militia officers. With the mission of building ranges and promoting rifle practice, the state of New York granted the NRA its initial charter (Sugarmann 1992, 25–26). The organization struggled for support and funding in the early years, but its efforts to promote marksmanship among citizen soldiers gained momentum after the turn of the twentieth century. Federal legislation signed in 1905 by President Theodore Roosevelt enabled the NRA "to purchase surplus military rifles at cost and sell them to members and civilian shooters" (Melzer 2009, 36). The Roosevelt administration also began to provide federal money to the NRA to hold shooting matches. Federal funding for these efforts continued until 1958 with only a short break during the Great Depression. A primary focus for the NRA during much of the early twentieth century therefore concentrated on competitive shooting. However, after World War II, the NRA developed a firearms safety program and began to draw in hunters as members. By 1950, approximately half its members identified as hunters so that by mid-twentieth century, firearms safety education and recreational shooting joined marksmanship training as the NRA's primary concerns (Melzer 2009, 36; Sugarmann 1992, 34; see also, Winkler 2013).

With the high profile political assassinations in the United States during the 1960s, the issue of gun control began to intensify in American society. In 1968, the US Congress passed the Gun Control Act with opposition from the NRA only on certain provisions. Despite the presence of Second Amendment fundamentalists within the NRA's structure, the sportsmen still dominated the organization and Franklin Orth, the NRA's Executive Vice-President in the wake of the assassination of President John F. Kennedy in 1963, even publicly supported some form of gun control, "arguing that no reasonable American could take a different stance" (Melzer 2009, 39). However, the growing faction of hardliners within the organization, led by Harlan Carter, took a different stance and worked to replace the leadership with like-minded members — an effort that was initially thwarted in 1976 when the intact leadership fired several dozen employees aligned with Carter. Yet, it was only a matter of time before Carter and his allies took control, staging a revolt before the NRA's annual meeting in Cincinnati in 1977 that replaced the organization's entire leadership. Carter was elected Executive Vice-President of the organization and his allies filled the remaining leadership positions. The coup marked a turning point in the history of the NRA, shifting its focus to the strident defense of gun rights.

In 1975, the NRA established its lobbying arm: the Institute for Legislative Action (ILA). Carter was the NRA-ILA's first director, and its lobbying efforts and influence only grew when he became Executive Vice-President in 1977 — a post in which he served until 1984. The NRA struggled during the late 1980s with leadership issues until it regained momentum with the election of Wayne LaPierre as Executive Vice-President in 1991. LaPierre continues to guide the organization through 2014. Since the 1970s, the NRA's membership has risen from one million to nearly five million members. Its public image was helped along by the role played by actor Charlton Heston who served as NRA President from 1998 to 2003. Although the modern NRA remains active in the areas of gun safety education, marksmanship training, and the promotion of recreational shooting, the organization has firmly dedicated itself to opposing any type of gun control legislation. "Today the NRA-ILA is where most of the organization's energy is directed" (Melzer 2009, 40). Spokespersons for the NRA have adopted a uniform, fundamentalist stance represented by the discourse of Second Amendment absolutism.

3. The paranoid style in politics

In the early 1960s, historian Richard Hofstadter detailed in a lecture (and subsequent essay and book chapter) a particular style employed in American politics that he termed "the paranoid style." Although not exclusive to any one political orientation — in fact, examples of the paranoid style exist across the political spectrum — Hofstadter formulated his description against the backdrop of the conservative movement led by US Senator Barry Goldwater and the style of politics practiced by associated right-wing groups. As Hofstadter (2008) describes, the paranoid style involves "a way of seeing the world and of expressing oneself" (Hofstadter 2008, 4) that entails the "qualities of heated exaggeration, suspiciousness, and conspiratorial fantasy" (Hofstadter 2008, 3). He explains:

> Webster defines paranoia, the clinical entity, as a chronic mental disorder characterized by systematized delusions of persecution and of one's own greatness. In the paranoid style, as I conceive it, the feeling of persecution is central, and it is indeed systematized in grandiose theories of conspiracy. But there is a vital difference between the paranoid spokesman in politics and the clinical paranoiac: although they both tend to be overheated, oversuspicious, overaggressive, grandiose, and apocalyptic in expression, the clinical paranoid sees the hostile and conspiratorial world in which he feels himself to be living as directed specifically *against him*; whereas the spokesman of the paranoid style finds it directed against a nation, a culture, a way of life whose fate affects not himself alone but millions of others. (Hofstadter 2008, 4)

As a historian, Hofstadter (2008, p. 6) is interested in the way this manner of expression "has been linked with movements of suspicious discontent". He details several instances of its use throughout the history of American politics, including examples contemporary to his times such as accusations of communist infiltration of the government circulated during the McCarthy era and the John Birch Society's argument that water fluoridation was a communist plot to poison Americans. Even though "nothing prevents a sound program or sound issue from being advocated in the paranoid style," the term carries an intentionally pejorative connotation, Hofstadter (2008, 5) notes, because "the paranoid style has a greater affinity for bad causes than good". One might alternatively argue that the paranoid style has a potentially transforming effect in that it can effectively shut down debate on legitimate issues by moving the discourse into the realm of ideologically distorted fantasy. Where democratic debate may genuinely entertain the pros and cons of adding fluoride to the public water supply, for example, the paranoid style moves the discourse into a realm marked by conspiratorial accusations and apocalyptic warnings that bear little resemblance to lived reality.

The paranoid style, as outlined by Hofstadter, can be thought of as a *style* insofar as it involves a manner or way of doing something — namely, a way of advancing a political position. Importantly, the political position (content of the message) can be separated from the style (manner) in which the message is conveyed. This usage of *style* accords with the concern in rhetoric with *how* ideas are expressed (as distinct from *what* ideas are expressed). Any issue could potentially be forwarded through the use of the paranoid style just as different styles could be used to forward the same issue. In politics, it is common to speak of the styles of politicians so that, for example, the issue of immigration reform could be advanced by a president who adopts a professorial style (think of President Obama) or a president who adopts a cowboy style (think of President Bush). Notably, the focus here is on individual variation in the way language is used, a concern shared by sociolinguists (Eckert and Rickford 2001). Despite the differences between the usages of *style* in rhetoric versus sociolinguistics (not to mention the numerous definitions employed within sociolinguistics alone), a common concern nevertheless focuses on the linguistic features or figures of speech employed by an individual speaker to convey a message. In other words, interest rests on how a message is conveyed, the manner in which it is done in an individual's discourse.

Yet there are additional dimensions to Hofstadter's (2008) paranoid style beyond concern with stylistics or the definitions of *style* that emphasize individual variation or expressive choice. These dimensions are especially relevant to the critical analysis of discourses in which the paranoid style appears. In particular, the paranoid style is not just a way of "expressing oneself" but also encompasses "a way of seeing the world" (Hofstadter 2008, 4). As Hofstadter (2008) explains, the paranoid style "has to do with the way in which ideas are *believed* and advocated" (Hofstadter 2008, 5; emphasis mine). In other words, more than a mere style of speaking, it is "a style of mind" (Hofstadter 2008, 3). It encompasses certain ideas and beliefs. In addition, although embodied at any given time in a particular spokesperson for a cause, there is an important group dimension to the use of the paranoid style. It is not simply a matter of a speaker employing individual stylistic choices. The paranoid style involves a *shared* system of beliefs and way of representing the world. Whereas paranoia in the clinical sense, as Hofstadter points out, infects the individual; paranoia in the political realm permeates the worldview of a social group, forming a system of beliefs that guide how the group represents and comes to understand the political landscape. In this way, the paranoid style acts not just as an individual rhetorical style, but as an *ideology* in the sense of a system of ideas and beliefs that guide representations of the world for a social group. The paranoid style effectively encapsulates a way of seeing and hence reasoning about the world.

In postulating the paranoid style as an ideology, I wish to underscore the symbolic dimension of ideology as a tool for expressing concepts, thoughts, ideas, and representations. Moreover, I wish to emphasize the plurality as well as the variety of ideologies — whether political, cultural, or linguistic — in play in society at any given time. Various systems of ideas and beliefs operate simultaneously to represent the world from different perspectives, intersecting and impacting representations in the process. Although not itself a political ideology, the paranoid style qua ideology can operate in the service of a political ideology, combining with it to express and formulate arguments that bolster a political position.

Underlying the paranoid style are several basic elements or ideological assumptions about the nature of the world and the in-group's political struggle in that world against opponents. Central among these is the image of "a vast and sinister conspiracy" (Hofstadter 2008, 29). The conspiracy is carried out against a culture or way of life with the intent to put an end to its existence. This is not the same as simply seeing an occasional plot or conspiratorial act within the flow of historical events (e.g. Watergate or an assassination plot). Instead, the paranoid style perpetuates the idea of an ongoing, "gigantic and yet subtle machinery of influence set in motion to undermine and destroy a way of life" (Hofstadter 2008, 29). For exponents of the paranoid style, conspiracy is viewed "as *the motive force* in historical events. History *is* a conspiracy" (Hofstadter 2008, 29; emphasis in the original). The conspiracy is set in motion by a well-organized, powerful force that is seen as an *enemy* and not just a political opponent. The enemy is viewed with extreme suspicion and is attributed vast power to control the flow of historical events through secret schemes and behind-the-scene plots that allow it to conduct acts of malice toward the persecuted way of life. It is as if the enemy stands outside history, "not caught in the toils of the vast mechanism of history" to instead manufacture, will, or deflect "the normal course of history in an evil way" (Hofstadter

2008, 32). The power the enemy is said to possess may include control of the media and educational system along with vast funding sources that allow it to disseminate (mis)information and control the public mind. The group that is persecuted by the enemy is therefore seen as the last defender of its way of life, making a final but determined stand in "a conflict between absolute good and absolute evil" (Hofstadter 2008, 31). As such, the Manichean struggle is viewed "in apocalyptic terms" so that the stakes involve "the birth and death of whole worlds, political orders, whole systems of human values" (Hofstadter 2008, 29). Importantly, the current moment always represents a crucial "turning point: it is now or never in organizing resistance to conspiracy" (Hofstadter 2008, 30). Leadership against the threat is therefore strident and militant, moving the conflict beyond the realm of political mediation and compromise.

5. Us vs. Them in the discourse of Second Amendment absolutism

Given its Manichean underpinnings, the paranoid style/ideology lends itself well to bolstering a discourse of absolutism. My claim is that the paranoid style provides a valuable set of ideological assumptions that are woven together with additional ideological threads to form the discourse of Second Amendment absolutism. In other words, various systems of thought form the fabric of this discourse, which, as a discourse in the Foucaldian sense of the term, provides an explanatory framework that structures knowledge and constitutes social identities central to the politics of gun rights in American society. The aim of the present analysis is therefore to unravel these various ideological threads and illuminate the assumptions that contribute to the arguments forwarded by the NRA. Since group identities are built upon the scaffolding provided by ideologies, I do this by focusing on the construction of the in-group and out-group in the discourse of Second Amendment absolutism.

In the discourse of Second Amendment absolutism, the world is divided into a simple binary between the in-group and out-group. Much of this divide follows the common imagery in American politics between Washington insiders and outsiders, where "Washington" metonymically represents the power center of the US government. Outside this power center exists what is depicted as the American mainstream comprised of the everyman. Many a political campaign has used the epithet of "Washington insider" against an incumbent candidate who has served in Washington while attempting to position the challenging candidate as an ordinary citizen uncorrupted by the halls of power. In his rhetoric, NRA Executive Vice-President Wayne LaPierre sets up a similar dichotomy to position the NRA's political opponent as Washington insiders that are out of touch with the rest of America, as seen in the excerpts that follow.

1. The national media and the political elites, they are all part of the same class that thinks they're smarter than we are. They know better than we do. They can tell us what to do or not, what to own or not, what to eat and drink or not, and how to live or not. (LaPierre 2013)
2. Anti-freedom elitists in academia, the media, rich foundations and government can do permanent damage to individual freedoms just as real as an insurrection or coup. (LaPierre 2002)
3. When it comes to those scheming bureaucrats in Washington, gun owners have had it. Our rights have been attacked before as the political elites and the media have often conspired to shame and blame American gun owners for violent crime. (LaPierre 2011)

The labels used to name the NRA's political opponents in these first three excerpts — "political elites," "national media," "anti-freedom elitists in academia," "rich foundations," "government," and "bureaucrats in Washington" — represent a broad and general swath of the sociopolitical landscape. Although the NRA is not shy about naming specific politicians or figures working for gun control regulations, much of the discursive process of constructing the political opponent in LaPierre's rhetoric involves naming a general, unspecified out-group that acts as a foil against which the NRA is defined. In this way, various interchangeable entities are lumped together as "part of the same class" that is attributed an "elite" status removed from the life and concerns of the everyman. Descriptors throughout the discourse underscore the elite status of this out-group, which is referred to in the following excerpts as "the ruling class."

4. Behind every anti-gun law…or candidate …or editorial…or movie …is a ruling class… (LaPierre 2008)
5. They're the ruling classes that all believe the same…elite…conceit — (LaPierre 2008)

Constructing the out-group as an elite ruling class underscores the perception that they control the reins of power. As Hofstadter (2008, 32) describes of the paranoid style, "Very often the enemy is held to possess some especially effective source of power: he controls the press; he directs the public mind through 'managed news'; he has unlimited funds…he is gaining a stranglehold on the educational system". Lumping together the media, government, and academia certainly covers the power bases in society. In the process of naming these various social and political institutions, LaPierre attributes a common viewpoint to them all — "the same elite conceit" — while erasing the diversity of opinion that undeniably does exist within and across those institutions. Moreover, the "conceit" attributed to these "elites" characterizes them as showing disdain and contempt for those supposedly under their rule.

Further in line with the paranoid style, the power attributed to the out-group is portrayed in terms of "a vast and sinister conspiracy" (Hofstadter 2008, 29). As seen earlier in (3), it is not just bureaucrats in Washington that form the opponent but "scheming bureaucrats." The conspiratorial nature of the out-group is further elaborated in the excerpts that follow.

6. If you consider the Constitution less relevant, if you ignore or distort the Second Amendment, if you conspire to make lawful firearms less accessible to lawful citizens, if you infiltrate school boards and churches and legislatures and foundations to advance an anti-freedom agenda of any kind — the fact that you were born on American soil won't mask the fact that you're an enemy of freedom and a political terrorist. (LaPierre 2002)
7. Already, they are conspiring in private. Re-grouping, planning, preparing, organizing, even waiting for the, quote "next Newtown" — the next tragedy to come, the next senseless, horrific crime to exploit. (LaPierre 2013)

Through word choice associated with the conspiracy frame — e.g. "conspire" and "infiltrate" — LaPierre forwards the notion in (6) that the NRA's political opponent has what amounts to a conspiratorial "anti-freedom agenda." The use of the word "infiltrate" in conjunction with the naming of "school boards and churches and legislatures and foundations" further solidifies the image of the out-group as controlling a variety of social institutions. Much like accusations of communist infiltration during the era of McCarthyism, the "anti-freedom" elites are said to "infiltrate" and control everything from schools to churches to government to private funding sources. The elites who are said to be in control, operating with a single agenda and mindset, "are conspiring in private" to take away gun rights, as seen in (7).

One could view this conspiratorial talk in metaphorical terms, and argue that LaPierre is simply adopting a rhetorical flourish to arouse the passions of movement followers. Certainly, this may very well be the case. My concern, however, is not whether LaPierre truly believes there is a vast and sinister conspiracy working against the NRA (in the technical sense of the term) or whether he intends it merely as a metaphor. The perlocutionary intent is the same in both scenarios — namely, the paranoid style aims to construct an absolutist stance that inflames tensions surrounding the debate over gun policy and walls off reasoned discussion of alternative viewpoints. Instead of debating gun policy proposals, attributing conspiratorial designs to a vast and powerful political opponent moves the discourse into the realm of vague themes and helps turn a political opponent into a mortal *enemy*, further helped with descriptions as seen in the following excerpts.

8. Together they form a sort of Taliban, an intolerant coalition of fanatics that shelter the anti-freedom alliance so it can thrive and grow. (LaPierre 2002)
9. The Constitution is pristine and inviolate. And those who promote that we be less free are political terrorists. (LaPierre 2002)

As seen in (8) and (9), the demonization of the political opponent qua enemy depicts those who propose gun control measures as "a sort of Taliban" or as "political terrorists" that form a "coalition of fanatics that shelter the anti-freedom alliance." Such inflammatory characterizations effectively strip gun regulation proponents of their place as legitimate members of the polis, and equate them with foreign enemies. In this way, the political struggle over gun rights is portrayed through a war-like frame as a conspiracy by the out-group to not just regulate firearms but to destroy the in-group as a foreign autocratic regime or terrorist organization might attempt.

10. Apparently, there is nothing the president will not do to get something — anything — through Congress to advance his agenda to destroy the Second Amendment. Nothing. (LaPierre 2013)
11. …they're coming after us with a vengeance to destroy us. To destroy us and every ounce of our freedom. (LaPierre 2013)
12. They use tragedy to try to blame us, to shame us into compromising our freedom for their political agenda. They want to change America, our culture and our values. (LaPierre 2013)

Whereas the core issue revolves around interpretation of the Second Amendment, the paranoid style amplifies that interpretive struggle as an "agenda to destroy the Second Amendment," as seen in (10). Yet the fears portrayed in the discourse go well beyond the Second Amendment. As Hofstadter (2008, 29) notes, the perception is that the enemy seeks "to undermine and destroy a way of life". Indeed, this is well represented in the discourse of Second Amendment absolutism where the ultimate fear is that "they're coming after us with a vengeance to destroy us" (11) where "destroy us" means, "They want to change America, our culture and our values" (12). In other words, the threat is not just one against the Second Amendment, but a threat perceived to endanger a culture or an entire way of life. This perception shifts the political conflict into a type of war — a *culture war*. "The paranoid tendency is aroused by a confrontation of opposed interests which are (or are felt to be) totally irreconcilable, and thus by nature not susceptible to the normal political processes of bargain and compromise" (Hofstadter 2008, 39). In this way, the idea of working together with proponents of gun regulation to balance the rights and responsibilities of gun ownership with concerns for public health and safety is replaced by the image of a pitched battle for what is perceived to be the social group's very existence.

The delineation of the enemy in the struggle over gun rights and regulations operates as a crucial foil for defining the in-group. In contrast to the image of the political other as an elite ruling class with vast power, the NRA positions itself as the little guy — a political outsider that lacks the resources of its foe. Of course, from an objective perspective, such a characterization appears undeniably at odds with the reality of the NRA's substantial resources and political influence (not to mention the fact that the NRA-ILA is headquartered in the DC area). Nevertheless, like the Washington outsider in those classic American political campaigns, the NRA claims to be the true representative of America. Where it lacks the vast power of the scheming enemy, it putatively makes up for it with the overwhelming support of the American public.

13. All over this country, people are more and more frustrated with Washington and the political and media elites. They are dismayed over a political debate that has nothing to do with addressing our problems and everything to do with advancing an old, tired, failed political agenda. Everywhere I go, I've learned that the NRA is truly at the heart of America's heartland. That we are in the middle of the river of America's mainstream. That what we want is exactly what most Americans want. (LaPierre 2013)
14. The political class and media class just don't get it. In a lot of ways, they've lost track of what this great nation is really all about. It's about US and people like us, all over this country. It's always been about "we, the people," not the political class, all the way back to our founding. (LaPierre 2013)
15. Today, the NRA is a record 5 million strong! Even as thousands of Americans join our cause every day, the media and political elites denigrate us. They cringe at the sight of long lines at gun shows. They mock Americans who are buying firearms and ammunition at a record pace. They scorn and scold the NRA. They don't get it because they don't get America. (LaPierre 2013)

As LaPierre states in (13), "the NRA is truly at the heart of America's heartland." The metaphor of a beating heart dovetails with the image of rural America to convey the notion that this locale is both geographically and symbolically the life force of America, distal to "Washington and the political and media elites." As he shifts to another metaphor to convey the same point, LaPierre states, "we are in the middle of the river of America's mainstream." Here, the river metaphor merges into the political connotation of "mainstream" as normal and conventional. The NRA is thereby positioned as representing the orthodox view on gun rights and regulation. As Morris (1992) notes, "A crucial feature of hegemonic consciousness is that it always presents itself as a set of values and beliefs that serves the general welfare" (Morris 1992, 363, quoted in Melzer 2009, 108–109). This is certainly evident in the NRA's discourse where its absolutist stance is positioned as the political center (rather than extremist fringe), claiming to represent "exactly what most Americans want."

In (13), (14) and (15), the pronouns *we* and *us* refer to both the NRA (including LaPierre and NRA members in the audience) and "people like us, all over this country." Further, through the allusion to "we, the people," and its intertextual echoes of the Declaration of Independence and connotations of the nation as a whole, the NRA becomes the true representative of "this great nation" in contradistinction to the ruling elites that represent heretical views and rule, presumably without consent, over "we, the people" on the issue of gun regulations. The oration in (14) places emphasis on "us" (represented by capitalization in the NRA's transcript), explicitly staking out a diametrical opposition to *them*. With these lines of a power imbalance drawn, the image of persecution is then filled in by the hand of "political elites" who are said, in (15), to "mock Americans," "denigrate us," and "scorn and scold the NRA." The feeling of persecution at the hands of the enemy serves to rally the in-group's sense of injustice.

In the paranoid style, the charge against a clearly delineated enemy is led by a militant leader; and LaPierre (among others in the movement) certainly fits the bill. Moreover, to effectively espouse the paranoid style's fantastical imagery of impending doom, the leader positions himself as a prescient figure with the ability to perceive the conspiracy and foresee the looming threat "before it is fully obvious to an as yet un-aroused public" (Hofstadter 2008, 31). As LaPierre notes:

16. At this gathering one year ago, I predicted that our freedom might soon face its greatest threat ever. I spent the past year warning gun owners all over this country that, if re-elected, President Obama would launch an all-out, historic assault against the Second Amendment and the personal freedom of hundreds of millions of law-abiding Americans. (LaPierre 2013)

As LaPierre contends in (16), the predictions and warnings he gave are coming to fruition in the current moment of political struggle.

Curiously, in the paranoid style, the present moment always seems to be the defining moment in the Manichean struggle of good versus evil. "Like religious millenarians, he expresses the anxiety of those who are living through the last days and he is sometimes disposed to set a date for the apocalypse" (Hofstadter 2008, 30). In actual fact, the specific political moment is largely irrelevant to the apocalyptic scenario painted by the militant leader, whether it is in 2013, as in (16) above, or in 2008 as seen in the following excerpt.

17. The Second Amendment is facing a perfect storm. In fact, the worst I've seen in thirty years. It's hard to believe it's been that long … I came to work at NRA in 1978. And it's taken three decades to crystallize for me: Behind every anti-gun law…or candidate …or editorial…or movie …is a ruling class that can't stand you taking responsibility for your own safety. (LaPierre 2008)

Where the actual threat against gun rights realistically waxes and wanes as the political winds change, the NRA's perception of threat remains constantly amplified so that regardless of the occasion, the "Second Amendment is facing a perfect storm." It is now or never to make the last stand; "it is now or never in organizing resistance to conspiracy" (Hofstadter 2008, 30). The portrayal of a constant level of imminent threat against gun rights serves much like a revivalist sermon to "portray that which impends but which may still be avoided" (Hofstadter 2008, 30). As long as movement supporters do not grow weary of the message, and come to perceive their world as constantly under attack, then the immediacy of the message works to rally the membership and mobilize new supporters to the cause. It also helps mold an absolutist, unbending stance on the issue.

When it comes to defining the cause of the NRA and movement followers, defense of the Second Amendment may be the core political issue but the cause is outlined in much broader terms as a fight for freedom. The ubiquitous theme of freedom resonates throughout the discourse of Second Amendment absolutism. Thus, instead of political arguments against particular gun control proposals, the discourse emphasizes a more general threat to freedom.

A term and concept such as *freedom* is sufficiently vague and positively valued by the national community as a whole so that it is difficult to argue against without being seen as opposing a universally accepted principle (see also, Burke 1945 on "god-terms"). To argue against freedom would be viewed as heretical, unpatriotic, and un-American. Thus, to attach a specific cause (such as the opposition to sensible gun regulations) under the generic banner of freedom is to position it as falling within the realm of "the general moral order, and hence not justified only by partisan, self-serving grounds" (van Dijk 1998, 258).

Furthermore, the vagueness of a term such as *freedom* allows for the accrual of different shades of meaning that vary with political orientation as different ideological attachments color its significance. As Melzer (2009, 131) points out, the gun rights movement is closely aligned with the main dimensions of conservative politics in the United States, including traditionalism, anti-communist militarism, and libertarianism (see also, Diamond 1995, 7). In particular, libertarianism in its conservative form helps undergird the strong theme of freedom found in the discourse of Second Amendment absolutism with its emphasis on self-ownership, liberty of action, and protection from interference (Vallentyne 2012). Where gun regulations interfere with individuals' autonomy by limiting their ownership or use of certain firearms in certain locations under certain conditions, *freedom* in the sense attributed to it by strict libertarianism is violated. As a result, the NRA is not merely fighting for gun rights, as the organization frequently emphasizes, but is fighting for freedom from governmental interference. This refrain is commonly heard within the discourse, as seen in the excerpts that follow.

18. So when they ask you to sign over some rights, you say this: [...] I'm the NRA, and I'll fight for freedom. (LaPierre 2002)

19. From liberty's defense, we will never back down. We will never surrender. We will always stand, we will always fight. We will always Stand and Fight for freedom! (LaPierre 2013)

In this way, with its rhetorical focus on freedom, the NRA fashions itself as the "largest and oldest civil rights organization in the United States" rather than simply a gun rights organization.

Through the libertarian principle of self-ownership, individuals are also seen as responsible for their own self-protection. This view merges with a gender ideology that defines masculinity in terms of a man's ability to protect himself against threats to his self-ownership and the subordinates in his household. To abdicate this responsibility to another entity, such as the government, is not only to give up one's freedom but also one's responsibility as masculine protector. Young (2003) summarizes this "logic of masculine protection" as follows. "The world out there is heartless and uncivilized, and the movements and motives of the men in it are unpredictable and difficult to discern. The protector must therefore take all precautions against these threats, remain watchful and suspicious, and be ready to fight and sacrifice for the sake of his loved ones" (Young 2003, 4, citing Elshtain 1987, 1992). In his examination of gender and the NRA, Melzer (2009) provides a similar description of this logic, which he links to the ethos of the American frontier and terms *frontier masculinity*. "Characterized by rugged individualism, hard work, protecting and providing for families, and self-reliance, frontier masculinity is the mythologized dominant version of manhood from America's frontier past" (Melzer 2009, 16). Frontier masculinity therefore represents a hybridization of libertarian principles with the logic of masculine protection, a perspective well voiced by LaPierre, as seen in the excerpts that follow.

20. There is nothing more good and right and normal than an honest American citizen owning a firearm to defend himself or protect her family. (LaPierre 2013)
21. And the ultimate underpinning of personal survival is the Second Amendment to the United States Constitution. The lesson of New Orleans is that all those

politicians who said government and police will be there to protect you in a disaster are naïve at best and liars at worst. The lesson of New Orleans is that you can't count on government to protect you. But you can count on the looters, robbers, rapists, and armed gangs to show up right on time, every time, to prey on the vulnerable, law-abiding, unarmed citizens. (LaPierre 2006)

22. More Americans today than ever before understand the principle of our Second Amendment: the freedom it gives to them as individuals, to be responsible for your own safety, protection, and your survival. Americans, throughout this country, are suspect of criminal attack. They've witnessed the slaughter of tyrants, and they know that terrorists are lurking and plotting to murder us. These aren't just distant fears, they're coming realities, gathering and approaching as certain as dark storm clouds. (LaPierre 2012)

Importantly, the logic of masculine protection and frontier masculinity — which can also be enacted by women, as the NRA avidly spotlights — is predicated upon the assumption of a hostile world that poses a constant threat to the safety of oneself and one's family. True to the paranoid style, the image of a hostile world is painted through the amplification of exaggerated threats represented by various bogeymen. The specifics are drawn from the latest news headlines. In (21), a speech delivered after Hurricane Katrina, the threat comes in the form of "the looters, robbers, rapists, and armed gangs" that threaten one's "personal survival." In (22), bogeymen are provided in the shape of "tyrants" and "terrorists" that "are lurking and plotting to murder us." Likewise, in LaPierre's speech at the 2013 annual meeting, allusions are made to the Boston Marathon bombers. As LaPierre underscores in (22), "These aren't just distant fears, they're coming realities, gathering and approaching as certain as dark storm clouds."

Appeals to fear draw from the Manichean vision of the world as a sharply divided contest between the forces good and evil. With evil lurking everywhere, "good guys with guns" are positioned as the only reliable form of protection for themselves and families against those threats. As one of the NRA's favorite sound bite arguments says:

23. …the only way to stop a bad guy with a gun is a good guy with a gun. (LaPierre 2013)

In addition, the Manichean template applies equally to the pitched political struggle qua (culture) war where the outlines of the debate are painted as an either-or choice between "freedom fighters" and "freedom haters." In language that resonates with Bush's "war on terror" narrative (Hodges 2011), LaPierre states the case as follows:

24. It's black and white, all or nothing, you're with us or against us. There are not flavors of freedom. You can't like yours, but not mine. There are not classes of freedom. You can't have more, or less, than me. And there is no temporary suspension of freedom. Once on loan, you never get it back. Americans who think freedom is negotiable or malleable are, by our Founding Fathers' standards, not Americans. (LaPierre 2002)

As implied in (24), those who propose even limited regulations on gun ownership and use are, by the standards set up by LaPierre, "not Americans." The Us versus Them dichotomy thereby sets up a political contest between two enemies disdainful of each other and suspicious of one another's motives.

6. Conclusion

In examining the sharp divisions constructed by the NRA through its spokesperson, Wayne LaPierre, my aim has been to illuminate key elements of a larger discourse of Second Amendment absolutism that buttresses the gun rights movement. As a discourse in the Foucauldian sense of the term, the discourse of Second Amendment absolutism carries with it a set of assumptions, explanations, and expectations about the struggle over gun rights and regulations in US society. Various ideological influences underpin this discourse, coming together to promote a way of thinking about the world in which certain social relations and cultural understandings are made possible, meaningful, and logical. The political tenets of conservative libertarianism and the gendered logic of frontier masculinity join together with the elements of the paranoid style to form the discourse. In particular, the paranoid style provides a substantial contribution that steers the discourse toward unbending extremism. Where there is genuine public concern and desire to find solutions that balance gun rights with public safety, gun rights absolutists see conspiracy, governmental plots to confiscate guns, and a threat to their very existence. In imposing sharp social divisions and sowing fear — and even hate — the discourse polarizes and leaves little room for common ground.

The implications of this for democratic debate over gun policy should be evident by now. In a debate dominated by extremist positions that paint political opponents as mortal enemies, productive dialogue that seeks to find widely acceptable solutions through the normal political process becomes increasingly difficult. Despite the NRA's claim to represent mainstream views on gun policy, such claims are belied by national polls that show most Americans support some regulation, such as background checks prior to the sale of firearms, while preserving the individual right to own firearms (Gallup 2013). Although the NRA leadership may speak for a relatively small number of extremists in the gun rights movement in staking out an absolutist stance against any form of regulation, the powerful discourse of Second Amendment absolutism that the NRA leadership and lobbyists promulgate impacts the debate as a whole. It impacts the debate not so much by joining the debate as by obfuscating and shutting it down. After all, to espouse Second Amendment absolutism per the discourse outlined above is to vilify any gun policy proposal as intolerable and beyond reasonable deliberation. Yet gun violence is an issue of real concern in American society, and finding real solutions depends upon fostering dialogue on policy questions in a manner that recognizes legitimate concerns on all sides without the heated exaggeration and conspiratorial fantasy of the paranoid political style.

References

Barthes, Roland. 1957. *Mythologies*. Paris: Edition du Seuil.

Burke, Kenneth. 1945. *A Grammar of Motives*. New York: Prentice-Hall.

Diamond, Sara. 1995. *Roads to Dominion: Right-Wing Movements and Political Power in the United States*. New York: Guilford.

Eckert, Penelope, and John Rickford (eds.). 2001. *Style and Sociolinguistic Variation*. Cambridge: Cambridge University Press. doi:10.1017/CBO9780511613258

Elshtain, Jean Bethke. 1987. *Women and War*. Chicago: University of Chicago Press.

Elshtain, Jean Bethke. 1992. "Sovereignty, Identity, Sacrifice." In *Gendered States: Feminist (Re) visions of International Relations Theory*, edited by V. Spike Peterson, 141–54. Boulder, CO: Lynne Rienner.

Fairclough, Norman. 1989. *Language and Power*. London: Longman.

Fairclough, Norman. 1992. *Discourse and Social Change*. Cambridge: Polity Press.

Fairclough, Norman. 1995. *Critical Discourse Analysis*. London: Longman.

Foucault, Michel. 1972. *The Archaeology of Knowledge*. London: Tavistock. doi: 10.1177/053901847000900108

Gallup. 2013. Guns: Gallup Historical Trends. Available at: http://www.gallup.com/poll/1645/guns.aspx. Accessed September 14, 2013.

Geertz, Clifford. 1973. *The Interpretations of Cultures*. New York: Basic Books.

Hall, Stuart. 1996. "The Problem of Ideology: Marxism without Guarantees." In *Stuart Hall: Critical Dialogues in Cultural Studies*, edited by David Morley and Kuan-Hsing Chen, 25–46. London: Routledge.

Hodges, Adam. 2011. *The 'War on Terror' Narrative: Discourse and Intertextuality in the Construction and Contestation of Sociopolitical Reality*. New York: Oxford University Press.

Hofstadter, Richard. 2008[1965]. *The Paranoid Style in American Politics*. New York: Vintage Books.

LaPierre, Wayne. 2002. NRA Annual Meeting Speech. Available: http://www.nraila.org/news-issues/speeches/2002-nra-annual-meeting-speech-by-wayne-lapierre.aspx?s=&st=&ps.

LaPierre, Wayne. 2006. NRA Annual Meeting Speech. Available: http://www.nraila.org/news-issues/speeches/remarks-by-wayne-r-lapierre,-nra-executive-vice-president,-at-the-nra-

2006-annual-meeting-in-milwaukee,-wi-52006.aspx?s=wayne+lapierre+annual+meeting &st=&ps.

LaPierre, Wayne. 2008. NRA Annual Meeting Speech. Available: http://www.nraila.org/news-issues/speeches/remarks-by-wayne-lapierre-at-the-137th-annual-meeting-of-members,-louisville,-kentucky,-may-17,-2008.aspx?s=&st=&ps.

LaPierre, Wayne. 2011. NRA Annual Meeting Speech. Available: http://youtu.be/A5vAViVDO7A.

LaPierre, Wayne. 2012. NRA Annual Meeting Speech. Available: http://youtu.be/D8rBHcCW8Jo.

LaPierre, Wayne. 2013. NRA Annual Meeting Speech. Available: http://youtu.be/iJQqr8PpG98.

Melzer, Scott. 2009. *Gun Crusader's: The NRA's Culture War*. New York: New York University Press.

Morris, Aldon D. 1992. "Political Consciousness and Collective Action." In *Frontiers in Social Movement Theory*, edited by Aldon D. Morris and Carol McClurg Mueller, 351–374. Yale: Yale University Press.

Sugarmann, Josh. 1992. *National Rifle Association: Money, Firepower, Fear*. Washington, DC: National Press Books.

Thompson, John. 1990. *Ideology and Modern Culture*. Cambridge: Polity Press. doi: 10.2307/591346

Vallentyne, Peter. 2012. "Libertarianism." In *The Stanford Encyclopedia of Philosophy* (Spring 2012 Edition), edited by Edward N. Zalta. Available: http://plato.stanford.edu/archives/spr2012/entries/libertarianism/.

Van Dijk, Teun A. 1998. *Ideology*. London: Sage.

Winkler, Adam. 2013. *Gun Fight: The Battle over the Right to Bear Arms in America*. New York: W. W. Norton and Company.

Young, Iris Marion. 2003. "The Logic of Masculinist Protection: Reflections on the Current Security State." *Signs* 29(1):1–25. doi:10.1086/375708

The politics of being insulted

The uses of hurt feelings in Israeli public discourse

Zohar Kampf
The Hebrew University of Jerusalem

Scholars of politeness admit that being insulted may be the result of the hearer's assumptions about the other's behavior and may not necessarily relate to the actual words or intentions of the speaker. Thus, it is surprising to find only a few accounts of how people are doing "being insulted" or of how, in public discourse, responses to insults are strategically employed for various ends. In this chapter, I analyze the meta-pragmatics of "hurt feelings" in order to understand how speakers do things with emotions and the role of hurt feelings in political democratic discourse. By examining instances in which public figures have stated their feelings of insult in Israeli public discourse (1997–2012), I show both how hurt feelings are strategically employed to protest against politically unacceptable acts, and how public actors sometimes explicitly refuse to be insulted, shifting the meaning of what is perceived as an insult by side-participants into a compliment. I conclude by discussing the consequences of manifesting hurt feelings in political discourse.

Keywords: insults, impoliteness, aggressiveness, perlocutions, political discourse, emotions

1. Introduction

In public discourse incivility is manifested in a range of forms, including hate speech and racist and populist discourses, all of which consist of language used offensively against specific social targets. Most scholarly attention has been directed to expressions of incivility produced in the discourse of the offenders — racists, extremists, or homophobes, for example (e.g. Van Dijk 1987; Boromisha-Habashi 2013) — or to various types of institutional discourses — in the media (e.g. Clayman and Heritage 2002; Lorenzo-Dus 2009) or in national parliaments (e.g. Pérez de Ayala 2001; Ilie 2010). However, very little work has been done on

DOI 10.1075/bct.93.05kam

the questions raised by the discursive construction of "being offended": How do public hearers confront insults? What kind of public discourse is constructed on insulted emotions? How are hurt feelings strategically employed for various ends in public discourse? To answer these questions, I integrate discourse analysis of meta-pragmatic comments on politicians' insulted feelings with political, cultural, and social theories. By analyzing the meta-pragmatics of hurt feelings, I aim to shed light on various aspects of "being insulted" (not to be confused with feeling insulted), including its verbal form; content; structure of participation, discursive functions; and, at the macro level, the status of hurt feelings in political democratic discourse. I begin by discussing what it means to be publically insulted and how hurt feelings can be analyzed in public discourse. I then present two models of democratic discourse — the confrontational and the emotional — and point out the status of insulted feelings within them. I then answer the questions of how and why public figures either express their emotions or, alternatively, refuse to do so. In my conclusions, I discuss the consequences of manifesting hurt feelings in political discourse.

2. Insulting vs. being insulted

Scholars of linguistic politeness admit that being insulted may be an outcome of a hearer's perception or construction of a speaker's behavior, with or without any relation to the offender's words and/or ill-intentions (Culpeper 2011). Holmes et al. (2008, 196) stress that insults (and other impolite verbal behavior) are "assessed by the hearer as threatening her/his face or social identity, and infringing the norms of appropriate behavior that prevail in a particular context and among particular interlocutors, whether intentionally or not". In his definition of impoliteness, Culpeper (2011) emphasizes the role of the hearer in perceiving insulting behavior as intentionally face-attacking. In the same vein, philosopher Jerome Neu (2008) draws a distinction between to insult and to be insulted. Whereas the former is "to assert or assume dominance, either intentionally claiming superiority or unintentionally revealing lack of regard," to be insulted "is to suffer a shock, a disruption of one's sense of self and one's place in the world" (vii). What is common to all definitions is the hearer's interpretation of someone else's words as defying an expectation or norm of civil behavior, resulting in a damaged face and a lower position in the social hierarchy.

Interestingly, these two consequences may be found in the etymologies of both the English and Hebrew words *insult* (originally from Latin) and *elbon* (originally from Aramaic). The modern meaning of insult — to offend, to taunt or to ridicule — metaphorically evolved from a physical and violent action, i.e. to leap or jump upon (Culpeper 2011). Accordingly, to be insulted is to suffer damage following physical action, in the early sense of the word, or following symbolic violence, in the contemporary, modern sense. In Hebrew, reference to *elbon* is found in the *Talmud*, where it is etymologically related to the word *aluv,* meaning miserable, poor, worthless or weak. To be insulted, in this sense, refers to the hearer's perception of his position as lowered (emotionally, materially, socially or physically) from what it was before a specific "insulting" act (verbal or non-verbal) was performed.

From a socio-pragmatic perspective, being insulted is associated with the realm of perlocutions, that is, the effect of speech acts on social relationships. Here I propose following either of two trajectories in analyzing expressions of hurt feelings, all of which move the perlocutionary consequences from the cognitive realm (feeling insulted) into the social and the political realms (being insulted). The first trajectory originated in argumentation theory with van Emeren and Grootendorst's discussion of the differences between the felicity conditions of illocutionary and perlocutionary acts (1984, 51–53) and in performativity theory with Judith Butler's emphasis on the consequences of illocutionary acts (1997). Whereas illocutions demand cognitive understanding to be felicitous, perlocutions require the hearer's acceptance of the speaker's intention to offend followed by an actual change in the world. This insight allows us, for example, to understand the perlocutionary effect of threats as intimidating when X avoids action Y following a threat, the effect of apologies as reconciling when X restores social relations with the apologizer, and a range of utterances as insulting when X signals his emotional damage in various ways. Thus, in doing being insulted a social actor can transform an emotion (whether sincerely felt or not) into a social practice, using it to achieve particular political goals.

As with other expressions of impoliteness, the public settings in which an insult occurs increase the chance that it will have the perlocutionary effect of being insulted (Culpeper 2011, 201–3). At least three conditions should be satisfied in order to result in a derogatory effect (see Kampf 2013). Firstly, the insult should be designed primarily as a media spectacle, aimed at informing the public of what the insulter thinks about the person insulted. In this case, informing side-participants of what is being said — to insult —"becomes the main purpose of what is being said" (Clark and Carlson 1982, 215). Secondly, the insult should be reported and documented by the media in a "public quotation archives", in some cases setting the public agenda for a few days, in others etched in public memory for longer periods. And, thirdly, the insult must grossly exceed the discursive expectations for respect (Neu 2008), not only in the eyes of the person being insulted but also for side-participants and overhearers. In this case, the insulting event turns into a degradation ceremony "whereby the public identity of an actor is transformed into something looked on as lower in the local scheme of social types" (Garfinkel 1956, 420–424).

The second trajectory for analyzing perlocutionary effects originated in literary theory as well as in reception and audience studies (e.g. Fish 1980; Radway 1984) and is attuned to modes of evaluating speech acts within different communities of practice. Social and political communities utilize distinctive and shared rules of language use and common strategies for interpreting and signifying messages, which are different from the means of production and interpretation implemented by other communities (Hymes 1972). According to this logic, specific communities also share rules, norms and repertoires of emotional behavior. More than being organic responses to certain stimuli, hurt feeling are cultural and political practices "produced in specific cultural and historical contexts and power relations" (Harding and Pribram 2002, 411). Thus, being insulted means expressing one's emotional response, in line with the constraints of the "structure of feeling" (Williams 1977) which governs a specific "community of feeling" (Berezin 2002).

Politicians, for example, possess distinctive modes for interpreting the words and deeds of their peers and thereby may be perceived as members of a political community of feelings (Kampf 2008). Earlier studies have pointed to discrepancies between evaluations of speech acts by politicians and those by members of the public: whereas what the public tends to judge is the sincerity level of public performances (Kampf 2012), within the political community evaluation of sincerity is suspended (Abadi 1990) or is, at most, relegated to a minor role, and may be replaced by other modes of judgment, some of which are "emotional". In the case of apologies made between politicians, the "embarrassment condition" is one of several required for achieving the perlocutionary effect of forgiveness (Kampf 2008): the more insulting the gesture — the more it is perceived by the forgiver as threatening the face and symbolic power of the apologizer — the greater the chances for the apology to be accepted. For laymen, this kind of emotional tradeoff (I was insulted, so you have to feel the same in order to grant absolution) leaves the impression that politics is "an esoteric world of internal squabbles, of Byzantine power struggle" (Thompson 2000, 99); for peer politicians, it is part and parcel of everyday politics. And for discourse scholars, this kind of emotional economy raises questions about the role of emotions in general and of being insulted in particular within public democratic arenas.

3. Being publically insulted: between confrontational and emotional politics

Emotional responses and manifestations of hurt feelings can be traced in all levels of political discourse. In global politics, we occasionally witness cases in which one state forces another to participate in "humiliation rituals" as a condition for "settling the score" following various types of diplomatic transgressions perceived as "insulting" (Kampf and Lowenheim 2012). These may include the UK's forced apology to Iran in 2007 for alleged British intrusions into Iranian waters by 15 British sailors and marines and the Swiss forced apology to Libya for arresting Muammar Gaddafi's son in 2009. In national politics, emotions play a part in the formation of relationships among social and ethnic groups. Political tensions within divided societies often result in controversies which cause emotional damage. Adopting the premises of the *politics of recognition* in many democratic nation-states enabled former marginalized and silenced groups to manifest their insulted feelings and to demand symbolic restitution for present transgressions, most of which are expressions of politically incorrect statements (Lakoff 2000). In parliamentary politics, the management of hurt feelings is part of the political game, aimed at pursuing greater symbolic power. As we shall see below, taking on the role of the insulted party enables politicians to improve their positions within the political pecking order, to acquire media attention and, in general, to gain greater political power (Kampf 2008).

Whether expressed in global, national or parliamentary politics, from the perspective of political democratic theory, emotions are regarded as a symbolic pollution of the ideal speech situation, i.e. of a rational and detached deliberation on public issues (Habermas 1989). According to Habermas' public sphere model, emotional enunciations manifested during political conversations may distort the rules of debate. Aggressive discourse may transform a rational exchange of ideas aiming at the public good into an emotional duel (Tannen 1998) and result in efforts made by the offender and/or side-participants to appease the insulted party.

An alternative to Habermas' ideal speech situation is the model for public discourse offered by communication theorist Michael Schudson (1997). After criticizing the sociable and problem-solving types of conversation, Schudson proposes that speech in democracies should instead be based on frequently hostile arguments between dissenting parties. Schudson praises the benefits of hostile discourse as a platform for engaging in politics, as long as all participants are adhering to the Gricean cooperative principle (1975). However, he admits that the effective management of antagonistic debate is based on the good will of all sides not to be insulted: "An argument out of control is a conversation where each statement's ambiguity is read in the most hostile way possible." (301). Thus, as in the

Habermassian model of deliberative democracy, emotions should be kept out of an efficient and engaging democratic debate.

In practice, political insulters may employ the argument that public communication should be based on the premises of rational, detached and hostile discourse. In Israel, public offenders tend to resort to the image repair strategy of *good intentions* (Benoit 1995) in trying to justify their provocative remarks and attempt to convince the public that their slanders have been made in an effort to effectively discuss "social problems". This strategy was utilized, for example, by Israeli singer Meir Ariel, who in 1998 called members of the LGBT community "perverts who spread diseases." Following the scandal which erupted around his homophobic remark, Ariel explained his slander in a media interview in terms of the hostile argument scheme:

> The issue I wanted to be raised here for discussion was how to exclude any manipulation on the part of someone being hurt from public debate… [My] purpose was to eliminate the manipulation of being insulted from political discourse and to keep only to the point of the issues. From now on, if you feel insulted and have something to say, say it; and if you don't have anything to say, keep your hurt feelings to yourself. (*Haaretz* September, 11, 1998)

Ariel reduces the offensiveness of his words by emphasizing his genuine good intentions to create a formula for improving public discourse ("to eliminate the manipulation of being insulted"). The insulted feelings expressed by members of the LGBT community are labeled "manipulation," shifting the blame for any emotional damage to the offended party, who is accused of oversensitivity ("keep your insulted feelings to yourself") and thus of polluting political discourse with sentiments. The insulter, according to Ariel, should be praised for his good intentions and political courage.

Another argument in favor of hostile discourse in which hurt feelings should be confronted rationally was made in several op-eds by Flemming Rose, the editor of the Danish newspaper *Jyllands-Posten*. In a column in the *Washington Post* following the publishing of the 12 caricatures that aroused the Muhammad cartoons controversy, Rose resorted to the strategy of *good intentions*: "Our goal was simply to push back self-imposed limits on expression that seemed to be closing in tighter" (*Washington Post*, February 19, 2006). Positioning the *Jyllands-Posten* as the savior of Danish democracy from the threats posed by Islamic restrictions on freedom of speech, Rose argued for the inevitability of hurt emotions in democratic, hostile debate. Accordingly, citizens in a democratic state have the right to feel insulted, but should acknowledge that their hurt feelings ought to come second to superior social values such as the freedom of speech and freedom of the press: "We cannot apologize for our right to publish material, even offensive material. You cannot edit a newspaper if you are paralyzed by worries about every possible insult." Rose reinforces his argument by stating that his own feelings are often hurt in his capacity as a news editor:

> I am offended by things in the paper every day: transcripts of speeches by Osama bin Laden, photos from Abu Ghraib, people insisting that Israel should be erased from the face of the Earth, people saying the Holocaust never happened. But that does not mean that I would refrain from printing them as long as they fell within the limits of the law and of the newspaper's ethical code. (*Washington Post*, February 19, 2006)

In recounting his own personal experience as an editor, Rose is employing the strategy of "deliberate self-positioning" (Harré and Van Lagenhove 1999) in the role of the insulted figure ("I am offended by things in the paper every day"). This strategy is aimed at convincing his readers that although everybody, including himself, feel offended at times, only institutional regulations ("the law and … the newspaper's ethical code") may restrict the freedom of speech. The benefits of growing a thick skin are apparent in the conclusion of his op-ed: "Since the publication of the cartoons, we have had a constructive debate in Denmark and Europe about freedom of expression, freedom of religion and respect for immigrants and people's beliefs." Here, as well, emotional enunciations should be kept out of an effective democratic debate.

Yet an alternative model, one which adopts a different line of critique of public discourse in contemporary democracies, acknowledges the inevitable presence of emotions, especially that of hurt feelings and victimhood, in raising, debating and understanding social problems. According to this emotional model, democratic public spheres in the late-modern era are divided into public "sphericules" (Gitlin 1998) consisting of various groups, each adhering to different values, norms and beliefs. In such fragmented societies, the normative basis of social relationships becomes fragile, leading to a growing inability to represent or discuss social and political issues via normative, rational and conventional tools (Giddens 1991). Expressions of emotions thus become a convenient and effective way to point out social transgressions and to tackle unsolvable issues (Ilouz 2003). Emotive language which emphasizes pain, anger and guilt dominates the center stage of public and political discourses that focus on wounded social relationships. Against this backdrop, expressing one's hurt feelings in public becomes a conventional means of protesting untoward acts made by others, of gaining sympathy from uninvolved audiences who can identify with the emotional suffering of the insulted person and, indeed, of earning media attention for the demands made by the insulted party.

In Israeli political discourse, the transformation from solidarity, from consent-oriented rules of debate, into disruptive emotional arguments has been situated at the outset of the 1990s by scholars (e.g. Blum-Kulka, et al. 2002) and journalists alike. In an editorial published by *Haaretz* in 1998, the editor lamented the growing trend of inserting feelings of victimhood into political discourse. Following a case in which politicians from the National Religious Party (*Mafdal*) made as a condition for the awarding of the Israel Prize to the novelist Amos Oz a public apology for an "insulting" column he had written against the Israeli settlers,[1] *Haaretz* characterized the shift in Israeli politics into one based on emotions: "This practice of insulted feelings seeking compensation is becoming a disgraceful habit in a society experienced in severe and bitter disputes. Oz should not apologize…" (*Haaretz,* March 11, 1998).

In what follows, I analyze several facets of the discourse of hurt feelings in Israel. Based on discourse analysis of news reports and broadcast interactions between 1997 and 2012,[2] I examine, first, how public figures manifest their insulted feelings on the levels of both form and content. Second, I identify the functions of insulted feelings, i.e., how emotions are strategically employed for protesting against politically unacceptable acts. I also demonstrate instances in which public actors have explicitly refused to admit that they were insulted, sometimes subverting the meaning of an alleged insult by transforming it into a compliment. Third, I discuss the relationship between stating one's insulted feelings in public and the two models of democratic discourse — the emotional and the confrontational.

1. Oz accused the settlers of being a "small sect, a messianic cult, close and cruel, [which] emerged a few years ago from a dark corner of Judaism, and … threatens to destroy all that was dear and sacred to us, and to impose a bloody wild and wacky war on us" (*Yedioth Ahronot,* June 8, 1989).

2. The dataset for this study was compiled from three different research corpuses. The first is a corpus of 841 news items reported in Israel between 1997 and 2004 and consisting of utterances related to political apology — demands for apology, apologies, evaluations of apologies, etc. Insults were found to be catalysts for demands for apology (Kampf 2008), and 39 instances in which offended parties or public actors realized meta-pragmatic comments of their hurt feelings were considered. The second research corpus consists of 900 news items published between August 2007 and August 2013 in *Haaretz* which contain one of the keywords "insulted" or "insulting" (*maaliv* or *elbon*). Forty cases that include meta-pragmatic comments on one's hurt feelings or the mentioning of the keyword in direct speech were considered. Finally, I have randomly collected news items from both TV and Internet news sites in which political insults were reported or discussed.

4. The uses of hurt feelings in Israeli political discourse

The analysis of the politics of hurt feelings in Israel must be prefaced by a description of the confrontational, sometime uncivil, Israeli speaking style. During the first decades of Israel's existence, the collective values dominating Israeli culture were manifested in the *dugri* style of speaking, characterized as assertive, direct and sincere "straight talk" (Katriel 1986). Studies conducted during the 1980s and the 1990s underlined the culturally ideological, anti-European and unique perceptions of politeness in Israeli society, including the absence of what Blum-Kulka (1992) called "normative scripts of politeness." Accordingly, in the Israeli speech community values of clarity and authenticity are appreciated more than elaborate relational face work. Blum-Kulka et al. (1985) showed that this unique understanding of what constitutes polite conversation was evidenced especially in close relationships, with styles of politeness varying greatly according to social situation. In the mediated political arena, a highly confrontational style was apparent by the 1990s. Blum-Kulka et al. (2002) argued that the antagonistic style of Israeli politicians may be shown to have its roots in traditional Jewish modes of dialectical argumentation.

Later studies have drawn attention to the erosion of a distinctive Israeli style of speaking, linking it to the decline of collective values in Israeli society. This process has, on the one hand, mitigated the abruptness of Israeli speech, with an increase in more elaborate and mitigated speaking styles, and, on the other, has led to the emergence of an offensive and hostile style of speaking, termed *kasah* (Katriel 2004). Defined as "a forceful, aggressive verbal blow aimed at one's interactional partner" (Katriel 2004, 208), *kasah* is associated with the growing factionalism and radicalization of Israeli society. In contrast to the *dugri* style, which presupposes shared values and thus shields social actors from feeling insulted, *kasah* is "interpersonally directed as a putdown" (Katriel 2004, 209).

Judicially, the Israeli criminal code includes a controversial law for protecting institutional actors from symbolic hostility. Entitled "Insulting Public Servants", the law determines that a person "insulting a public servant or official…on duty, is subject to imprisonment of six months" (Section 288). Although this law has been highly criticized over the years for its role in restricting freedom of speech,[3] Israeli officials continue to enjoy a law which protects them from being insulted. The institutional efforts to restrict the boundaries of incivility also find expression in the ethical codes of the Israeli parliament (*Knesset*), which instruct politicians to protect the dignity of the Knesset and its members and conduct themselves in a way that respects their role as MKs. Such rules are also found in Israeli media

3. e.g. http://www.the7eye.org.il/43877.

regulations, instructing political interviewers, for example, not to be rude or to harass interviewees, and not to sacrifice politeness in the name of truth and justice (Kampf and Daskal 2013).

In spite of the efforts to fight incivility, public spectacles of insults are rather frequent in Israeli public discourse. This trend is evident, for example, in a growing number of citizens' complaining against broadcasters perceived as treating politicians in insulting ways (Kampf and Daskal 2011), and a growing number of politicians complaining to the Knesset's Ethics Committee about the insulting behavior of their peers.[4] As we shall see below, this trend is further evidenced in the variety of strategic uses of hurt feelings in political and media discourses. Against this backdrop, it is of interest to analyze the politics of being insulted and the uses of hurt feelings in public discourse by asking how politicians cope with insults, whether intentional or not and how their meta-pragmatic comments about their hurt feelings fall into one of the two models of public discourse. In line with the emotional model of democracy, hurt feelings are manifested as a protest against politically disrespectful acts; in line with the argumentative model, insulted feelings are sometimes explicitly denied by political figures, although less frequently than the former.

4.1 Emotional politics: Hurt feelings as a tool for protesting and for gaining visibility

Hurt feelings are frequently utilized in Israeli political discourse as a means for expressing one's discontent with or dissent from the disrespectful behavior of others, for presenting a political rival as deviant, for earning media attention and for gaining sympathy from overhearers who can identify with the emotional suffering of the insulted person. By manifesting insulted feelings, a speaker is framing action X as a politically unacceptable act (see Olshtain and Weinbach 1993), one that expresses lack of respect for the speaker or the group s/he represents. The motivations behind *politically unacceptable acts* (PUA) vary, ranging from the response to a specific political policy (e.g. an anti-social financial budget, the ruling of an untoward law) and offensive words (e.g. reference to Israeli Arabs in official state documents as "minority groups", or calling a Moroccan-born candidate for an official position a "thug") to seemingly disrespectful behavior or attitudes (e.g. the pejorative speech of the Minister of Defense in the Foreign Affairs and Defense Committee; criticism of journalists against the President's pretentious birthday party).

4. http://www.knesset.gov.il/committees/heb/docs/ethics_15.pdf.

Public figures have a number of ways to discursively manifest their insulted feelings following a PUA. Several recurrent patterns were found in the corpus:

- *[PUA] is an insult to [OFFENDED PARTY].* The conventional expression of hurt feelings includes a reference to both the unacceptable act and a specific offended party. For example, following the social protest in Israel in 2011, recommendations were published by a committee assigned to suggest solutions to the protestors' demands. In his response to the recommendations, the Israeli workers union leader, Menachem Eyni, protested: "The attitude in the report to the contractor's workers [PUA] is an insult (*elbon*) to all those who desire social justice" [OFFENDED PARTY]. (*Haaretz,* October 4, 2011)
- *[PUA] is an insult to intelligence.* Instead of naming a specific insulted person, the speaker uses the noun "intelligence", thus emphasizing the pejorative nature of the PUA and attributing the insulted feelings not only to a particular person but generally to any intelligent person. For example, in his response to an argument made by an energy company during a negotiation on taxing the rates of natural gas, the Israeli Minister of Finance, Yuval Steinitz, argued in the name of the public that "the claim that the tax increase is retroactive [PUA] is an insult (*elbon*) to intelligence" (*Haaretz,* November 8, 2010).
- *[PUA] is insulting.* Another recurrent verbal form includes an explicit or anaphoric *it* reference to the PUA, without any attribution to an offended party. This may be another strategy for increasing the number of insulted figures by including virtually everyone. Thus, for example, in response to a draft policy paper about the enlisting of ultra-religious Jews in the Israeli army, presented by the leading Likud party to the secular party Yesh Atid, the party spokesman declared that "the draft [PUA] is insulting (*ma'aliv*)" (*Haaretz,* August 1, 2013).
- *Threatening or demanding restitution following insults.* Although this strategy for expressing one's insulted feelings has no conventional verbal pattern, insulted figures do attach a threat or a demand for apology following their public announcement of their hurt feelings. This strategy can be understood as one discursive move in the "economy of emotions", which aims at redressing the emotional damage caused by the offender by causing him an equal emotional damage. One example was found in a letter sent to the editor of *Haaretz* three weeks after the publication of a photograph of an Israeli aircraft fighter appended to an article discussing atrocities in the 20th century. Under the title "An insult (*elbon*) to the IDF and all of us", the letter conveyed the writer's suggestion to *Haaretz*: "I think you should apologize to the readers for the insult (*elbon*) [with which] you have insulted (*he'elavtem*) the IDF and all of us" (*Haaretz,* October 2, 2009).

Moving from content and form to the structure of participation in the discourse of hurt feelings, insulted figures were found to be members of one of the three institutions characteristic of the nation-state — politicians, journalists, and citizens — or an international political actor. In most cases, the insulter possessed greater power in the political or social hierarchy than did the insulted party, a state of affairs attesting that hurt feelings are mostly used by the less powerful for protesting against the unacceptable acts of the more powerful. One blatant example of protest by the powerless against the political establishment occurred a few days before the 2001 elections in Israel. In his effort to appease the Israeli Arab population and to convince them to vote for his Labor party, Prime Minister Ehud Barak personally telephoned Arab citizens and apologized for the October 2000 events (in which 13 Israeli Arabs were killed by police during protests). In a news item that surveyed the responses to Barak's calls among the Arab population in Israel, Husam Abass, a citizen from Umm El-Fahem, lamented: "Now he remembers? On Election Day? It's insulting (*maaliv*)" (*Haaretz,* February 7, 2001). This response demonstrates how insulted feelings may be expressed by citizens to protest PUA, and further suggests that even appeasing and reconciliatory gestures may be perceived as insulting, if the emotions involved are judged as insincere.

Moving from the public arena into the political sub-field, we find that being insulted serves as an important strategy for pursuing power by threatening the face of political rivals, by positioning oneself as the "just" person in a debate and by gaining greater media visibility. Members of the political "community of feelings" resort in distinctive ways to the management of disputes, which serve their continuous efforts to gain and maximize symbolic power at the expense of other members within the community. First, they may promote conflictual situations by doing being insulted. The following transcript demonstrates how the insistence on a particular interpretation of a rival's words leads to a dispute in which the interpreter performs the role of the insulted in order to initiate a public denunciation of the allegedly insulting politician.[5] The dispute erupted at a meeting of the Education Committee of the Israeli Knesset in 2008. During a speech by the chairman of the Israeli Teachers' Union, the Minister of Education, Yuli Tamir, whispered a comment concerning the former director of the Ministry, Ronit Tirosh, who happened to be sitting next to her. Tamir complained that she was working to clean up the "garbage and shit" that Tirosh had left behind in the Ministry. In response to this impolite form of criticism, Tirosh made a "scene" (Goffman 1959) and treated Tamir's words as a personal insult.

5. The following example was first introduced in Kampf and Blum-Kulka (2011).

"She is calling me a piece of shit"
Yuli Tamir (the Minister of Education and a professor of political philosophy)
Ronit Tirosh (the former director of the Ministry of Education, and a Likud MK)
July 8, 2006, the Education Committee of the Israeli Knesset

1. Tirosh: [honored chairman, the minister] of education has just called me- >called me< a piece of shit.
2. Tamir: [no, that is not what I said]
3. Tirosh: [I wasn't speaking to her]
4. Tamir: [I said that the garbage and shit you] left-
5. Tirosh: [it is precisely, it is recorded]
6. Tamir: [I said that the ga::rbage,]
7. Tirosh: [I can't believe it] I am sitting here and listening (.) and she is calling me a piece of shit

4 turns of dueling omitted

12. Tirosh: [honored chairman, I pro::test. She will not call me shit. I am asking that on the education committee, a university professor, I am [sitting and listening
13. Tamir: [sorry]
14. Tirosh: [to the chairman of the teachers union]
15. Tamir: [according to the]
16. Tirosh: and she is calling me a piece of shit
17. Tamir: your personal bitterness cannot be a work plan, there is nothing you can do

The committee chairman hushes them up and encourages the Teachers' Union chairman to finish his address.

Following her dramatic announcement of the insult by the Minister of Education (turn 1), Tirosh rejects Tamir's explanation that she has been misinterpreted. In fact, during the entire interaction, she refuses to negotiate regarding the apparent misunderstanding and chooses to simply ignore Tamir's words, treating her as a non-ratified participant (Goffman 1981) and directing her own protest to the committee chairman and other participants. This strategy can be understood in Garfinkel's (1956) terms as an effort to degrade the Minister of Education: by denouncing Tamir and ignoring her at the same time, Tirosh tries to build up a coalition of denunciation against Tamir which could result in a loss of status not only here, but — with the help of the media — in the general public. It is interesting to note that Tirosh ignores the potential threat to her own political face in being called "a piece of shit" (she uses this phrase no less than four times), or in taking part in such a quarrel. The utilitarian logic of "doing being insulted" in this case is that damaging the face of the rival may benefit the insulted, despite the potential damage to her own face as being part of an embarrassing situation.

A second example focuses on the ways in which the offended party invests effort to keep the insult on the public agenda in order to gain greater public exposure in the competitive mediated political arena.[6] Involving two allied politicians,

6. See Kampf (2008) for an elaborated analysis of the event.

this incident at the 2002 Labor Party convention began with an insult directed by Minister Benjamin Ben-Eliezer, the Labor Party chairman, at Dalia Itzik, the Minister of Industry and Trade. Itzik had spoken against Labor continuing to sit in the unity government with the right-wing Likud Party, and Ben-Eliezer, a supporter of the unity government, went to the podium and called her critical remarks "a big bluff" (*Yediot Aharonot,* October 4, 2002); in response, Itzik demanded an apology. Ben-Eliezer, who needed Itzik's support in order to stabilize his position as party chairman, subsequently made two separate apologies, both rejected by the offended party. After Itzik refused to accept his telephone apology, Ben-Eliezer made a second attempt to placate her: in front of the entire assembly of Labor Party government ministers, Ben-Eliezer turned to Itzik and said:

> I love you Dalia. You are an excellent minister. I apologize for the thing I said that hurt you at the party convention (*Haaretz,* October 4, 2002).

Alongside a realization of an IFID ("apologize") and an acknowledgment of responsibility for the misdeed ("for the thing I said that hurt you"), Ben-Eliezer also supported Itzik's political positive *face* by expressing his affection ("I love you") and calling her by her first name. After attempting to secure solidarity with the offended, he further reinforced her political face by complimenting her professional virtues. However, despite these efforts, Itzik rejected this apology, too, and made her forgiveness conditional on one more statement, to be performed publicly before a large audience. Itzik's refusals and insistence on a spectacle of public apology can be understood as a means for keeping the chairman's debt to her on the public agenda, as evidenced in her comment to Ben-Eliezer after he had fulfilled her demand: "Your offence was very helpful. I should have sent you a huge bouquet of flowers" (*Haaretz,* October 4, 2002).

Itzik's reference to the advantages that resulted from being insulted may indicate that her taking offense was not authentic, but rather a calculated attempt to gain political points and at the same time detract from the political power of Ben-Eliezer. Like Tirosh in the previous example, Itzik violated the sincerity condition by doing being insulted, and she justified her recurring refusals and her demands for reparation for the transgression in terms of giving equal publicity to the "insulting" statements. Her self-positioning as a victim within the political community of feelings earned her a higher position in the political hierarchy as a person central enough to be awarded absolution. Within the broader political field, keeping the insult on the public agenda granted her greater public exposure in the mediated political arena.

4.2 Confrontational politics: Choosing not to be insulted

In this section, I discuss instances demonstrating the confrontational model of politics in which political actors refused to be insulted by others' allegedly politically unacceptable acts. According to the hostile, argumentative model of democracy (Schudson 1997), the expression of emotions should be avoided when engaging in efficient political discourse: effective management of political debate is based on the good will of all participants not to be insulted, even when the debate becomes somewhat aggressive. In line with this model, the analysis of hurt feelings in Israeli public discourse shows that at times political actors (1) transform insults into compliments or (2) state publically that they were not offended by what others interpreted as an insult.

Cases in which political actors subversively transform an explicit insult into a compliment were discussed by Butler (1997) in her *Excitable Speech*. She found that a derogatory label stuck on someone by an insulter "runs the risk of inaugurating a subject in speech who comes to use language to counter the offensive call" (Butler 1997, 2). One mode of countering insults is to "recycle" an injurious name: the use of discursive strategies such as *resignification* and *revaluation* (Butler 1997, 14) on the part of the targeted person or group may transform the malicious meaning of a term into a tolerable one, and may be understood as a perlocutionary act that thwarts the original intention to hurt.

One such case is the 2013 campaign slogan of the Israeli left-wing party *Meretz*: "Leftists go home!" (*Smolanin habyta!*). During the 2000s, against the backdrop of the second Intifada and the deteriorating prospects of a peace agreement with the Palestinians, the term "Leftist" was loaded with derogatory meaning in Israeli public discourse. In rightwing internet "readers' comments" and in protests against negotiations with the Palestinians,[7] the slogan adopted by *Meretz* had been frequently used to label left-wingers and human-rights activists. The derogatory effect was reinforced by the use of the homophonic resemblance between the Hebrew word "left" (*smol*; שמאל) and the English word "small" (small; סמול): the words were exchanged in rightwing propaganda slogans. In appropriating the offensive slogan for its own campaign, *Meretz* aimed at resignifying the meaning of the term "left", investing it with positive meaning as part of a strategy to restore respect for political leftist values among their own electorate.

A second example of insult transformed into compliment is a bumper sticker distributed in the 1999 elections by supporters of the right-wing *Likud* party in

7. One reflexive comment testifying to this process was made by the musician Aviv Geffen in an interview on "Meet the Press" during the 2010 Remembrance Day of the Yitzchak Rabin assassination: "To be called a leftist today is a curse". See: http://www.mako.co.il/news-channel2/Meet-the-Press/Article-85fa714e91efb21004.htm.

response to an offensive speech made by the Israeli actress Tiki Dayan at a Labor party convention. In her speech, Dayan turned to her supporters and said,

> Friends, we are talking here about a different people, don't you understand? We are talking about people who were turned into the most important ones here, [but they are] people from the marketplace, riffraff [*asafsuf*][8]

A few days later, stickers were distributed in Israel, reverberating two words from Dayan's speech: "I am a proud member of the riffraff" (*Ani afsfuf Ge'he*) and "I am a member of the riffraff from the marketplace and vote for Netanyhu (*Ani afsfuf meha-shuk ve-matzbiha le-Netanyhu*)".[9] In this case as well, the goal of the campaigners was to purge the derogatory meaning from the word *asfsuf*, while reminding the Israeli public which party was politically responsible for the offense. Interestingly, the idiom "I am a proud member of the riffraff " became popular in Israeli public and political discourse and is still widely used as a means of positively representing oneself as part of "the common people".

Emotional politics are also circumvented by the public denial that an allegedly disrespectful statement or behavior was actually insulting. Asserting one's refusal to be hurt was also found to be accepted practice within the political community of feelings. Based on 30 interviews with Israeli parliament members at the outset of the 2000s, it was found that political verbal aggression without malicious intention to offend is a necessary strategy in parliamentary discussions for gaining media and political visibility. The political script according to which insults are not meant to hurt the feelings of peers was acknowledged by political hearers, who admitted that they are not insulted at the political level by aggressive assaults since, in the course of their own political socialization, they have developed a thick skin (Livneh 2005).

Denying emotional damage was also found to be a strategy for thwarting journalistic efforts to personalize political relationships in their reporting. Political figures tend to shift the discussion of a potential insult away from their hurt feelings to broader social and political issues, such as the importance of freedom of speech in a democracy or of social tensions that should be pacified. An example of this strategy is provided by the response of Amir Peretz, a Sephardic (north-African in origin) candidate for the chair of the Labor party, to the words made by

---

8. The word *asafsuf* was first mentioned in the Bible. During the first stage of the exodus from Egypt, the Israelites were joined by "a mixed multitude" (Exodus 12:38; Numbers 11:4). In Biblical Hebrew *asafsaf*, "the mixed multitude", refers to the non-Jews who accompanied the Israelites on their journey; in Modern Hebrew the word *asafsuf* has the meaning of an illiterate and ignorant mob.

9. See: http://stickerim.blogspot.co.il/2009/01/blog-post_09.html.

his Ashkenazi (European in origin) party member, Isaac Herzog. In an American diplomatic cable leaked by *WikiLeaks* and published by *Haaretz* in 2011, Herzog was quoted as telling a senior American diplomat that one of the reasons why the Labor party did not score high on the polls was the public perception of Peretz as "inexperienced, aggressive and Moroccan" (*Haaretz,* April 13, 2011). In a journalistic effort to elicit his response, Peretz was invited to an interview on "Meet the Press". At the outset of the interview, journalist Dana Weiss stated that, although Peretz was now deemed to be more suitable than in the past to serve as the chair of the Labor party, there were always voices ready to remind the public that he was born in Morocco, awakening the "ethnic demon" (a metaphor for describing the tensions between Ashkenazi and Sephardic Jews in Israel). The relevant sections of the program are given below, with the turns numbered.

"I really wasn't insulted"
Dana Weiss (interviewer)
Amir Peretz (Labor party's chair candidate)
April 16, 2011, Meet the Press, Channel 2

1. Weiss: …then, and then came Buji Herzog, WikiLeaks and Haaretz and spoiled your plan? suddenly the ethnic demon is running wild again? suddenly your origin and the road you've traveled are illegitimate? Is this an insult?
2. Peretz: I want to tell you one thing. I hear this question, are you insulted? Not insulted? No. I really wasn't insulted. I'll tell you why-

Nine turns in which Weiss tried to focus on the personal relationship between Herzog and Peretz are omitted

11. Peretz: I want to talk, I want to talk, really. We have a chance once and for all to discuss an issue that is so deep, so important, and I want us to take it to somewhere else. Look what happened. You see. there is an argument within Zionism, and that is the real issue¯ […] I, want, people, not to be judged by their place of origin.

In spite of the interviewer's effort to frame the case as a political squabble (turn 1 and the later interruption "but you refused to answer his calls…"), Peretz refuses to stay within the frame of personalized politics, proposing instead a new frame for the interview, one that focuses on the public good ("that is the real issue"). First, Peretz resorts to the strategy of voicing (Lauerbach 2006) in order to refute the claim that he was insulted (turn 2: I hear this question, are you insulted?). Then, in turn 8, he reframes the personalized discussion about his feelings into a discussion about the society by using first-person, inclusive pronouns ("*We* have a chance once and for all to discuss an issue that is…so important") and by explicitly introducing a topic shift ("I want us to take it to somewhere else"). From this point on, Peretz avoids the personal quarrel: he offers his view on the origin of the social problem and suggests its solution ("[that] people in Israel not be judged by their place of origin"*)*. The utilitarian logic behind not "being insulted" in this case is that the personal conflict may damage Peretz's face. Changing the focus from personal politics to possible solutions of social problems may indeed help a politician to reposition himself as experienced and responsible, someone who aims at promoting the "social good" at the expense of personalized and cynical politics.

5. Conclusions: Being insulted and the ethics of emotional discourse

In this chapter, I have treated the expression of insulted feelings as a perlocutionary act that allows shifting the traditional focus of speech act theory from conventions to interpretations and consequences. Taking offense is an act that essentially relates to interpretation, thus inviting a focus on the offended party's perspective and an analysis of how to do things with emotions. In our research, emotional responses were first identified as perlocutionary acts through meta-pragmatic comments made by insulted figures, and second, by the singular modes of decoding insulting words, specific to the political community of feelings.

Hurt feelings were found to be strategically employed by public actors within two models of public discourse: the confrontational and the emotional. Following the establishment of the two models, I demonstrated how political actors meta-pragmatically speak about their insulted feelings, or, refuse to share with their audiences — journalists and the public — how they feel about allegedly offensive acts. Within emotional politics, "doing being insulted" was found to be an effective means for protesting and framing the actions of others as politically unacceptable acts; within confrontational politics, insisting that one has not been insulted was found to be a counter strategy for confronting insults and a useful means of avoiding personalized politics.

Both models for expressing feelings or avoiding their expression have consequences for the normative management of public discourse in democratic states. On the one hand, being frequently insulted may have a chilling effect on the motivation of public figures to express their views. The main argument against emotional politics is that it allows certain groups or actors to position themselves on a regular basis in the role of the victim and to acquire moral superiority by pointing their finger at and attributing blame to social and political offenders. Such discursive relationships have harsh consequences for democracies, as they may limit freedom of speech and freedom of press, thwarting the possibility of discussion and resolution of social and political problems. On the other hand, confrontational politics compel political actors to grow an elephant-like thick skin, thus transforming political debates into an aggressive exchange between two or more warring parties, with no one admitting to being offended. This state of affairs is dangerous, as it suggests that participants in democratic discourse are either servile or arrogant (Neu 2008), the servile immune to any kind of disrespectful behavior and ready to swallow any type of humiliation, the arrogant unaware of or unbothered by any use of offensive language. As I have tried to demonstrate in this chapter, contemporary public discourse includes both models. Although expressions of emotions may be problematic from both perspectives, they may have advantages as well. Democracies may enjoy the advantages of hurt feelings as moral emotions which allow different perspectives and values in a society to be voiced and discussed within the problem-solving frame of the open, public arena.

References

Abadi, Adina. 1990. "The Speech Act of Apology in Political Life." *Journal of Pragmatics* 14(3):467–471. doi:10.1016/0378-2166(90)90102-J

Benoit, L. William. 1995. *Accounts, Excuses, and Apologies: A Theory of Image Restoration Strategies*. Albany, NY: State University of New York Press.

Berezin, Mable. 2002. "Secure States: Towards a Political Sociology of Emotion." In *Emotions and Sociology*, edited by Jack Barbalet, 33–52. London: Basil Blackwell.

Blum-Kulka, Shoshana. 1992. "The Metapragmatics of Politeness in Israeli Society." In *Politeness in Language: Studies in Its History, Theory and Practice*, edited by Richard J. Watts, Sachiko Ide, and Konrad Ehlich, 255–281. Berlin: Mouton de Gruyter.

Blum-Kulka, Shoshana, Menahem Blondheim, and Gonen Hacohen. 2002. "Traditions of Dispute: From Negotiations of Talmudic Texts to the Arena of Political Discourse in the Media." *Journal of Pragmatics* 34(10–11):1569–1594.
doi: 10.1016/S0378-2166(02)00076-0

Blum-Kulka, Shoshana, Brenda Danet, and Rimona Gerson. 1985. "The Language of Requesting in Israeli Society." In *Language and Social Situations*, edited by Joseph P. Forgas, 113–136. New York: Springer Verlag. doi:10.1007/978-1-4612-5074-6_7

Boromisza-Habashi, David. 2013. *Speaking Hatefully: Culture, Communication, and Political Action in Hungary*. University Park, PA: Pennsylvania State University Press.

Butler, Judith. 1997. *Excitable Speech: A Politics of the Performative*. New York: Routledge.

Clark, Herbert H., and Thomas, B. Carlson. 1982. "Hearers and Speech Acts." *Language* 58(2):332–373. doi:10.1353/lan.1982.0042

Clayman, Steven E., and John Heritage. 2002. "Questioning presidents: Journalistic deference and adversarialness in the press conferences of US Presidents Eisenhower and Reagan." *Journal of Communication* 52(4): 749–775. doi:10.1111/j.1460-2466.2002.tb02572.x

Culpeper, Jonathan. 2011. *Impoliteness: Using Language to Cause Offence*. Cambridge: Cambridge University Press. doi:10.1017/CBO9780511975752

Fish, Stanley. 1980. *Is There a Text in This Class?* Cambridge: Harvard University Press.

Garfinkel, Harold. 1956. "Conditions for Successful Degradation Ceremonies." *American Journal of Sociology* 61(5):420–424. doi:10.1086/221800

Goffman, Erving. 1959. *The Presentation of Self in Everyday Life*. Garden City, NY.

Goffman, Erving. 1981. *Forms of Talk*. Philadelphia: University of Pennsylvania Press.

Giddens, Anthony. 1991. *Modernity and Self-identity: Self and Society in the Late Modern Age.* Stanford, CA: Stanford University Press.

Gitlin, Todd. 1998. "Public Sphere or Public Sphericules?" In *Media, Ritual, and Identity*, edited by James Curran, and Tamar Liebes, 198–175. London: Routledge.

Grice, H. Paul. 1975. Logic and conversation. In *Syntax and Semantics III: Speech Acts*, edited by Peter Cole and Jerry L. Morgan, 41–58. New York, NY: Academic Press.

Harding, Jennifer, and E. Deidre Pribram. 2003. "The Power of Feeling: Locating Emotion in Public." *European Journal of Cultural Studies* 5(4):407–426. doi:10.1177/1364942002005004294

Harré, Rom, and Luk van Lagenhove. 1999. *Positioning Theory: Moral Contexts of International Action.* Oxford: Blackwell Publishers.

Holmes, Janet, Meredith Marra, and Stephanie Schnurr. 2008. "Impoliteness and Ethnicity: Māori and Pākehā Discourse in New Zealand Workplaces." *Journal of Politeness Research* 4(2):193–219.

Hymes, Dell. 1972. *On Communicative Competence.* Philadelphia: University of Pennsylvania Press.

Ilie, Cornelia. 2010. "Strategic Uses of Parliamentary Forms of Address: The Case of the UK Parliament and the Swedish Riksdag." *Journal of Pragmatics* 42(4):885–911. doi: 10.1016/j.pragma.2009.08.017

Illouz, Eva. 2003. *Oprah Winfrey and the Glamour of Misery: An Essay on Popular Culture.* New York: Columbia University Press.

Lakoff, T. Robin. 2000. *The Language War.* Berkeley: California: University of California Press.

Lauerbach, Gerda. 2006. "Discourse Representation in Political Interviews: The Construction of Identities and Relations through Voicing and Ventriloquizing." *Journal of Pragmatics* 38(2):196–215. doi:10.1016/j.pragma.2005.06.015

Livneh, Ariel. 2005. "Two Loaded Contexts of Physical and Verbal Aggression in the Eyes of the Beholders — Professional Basketball Games and Parliamentary Sessions." Ph.D. Thesis, Bar Ilan University, Israel.

Lorenzo-Dus, Nuria. 2009. "You're Barking Mad, I'm Out": Impoliteness and Broadcast Talk." *Journal of Politeness Research* 5(2):159–187.

Habermas, Jürgen.1989. *The Structural Transformation of the Public Sphere.* Cambridge, MA: MIT Press.

Kampf, Zohar. 2008. "The Pragmatics of Forgiveness: Judgments of Apologies in the Israeli Political Arena." *Discourse & Society* 19(5):577–598. doi:10.1177/0957926508092244

Kampf, Zohar. 2013. "Mediated Performatives." In *Handbook of Pragmatics*, edited by Jan-Ola Östman, and Jef Verschueren, 1–24. Amsterdam: John Benjamins. doi: 10.1075/hop.17.med1

Kampf, Zohar, and Blum-Kulka, Shoshana. 2011. "Why Are Israeli Children Better at Settling Disputes than Israeli Politicians? In *Politeness across Cultures*, edited by Francesca Bargiela-Chiappini, and Dániel Kádár, 85–105. Basingstoke: Palgrave Macmillan

Kampf, Zohar, and Daskal, Efrat.2011. When the Watchdog Bites: Insulting Politicians on Air. In *Talking Politics in Broadcast Media*, edited by Mats Ekström, and Marianna Patrona, 177–200. Amsterdam/Philadelphia: John Benjamins. doi:10.1075/dapsac.42.14kam

Kampf, Zohar, and Nava Löwenheim. 2012. "Rituals of Apology in the International Arena." *Security Dialogue* 43(1):43–60. doi:10.1177/0967010611431095

Kampf, Zohar, and Daskal, Efrat 2013. "Too Hostile, too Deferential: Processes of Media Answerability in the Wake of Political Interviews." *Journalism* 14(4):522–540. doi: 10.1177/1464884912448902

Katriel, Tamar. 1986. *Talking Straight: Dugri Speech in Israeli Sabra Culture*. Cambridge, U.K.: Cambridge University Press.

Katriel, Tamar. 2004. *Dialogic Moments: From Soul Talks to Talk Radio in Israeli Culture*. Detroit: Wayne State University Press.

Neu, Jerome. 2008. *Sticks and Stones: The Philosophy of Insults*. Oxford: Oxford University Press.

Olshtain, Elite, and Liora Weinbach. 1993. "Interlanguage Features of the Speech Act Complaining." In *Interlanguage Pragmatics*, edited by Gabriel Kasper, and Shoshana Blum-Kulka, 108–122. Oxford: Oxford University Press.

Pérez de Ayala, Soledad. 2001. "FTAs and Erskine May: Conflicting needs? — Politeness in Question Time." *Journal of Pragmatics* 33(2):143–169. doi: 10.1016/S0378-2166(00)00002-3

Radway, Janice. 1984. *Reading the Romance: Women, Patriarchy, and Popular Literature*. Chapel Hill: University of North Carolina.

Schudson, Michael. 1997. "Why Conversation is Not the Soul of Democracy." *Critical Studies in Media Communication* 14:297–309. doi:10.1080/15295039709367020

Tannen, Deborah. 1998. *The Argument Culture: Stopping America's War of Words*. New York: Ballantine Books.

Thompson, John B. 2000. *Political Scandal*. Cambridge: Polity. doi: 10.1016/B0-08-043076-7/04377-1

Van Dijk, Teun A. 1987. *Communicating Racism: Ethnic Prejudice in Thought and Talk*. London: Sage.

Van Eemeren, Frans H., and Rob Grootendorst. 1984. *Speech Acts in Argumentative Discussions: A Theoretical Model for the Analysis of Discussions Directed Towards Solving Conflicts of Opinion*. Dordrecht: Floris Publications.

Williams, Raymond. 1977. *Marxism and Literature*. Oxford: Oxford University Press.

Representing “terrorism”

The radicalisation of the May 2013 Woolwich attack in British press reportage

Matthew Evans and Simone Schuller
University of Huddersfield

This chapter uses critical stylistics to analyse the British press’s use of the term “terrorism” in their reporting of the murder of Fusilier Lee Rigby outside the military barracks in Woolwich, London on 22nd May 2013. It considers academic definitions of “terrorism” and compares these to the use of the term in newspaper reports on the attack. The authors seek to understand how the Woolwich attack is fit into a complex and contested concept such as terrorism. A close reading of a small corpus of national newspaper articles was used to identify common themes in the way the incident is portrayed, with critical stylistic analysis being applied to investigate how the term “terrorism” is used in context. The study highlights how the application of the “terrorism” label is justified within the articles despite the scarcity of information regarding the attack and persons involved at the time of their publication.

Keywords: terrorism, media, Woolwich, critical stylistics, newspaper corpora

1. Introduction

On 22nd May 2013, two men attacked and murdered Fusilier Lee Rigby outside a military barracks in Woolwich, London. Precise details of the incident and the individuals involved were not immediately clear, but eyewitness reports were available almost instantly through television news channels and social media networks such as Twitter. The considerable impact of these initial reports was due in part to the two suspects’ apparent desire to be filmed at the scene and to gain media coverage for their actions. Much of the reportage focused on a cameraphone recording taken by an eyewitness, in which one of the suspects justified the attack as a response to British military involvement in Muslim countries. A meeting of COBRA, the British government’s emergency committee, was called, while the

DOI 10.1075/bct.93.06eva

British Prime Minister, David Cameron — away on a state visit to France — said in his initial response to the attack that there were "strong indications that it [was] a terrorist incident".[1]

Coverage of the attack in the next morning's national newspapers concentrated on the implications of the suspects' apparent background and beliefs. Despite the fact that details concerning the incident and the identities of those involved remained uncertain, many publications were quick to label it a terrorist attack. This response raises questions about the way a contested concept such as "terrorism" is portrayed and how the media plays a role in shaping public understandings of it. The present study looks at the way that terrorism was represented in initial articles reporting on the Woolwich attack and how use of the term "terrorism" was –consciously or not– justified in context.

It should be noted that we do not seek to defend or justify the suspects' actions; rather, the discussion in this chapter is based on our conviction that an attack such as that carried out in Woolwich can be immoral and unjustifiable without necessarily being terrorist. We believe that the "terrorist" label is sometimes applied hastily and rashly in such cases. The coverage of Woolwich is of particular note due to the sheer volume of attention given to it and the rapidity with which media used "terrorism" and related terms such as "terror", "terrorist(s)" and "anti-terrorism". This eagerness to label the attack "terrorist" prompted a number of press commentators, including *The Guardian*'s Glenn Greenwald (2013), to critique this aspect of the coverage. As such, it is a suitable case study for an investigation into representations of terrorism.

Our approach in this study combines our backgrounds in linguistics and conflict studies to analyse reports on the Woolwich attack in the British national newspapers. Sections 2.1 and 2.2 of this chapter describe the linguistic approach, which uses corpus techniques to build a dataset, and the critical stylistic (Jeffries 2010) tools used to analyse how "terrorism" and related terms are used in the articles. Section 2.3 gives a brief overview of definitions of terrorism in order to establish a conceptual framework against which our data is examined, and highlights those aspects that are particularly relevant to our data. Section 3 presents the findings of these combined approaches, based on a number of overarching themes we identified in how the Woolwich attack was presented as terrorist, and augmented by the use of critical stylistic methods to look at the particular way in which "terrorism" and related terms are applied in the data. Section 4 summarises our findings, and suggests possible areas for further research.

1. Video available at http://youtube/Nb2LFId971M (accessed 4th March, 2014).

2. Background and methodology

2.1 Creation of the corpus

Our research corpus comprises articles from the British national newspapers of 23rd May, 2013, the day after the Woolwich attack. The main reason for selecting this data was that it would allow us to put ourselves in the position of someone reading the first printed news of the attack. While there was plenty of coverage across different types of media between the time of the incident and the publication of the newspapers, we felt that these articles — while still based on a very limited amount of accurate, detailed information about the attack — would represent a more "considered" response to the incident, with writers and editors having had the opportunity to decide how to represent it and, crucially, whether or not to label it terrorist. By focusing on these newspaper articles, decisions on what data to include or exclude were made simple: we compiled a complete dataset by gathering all articles on the topic from each of the morning editions of the popular British national newspapers. This dataset comprises a range of types of articles: some are comparatively objective, factual news reports, while others are more subjective editorials or opinion pieces, providing personal responses to the attack. The national newspapers also cover the range of the mainstream British political spectrum, allowing us to gain a fair impression of the response across ideological standpoints. A key point to make here is that we do not aim to make comparisons between different publications, except in instances where a particular "theme" in the reporting of terrorism is especially prevalent in a particular newspaper. Due to the small amount of data and our hunch that the phenomenon we are investigating — an eagerness to apply the "terrorist" label — exists across publications, we wish instead to base our analysis on the kind of impression our hypothetical reader would have gained from an overview of the range of national newspapers on the morning of 23rd May 2013.

Our data was compiled using Nexis UK by LexisNexis,[2] a research tool that allows users to search for particular terms in various corpora, including newspapers. The national newspapers available through Nexis UK are *The Daily Mail, The Express, The Guardian, The Independent, The Mirror, The Sun, The Telegraph* and *The Times*, which account for eight of the nine most widely-read national newspapers in the UK.[3] The eight publications represent both relatively liberal

2. See http://www.lexisnexis.com/uk/nexis for more information on Nexis UK.

3. Statistics on the combined readership for physical and website titles compiled by Press Gazette, available at http://www.pressgazette.co.uk/uk-newspapers-ranked-total-readership-print-and-online (accessed 4th March, 2014). The remaining publication, *The Daily Star*, is not available through Nexis UK. Although *The Daily Star* is missing, it is not dissimilar to the included titles — in particular *The Sun*, which is also both a tabloid and relatively conservative.

(*The Guardian, The Independent, The Mirror*) and conservative (*The Daily Mail, The Express, The Sun, The Telegraph, The Times*) aspects of the British press, as well as the different formats of British newspapers: tabloids (*The Sun* and *The Mirror*), mid-markets (*The Daily Mail, The Express*) and broadsheets (*The Guardian, The Independent, The Times, The Telegraph*). Therefore, we felt that the national newspaper data available through Nexis UK would provide us with a thorough overview of the coverage of the attack.

The next step in the creation of the corpus was to compile the articles to include in our study by searching Nexis UK for newspaper articles published on 23rd May 2013 that contained the search term "Woolwich". In total, 41 articles contained the search term, and by reading through them we determined that all 41 were relevant to our research. Each publication accounted for between three and nine separate articles, with combined articles for each publication containing between 2,439 and 6,401 words.[4] Clearly, there is variation in the quantity of words used in each publication's reporting of the attack; however, we felt that each is adequately represented, and that trying to even up the representation of each publication by hand-picking articles would be an arbitrary process leading to a diminished dataset.

Once we had gathered our data, we read through each article, compiling all sentences containing variations on the lemma **terror*: "terror", "terrorist(s)", "terrorism", "counter-terror", "counter-terrorist", "counter-terrorism", "anti-terror". These sentences were placed together in a concordance database, allowing us to see "all of the occurrences of [our] search term, presented with the context they occur in" (Baker et al. 2009, 42–43). This made it easier for us to look at each occurrence of **terror* in depth. Occurrences were labelled according to word class, allowing us to separate out, for example, occurrences of "terrorist" that were nouns and occurrences that were adjectives. Further analysis was undertaken using critical stylistic tools, to look at the use of naming, modality, and presupposition. Due to the relatively small amount of data used in this study, we do not seek to make claims for the statistical significance of patterns found; rather, this use of basic corpus methods allowed us to focus on particularly interesting features of the data. Our approach went hand-in-hand with a concurrent close reading of the articles, which enabled us to identify salient themes in the way that the Woolwich attack is represented as a terrorist incident: the suspect's recorded monologue, the political response, references to previous terrorist incidents, the establishment of an allegedly new brand of terrorism and references to al-Qaeda. Here, the concordance database was helpful again, since it allowed us to mark each concordance for its significance to a certain theme. The identified themes are examined in more detail in Section 3.

4. For a full list of articles and figures, see Appendix.

2.2 The critical stylistic approach

The linguistic analysis in Section 3 uses methods of analysis associated with critical stylistics (Jeffries 2010). Critical stylistics builds on work in Critical Discourse Analysis (CDA), which uses a variety of methods of analysis to help "show up [...] connections between language, power and ideology" (Fairclough 1989, 5). This approach can help the researcher to understand the use of a particular term in a particular context: for example, L'Hote (2010) looks at the particular meaning of "globalisation" in Labour manifestos, and Edwards (2012) explores the meaning of "indigenous" and "white" in British National Party manifestos. Such research uses a wide range of linguistic "tools" of analysis to answer the question "What is the text doing?" — critical stylistics represents an attempt to inventorise the particular tools that can be used in such an attempt (Jeffries 2010, 15). Three of these — naming, modality and presupposition — are used here to analyse the way "terrorism" is represented in the corpus of the articles. Each of these plays a role in producing a text's representation of reality (Jeffries 2010, 14) and is, therefore, helpful in analysing how the newspaper articles portray the Woolwich attack as terrorist. Specific reasons for the choice of these particular tools are provided below.

Naming looks at the way that speakers and writers name particular entities, focusing on noun phrases and the information included within them. This can be through the simple choice of which noun to use to refer to someone/thing, e.g. "student", "woman" or "activist", a straightforward part of everyday language that "can serve many different psychological, social or political purposes" (Reisigl and Wodak 2001, 47). Modification of the chosen noun can make things more complex, and allow a text producer to "package up" their own opinions and assumptions about the referent (Jeffries 2010, 19) into the noun phrase, e.g. "the lazy student, who never gave her essays in on time". Given how little was known about the attackers' identities when the newspapers went to press, the way that they are named in the articles is of considerable interest.

Modality has to do with "the degree of assurance or commitment with which a speaker vouches for a proposition" (Fowler 1986, 57). By looking at, amongst other features of grammar, modal auxiliary verbs such as "may", "might", and "could", the researcher is able to look at what a writer or speaker hypothesises, and how confidently hypotheses are stated. For example, note the difference between "the protests *may* bring about regime change" and "the protests *will* bring about regime change". Text producers can also represent a proposition as straightforwardly "true" through categorical assertions: these are statements containing no modality, such as "the protests brought about regime change". As with naming, analysis of modality will help to demonstrate the way in which the articles discuss an event which was, at that point, very recent, and about which details were sketchy.

Presupposition differs from naming and modality in that it is not as simple to "read off" of a text. Presuppositions are assumptions built into a text, and are caused by a variety of linguistic triggers. This "hidden" quality makes presuppositions "less amenable to comment, debate or scrutiny" (Jeffries 2010, 102). Existential presuppositions are closely related to naming: by referring to something with a definite noun phrase ("the terrorist activist", "his taste in clothes"), a text producer presupposes that the referent exists. Logical presuppositions, meanwhile, are triggered in a number of ways. The most common of these are change of state verbs such as "stopped" ("he stopped discussing politics" presupposes he talked about politics before), factive verbs ("she understood the difficult situation", where what follows the verb "understood" is presupposed to be true) and iterative words, which presuppose that something must have happened more than once ("there was another terrorist attack", where "another" presupposes that there was a previous terrorist attack). What is vital to note is that a presupposition is a "taken-for-granted, implicit claim embedded within the explicit meaning" (Richardson 2007, 63). As such, presuppositions give writers working within the medium of news articles the opportunity to express potentially contentious ideas in an implicit way.

2.3 Definitions of "terrorism"

Due to its politicised and stigmatising nature, "terrorism" has always been a contested concept. Hoffman's comprehensive definition (2006, 40) argues that an act can be understood as terrorist if it is

> ineluctably political in aims and motives; violent — or, equally important, threatens violence; designed to have far-reaching psychological repercussions beyond the immediate victim or target; conducted either by an organization with an identifiable chain of command or conspiratorial cell structure (whose members wear no uniform or identifying insignia) or by individuals or a small collection of individuals directly influenced, motivated, or inspired by the ideological aims or example of some existent terrorist movement and/or its leaders; and perpetrated by a subnational group or nonstate entity.

A number of the factors listed by Hoffman are relevant to assessing the reportage of the Woolwich attack. Firstly, as is shown in more detail in Section 3.1, most articles in our study focus on the alleged political *aims* of the attackers, while ignoring the *motives* and *justifications* given by one of the suspects in the cameraphone recording. Thus, in contrast to traditional conceptions of terrorism, which are intrinsically linked to both the motivations and goals of groups branded as terrorist, the understanding of the term promoted by the newspaper articles is relatively detached from any political motives. As discussed in more detail in Sections 3.1 and

3.2, this reductive and seemingly depoliticised concept of terrorism has important implications regarding the potential legitimacy of attacks labelled as terrorist, since it effectively removes any possibility of explaining or justifying these attacks.

Another interesting aspect of Hoffman's definition is the condition that a terrorist act is "conducted either by an organisation with an identifiable chain of command […] or by individuals or a small collection of individuals directly influenced, motivated, or inspired by the ideological aims or example of some existent terrorist movement and/or its leaders" (ibid.). It is worth noting that the first edition of Hoffman's *Inside Terrorism*, published in 1998, did not mention the second possibility, i.e. that a terrorist act may be committed by individuals who do not have direct links to any terrorist organisation, but who have simply been "inspired" by such a movement. While this recent development in the evolution of the term "terrorism" has obviously been prompted by the circumstances of terrorist attacks committed in recent years, it also carries a risk of the "terrorist" label being applied to certain events or individuals without a thorough examination of their political and organisational background, since it allows for a much looser connection between a terrorist organisation and the actual perpetrators of an attack. Section 3.4 examines how the articles in our study bridge the gap between conventional definitions of terrorism and the circumstances of the Woolwich attack by referring to a "new" kind of terrorist threat. More specifically, Section 3.5 analyses the frequent links made between the attackers and the radical Islamist terrorist organisation al-Qaeda, despite the absence of information about any actual involvement of the suspects with this or any other terrorist movement at the time of the publication of the articles.

Interestingly, Hoffman does not refer to the targets of a terrorist attack apart from his statement that "terrorism is specifically designed to have far-reaching psychological effects beyond the immediate victim(s) or object of the terrorist attack" and that it intends to intimidate a wider "target audience" (2006, 40–41). This notion of terrorism carrying repercussions that reach beyond the actual victim of the attack is explored in Section 3.2, which shows how the articles in our study frame the London/British public as a whole as the target of the attack.

Other authors' definitions of terrorism are more specific with regard to the characteristics of the immediate targets of a terrorist attack. They define terrorism as "the deliberate, negligent, or reckless use of force against noncombatants" (Rodin 2004, 755) and suggest that an act can be considered terrorist only if "it is directed indiscriminately against non-combatants" (Novotny 2007, 23). However, in his monologue, the Woolwich attacker makes clear that the victim was deliberately targeted due to his apparent professional background as a member of the

British armed forces (*Sun 4*).[5] This aspect was seized on by the media as another reason why the attack constituted a terrorist incident, with much of the reportage focusing on the victim's professional background, the proximity of the attack to the Woolwich barracks where the victim was stationed, and the fact that he was wearing a "Help for Heroes" T-shirt,[6] implying that this made him easily recognisable as a soldier. Several papers praised the "fallen hero" (*Mirror 3*) or, more generally, "our brave soldiers" (*Sun 2*), calling for solidarity with and support for the British armed forces in the aftermath of the attack. If, however, the implication is that the victim was targeted specifically due to his profession, the application of the "terrorism" label has to be questioned based on the definitions of terrorism provided above. After all, an attack targeting an (even off-duty) soldier of a nation at war, which is according to the attacker's monologue perceived as an occupying force abroad, would have to be considered a — however unjustified or inappropriate — measure of warfare, not terrorism.[7]

This suggests three different possibilities for the framing of the Woolwich attack. The attack could be viewed as a terrorist attack, although it appears not to fit comfortably into academic definitions of terrorism. As shown above, it might alternatively be portrayed as an example of warfare — an attack that contributes to one side's actions in an on-going war and is thus, at least in the minds of its perpetrators, legitimate and justifiable. Thirdly, the incident could be seen as simply a violent crime: an unprovoked, physical, and deadly attack on an apparently innocent passerby. These three categories are not mutually exclusive — as shown in Section 3.2, the media reportage on the Woolwich attack also frames the incident as part of a larger conflict (or 'war') between Islam and the West/Britain. However, the predominant characterisation of the incident as one or the other carries considerable

5. Individual articles from our dataset are referred to by an abbreviation of parent title and ordering in the Appendix, e.g. this quote attributed to *Sun 4* is taken from the fourth article listed in the *The Sun* section of our Appendix ("You and Your Kids Are Next").

6. "Help for Heroes" is a UK charity providing support to British soldiers wounded in service.

7. Conversely, an argument can be made for regarding even unintentional attacks against non-combatants in the course of conventional warfare (usually referred to as collateral damage) as terrorism (Rodin 2004). Political commentator Glenn Greenwald poses a similar question in response to the initial news reporting on the Woolwich attack: "The US, the UK and its allies have repeatedly killed Muslim civilians over the past decade (and before that), but defenders of those governments insist that this cannot be "terrorism" because it is combatants, not civilians, who are the targets. Can it really be the case that when western nations continuously kill Muslim civilians, that's not "terrorism", but when Muslims kill western *soldiers*, that is terrorism?" (Greenwald 2013). Hoffman's definition of terrorism deliberately — although not entirely convincingly — counteracts this line of argument by limiting terrorism to acts "perpetrated by a subnational group or nonstate entity" (2006, 40).

implications regarding the legitimacy and wider significance of the attack. Our study aims to highlight the fact that despite the scarcity of details regarding the background of the attack and persons involved at the time of the publication of the articles, a characterisation of the incident as an act of terrorism seems to have been favoured by the media over a portrayal of the incident as a criminal act.

3. Themes of terrorism in the corpus

3.1 The suspect's monologue

The suspect's monologue in the eyewitness recording suggests a fundamentalist Muslim motivation for the attack. Making allusions to the Koran, the suspect explains that the victim was killed for being a member of the British armed forces, as "Muslims are dying daily by British soldiers" (*Sun 4*). Insisting that he and others will "never stop fighting you until you leave us alone" (ibid.), he calls for British citizens to remove their government, and for British troops to be withdrawn from Muslim countries, "so we can all live in peace" (ibid.). These words probably constitute one of the main reasons for the incident instantly being viewed as a terrorist attack, rather than as a brutal but possibly 'random' crime. However, this reaction demonstrates an increasingly narrow understanding of 'terrorism', with the concept being linked mainly to religious fundamentalism, in particular in the context of 'Islamic terrorism'.

The majority of articles in our study concentrate on the parts of the attacker's monologue that contain threats of violence against British society and references to Islam and the Koran, a tendency that is immediately noticeable in some of the headlines, such as "Terror Fanatics Behead Soldier [...] By Almighty Allah, We Will Not Stop Fighting You" (*The Daily Express 8*) and "You and Your Kids Are Next: Terror on our Streets" (*Sun 4*). They largely gloss over passages that correspond with Hoffman's requirements regarding the "ineluctably political" motives of a terrorist attack (2006: 40). Only *The Sun* published the full monologue, which contains the following justificatory remarks:

> So what if we want to live by the Sharia in Muslim lands? Why does that mean you must follow us and chase us and call us extremists and kill us. Rather you lot are extreme. You are the ones that when you drop a bomb you think it hits one person? Or rather your bomb wipes out a whole family? (*Sun 4*)

This part of the speech seems to contain the bulk of the evidence of the suspects' motives for carrying out the attack. However, the fact that only one of the eight publications decided to print this part of the monologue shows that while the suspects' aims (the removal of British troops and the British government) are highlighted, the motivation and reasoning behind the attack (Muslim civilians being attacked and killed by British troops) are ignored. It appears that motives are deemed irrelevant in the classification of the attack as a terrorist incident.

As a result, the idea of terrorism constructed by the articles is one that does not acknowledge its possible use as a political and ideological instrument: the terrorism of the Woolwich attack is an almost *depoliticised* terrorism. No space is provided for discussion of the suspects' potential reasons for feeling threatened or oppressed, and thus the characteristic of terrorism as 'the weapon of the weakest' that aims to "create power where there is none" (Hoffman 2006, 41) is lost. Instead of the politically-charged act of self-defence seemingly intended by the suspect, readers are encouraged to view the attack as an evil act of irrational and unmotivated violence. This portrayal of a terrorist attack contrasts sharply with Hoffman's definition of terrorism, which frames terrorist acts as rational actions based on political motives to reach political aims. The outcome of this discrepancy is clear: by labelling the incident as terrorist, while at the same time making it seem irrational by stripping it of its political background and motives, the attack is being firmly established as illegitimate and unjustifiable.

The dismissal of the suspect's political reasoning also aligns with a particular image of Islamic terrorism. While the phenomenon can be perceived as a reaction to 'Western' actions, such as military involvement in Muslim countries or attempts to influence government systems in such states (which ties in with the attacker's explanations), others frame it as an inherently Islamic phenomenon, with violence and the deliberate killing of non-Muslims being "sanctioned by the Koran".[8] For example, *Mail 3* discusses the alleged fact that "The head and the sword have a specific place in the rhetoric, heraldry and history of Islam", enabling jihadist interpretations that are used to justify terrorist acts. The conception of Islam as inherently violent is stated explicitly by Tommy Robinson, then leader of the English Defence League and a prominent critic of Islam, in his response to the Woolwich attack: "Our next generation are being taught through schools that Islam is a religion of peace. It's not. It never has been. What you saw today is Islam" (quoted in *Guardian 5*). By ignoring the attacker's justification of the murder, this second image of a violent and dangerous radical Muslim fanaticism is supported, giving the impression of a fanaticism possibly stemming from the alleged inherent violence of Islam itself, rather than from an — at least in the suspect's view — rational desire for self-defence.

8. Perhaps the most popular academic work depicting Islam as an inherently violent religion is Samuel Huntington's *The Clash of Civilizations and the Remaking of World Order* (1996). Since the 9/11 attacks in 2001, numerous works following the same line of argument have been published.

3.2 Political response

In his initial speech reacting to the attack, Prime Minister David Cameron stated that there were "strong indications that [the attack was] a terrorist incident".[9] Despite this seemingly tentative approach — "there are strong indications" — the speech made clear that the incident was being viewed and treated as a terrorist attack. This was further underlined by the fact that Home Secretary Theresa May called a meeting of the Whitehall emergency committee, COBRA, immediately after the attack.

The Prime Minister went on to praise the "absolutely indomitable British spirit that we will not be cowed", which would ensure that "the terrorists will never win".[10] Large sections of Cameron's speech employed an 'us vs. them' rhetoric which contrasted allegedly Western or British values, such as democracy, freedom and resilience, with Muslim fanaticism and extremism. Reportage also employed this 'us vs. them' opposition, framing the whole population of Britain/London as the target of the attack: "Britain must stand united against the terrorists" (*Sun 2*), "Islamist terrorism returned to Britain's streets" (*Telegraph 4*), "Soldier Hacked to Death in London Terror Attack" (*Times 3*). Articles also reported Boris Johnson's response to the attack, in which he observed that "Londoners have been through terror before" (*Telegraph 3*). This is in line with the conception of terrorism as targeting a wider audience beyond the immediate victim, such as the general population of a particular country (Hoffman 2006, 40–41). The attacker himself contributed to this view by depicting the attack as part of an on-going confrontation between "us" (in this case referring to Muslims) and "you people" (i.e. the British public) in his monologue (*Sun 4*). He framed the attack as mirroring the alleged aggression of British forces against Muslims abroad, as opposed to an incident that only involved the attackers and the victim.[11]

Both media reports and political responses bought into this portrayal of the attack as part of an ongoing conflict, although the causes and effects were of course reversed: while the suspect framed the attack as a response to British aggression abroad, British politicians and media cited attacks like this as necessitating resilience and retaliation, e.g. through the ongoing "war on terror". This view of the attack as part of an ongoing "war" might also help to explain why the suspect's

9. Video available at http://youtu.be/Nb2LFId971M (accessed 4th March, 2014).

10. Ibid.

11. Interestingly, the suspect changed his stance towards the end of his speech, and, after calling for the removal of "your government" from power, called for the return of "*our* troops" from Muslim countries, thereby briefly making himself part of the UK society he had been depicting as his adversary (*Sun 4*).

stated motives and justifications of the attack as self-defence were not given much attention, as highlighted in Section 3.1. Inevitably, the 'other side's' motives and claims for legitimacy tend to be disregarded in an ongoing conflict, their actions tending to be portrayed as irrational and unjustified. However, media and political responses could have decided to initially take a more neutral stance by refusing to 'take sides', thus denying the suspects their apparent wish to frame the attack as part of an ongoing, larger conflict until further details about the incident and persons involved emerged.

While depicting the attack as one aimed against the British public in general, both politicians and the media were eager to highlight that this 'British public' also included British Muslim communities. In his initial reaction, Cameron claimed that "people across Britain, *people in every community*, I believe, will utterly condemn this attack" (our emphasis).[12] His second speech on the issue, delivered on 23rd May 2013 in front of 10 Downing Street, again referred to the suspects' alleged aim of creating divisions within British society: "The people who did this were trying to divide us. They should know: something like this will only bring us closer together and make us stronger".[13] Interestingly, the lines along which these divisions could occur are never explicitly stated — it is assumed that the audience are familiar enough with British ethnic and religious tensions and the rhetoric surrounding the 'war on terror' to understand the statements as a reference to British Muslim communities and other parts of British society.

A number of articles in our study voice similar sentiments regarding the suspects' alleged intention to create divisions within British society (e.g. the main body of *Sun 1* and Anita Baig's accompanying 'My View' section) and highlight the role of British Muslims as part of the targeted 'British public'. Some papers also raise concerns about the potential of retributive violence against British Muslim communities in reaction to the incident: "Hundreds of hooded protesters from the English Defence League marched through Woolwich after their leader Tommy Robinson urged people to 'take to the streets'" (*Express 5*), "Scores of supporters of the English Defence League threw bottles at police and chanted anti-Muslim slogans in Woolwich hours after the murder of one man and the shooting of his two suspected assailants" (*Guardian 5*). Like the Prime Minister's speeches, newspaper articles stating that, for example, "the grisly incident in Britain was met with complete shock, including among our Muslim community who coincidentally may share the religion of the attackers" (*Mirror 3*) draw a clear distinction between 'good' British Muslims and the allegedly inherently violent, radicalised Muslims

12. Video available at http://youtu.be/Nb2LFId971M (accessed 4th March, 2014).

13. Video available at http://www.youtube.com/watch?v=ogDnG9k62YE (accessed 4th March, 2014).

perceived as the 'Other'. Muslim organisations in the UK joined this discourse by issuing statements condemning the Woolwich attack and asserting that "this truly barbaric act has no basis in Islam" (Muslim Council of Britain 2013). However, this leaves very little space for the voices of British Muslims who condemn the attacks as an instrument of violence and perceive themselves as part of British society — while at the same time perhaps agreeing to some extent with the attacker's depiction of a Muslim world subjected to Western domination and aggression.

3.3 References to previous terrorist incidents

One of the most insidious ways in which the newspapers construct the attack as an incident of 'terrorism' is through references to earlier attacks widely accepted to have been terrorist. This is done primarily through connections to previous terrorist attacks with a radical Islamist background. These connections take advantage of readers' background knowledge of incidents which took place months or — in most cases — years beforehand, and which have had sufficient time to be understood and classified as terrorist. As a result, readers are encouraged to understand the extremely recent and — at the time of publication — unanalysed attack in Woolwich as simply another example of terrorism.

References to previous attacks are linguistically constructed in a number of different ways. Connections are frequently made through naming. For example, many of the articles refer to 'Islamic terrorists' or 'Islamic terrorism', denying the reader an opportunity to argue that the terrorism in question was not 'Islamic', or that the attack discussed was not a terrorist incident despite its fundamentalist Islamic elements. Instead, the 'Islamic' nature of the 'terrorists' is packaged up into a concrete entity (Jeffries 2010, 19). A reader could argue with a proposition such as 'They were Islamic terrorists' or 'The terrorism was Islamic', but both aspects are presupposed in "Islamic terrorists murder soldier" (*Mirror 1*) and "Islamic terrorism is spreading" (*Sun1*). Thus, readers' preconceptions regarding a link between terrorist incidents and a fundamentalist Islamist agenda are activated, making it seem more likely that the event described in these terms is indeed a terrorist incident. As discussed before, the Islamic background of the attack constitutes perhaps the main reason why it was almost inevitably regarded as terrorist in the first place — a logic that is further reinforced by packaging up the two concepts into one unquestionable entity.

The *Telegraph* articles make particularly extensive use of naming to link the Woolwich attack to previous terrorist incidents. *Telegraph 3* labels the incident "the first terrorist murder on the British mainland since the 7/7 suicide bombings" and refers to "the attack, which had chilling echoes of a plot to behead a soldier foiled in Birmingham in 2007". Note that although each of the passages consists of a single noun phrase ("murder" and "attack" are the head nouns, postmodified by prepositional phrases and relative clauses containing other noun phrases), they both contain much that might be considered contentious — was the murder 'terrorist'?; did the attack have 'chilling echoes' of the previous plot? The fact that these details are packaged up into noun phrases makes it hard for the reader to argue with them (Jeffries 2010, 19). *Telegraph 4* also makes the link to the 7/7 bombing explicit by labelling the attack "Britain's worst act of terrorism for eight years" and "the first terrorist murder on British soil in eight years". In these examples, the vaguer allusions to 7/7 force the reader to draw an inference linking it to the Woolwich attack. This comparison is also noteworthy in that, as the *Telegraph* acknowledges, much more time has passed since 7/7: there has been plenty of opportunity for in-depth analysis of that attack, and for a definition of terrorism to be attributed and adequately argued for, whereas the Woolwich attack had happened only the day before readers were presented with these connections.

Perhaps the most explicit way in which connections are made with previous attacks is through categorical assertions, which are notable for their lack of modality: there is no question of possibility or desirability — a statement is presented as a fact, without "any expression of tentativeness" (Fowler 1991, 127). Such statements are often used to note the apparently familiar nature of the attacks. Interestingly, many examples refer back to attacks that were plotted but ultimately unsuccessful. For example, *Mail 3* states that "The Woolwich terror attack has chilling echoes of a previous plot to kidnap and behead a British Muslim soldier".[14] Here, as in the earlier example from the *Telegraph*, the rather poetic idea that the attack carried 'echoes' that were 'chilling' is presented as though it were a fact: the verb 'has' is not modified by a qualifier such as 'might' or 'for some people'. That the particular plot referred to was unsuccessful is made clear in a similar statement in *Guardian 1*: "Yesterday's incident was [...] reminiscent of a past and disrupted plot by violent jihadists in Birmingham in 2007". Note that the naming in this instance is more tentative, with the Woolwich attack labelled as "yesterday's incident". However, the implication of terrorism is made through the use of the complement that notes its similarity to a previous plot, and more specifically one concocted by "violent jihadists". Although the planned attack referred to in the *Sun* and *Guardian* excerpts was unsuccessful, a sense of fear is inspired through the suggestion that such plots are not uncommon, and that there could easily have been more such incidents. Yet

14. Interestingly, while several other papers also refer to this failed plot to kidnap and murder a British soldier in 2007, only *The Guardian* and *The Daily Mail* explicitly state that the plot targeted a *Muslim* soldier, with the aim of deterring Muslims from joining the UK armed forces. The *Express* implicitly acknowledges this by citing the motive behind the planned attack, while the *Telegraph* and *Independent* both mention the incident without referring to the target's religious background.

the grounds for making these connections are not strong — note that no explicit connections are made linking the Woolwich suspects to individuals or organisations responsible for previous attacks or plots.

Similar in effect to statements regarding reminiscence and echoes is the use of presupposition in the article. This can be seen in statements about how terrorism 'returned', which trigger a logical presupposition about an earlier state of affairs (Jeffries 2010, 95). In these instances, 'return' is an iterative word, which hints that something has occurred on more than one occasion (Jeffries 2010, 95): "Terrorism returned to the streets of Britain yesterday" (*Independent 4*), "Islamist terrorism returned to Britain's streets" (*Telegraph 4*). In each instance, the subject — the entity that is doing the returning — is 'terrorism' or, more specifically, "Islamist terrorism". The referent in each adverbial is also identical — "the streets of Britain", "Britain's streets". The use of a broad concept — terrorism — makes these statements especially powerful, its non-human, intangible nature making it all the more difficult to comprehend or control.

In a similar way, connections are made between the Woolwich attack and attacks committed by the IRA during the Troubles and subsequent peace process in Northern Ireland. Unsurprisingly, none of the newspapers suggests any tangible connections between individuals or organisations involved in each. The only concrete link made is the geographical coincidence of both parties having attacked personnel from the same military barracks in Woolwich, since the nearby King's Arms pub, which was commonly frequented by military personnel, was bombed by the IRA in November 1974. Often, connections between the IRA's and the suspects' attacks are presupposed. For example, *Telegraph 9* states that "Troops stationed in Woolwich have been targeted by terrorists before. In November 1974, the area was the scene of an IRA attack". There is another iterative trigger here, with 'before' presupposing that something similar to what is stated in the proposition (the targeting of Woolwich troops by terrorists) must have happened previously, i.e. before the 2013 attack — indeed, this is explicated in the following sentence. Similarly, Prime Minister Cameron stated in his initial speech that Britain had "suffered terrorist attacks before, terrorist attacks from the IRA, terrorist attacks from Islamic extremists",[15] and *Mail 1* reports on Mayor of London Boris Johnson's reaction to the attacks, which referred to how Britain had suffered "terrorist attacks before at the hands of the IRA", thus implying some kind of continuity between IRA terror and Islamic threat. Readers may wish to question the relevance of these connections: could there be any real connection between attacks

15. Transcript available at http://transcripts.cnn.com/TRANSCRIPTS/1305/22/ctw.01.html (accessed 4th March, 2014).

committed by the IRA and the 2013 attack? What certainly *is* implied is that the 2013 incident also represents an act of terrorism.

3.4 A new brand of terrorism

In many regards, the Woolwich attack does not fit conventional conceptions of 'terrorism'. The articles in our study deal with this by seeking to categorise the attack as belonging to a particular, *new* strand of Islamic terrorist activity, in line with Hoffman's definition of terrorism which includes attacks being committed by "individuals or a small collection of individuals directly influenced, motivated, or inspired by the ideological aims or example of some existent terrorist movement and/or its leaders" (2006, 40).

The most striking way in which this is done, across the articles, is through the simple use of the adjective 'new': "Yesterday's incident was a new style of terrorist attack in Britain" (*Guardian 1*), "This new brand of terror poses a daunting challenge to the police and security" (*Sun 2*), "Dubbed the 'Nike terrorists' […] Britain has faced a new generation of Islamic extremists" (*Telegraph 7*). The use of 'new' to pre-modify the head nouns in each of these examples effectively deals with any qualms readers might have about the status of the attack: if something about what happened in Woolwich seems not to fit with the reader's concept of terrorism, then that is because it is a 'new', unfamiliar kind. This links in with a number of instances in which this new kind of terrorism is contextualised within the history of terrorist attacks and the 'war on terror'. For example, *Sun 2* states that "events in Woolwich also reveal how the war on terror has entered a chilling new phase". Thus, while the Woolwich attack may represent something new, it is nonetheless part of the larger narrative of the "war on terror" and the attacks this "war" is responding to, among them the 9/11 attacks on the World Trade Centre and the 7/7 bombings in London. The idea of the Woolwich attack as an evolutionary step in terrorism is also hinted at by quotes attributed to Scotland Yard's John O'Connor: "Terror experts said that the murder […] represents a 'new round of terror threats in this country'" (*Express 8*), "He added […] 'You're into a new round of terror threats in this country, particularly as you don't know the full extent of it'" (*Telegraph 7*). Here the suggestion is that what might seem too unfamiliar to be classed as terrorism is, in fact, simply a "new round" of the same threat to society.

The two defining characteristics of the 'new terrorism' cited by most newspapers are the inclusion of attacks committed by individuals working without direct links to an existing terrorist organisation, and the increased likelihood that the individuals concerned may be citizens of, or permanently live in, the Western countries in which they conduct their attacks. Firstly, the individualist nature of the new kind of terrorism is represented through the use of 'lone wolf' as an adjective. This aspect of the suspects' portrayal presents a frightening possibility — that monitoring relatively familiar terrorist organisations is not enough: "The police and security services have [...] been under constant threat of the lone wolf terrorist" (*Telegraph 7*), "Counter-terrorism officers and security officials will fear that the Woolwich attack fits the category of crime they can do little to thwart: random, lone-wolf, unsophisticated attacks" (*Guardian 4*). Secondly, the 'homegrown' characteristic seems to have been inspired mainly by the recorded monologue of one of the suspects. All papers highlight the suspects' British/London accent, with *Telegraph 1* observing that "their British accents suggested that they were 'homegrown' terrorists". *Sun 1*, meanwhile, notes that "Britain's spooks and anti-terror cops appear to have been caught unawares by the mid-afternoon atrocity committed by homegrown fanatics". The use of 'homegrown' in the pre-modification of 'terrorists' and 'fanatics' differentiates them from other, more conventional and familiar, 'foreign-grown' terrorists. The focus on this aspect of the attackers suggests that the reports find the suspects' apparent nationality or place of residence to be of significance. Allusions to the unlikeliness of their accent help to 'sell' the incident as a terrorist one.

Both characteristics — attacks being committed by individuals without direct links to terrorist organisations and those individuals' origin within the countries in which they commit an attack — also apply to several terrorist incidents without any Islamic or religious background.[16] However, the image of the 'lone-wolf, homegrown terrorist' has recently been applied in particular to attacks committed by Muslims who were born and/or have spent a considerable part of their lives in Western countries. The radicalisation of Muslims and their potential development into 'homegrown terrorists' are thus depicted as today's main terrorist threat, with other forms of terrorism and acts of violence committed by non-state actors receiving comparatively little attention.

3.5 References to al-Qaeda

As outlined above, all papers in the corpus link the attack to an alleged larger Islamist threat to the UK, with most drawing an explicit link between the suspects and the radical Islamist organisation al-Qaeda. These references are made in spite of the lack of information available as to whether the two suspects had at any point actually been members of this or any other terrorist organisation. Lacking

16. Examples include the bombing and shooting attack in Norway committed by far-right extremist Anders Behring Breivik in 2011, the anti-government Oklahoma City Bombing in 1995, and Franz Fuchs' xenophobia-inspired wave of letter bombs against Austrian politicians and public figures in 1993.

any concrete evidence of al-Qaeda involvement, the articles frequently highlight the existence of al-Qaeda propaganda outlets such as websites and magazines that have made calls for violent attacks against non-Muslims (e.g. *Daily Mail 1* and *3*, *Telegraph 1* and *7*). The idea that the Woolwich suspects had been inspired by such materials was, at this early stage, merely a suspicion, as noted in *Telegraph 1*: "The atrocity certainly fits Al-Qaeda's blueprint for home-grown terrorism, whereby its supporters have been urged to carry out individual attacks". However, making connections to an organisation with which readers would already be familiar, and which they would already regard as terrorist, adds weight to the idea of the Woolwich attack as terrorist.

As with the references to previous terrorist attacks, connections of this sort allow the articles to place Woolwich in a familiar context of (Islamic) terrorism, knowing that readers would be familiar with al-Qaeda, a name that is by now synonymous with Islamic terrorism in the "West". Assumptions that the suspects were connected to, or inspired by, al-Qaeda are sometimes also placed in their naming: "two al-Qaeda-inspired Islamist terrorists" (*Telegraph 4*), "One of the terrorists — both thought to be al-Qaeda 'lone-wolves'" (*Sun 3*). In the *Telegraph* example, "al-Qaeda-inspired" is included in adjectival form in the pre-modification of the noun "terrorists" (which itself is explicit in assuming the terrorist nature of the attacks). Placing the idea of al-Qaeda inspiration in the noun phrase rather than stating the proposition — "the terrorists were inspired by al-Qaeda" — allows the reporter to state the matter as something inherent to the suspects. However, no references to al-Qaeda were made by the suspect in his monologue. The *Sun* example is more speculative, with the relative clause "[who are] both thought to be al-Qaeda 'lone-wolves'" post-modifying the noun "terrorists". Here, the modal lexical verb "thought" serves to make it clear that links with al-Qaeda are currently speculative. Further, there is a lack of specificity here as to *who* thinks that the suspects are al-Qaeda "lone-wolves": this could just be idle speculation on the part of the newspaper.

The speculative nature of any possible connections with al-Qaeda is acknowledged by the reports' use of modality in making such links: while there are plenty of categorical assertions stating clearly that the suspects *are* terrorists, speculation regarding al-Qaeda is played down through modality. Where the possibility of al-Qaeda having had a role in, or been an inspiration for, the attacks is discussed, modality is used to mitigate the reporter's certainty: "while many *may* be inspired by al-Qaeda, they operate without command or control from the terror group" (*Telegraph 7*), "Another *possibility* [...] is that the minds of the killers of the British soldier were poisoned in a mosque or even in prison, an increasingly popular recruiting ground for groups linked to al-Qaeda" (*Mail 3*) (our emphasis in both quotes). Referring to the murder in Woolwich and other, apparently similar, planned attacks, the use of the modal auxiliary "may" in the example from the *Telegraph* recognises that a connection is only a possibility, with the main clause (starting at "they operate…") making it clear that a direct relationship is unlikely. In the *Mail* example, the idea that "groups linked to al-Qaeda" may have had an influence is defined as merely "another possibility", thus noting that this is speculation. While the use of modality in these examples means that readers are not being misled as to the certainty of al-Qaeda's relevance to the story, the very mention of such a possibility — with no genuine evidence on which to base such speculation — helps establish the sense of a real threat consistent with previous attacks with which readers will be familiar. This is also noticeable in the *Telegraph 1* statement discussed above, in which the reporter states that "The atrocity *certainly* fits al-Qaeda's blueprint for home-grown terrorism" (our emphasis). Here, the adverb "certainly" slightly diminishes the confidence of the statement, but nonetheless implies that some link to al-Qaeda is present.

4. Conclusion

Our contention before starting this research was that an attack such as the one carried out in Woolwich can be too readily framed as "terrorist". Linguistic analysis of a number of themes in the reportage of the attack has backed up this contention. While it is natural that newspapers will not stick vigorously to academic definitions and arguments regarding the conception of terrorism, the articles provide evidence of negligent handling of what is a powerful and divisive term.

In some instances, the simple choice of which information to highlight and which to disregard helped to frame the incident as terrorist. In particular, the quotes selected from the suspect's monologue helped to establish an "us vs. them" narrative, while ignoring the explanations provided with regard to the attackers' political motivation. Elsewhere, naming choices helped both to contextualise the attack historically and to identify it as indicative of a frightening future. Explicit links were made to previous — albeit unrelated — attacks through the use of presupposition, while terms such as "new" and "lone-wolf" helped to "update" readers' understanding of terrorism and paper over the cracks caused by the divergence between the Woolwich attack and past instances of terrorism that align more neatly with conventional conceptions of the phenomenon. The use of categorical assertions to make connections to previous Islamic terrorist attacks, and the hypotheses of links to al-Qaeda, helped to ground the attack in a familiar description of Islamic terrorism. Ultimately, the journalists' willingness to apply a very specific and highly-modified definition of terrorism to the attack backs up Glenn Greenwald's (2013) suggestion that with regard to the attack in Woolwich "the term [terrorism] has no real definition [...] beyond 'violence engaged in by Muslims in retaliation against western violence toward Muslims'".

Key to these findings has been the approach taken. The close reading of a fairly small dataset enabled us to identify key themes that occurred across publications, each of which bore fruitful linguistic analysis. Basing the latter on a thorough, tagged concordance list gave our findings a foundation of rigour. The use of a defined set of linguistic tools showed up the ways in which minor grammatical choices can help produce persuasive arguments. Future work on the subject of 'terrorism' could take this approach further, using a larger corpus and making greater use of corpus tools such as keywords and collocations to provide the means for meaningful statistical analysis, for example in exploring what adjectives are frequently used in the pre-modification of 'terror'. It would also be of interest to further explore some of the themes discussed in the analysis here — for example, the way that links are posited between seemingly very different incidents, such as the IRA attacks and the crime committed in Woolwich.

References

Baker, Paul, Andrew Hardie, and Tony McEnery. 2009. *A Glossary of Corpus Linguistics*. Edinburgh: Edinburgh University Press.

Edwards, Geraint O. 2012. "A Comparative Discourse Analysis of the Construction of 'In-groups' in the 2005 and 2010 Manifestos of the British National Party." *Discourse & Society* 23(3):245–258. doi:10.1177/0957926511433477

Fairclough, Norman. 1989. *Language and Power*. London: Longman.

Fowler, Roger. 1986. *Linguistic Criticism*. Oxford: Oxford University Press.

Fowler, Roger. 1991. *Language in the News* London: Routledge.

Greenwald, Glenn. 2013. "Was the London Killing of a British Soldier 'Terrorism'?" <Available at http://www.theguardian.com/commentisfree/2013/may/23/woolwich-attack-terrorism-blowback> [Accessed 4 March 2014]

Hoffman, Bruce. 2006. *Inside Terrorism*. Columbia: Columbia University Press.

Jeffries, Lesley. 2010. *Critical Stylistics: The Power of English*. Hampshire: Palgrave Macmillan.

L'Hote, Emilie. 2010. "New Labour and Globalization: Globalist Discourse with a Twist?" *Discourse & Society* 21(4):355–376. doi:10.1177/0957926510366212

Muslim Council of Britain. 2013. "Muslims Condemn Attack on Soldier in Woolwich" <Available at http://www.mcb.org.uk/index.php?option=com_content&view=article&id=2333> [Accessed 4 March 2014]

Novotny, Daniel D. 2007. "What is Terrorism?" In *Focus on Terrorism* (Volume 8), edited by Edward V. Linden, 23–32. Hauppauge: Nova Science Publishers.

Reisigl, Martin, and Ruth Wodak. 2001. *Discourse and Discrimination: Rhetorics of Racism and Anti-Semitism*. London: Routledge.

Richardson, John E. 2007 *Analysing Newspapers: An Approach from Critical Discourse Analysis*. Hampshire: Palgrave Macmillan.

Rodin, David. 2004. "Terrorism without Intention." *Ethics* 114:752–771. doi:10.1086/383442

USC United States Code, 22 USC § 2656f "Annual Country Reports on Terrorism" <Available via Cornell University Legal Information Institute at http://www.law.cornell.edu/uscode/text/22/2656f> [Accessed 4 March 2014]

Appendix

Newspaper	Articles	Total no. of words
The Daily Mail	1. Chilling Rant into Cameraphone 2. Crazed Animals? How News of the Savage Attack Exploded on Twitter 3. Were They Inspired? 4. Female Gun Cops who Aren't Afraid to Pull the Trigger	4,013
The Daily Express	1. Mum Confronted Knifemen 2. Chilling Echo of Kidnap Plot 3. Brave Mother Tried to Get Men to Hand over Knives 4. Defiant Queen Vows to Still Visit Woolwich 5. Fear for Asians as EDL Tries to Stoke Reprisals 6. 'They Were Hacking Away at Him. He Never Had a Chance' 7. Soldier from Barracks Killed by IRA Bombers 8. Terror Fanatics Behead Soldier: Barbaric Attack on British Street; Victim Wore Help for Heroes T-Shirt; By Almighty Allah We Will Never Stop Fighting You	3,569
The Guardian	1. 'You People Will Never Be Safe': British Soldier Dead in Suspected Terror Attack near London barracks; Knife Attack 'an Eye for an Eye' Says Suspect in Camera Footage; Killing in Street Is 'Absolutely Sickening' Says Prime Minister 2. 'We Saw the Meat Cleaver. They Were Hacking at this Poor Guy': After the Horrific Terror Attack which Left One Man Dead the Suspects Stood in the Busy Street, Asked Passers-by to Take Pictures, and Stayed until the Police Arrived 3. Eyewitness: 'He Talked about War and Killing Police' 4. An Attack that the Security Services May Have Been Powerless to Prevent; Killing May Have Been Work of 'Self-Starters'; Terror Threat level Remains Substantial, Officials Say 5. EDL Protestors Clash with Police	4,487

Newspaper	Articles	Total no. of words
The Independent	1. One Woman Was Crying: 'They Killed Him. They Killed Him': Dazed Residents Are Still Coming to Terms with the Shocking Scenes They Witnessed 2. A Worrying New Face of Islamist Threat to the UK 3. Prime Minister Vows That Britain Will 'Never Buckle' 4. 'Sickening, Deluded and Unforgiveable': Police Shoot Two Men after Soldier Is beheaded in Busy Woolwich Street; PM and Mayor Lead Chorus of Outrage as No 10 Terror Committee Meets; Bloody Attack Brings Terror to Capital's Streets	2,860
The Mirror	1. You Will Never Be Safe: Beheaded on Our Streets; Islamic Terrorists Murder Soldier and Give Grim Warning 2. 'Let Me Pass…Let Me Pray for Him': Beheaded on our Streets; Courage of Woman who Stood Up to Boasting Butchers 3. Panic and We're Lost 4. May Orders Top Security at Barracks	2,749
The Sun	1. No Clues, No Warning: Terror on our Streets; Passers-By Confront Bloody Fanatics 2. Beyond Belief 3. As Woman Strokes a Beheaded Soldier, His Killer Cries for Jihad: Machete Maniacs Murder Squaddie 4. You and Your Kids Are Next: Terror on our Streets; Chilling Video of Machete Killer; Blood-Stained Nut's Rant; He Made Witness Film It	3,965
The Telegraph	1. This Savage Attack Must Not Shake our Resolve 2. Mother Tells Terrorists to Drop Weapons: Life on Line — The Woman who Defied Killers as They Waited for Police 3. An Eye for an Eye, a Tooth for a Tooth. We Won't Stop Fighting until You Leave Us Alone; Two Islamist Terrorists Attempt to Behead Soldier with a Knife and Meat Cleaver after Murdering Him on a London Street 4. Slaughtered 'Like a Piece of Meat' on the Daytime Streets of London 5. 'Back Victim by Buying T-Shirt': Help for Heroes 6. We Will Never Buckle under this Sickening Attack, Says PM: Political Response 7. New Threat to Britain: Lone Wolves under the M15 Radar; Out of Nowhere, without Command or Control from Terror Groups, Attackers Escape Notice 8. Men Described as 'of Muslim Appearance' 9. Security Tightened at Army Bases across the Capital	6,401
The Times	1. Soldiers Are 'Locked Down' in Barracks 2. 'They Were Crazy, Chopping at This Guy Like He Was a Piece of Meat' 3. Soldier Hacked to Death in London Terror Attack: Police Shoot Two Islamists outside Barracks; Soldier Is Hacked to Death in Terror Attack; Assailant Rants to Camera after Killing	2,439

"Threatening other" or "role-model brother"?

China in the eyes of the British and Hungarian far-right

Anna Szilágyi
Savannah College of Art and Design

In the late 2000s far-right parties made significant gains in numerous countries of the European Union. Sharing the same agenda and discourse of discrimination, many of these parties collaborate today at the European level as well. Yet, it is unclear whether the contemporary European far-right is indeed homogenous in terms of ideology. This project in critical discourse analysis shows that the far-right in the EU is actually characterized by ideological diversity. The chapter compares and contrasts how China, an emerging great power with a booming economy, has been portrayed in the early 2010s by far-right parties in the UK and Hungary. By identifying major references, metaphors, frames and argumentation schemes, the author concludes that despite belonging to the same party family, and being actual political allies, the British National Party (BNP) and the Jobbik party in Hungary construct fundamentally different images of the "Chinese Other". The far-right in the UK, a major Western power, presents China clearly in hostile terms, mainly as a "dangerous, threatening intruder" into the British market. Additionally, in the discourse of the British far-right China is primarily identified as a communist dictatorship and used as a metaphor of oppression in the domestic UK context. Meanwhile, in Hungary, a post-communist country in Eastern Europe and a relatively recent member of the European Union, an opposite picture of China is constructed by the far-right. Here, China serves as a tool to distance Hungary from the West. China is positioned by the Hungarian far-right as a state where communism has lost its significance. By stressing the Asian origin of Hungarians, brotherhood is claimed among Hungarians and Chinese and China is presented as a "role model country" which successfully resisted "Western dominance".

Keywords: far-right, China, ideological cleavages, Eastern and Western Europe

DOI 10.1075/bct.93.07szi

1. Introduction

The European parliamentary elections that took place in 2009 in the midst of the global financial crisis demonstrated clearly that the far-right is on the rise within the European Union (EU). For the first time, right-wing extremists made gains by winning parliamentary seats simultaneously in 14 member states of the EU, including Austria, Belgium, Bulgaria, Denmark, Finland, France, Greece, Hungary, Italy, Latvia, the Netherlands, Slovakia, Romania and the UK. In these countries the far-right attracted voters with similar agendas and rhetoric. Far-right parties of Europe commonly combine heavy nationalism with racism and/or xenophobia, opposing the national communities they believe to represent (the "*we*", the "*us*", the "*our*") to ethnic, religious and sexual minorities in hostile terms.

Yet, it remains a question whether the ideological universe of the booming European far-right is indeed homogenous. Fieschi (2000) articulated skepticism already after the European Parliamentary elections in 1999 in which 6 far-right parties succeeded. She pointed to their inability to form stable coalitions and cooperate, explaining this otherwise unusual trend within the EU with the extreme nationalism of the parties: "The difficulties encountered in attempts to form parliamentary groups are indicative of the primacy of nationalism which undermine any potential for ideological alliances" (Fieschi 2000, 518).

Reviewing systematically the characters and organizational forms of European far-right parties in more recent times, Minkenberg (2011) also stressed the relevance of diversity. He argued that we are actually "concerned with a large variety of widely different ideological and organizational forms of right-wing radicalism that require a differentiated approach" (Minkenberg 2011, 37). According to Minkenberg, among other things, an East-West division makes the European far-right movement divergent. As he observed, compared to their Western counterparts, far-right parties of the post-communist East are less developed in terms of organization, more past-oriented and rather militant.

We also see that Western and Eastern European far-right actors do not necessarily construct enemies of identical groups. The overview of contemporary far-right agendas by Wilson and Hainsworth (2012) illustrates this tendency well. Although some far-right parties in the West — the French Front National for instance — evoke anti-Roma sentiments, the Western European far-right creates hostile 'others' primarily of immigrants. Meanwhile, in the post-communist East the Roma population is the main target of many far-right parties. Additionally, unlike their Eastern counterparts, far-right political actors in the West generally refrain from expressing anti-Semitism and pro-Nazi sympathies publicly (but see Sotiris this issue). Similarly, homophobia is more central in the rhetoric of the Eastern than Western far-right.

Occasionally, even East-West incidents take place because of such divisions. For instance, in 2011 the British National Party (BNP) had to expel his its regional secretary, Chris Hurst after he gave a Nazi salute at a popular far-right festival in Hungary. The politician's explanation was that he "did what everybody else in the club was doing" in Hungary (Teed 2011).

However, there are also far-right political formations in Eastern and Western Europe who claim unity. Several far-right parties — including the British National Party and the Hungarian Jobbik party — participate in the Alliance of European National Movements (AENM). This organization was established in 2009 with the aim to facilitate a pan-European far-right collaboration. Members of the AENM stress that they have a "common responsibility" and engage in a "common fight" (AENM 2009). They also celebrate the existence of a "likeminded Nationalist community throughout Europe" (BNP 2013).

The trend that the discriminatory far-right discourses are structured by the same linguistic and rhetorical patterns in different national contexts also points to the ideological unity of the parties in question (for a comprehensive overview of the far-right rhetoric see Reisigl, and Wodak 2001). However, it is important to stress that the salient rhetorical overlaps between far-right discourses have been primarily observed in the context of the parties' domestic agendas. We indeed see that the different far-right actors employ an identical discursive repertoire when they discriminate minority communities at home. Yet, it is possible that the ideological diversity of the contemporary European far-right could be better mapped if we explore the "othering" strategies of the relevant parties in international contexts.

Within the social science study of "otherness" two major traditions can be distinguished. On the one hand, the 'self-other' nexus *within the society* has been widely analyzed. Many studies on the discriminatory discourse of the European far-right follow this line of research and study how the relevant political actors and/or their partisan media construct *internal others* of minority communities who exist within a society (i.e., immigrants, religious and ethnic groups) (Wood and Finlay 2008; Krzyzanowski and Wodak 2009; Bársony et al. 2011; Kovács and Szilágyi 2013).

On the other hand, the "self-other" relationship has been studied in the *transnational context* as well. The role that *external others* (i.e., nations, states and civilizations) play in the identity formation of their counterparts has been examined globally by cultural theorists, political scientists, media and international relation scholars (Said 1978, 1981; Neumann 1999; Lee et al. 2002).

In this chapter, I analyze the "othering" strategies of Eastern and Western European far-right parties in the transnational context. I compare and contrast how UK's British National Party (BNP) and the Hungarian Jobbik party — who are actual political allies and regularly promote each other in public — relate to a significant global entity, China.

Why is China important in this context? Due to the economic reform process launched in the late 1970s by the country's paramount leader Deng Xiaoping, the world witnessed China's tremendous growth in the past decades. While remaining an authoritarian communist state, the People's Republic of China (PRC) has transformed into the world's leading exporter and second largest economy. In the past 30 years, the average growth rate in China was the highest in the world. The country is expected to surpass the current number one economy, the United States before the end of the 2010s (OECD 2012). China also owns the world's largest foreign exchange reserves in the era of global financial crises and widespread national debt crises among Western countries. There is not much doubt that China's boom will fundamentally reshape global politico-economic realities. The rise of China is a "world challenge" according to Jacques (2009), bringing gradually a "global shift" in Halper's view (2010), and "shaking the world" in the opinion of Kynge (2006).

How do far-right parties in Eastern and Western Europe relate to this significant global development, China's rise? To answer this question, I explore what picture of China is constructed by them, respectively.

I analyze all the accessible and relevant texts that were published on the BNP's official website between 2011 and 2013, mapping what China and its emerging economic and political power means for the far-right in a leading Western country like the UK. In the case of post-communist Hungary, I explore all the accessible articles related to China that appeared between 2010 and 2012 on *Barikad.hu*, a major Hungarian far-right online portal, a political mouthpiece of the Jobbik party.[1]

Following the categorization elaborated in the literature on the rhetoric of "othering" (Reisigl and Wodak 2001), I primarily focus on two units of discourse. First, I study references that were made about China in the relevant media texts. In other words, I explore how China was named by the two far-right outlets, with a special focus on replacements (i.e., when instead of *China* references are made to a "rising superpower", "eastern giant" or "authoritarian state"). Second, I identify argumentation schemes that emerge frequently in the texts, displaying how the outlets argued for or against China.

Additionally, I pay attention to the key metaphors and frames which appeared and were evoked in the texts in the context of China. In the case of the latter I build upon the linguistic conceptualization of frames, developed by George Lakoff (2004). In Lakoff's political discourse analysis, frames are mental structures that

1. *Barikad.hu* has recently changed its name to *Alfahir.hu*. However, during the analyzed period the portal was accessible under the domain name *Barikad.hu*. Therefore, in this chapter I refer to the domain name *Barikad.hu*.

determine how people perceive the outside world. As he explained, words activate a frame or a group of frames in the human mind. In this chapter, I show what frames were recently evoked by the British and Hungarian far-right in the context of China and what the underlying meanings of these frames are.

The chapter is divided into three parts. First, the representation of China by the British far-right will be discussed. Second, I introduce the constructions which the Hungarian far-right developed as a response to China's boom. Third, I interpret the results of the present analysis by critically comparing and contrasting the discourses on China by the two far-right groups.

2. The "other" as "threat": China in the discourse of the British far-right

2.1 Political background

This section focuses on the BNP's official website, the *Bnp.org.uk* which provides up-to-date materials about the policies and ideological standing of the party. The British National Party was established in 1982. Although this far-right party had been able to achieve only a limited electoral success for the past few decades, in recent times its position has strengthened. Importantly, in the elections for the European Parliament in 2009 the BNP won 6% of the votes and could send two delegates to the EP. Yet, the political significance of the BNP has remained relatively low compared to more mainstream British parties.

The BNP presents itself "as a defender of British way of life" (BBC 2010) and popularizes anti-immigration and anti-globalization agendas. Until 2001, the party had argued for the forced "repatriation" of all non-white people from the UK, while afterwards it campaigned for the "voluntary resettlement" of immigrants and British citizens of foreign descent (BBC 2010.). The party's current president, Nick Griffin faced court on racial hatred charges (BBC 2010.).

At the same time, under Griffin's leadership, which arose in 1999, the BNP's image has transformed in important regards due to his strategic efforts to mask the party's racist ideology (Copsey 2004). Accordingly, the contemporary discourse of the BNP may seem misleadingly 'moderate' at first glance (Richardson 2011). The comparison of BNP manifestos from 2005 and 2010 also showed that in terms of language use the BNP is "growing more sophisticated in its knowledge of techniques of disguising racial prejudice" (Edwards 2012, 256).

2.2 Overview

Since the BNP rarely discussed China in whole articles, by using the site's electronic archives, I explored every accessible text in which the PRC was mentioned on the party's webpage between 2011 and 2013. The interest of the BNP in China obviously increased in the analyzed period. China came up only in 13 articles in 2011, while 34 articles referred to the country in 2012 and the number climbed to 55 in 2013. Yet, in terms of the portrayal of the PRC, no significant change was observed. The representation of China was predominantly negative throughout the whole analyzed period.

Table 1. 1 Articles in which China was mentioned, *Bnp.org.uk* (2011–2013)

	2011	2012	2013
Total	13	34	55

It should also be stressed that besides the PRC, some of the relevant articles were also related to the Chinese diaspora in the UK. Similar to the immigration of other groups (Wood and Finlay 2008), Chinese immigration to the UK was presented by the BNP as a major threat for Britain. To reinforce this positioning, metaphors of "natural disasters" and "military invasion" were utilized in the texts. Such metaphors structure the discriminatory political and media discourses on immigration in other Western European countries as well (Reisigl, and Wodak 2001, 59). Immigrants from China and other countries were identified as a "flow" in one text ("Number of asylum seekers continues to rise" 21 October 2011). Another article stated that "We are being swamped by a tsunami of Chinese" ("Ying Tong Tiddle Eye Poh" 14 February 2013).

As we see, in the context of Chinese immigrants, plural pronominal forms were opposed (e.g., "we", "our", "us" versus "they", "them", "they"), sharpening a "self" vs. "other" division between British and Chinese in this way. This opposition was further reinforced when references involved derogatory terms: "Time to close our borders and stop these Chinese hordes from destroying our home" ("Ying Tong Tiddle Eye Poh" 14 February 2013).

A reference was made to "the Cantonese speaking Chinaman" and recent Chinese immigration was described as: "A new Mandarin speaking Chinese is knocking on our door" ("Ying Tong Tiddle Eye Poh" 14 February 2013). The role of the collective singular in discriminatory discourse was highlighted in various contexts (Langmuir 1990, 333; Reisigl and Wodak 2011, 57). The references to "the Chinaman" or to "a Chinese" implied that Chinese people lack individuality and all pose a threat to the UK.

2.3 The "intruder China"

The PRC was presented by the BNP's website in a univocally negative way too. Just as in the context of Chinese immigration, the "topos of danger or threat" was frequently applied regarding China. This topos, a common element in the various far-right discourses, was explained by Reisigl and Wodak (2001, 77) as follows: "If there are specific dangers and threats, one should do something against them". Although the threat-topos is indeed widely used by the different far-right parties, it is important to stress that this argumentation scheme also dominates the representation of China by mainstream politicians, press, and intellectuals in the US and Western Europe (Pan 2004; Barr 2011).

The texts on the BNP's website implied that China's growth is a challenge to Britain: "Most factories closed down and moved to China some time ago!" ("Survival of the British State", 8 January 2013). The image of the "China threat" was created in other realms too. In one piece, it was stressed that Europe is bombarded with "massive and unchecked food import from China" ("Movimento dei Forconi", 22 February 2012). It was argued that European industries struggle because their economies are overwhelmed with Chinese products. Regarding the London Olympics in 2012, one piece stressed that even national symbols of Britain are produced by the PRC: "Let's fly the China flag for Britain." ("Flying the flag for Britain…but which one?", 25 July 2012).

It was also argued that the PRC's growth, lacking environmental considerations, harms the whole world: "While we are trying to protect our own environment, our own corner of the world, big business is destroying the rest of the world" ("More concrete than you can shake a stick at", 9 February 2013). In this text, China was identified as an "ecological terrorist", evoking the sense of threat and danger in an environmental context.

China's economic success and richness were stressed as well, contrasted with the "misery" of English people, evoking a sense of "inferiority": "China, a country with almost 150 billionaires" ("Foreign aid", 22 March 2013), "We British are now paupers. These Chinese are dripping wealth we can only imagine" ("Ying Tong Tiddle Eye Poh", 14 February 2013). In the context of the "Chinese affluence" frame, "intrusion" was also evoked. Chinese were described as people who "buy up Britain", "steal the Nation from its indigenous peoples" ("Chinese Whispers", 24 October 2013).

As we see, the discourse of victimhood — which commonly emerges in the various far-right rhetoric (Reisigl and Wodak 2001, 74) — and used by the BNP as well (Edwards 2012) –was employed by the party to describe the relation between the two entities in question. Indeed, the British were described as the victims of the Chinese by the BNP: "Of course it is no benefit to the indigenous British to be exploited by unaccountable Chinese communists" ("Chinese Whispers", 24 October 2013). As the previous excerpt also demonstrates, the BNP often refers to "the indigenous British" instead of the British (Edwards 2012, 23). In China's context this identification evoked the threatening frame of colonization of the British by the Chinese.

2.4 The "Red China"

The references in the analyzed texts most often pointed to the communist and, therefore, oppressive character of the Chinese regime. The articles identified China as "communist China", "Marxist dictatorship", "Red China", "human rights abuse and torture capital of the world", "totalitarian society" ("Ying Tong Tiddle Eye Poh", 14 February 2013; "Nationalist Online" 7 January 2013; "Compulsory abortion, Reducing the National Debt the UKIP way!", 18 December 2012; "Communist takes over European presidency" 22 July 2012; "Shaping Society", 26 May 2013).

Yet, primarily it was not the international context in which the previous constructions emerged. The BNP press releases used China in the domestic UK context as a metaphor of dictatorship and oppression: "This sounds more like Red China than a democratic Britain" ("Compulsory abortion, reducing the national debt UKIP way!", 18 December 2012). The claim was frequently made that the political conditions in contemporary UK resemble those in China. Parallels were drawn between the state treatment of the British far-right media and the censored Chinese press: "In Britain, just as in China, publications that seek political reform are persecuted by the government" ("Nationalist Online", 4 January 2013).

Both the leaders of the UK and the EU were stigmatized by the BNP for being "Marxists". One piece associated the economic stagnation of Europe with the Marxism of the EU leaders due to which they allowed China to enter European markets: "These industrial economies [economies of Western Europe] were doing OK until the EU decided with their infinite wisdom and pro Marxist agenda that they wanted to help pollute this planet more and in turn they de-stabilized the Euro by opening up this lucrative market to the human rights abuse and torture capital of the world — China!" ("The Impending Euro Collapse", 30 December 2011).

While making such claims, the texts on the BNP's website also suggested that the UK should leave the European Union. However, the only major global power with the BNP could identify with was still Europe. Britain was primarily defined in the texts not as a Western but as a European power, as opposed to both the United States and China: "Unfortunately Europe is part of a globalized world. At the global level, it is competing with economies such as the United States or China" ("Europe on the edge of a precipice", 4 September 2012). As we see, the articles distanced Europe, and the UK within it, from the US and China equally.

3. The "other" as "brother": China in the discourse of the Hungarian far-right

3.1 Political background

Similarly to other former communist countries, Hungary's far-right entered the political arena after the transition to democracy in 1989, exploiting the opportunities offered by the new political order. Yet, it was not until the recent emergence of the political party Jobbik (*Jobbik* literally means "more right" and "better" at the same time) that this ideological camp could achieve significant influence in Hungarian politics.

Within a few years, Jobbik grew into a major political player in the late 2000s. The party made an electoral breakthrough in the European Parliament election in 2009, sending three delegates to the EP. A year later, in the Hungarian parliamentary elections, Jobbik received almost 17 percent of the votes, becoming the third largest political party in Hungary, occupying 47 seats (12 per cent of the total) in the national assembly. In the parliamentary elections in 2014, *Jobbik* increased its share of vote to 21 percent, becoming the second most popular party in Hungary.

Along with other structural factors, the deepening economic problems could form the background for the rapid emergence of the party. Jobbik's popularity began to grow spectacularly after the outbreak of the global financial crisis in 2008 which hit Hungary severely. The party combined a discriminatory — anti-Roma, anti-Semitic, anti-Israel, and anti-gay — nationalist political rhetoric with a harsh anti-globalization and anti-Western agenda, demanding Hungary's breakup with the major financial, political and military institutions of the West (e.g., the IMF, the EU, NATO). Jobbik also argued that Hungary should replace the West in terms of geostrategic orientation and, instead, build up a new strategic relationship with Eastern powers, including China.

In order to boost its popularity, Jobbik relied heavily on the media. This section of the article explores one of the major outlets which played a prominent role in the promotion of the party's agenda, *Barikad.hu* [Barricade.hu]. This far-right online portal (running currently under the name *Alfahir.hu*) provides up-to-date news and analyses about Hungarian and international politics.

3.2 Overview

Between 2010 and 2012 *Barikad.hu* wrote frequently about China (Table 2.1). The number of the published news stories steadily grew within the analyzed period: 48 were provided in 2010, 144 in 2011 and 184 in 2012. A similar trend can be observed in the case of editorials, op-eds and interviews: 13 were published in 2010,

26 in 2011, and 17 in 2012. Additionally, in 2011 *Barikad.hu* published a series of articles about Hun Hungarians who migrated from Asia to Europe in ancient times, referring in these to China too. 38 such pieces appeared in 2011 and another 18 pieces about Huns were published on the website in 2012.

Table 2. 1 Distribution of articles related to China by genres, *Barikad.hu* (2010–2012)

	2010	2011	2012
News stories	48	144	184
Editorials, op-eds, interviews	13	26	17
Articles about Hun history in China	0	38	18
Total	61	208	219

The portrayal of China by *Barikad.hu* between 2010 and 2012 can be characterized as positive (Table 2.2 and Table 2.3). Only 10 out of 48 in 2010, 12 out of 144 in 2011 and 11 out 184 news stories in 2012 covered problematic issues in connection with China. All the other articles focused on topics which can be characterized as neutral or positive. As regards editorials, op-eds and interviews, in 2010, only 2 out of 13 pieces were negative in their attitude towards the PRC. Within the period considered the largest number of op-eds, editorials and interviews, 26, appeared on the website in 2011, yet, in the same year virtually no article mentioned anything negative in connection to China. And in 2012 only 1 out of 17 articles articulated some criticism (Table 2.3).

Table 2. 2 Distribution of news stories that could contribute to a negative image of China, *Barikad.hu* (2010–2012)

	2010	2011	2012
Negative news	10	12	11
Neutral/positive news	38	122	173
Total	48	144	184

Table 2. 3 Distribution of op-eds, editorials and interviews on China by attitude, *Barikad.hu* (2010–2012)

	2010	2011	2012
Positive attitude	11	26	16
Neutral attitude	0	0	0
Negative attitude	2	0	1
Total	13	26	17

3.3 The "nominally communist China"

In 2010, two extensive interviews were published on Barikad.hu with party leaders of Jobbik who attempted to clear China's image from its "red" connotations. Evoking anti-Western and anti-Semitic sentiments, the president of the party, Gábor Vona argued that "Otherwise by today, Chinese communism has totally transformed. Nowadays I would rather describe China as a state-capitalist system with whom I seek contact much more happily than with its globalist and Zionist competitors"[2] ("Vona Gábor: Nem egy puhuló párt képét mutatjuk", 16 November 2010). Another politician of Jobbik, responsible for the party's foreign policy, Márton Gyöngyösi was asked in an interview: "Do you think that any sane Chinese would care that he lives in a country which is nominally communist?"[3] ("Új magyar külpolitika kell: arccal a Kelet felé! — Interjú Gyöngyösi Mártonnal" [New Hungarian foreign policy is needed: face the East! — Interview with Márton Gyöngyösi] 20 May 2010).

The frame of "nominal communism" was evoked in the context of China in other articles of *Barikad.hu* as well. For instance, in an editorial it was argued that "communist China actually sent Marxists dogmas to the garbage heap of history, creating such an effective capitalist system that it can beat main capitalist countries of the world one by one"[4] ("Nagy a zűrzavar — semmi sincs rendben" [There is a big chaos, nothing is all right] 4 October 2012).

As the last excerpt illustrates, the Chinese regime was presented quite positively by *Barikad.hu*. The PRC was regularly compared to the West — both to the European Union and the United States — and it was commonly suggested that China is more successful than these entities. In this regard, China was also positioned as a role model for Hungary, representing a hope that a "non-Western" way of prosperity can indeed be achieved.

2. The orgininal Hungarian excerpts:
"Egyébként a kínai kommunizmus mára teljesen átalakult. Ma már inkább államkapitalista rendszernek nevezném Kínát, amellyel sokkal szívesebben keresek kapcsolatot, mint globalista és cionista versenytársaival."

3. "Ön szerint érdekli bármelyik épp-elméjű kínait az, hogy nevében kommunista államban él?"

4. "...a kommunista Kína pedig gyakorlatilag a történelem szemétdombjára dobta a marxi dogmákat, olyan hatékony kapitalista rendszert hozva létre, hogy azzal a világ fő kapitalista országait győzi le egymás után."

3.4 The "role-model China"

In the first months of 2010, Márton Gyöngyösi and another leading politician of Jobbik published three op-eds on *Barikad.hu* which urged an "Eastern turn" for Hungary ("Stratégiai fordulat Kelet felé" [Strategic turn towards East] 25 January, 1 February, 9 February). They described the West as an "aging" ("elöregedő") and "decadent" ("dekadens") power with "lopsided identity and cohesion" ("identitásában és belső kohéziójában megroggyant"). In contrast the East, including China, was presented by the authors as an entity which is "getting muscular" ("egyre izmosodó") and "representing an economic and demographic advantage" ("gazdasági, demográfiai fölényt képviselő").

Such oppositions appeared frequently in the articles of *Barikad.hu*. References were made to the "declining West" ("hanyatló Nyugat") and the "dying West" ("halódó Nyugat") versus the "emerging giant" ("emelkedő óriás") as well as to the "mouse" West versus the "elephant" China ("A Nyugat és Kína erkölcse" ["The morality of the West and China"] 29 January 2011; "Az egér és az elefánt" [The mouse and the elephant] 26 July 2011). Besides, the representation of the PRC often combined common positive stereotypes of "orientalism" — I use this term in the way Said (1978) famously elaborated it — with naïve propagandistic clichés. In a similar fashion, the outlet proposed derogatory occidentalist stereotypes.

For example, "the self-destructive individualism, the bloody political correctness of the West" was compared with "eternal basic values of Confucian ethics, the respect towards tradition and hierarchy, the love of family and the appreciation of work"[5] in the East ("A magyar sajtó Kína-vitája" [China-debate in the Hungarian Press] 2011 June 30). Evoking also stereotypes of individualism versus collectivism, an anti-gay article praised the plan to make support of elderly parents legally obligate in China "for putting into practice the ideas of great scholars of the antique Chinese world and Confucius"[6] ("A Nyugat és Kína erkölcse" ["The morality of the West and China"] 29 January 2011).

Leaders of the Chinese Communist Party and post-communist Hungary were also opposed. In one piece the "selfishness" and the "exploitative character" of Hungarian left-liberal government were contrasted with the "healthy nationalism" of Chinese leaders "whose one goal is to make Chinese people proud of their

5. "A nyugati, önpusztító individualizmus és gyilkos politikai korrektség, a cionista érdekek mindenek fölött történő érvényesítésével áll szemben a konfuciánus etika olyan örök alapértékei, mint a hagyományok és a hierarchia tisztelete, a család szeretete, a munka megbecsülése."

6. "Kínában a kormány az elmúlt években egyre inkább fedezi fel az antik kínai világ nagy tudósának, Konfúciusznak a tanait és alkalmazza a gyakorlatban… Ma nyugati országokban a bíróságok azzal foglalkoznak, hogy minél jobban védjék a homoszexuálisok jogait…"

country"[7] ("Nyugalom! Kína nem Egyiptom" [Don't worry: China is not Egypt] 17 February 2011). Leaders of the European Union were also contrasted to Chinese politicians for being "incomprehensible, bureaucratic and stubborn" ("érthetetlen, bürokratikus, és önfejű") ("Kínai pofon" [Chinese smack] 22 September 2012). Similarly, several articles compared Chinese and US politicians. One journalist argued that while US leaders have law degrees, Chinese politicians studied engineering and therefore, unlike their American counterparts, "they always focus on the simplest and fastest solutions"[8] ("Sárga veszedelem? Attól függ kinek" [Yellow peril? Depends for who] 18 January 2011).

Moreover, China's model of market-authoritarianism was also positively contrasted with Western liberal democracy that was identified by *Barikad.hu* as "facade-democracy" ("látszatdemokrácia") ("Hu és Palin. Te kit választanál?" [Hu and Palin. Who would you choose?] 12 July 2011). Journalists praised the Chinese regime for its economic achievements: "They [the Chinese leadership] lift hundreds and hundreds of millions from poverty yearly"[9] ("Nyugalom! Kína nem Egyiptom" [Don't worry: China is not Egypt] 17 February 2011). The boom of China was also compared to the economic stagnation of the West in political terms: "To the West's sadness, Chinese autocracy is popular. It is very popular. So much so, that in China significantly more people support the existing regime instead of democracy of which daily functioning and outcomes they see in America where — just like here [in Hungary] — hundreds of thousands lose their homes and end up under highway bridges"[10] ('Nyugalom! Kína nem Egyiptom' [Don't worry: China is not Egypt] 17 February 2011).

Besides promoting China's model of development versus Western liberal democracy *Barikad.hu* also claimed that unlike the West, China does not interfere with other countries' internal affairs. *Barikad.hu* argued that under the tutelage of China, Hungary could achieve a greater level of national independence.

---

7. "...a kínai vezetés első számú célja nem gyurcsányista, azaz nem a saját és környezetének meggazdagodása a nép kizsigerelése révén ... egészséges nacionalizmusuk egyik célja, hogy Kína népe büszke lehessen országára."

8. "...egy problémánál elsősorban a lehető legegyszerűbb és leggyorsabb megoldásra összpontosítanak."

9. "Évente emelnek ki száz és száz milliókat a szegénységből..."

10. "A Nyugat bánatára a kínai autokrácia népszerű. Nagyon népszerű. Olyannyira, hogy Kínában jóval több híve van a fennálló rendszernek, mint a demokráciának, amelynek napi működését és annak eredményeit láthatják Amerikában is, ahol — hasonlóan hozzánk — emberek százezrei vesztik el házukat és költöznek az autópályák felüljárói alá."

3.5 The "non-interfering China"

China's foreign policy of non-interference was promoted by *Barikad.hu*. It was highlighted that the US has to compete "with a China led by hydrograph President Hu Jintao whose modesty is fabulous… Hu's philosophy includes the non-interference with other countries' affairs and the peaceful, non-military resolution of conflicts"[11] ("Hu és Palin. Te kit választanál?" [Hu and Palin. Who would you chose?] 12 July 2011). China's policy of non-interference was also often contrasted with the West's "dictatorial attitude". To highlight Western disrespect of sovereignty, one editorial used the example of English language newspapers which "are filled with different forms of "must" (has to, must, should, should have to, need to) in a way that the imperative forms apply to states and countries that are outside of the Western sphere"[12] ("Hé, Nyugat! Elég a "kell"-ből!" [Hey, West! It is enough of "must"] 7 February 2011). The journalist of the piece also asked: "When — just to mention one counter-example — had the English language Chinese newspapers written about the "musts" of non-Chinese governments? Never, because China does not interfere with sovereign countries' issues".[13]

The argument was often made that, in turn for China's respect towards the sovereignty of other countries, Hungary should remain silent regarding those issues which are considered sensitive by the Chinese government. One editorial warned that Hungary should not behave as a "barking dog" ("csahos kutya") of the West ("Így kell Kínába utazni: Belgium példát mutat" [How to visit China: Belgium sets an example] 21 October 2011).

Western concerns about human rights issues in China were described as "insincere" and "self-serving". To highlight this, cases of Tibet and Palestine were contrasted by the anti-Israel *Barikad.hu*. For example, one editorial highlighted that although the Hungarian right-wing government condemned China because of Tibet, "at same time the great defenders of right forgot to stand up for the rights of Palestinians although even the UN thinks that they are oppressed by an invad-

11. "Azzal a Kínával, amelyet a vízmérnök végzettségű Hu Csin-tao elnök vezeti, akinek szerénysége közmondásos. Még soha nem adott senkinek interjút. … Hu filozófiája a más országok belügyeibe való be nem avatkozás és a vitás kérdések békés, nem katonai úton történő megoldása."

12. "… a szövegben — és ez főként az angolszász lapokra vonatkozik — hemzsegnek a „kell" (has to, must, should, should have to, needs to) legkülönbözőbb formái úgy, hogy a parancsoló és felszólító mód a nyugati szférán kívül fekvő államokra és politikusokra vonatkozik."

13. "Vajon — hogy csak egyetlen ellenpéldát idézzünk — az angol nyelvű kínai lapok mikor írták azt, hogy a nem kínai kormányoknak mit „kell" tenniük? Soha, mert Kína nem avatkozik be szuverén országok belügyeibe."

ing power"[14] ("Orbán kínai látogatásával történelmet ír a Jobbik" [Orbán's visit to China is a historic achievement for Jobbik] 2 November 2010).

As we see, *Barikad.hu* provided several arguments explaining why Hungary should view China and not the West as a strategic ally. Importantly, besides economic and geopolitical considerations, the necessity of co-operation was proposed in ethnic terms too. *Barikad.hu* presented the Hungarian State as opposed to the West, as an Eastern nation with "Eastern values", engaging in heavy "self-orientalization" (Ong 1999).

3.6 "Sibling China"

The idea that Hungarians and Chinese are ethnically related was elaborated by the outlet on the grounds of "Turanism", an ideology that became influential at the beginning of the 20th century amongst Hungarian nationalist movements. The term "Turanian" was introduced in the 19th century by the German linguist Max Müller who believed that there is a non-Indo-European and non-Semitic family of languages, the "Turanian", spoken by populations of Southeast Europe, Turkey, Iran and Central Asia. Although Müller's theory was later refuted by linguists, the concept of "Turanism" lived on as a geopolitical category explored by linguists and ethnographers. "Thanks to the resulting Turanism, Hungarian research on Tibet could assume a leading role and Hungarian orientalists remain authoritative in their field" (Ungváry 2010, para 1).

However, "Turanism" also transformed into a political category, being frequently used by Hungarian nationalists and far-right actors in the first half of the 20th century to distance Hungary from the West. Following this tradition, today Jobbik's whole foreign policy is still embedded in the ideology of "Turanism". Jobbik argues that Hungary should leave the European Union and form a "new Turanian alliance" with Central Asian states (Ungváry 2010, para 8) and advocates co-operation with Turkey and Iran.

On the grounds of "Turanism", the Hungarian far-right traditionally rejects the scientifically valid linguistic theory about the Finno-Ugric origin of Hungarians. In the late 2000s, Jobbik still demanded the revision of the Finno-Ugric linguistic theory from the Hungarian Academy of Sciences. The party also backed the civic organization of the so-called Turanian "tribal conventions" in rural Hungary in 2008, 2010 and 2012. According to the organizers, in the recent years, these were attended by circa 100,000 local and international visitors (Magyar-Turán Alapítvány, n.d.).

14. "… miközben a nagy jogvédők elfeledettek kiállni a palesztinok jogai mellett, holott őket az ENSZ szerint is egy megszálló hatalom nyomorgatja."

Although "Turanism" originally means ethnic and cultural affinity between Hungarians and the Turkic, Tibetan, Japanese, and Korean people, Jobbik uses the concept more broadly as "Asianness". Accordingly, the party expended the ideology of "Turanism" to China as well, implying that there is ethnic kinship between Hungarians and Chinese too.

Accordingly, in the articles published by *Barikad.hu* about China, Hungarians were identified as the "only nation in Europe of Asian origin" ("Európa egyetlen ázsiai eredetű népe") whom Asian people consider as "friend and sibling" ("barát és testvér") ("Stratégiai fordulat Kelet felé — 3. rész" 9 February 2010). In an interview with the president of Jobbik, the Europeanness of Hungarians was presented as a question of location, as opposed to their Asian roots: "Hungary has a double identity. Because of its geographical position it is a European nation but we shall know that its roots can be found deep in the East, we are an Eastern nation"[15] ("A hazámban szeressenek — ne Brüsszelben!" [I should be loved in my home country not in Brussels!] 7 March 2010).

Additionally, in 2011, a series of articles were published by *Barikad.hu* about the Chinese roots of Hun Hungarians. No less than 38 such pieces appeared in 2011 and another 18 pieces about Huns were published on the website in 2012. The articles about the Huns in China not only attempted to provide further evidence to support the idea of Hungarians' Hun ancestry, but, importantly, also suggested that there exists a kinship between Hungarians and Chinese. Therefore, the pieces about the Huns could reinforce the positive image of China which was primarily created by news stories, editorials and interviews.

4. Summary

In this chapter, I compared and contrasted the images of China that were created by the British and Hungarian far-right. In the case of the UK, I studied all relevant and accessible articles on the official website of the BNP between 2011 and 2013. In the case of Hungary, I analyzed the accessible articles that were published by the major online portal of the Hungarian far-right, *Barikad.hu*, between 2010 and 2013. I explored references, metaphors, argumentation schemes and frames which appeared in the context of China. My results indicate that the Hungarian and the British far-right constructed fundamentally different images of China (Table 3.1).

First, the BNP's website reinforced the image of "Red China", while in the articles of the Hungarian online portal, the PRC was presented as a "nominally

15. "Magyarország kettős identitással rendelkezik. Földrajzi helyzetéből adódóan európai nemzet, de tudni kell, hogy a gyökerei mélyen keleten találhatóak, keleti nép vagyunk."

communist" country. In the BNP's texts, China functioned as a metaphor of dictatorship and oppression in the domestic UK context and was identified as a communist country. *Barikad.hu* attempted to position China as a state where communism lost its significance.

Second, the BNP's website was highly critical of the Chinese regime. Britain was identified by the BNP as a European power, opposed to both the United States and China. At the same time, *Barikad.hu* portrayed China's system of market-authoritarianism as a non-Western and anti-Western role model for Hungary. The PRC was regularly opposed to the West by *Barikad.hu* — both to the European Union and the United States — suggesting that China is more successful than these entities.

Third, the BNP's website portrayed China as a "dangerous intruder" into English markets and as a potential colonizer who constitutes a threat to the UK. Conversely, the online portal of the Hungarian far-right argued that Hungary should view China as a strategic partner. *Barikad.hu* claimed that only with the help of China can Hungary resist the West.

Fourth, on the BNP's webpage, Chinese people appeared to be "hostile aliens". The BNP's website identified Chinese as threatening "others" and presented the UK as a European power. In the Hungarian far-right press, kinship, i.e. racial relations, were discussed and China was positioned positively as a "sibling". *Barikad.hu* also identified the Hungarian State as an Eastern nation.

5. Conclusions

The sharp differences in the portrayal of China by the British and Hungarian far-right most likely mirror the distinct identities and political interests of the two parties. Despite the fact that they belong to the same political party family and that they are actual political allies, the British National Party and the Hungarian Jobbik view China fundamentally differently.

Barikad.hu is the mouthpiece of a far-right party which, on the one hand, wants to establish close ties with the PRC and, on the other hand, given its own political

Table 3. 1 Images of China constructed by *Barikad.hu* (2010–2012) and *Bnp.org.uk* (2011–2013)

	British Far-Right Media	**Hungarian Far-Right Media**
Representation of China	*"communist"* *"negative example"* *"dangerous intruder"*	*"nominally communist"* *"role model"* *"strategic partner"*
Presentation of Chinese	*"threatening aliens"*	*"siblings"*

profile, rejects the West. Jobbik may also sympathize with China's combination of economic development and authoritarian political system.

In 2010, Jobbik came up with the strategic agenda to position the PRC as major ally of Hungary. This idea could meet widespread resistance among far-right supporters. First, criticism of the ancient regime and harsh anti-communism had been important elements in the ideological universe of Hungarian far-right publics, in which strategic co-operation with a communist power hardly fits. Second, extreme nationalism is a common characteristic of far-right movements and the Hungarian far-right is no exception. Accordingly, it rejects any "foreign interference" into domestic affairs by "global players". Third, the Hungarian far-right, just as the far-right in general, is driven by xenophobia, and thus, views other ethnic groups, nations and civilizations with hostility.

In order to counter these long-standing far-right discourses and strategically consolidate China's image in the eyes of its supporters, the articles of *Barikad.hu* stressed that today's China is only a nominally communist county. Moreover, *Jobbik*'s online media promoted China's market-authoritarian system, versus Western neo-liberalism, as a true role-model for Hungary. China and the West were also opposed to clear up the fear of "Chinese intrusion". *Barikad.hu* suggested that with the help of China, Hungary can "regain its independence from the West". Finally, to reduce xenophobic sentiments, the West and Hungary were opposed in racial terms as well. Myths of Huns who migrated from Asia to Europe in ancient times were evoked. This way it was implied by *Barikad.hu* and Jobbik's politicians that, unlike with Western people, Hungarians are racially related to the Chinese and therefore China should be viewed by them as a "brother" nation.

The British National Party's website presents the official party line. Unlike *Jobbik*, the BNP does not attempt to identify itself with any major political or ethnic/racial entity other than the UK, regardless of whether it is Western or Eastern. The party, to a lesser or greater degree, rejects all key global players, including the EU, the US, and China. As the "defense of British interests" is stressed in the party's rhetoric, it portrayed the growing global significance of China as a threat to the UK. China embodied various threats in the BNP's discourse, including an "economic threat" as well as an "environmental threat". In addition, since opposing immigration is a crucial element in the party's program, China was also presented by the BNP as a country from which immigrants "intrude" on Britain.

The BNP also used China for the reinforcement of its own image. While the party presents itself as a "defender of national interests", the politicians of the EU and the UK are positioned by the BNP as "traitors" who serve Chinese interests instead of national interests. In addition, China was used by BNP for strategic stigmatization of mainstream British political elites as "reds" and "oppressors". The way in which BNP used China as a metaphor of oppression in a domestic context supports the observation of Atton: "The BNP is anti-multicultural, anti-equality and anti-freedom, yet its discourse uses the tropes of multiculturalism, equality and freedom to maintain an ideological space where racism and repression may appear natural and commonsensical" (2006, 586).

The Hungarian Jobbik party uses the same tropes of multiculturalism, equality, and freedom in the context of the West rather than the Chinese context. The West is presented by the Hungarian far-right as a "dictator", "intruder", and "colonizer". China is praised on the same grounds for not interfering with other countries' affairs. Although both parties describe the democratically elected governments of their home countries as "oppressors", the role of China in this positioning is distinct in the two cases. The BNP suggests that the political systems of Britain and China are actually similar. Conversely, Jobbik contrasts Hungarian and Chinese politicians — as well as Western and Chinese politicians —, praising the previous and bashing the latter.

The findings of this research highlight that the contemporary European far-right is indeed characterized by ideological diversity. It also seems that the divergence in question can be better observed if the "othering" strategies of the far-right parties are explored and contrasted in an international, rather than a domestic context. Parties of the far-right in Europe discriminate minority communities at home by introducing similar — racist and exclusionary — ideologies and rhetoric. However, the same parallelism cannot necessarily be observed when geopolitical issues, "global others", are considered.

This chapter reinforces the idea that there are ideological cleavages between the far-right parties of Eastern and Western Europe. The comparison of the British and Hungarian far-right discourses on the booming China shows that right-wing extremists in Europe may belong to the same party family, can even form political alliances, but primarily view the world through their own distinct prisms. Yet, from the analysis of two cases, only limited conclusions can be drawn. Further research, focused on different parties, should explore the general relevance of the East-West division in the world of the European far-right. Besides China, the representation of other global powers (e.g., the US, the EU) by various far-right parties could be compared and contrasted to map how widespread the ideological gaps in question are. Last but not least, it would be important to study whether similar divisions exist not only between, but also within, the circles of Eastern and the Western European far-right parties.

Acknowledgement

The first draft of this chapter was presented at the annual conference of the International Association for Media and Communication Research, Dublin, Ireland, June 25–29, 2013.

References

AENM. 2009. "Political Declaration." September 9. http://aemn.eu/political-declaration/ [accessed 16 February 2014].

Atton, Chris. 2006. "Far-Right Media on the Internet: Culture, Discourse and Power." *New Media & Society* 8:573–587. doi:10.1177/1461444806065653

Barr, Michael. 2011. *Who's Afraid of China? The Challenge of Chinese Soft Power*. London and New York: Zed Books.

Bársony, Fanni, Gyenge Zsuzsanna, and Ádám Kovács. 2011. "Kit érdekelnek a programok? A Jobbik kisebbségképe és annak médiareprezentációja a 2010-es országgyűlési választások kampányidőszakában" [Who Cares about Programs? Jobbik's Image of Minorities and Its Media Representation during the 2010 Parliamentary Election Campaign]. *Médiakutató*, Spring. http://www.mediakutato.hu/cikk/2011_01_tavasz/05_jobbik_kissebsegkepe [accessed 17 February 2014].

BBC. 2010. "Profile: British National Party." March 25. http://news.bbc.co.uk/2/hi/uk_news/politics/election_2010/8535920.stm (accessed 16 February 2014).

BNP. 2013. "Youth Leadership Training — A weekend in Hungary." October 21. http://www.bnp.org.uk/news/national/youth-leadership-training-weekend-hungary [accessed 16 February 2014].

Copsey, Nigel. 2004. *Contemporary British Fascism. The British National Party and the Quest for Legitimacy*. New York: Palgrave McMillan.

Edwards, Geraint O. 2012. "A Comparative Discourse Analysis of the Construction of 'In-Groups' in the 2005 and 2010 Manifestos of the British National Party." *Discourse & Society* 23(3):245–258. doi:10.1177/0957926511433477

Fieschi, Catherine. 2000. "European Institutions: The Far-Right and Illiberal Politics in Liberal Context." *Parliamentary Affairs* 53(3):517–531. doi:10.1093/pa/53.3.517

Halper, Stefan. 2010. *The Beijing Consensus. How China's Authoritarian Model will Dominate the Twenty-First Century*. New York: Basic Books.

Jacques, Martin. 2009. *When China Rules the World. The Rise of the Middle Kingdom and the End of the Western World*. London: Allen Lane.

Kovács, András, and Anna Szilágyi. 2013. "Variations on a Theme: The Jewish 'Other' in Old and New Antisemitic Media Discourses in Hungary in the 1940s and 2011." In *Analysing Fascist Discourse, European Fascism in Talk and Text*, edited by Ruth Wodak and John E. Richardson, 203–227. New York: Routledge.

Krzyzanowski, Michal, and Ruth Wodak. 2009. *The Politics of Exclusion. Debating Migration in Austria*. New Brunswick, New Jersey: Transaction Publishers.

Kynge, James. 2006. *China Shakes the World. The Rise of a Hungry Nation*. London and New York: Weidenfeld and Nicolson.

Lakoff, George. 2004. *Don't Think of an Elephant! Know your Values and Frame the Debate: The Essential Guide for Progressives*. White River Junction, Vt.: Chelsea Green.

Langmuir, Gavin I. 1990. *Toward a Definition of Antisemitism*. Berkley: University of California Press. doi:10.1515/9783110858914.86

Lee, Chin-Chuan, Joseph Man Chan, Zhongdang Pan, and Clement Y. K. So. 2002. *Global Media Spectacle. News War over Hong Kong*. Hong Kong: Hong Kong University Press.

Magyar-Turán Alapítvány. n.d. "Mi a a Kurul-Táj?" http://kurultaj.hu/kurultaj/ (accessed 4 September 2014).

Minkenberg, Michael. 2011. "The Radical Right in Europe Today: Trends and Patterns in East and West." In *Is Europe on the "Right" Path? Right-Wing Extremism and Right-Wing Populism in Europe*, edited by Nora Langenbacher and Britta Schellenberg, 37–55. Berlin: Friedrich-Ebert-Stiftung.

Neumann, Iver B. 1999. *Uses of the Other. "The East" in European Identity Formation*. Minneapolis: University of Minnesota Press.

OECD. 2012. "Looking to 2060: A Global Vision of Long-Term Growth." OECD Economics Department Policy Note, No. 15. http://www.oecd.org/economy/outlook/2060policynote.pdf [accessed 16 February 2014].

Ong, Aihwa. 1999. *Flexible Citizenship: The Cultural Logics of Transnationality*. Durham: Duke University Press.

Pan, Chengxin. 2004. "The 'China Threat' in American Self-Imagination: The Discursive Construction of Other as Power Politics." *Alternatives: Global, Local, Political* 29(3):305–331. http://www.jstor.org/discover/40645119?sid=21105021436911&uid=4&uid=2134&uid=3738216&uid=70&uid=2

Reisigl, Martin, and Ruth Wodak. 2001. *Discourse and Discrimination, Rhetorics of Racism and Antisemitism*. London and New York: Routledge.

Richardson, John E. 2011. "Race and Racial Difference: The Surface and Depth of BNP Ideology." In *British National Party — Contemporary perspectives*, edited by Nigel Copsey and Graham Macklin, 38–61. Abingdon, Oxon and New York: Routledge.

Said, Edward W. 1978. *Orientalism*. New York: Pantheon Books.

Said, Edward W. 1981. *Covering Islam. How the Media and the Experts Determine How We See the Rest of the World*. London: Routledge & Kegan Paul.

Teed, Paul. 2011. "'I'm no Nazi,' says BNP Candidate Snapped at Far Right Concert." *Your Local Guardian*, August 5. http://www.yourlocalguardian.co.uk/news/local/richmondnews/9180961._I_m_no_Nazi___says_BNP_candidate_snapped_at_far_right_concert/ [accessed 16 February 2014].

Ungváry, Krisztián. 2010. "Turanism: The 'New' Ideology of the Far Right." February 5. *The Budapest Times*. http://budapesttimes.hu/2012/02/05/turanism-the-new-ideology-of-the-far-right/ [accessed 19 February 2014].

Wilson, Robin, and Paul Hainsworth. 2012. "Far-Right Parties and Discourse in Europe: A Challenge for our Times." Brussels: European Network against Racism.

Wood C., and W. M. L. Finlay. 2008. "British National Party Representations of Muslims in the Month after the London Bombings: Homogeneity, Threat, and the Conspiracy Tradition." *British Journal of Social Psychology* 47:707–726. doi:10.1348/014466607X264103

Political crisis and the rise of the far right in Greece

Racism, nationalism, authoritarianism and conservatism in the discourse of Golden Dawn

Panagiotis Sotiris
University of the Aegean

The electoral rise of Golden Dawn from obscurity to parliamentary representation has drawn attention to its particular neo-fascist discourse. In sharp contrast to the tendency of most far-right movements in Europe to present themselves as being part of the political mainstream, Golden Dawn has never disavowed its openly neo-Nazi references. Its political and ideological discourse combines extreme racism, nationalism and authoritarianism along with traditional conservative positions in favour of traditional family roles and values and the Greek Orthodox Church. The aim of this chapter is twofold: on the one hand to situate the ideology and discourse of Golden Dawn in a conjuncture of economic and social crisis, a crisis of the project of European Integration, and examine it as part of a broader authoritarian post-democratic and post-hegemonic transformation of the State in contemporary capitalism; on the other hand to criticize the position suggested recently that Golden Dawn was also the result of the supposedly "national-populist" discourse of the anti-austerity movement. On the contrary, we will insist on the opposition between the discourses and practices of Golden Dawn and the anti-austerity movement in Greece.

Keywords: Golden Dawn, far-right, racist discourse, nationalism, anti-austerity protests, political crisis, Greece.

1. Introduction

On the night of September 18th 2013, in a working class borough near Piraeus, a member of the local Golden Dawn chapter murdered Pavlos Fyssas, a 34-year-old rapper. It was not the first murder by a Golden Dawn member or supporter, the neo-fascist organization having a long history of violent attacks (Psarras 2012;

DOI 10.1075/bct.93.08sot

Xenakis 2012). Golden Dawn has always targeted left-wing militants. In June 1998, a group of Golden Dawn members attacked three left-wing militants nearly killing one of them. Antonios Androutsopoulos, Golden Dawn second in command at the time, was condemned and imprisoned for this attack. Moreover, just a few days before Fyssas' murder Golden Dawn violently attacked and injured a group of Communist Party members.

However, it was the first time, after its impressive electoral rise in the 2012 elections, when it rose from obscurity to being an important political force, that Greek society fully realized the violence of this political organization. On September 28, 2013, a process of judicial investigation against Golden Dawn as a criminal organization was opened and its leadership was arrested and charged. However, despite this judicial process and the fact that a large part of Golden Dawn's leadership remains in custody awaiting trial, the electoral influence of Golden Dawn increased in the combined European Parliament and local elections in May 2014. In what follows, I will discuss the political discourse of Golden Dawn in light of the evolving social and political situation in Greece, the intensification of social and political antagonism and the deepening of social and political crisis.

2. Theoretical framework — methodology.

In terms of theoretical framework, I will argue for a Marxist orientation inspired by Gramsci and Althusser (Gramsci 1971; Althusser 2014), which treats social and political reality in terms of conflicting hegemonic strategies and theorizes discourses as ideologically contested terrains, traversed by class antagonisms and power strategies, reflecting in their unavoidably contradictory character the changing balance of class forces. In such a conception, language and discursive practices are historical, social and political phenomena and forms of social practice (Pêcheux 1982; Lecercle 2006). Such an approach is compatible with more critical approaches to discourse analysis that attempt to situate discourse at the intersection of language, power, and ideology (Fairclough 1989, 1995; Wodak and Meyer 2001; Weiss and Wodak 2003).

In terms of methodology, a selection of Golden Dawn's position texts, either party texts or individual contributions on the party program, ideology and specific political questions are analyzed. These texts offer an overview of the nodal concepts and discursive practices that delineate the ideology of Golden Dawn. These include three major policy documents (Golden Dawn 2012a; Golden Dawn 2012b; Ios 2013), that offer the general ideological outlook of Golden Dawn and its major political positions, plus a series of articles from Golden Dawn's websites on subjects such as globalization, the Greek crisis, racism, and the role of women in society.

In terms of secondary references to the discourse of Golden Dawn, I also make use of recently published literature on Golden Dawn (Psarras 2012; Chasapopoulos 2013; Papaioannou 2013), which includes extended references to political texts, declarations and interventions by Golden Dawn. I also rely on specific discourse analytic studies (e.g., Paraskeva-Veloudoyanni 2013 on speeches by Golden Dawn's leader N. Michaloliakos). However, since my background is in social theory and political philosophy, my approach is not quantitative or statistic, but qualitative. (The texts by Golden Dawn are used in a selective and indicative manner), as examples. My aim is to bring forward and highlight the main ideological conceptions and metaphors underlying the political discourse of Golden Dawn, based upon my theoretical choice to view the rise of Golden Dawn as the rise of a neo-fascist party in a very particular historical conjuncture of acute social and political crisis. However, I believe that my approach is within the contours of the broader interdisciplinary and multidisciplinary character of discourse analysis (van Dijk 1991, 1997). I attempt to situate the analysis of the discourse of Golden Dawn in the broader context of a landslide change in relations of political representation that shattered the post-1974 Greek party system and of an evolving crisis of hegemony that fuelled not only the Left, but also this particular version of the Far-Right.

Moreover, the main aim of this chapter is not simply to bring forward the main elements of Golden Dawn's discourse, but also, on a meta-analytical level, to discuss and critique the recent positions that have argued that Golden Dawn emerged from the context of protest movements in Greece (Frangoudaki 2013; Pantazopoulos 2013). In particular, we want to criticize as erroneous the position that the rise of Golden Dawn was fuelled by the supposed "nationalist" and "populist" elements in the discourse and ideology of recent protest movements in Greece. In contrast, we argue that the "national" and "popular" elements in the discourse and ideology of protest movements in Greece are democratic and egalitarian in nature, expressing a demand for justice and popular sovereignty.

3. The discourse(s) of Golden Dawn

In what follows, we attempt to examine some important aspects of the discourse of Golden Dawn, its main elements, and the basic discursive strategies we can discern in the texts and public interventions from the part of Golden Dawn cadre.

3.1 The core ideology of Golden Dawn: National Socialism

Golden Dawn, in sharp contrast to other Far-Right formations in Europe that despite their historic links to neo-fascism have presented themselves as right-wing conservative movements that accept the basic tenets and institutional arrangements of liberal democracy (Georgiadou 2008; Hainsworth 2008), has from the beginning been a neo-Nazi and neo-fascist party. The core ideology of Golden Dawn is openly neo-Nazi, in the sense that it explicitly refers to national-socialist ideology and the legacy of Nazi Germany. Chr. Pappas, a Golden Dawn member of the Greek parliament currently on trial, in 1983 openly referred to Golden Dawn's membership as "We National-Socialists" and vowed to the final victory that would lead to the "national-socialist cosmogony" (Papaioannou 2013, 34). Golden Dawn members refer to themselves, in their original statute from the 1980s, as "Greek National Socialists" hailing "Hitler's Germany" as the "most glorious example of all" (Ios 2013). They have glorified figures from the Nazi era, including Hitler himself, and pictures of prominent Nazi figures have frequently appeared on the cover of Golden Dawn's publications (Chasapopoulos 2013). They have cultivated political relations with neo-Nazi groupings in Europe and South Africa (Psarras 2012). This neo-Nazi orientation is also reflected in the organizational model of Golden Dawn that is based upon paramilitary rules and its reproduction of Nazi rituals, including the obligatory use of the Nazi salute (Ios 2013), the insistence on a uniform style of dress and of course the ritualistic parades and mass rallies.

3.2 The cult of origins

Julia Kristeva has stressed the importance of the "cult of origins" associated with the resurge of nationalism and racism since the early 1990s and the crisis of other more progressive ideologies. For Kristeva, the cult of origins is a form of hatred, both against those who do not share the same origin and also "hatred of oneself" in his or her current condition withdrawing "into a sullen, warm, private world, unnameable and biological, the impregnable 'aloofness' of a weird primal paradise — family, ethnicity, nation, race"; as "defensive hatred the cult of origins easily backslides to a persecuting hatred" (Kristeva 1993, 3). However, as Daniel Woodley has stressed the "integral nationalism" associated with fascist ideology and political practice "reflects not just the compensatory appeal of shared identity and reciprocity in an age of increased insecurity, nor the demand for cultural renewal, but the internal rationalization of a domesticated human economy through a set of normalizing practices designed to protect and improve the biological inheritance and geopolitical living space of the group" (Woodley 2009, 175).

This can help us with the particular version of nationalism and "cult of origins" in the discourse of Golden Dawn. They present themselves as "Greek Nationalists" that "have the Nation-Race at the core of their Belief" (Golden Dawn 2012, 15). They present the "Nation-Race", and in particular the Greek Nation, in its supposed "original continuance from the Greeks of the Classical Age" (Golden

Dawn 2012, 12), as the basis of a "National State", insisting that "we respect the Idea of the State only in the case that the State has a National Substance and Content and serves the Popular Community" (Golden Dawn 2012, 12). Both in the party's website and its publications, there are numerous texts commemorating important moments in the history of "Hellenism", from the wars of Athens and Sparta against the Persian Empire, to the fall of the Byzantine Empire, to the Greek War of Independence (1821–9), to the victory "against communism" in the Greek Civil War (1946–9). The discourse of the leadership of Golden Dawn and Michaloliakos in particular is full of historical references to this supposed continuity of the Greek nation (Paraskeva-Veloudogianni 2013, 92–102). Each year Golden Dawn organizes a mass rally in Thermopylae commemorating the famous battle between the Spartans and the Persians in 480 BC. This identification with history, especially Sparta, is evident in Michaloliakos' reference to local organizations of Golden Dawn as "little Thermopylae" in a speech at Thermopylae in 2012 (Paraskeva-Veloudogianni 2013, 212). Golden Dawn's programmatic texts refer to a society ruled in an authoritarian-aristocratic manner — hence the many references to ancient Greece and particularly Sparta — based upon principles of racial purity (Psarras 2012). Loyalty to the nation is presented not in terms of democratic participation and collective deliberation but only in terms of "honor", one of the words most often repeated in the speeches of Michaloliakos (Paraskeva-Veloudogianni 2013, 207–245). It is interesting to note that the main catch-phrase of Golden Dawn, always repeated in mass rally, is "Blood — Honor — Golden Dawn", which is also an obvious reference to the "Blut und Ehre" motto of the Hitler Youth in Nazi Germany.

It is obvious from the above, that Golden Dawn's discourse on nation and race attempts to incorporate Golden Dawn within the context of the national narrative. It reproduces the constituting myth of the continuity of the Greek nation. At the same time it contributes to a particular discursive (re)construction of national identity (Wodak et al. 2009) which legitimizes its own version of a paternalistic authoritarian society.

3.3 Racism and anti-Semitism

Virulent racism and anti-Semitism have been integral aspects of fascist ideology and political practice (Woodley 2009) and Golden Dawn is not an exception to this trend. There are many references to the priority of race and the need to protect the purity of race and oppose its potential genocide (Papaioannou 2013). There is an open and explicit anti-Semitism and in many speeches of Michaloliakos, the Jew is used as a "metonymy of evil [...] that doesn't require further explanation" (Paraskeva-Veloudogianni 2013, 84). Chr. Pappas has described "international Judaism" as attempting to "poison the nations" (Papaioannou 2013, 34.). "Hellenism" and "Zionism" are presented as enemies from Antiquity (Antepithesi 2014). In some way, it reproduces the sharp distinction between a positive national Self and a negative Other, which was characteristic of Nazi discourse (Kohl 2011).

Their approach to immigration is openly racist demanding the immediate arrest and mass deportation not only of all undocumented immigrants but also of those that they describe as immigrants with "illegally received documentation" (Golden Dawn 2012a, 18). Practically, they are targeting the majority of immigrants living in Greece, insisting that every illegal immigrant steals the job of a Greek worker. As with most Centre, Centre-Right and Right-wing parties and Media, they always use the term "lathrometanastes" when referring to immigrants, a pejorative term that uses as a compound the adjective that in Greek is also used for contraband merchandise (lathro > lathraios meaning contraband and illegal). The texts and speeches of the leadership of Golden Dawn are full of references to immigrants as "parasites" and "alien bodies" depicting them as a threat to the supposed purity of the "blood" and the historical continuity of the Greek nation (Paraskeva-Veloudogianni 2013, 70–6). The use of bodily metaphors is a characteristic trait not only of racist discourse, but also of other forms of political discourse (Musolff 2004) and the repetition of the "parasite" metaphor follows an important pattern of Nazi discourse, and in particular of Hitler's texts that tended to present the nation as a body in danger of disease because of foreign parasites (in the case of Germany presenting the Jews as parasites), attempting to legitimize racism and even genocide as cures (Musolff 2007, 2008). Immigrants are almost always presented as "dirty" and in most cases of racist violent attacks orchestrated by Golden Dawn the immigrants have been called "dirty" or "dirty animals" (Papaioannou 2013, 91). Of particular importance regarding the strategies of discursive manipulation (van Dijk 2006) adopted by Golden Dawn is the constant reversal regarding who is the victim of racism exemplified in the repeated theme of "racism against the Greeks" (Mastoris 2013; Paraskeva-Veloudogianni 2013) through a repeated reference to Greeks being the victims of attacks by immigrants, lacking access to social services, and being the victims of conspiracies.

As part of its recent attempt to present itself as a popular anti-austerity party, Golden Dawn has placed a lot of emphasis on practices of social solidarity, but "for Greeks only" (Psarras 2012). This has taken the form of well-publicized food hand-outs "only to Greeks", the supposed help it offers to "make neighbourhoods safe" and the highly controversial attempt to create blood banks "by Greeks and only for Greeks", evoking all the racial and Nazi references to the necessary purity of blood (RED 2012).

3.4 "A conspiracy against the nation"

Racism and ant-Semitism also take the form of a description of geopolitics as a conspiracy against the nation. Their approach to international relations is based upon variations of a conspiracy-theory approach, with strong anti-Semitic bias (Karaiskos 2012) and references to the "behind the scenes activity of American-Zionists" (Golden Dawn 2012a, 4). The crisis is presented as a conspiracy against Greeks aiming at their "biological extermination" and "genocide" (Epitideios 2012). Golden Dawn laments the "racism against Greeks" (Mastoris 2013) and they insist that there is an ongoing common effort by the EU, international plutocrats and the "American-Zionist bloc" to use Greece as an example and experiment (Meintanas 2013). Michaloliakos' speeches are often full of references to "conspiracies", presenting globalization as a conspiracy against Greece following a common pattern in west-European far-right parties (Paraskeva-Veloudogianni 2013, 85–89). This is also accompanied by an attempt to link all supposed enemies into a single conspiracy against Greece. We can use as an example a speech by Michaloliakos in February 2013 at Golden Dawn's annual rally commemorating the January 1996 crisis with Turkey (which almost led to military confrontation). In it, Michaloliakos attempts to combine nationalist anti-Turkey rhetoric with anti-Americanism, anti-Semitism (through a pejorative reference to the alleged Jewish descent of the then deputy minister for Foreign Affairs) and anti-immigration policies, linking the Turkish occupation of Greek-Cypriot areas after the 1974 invasion to the supposed "occupation" of neighbourhoods of Athens by immigrants (Paraskeva-Veloudogianni 2013, 224–225).

Such a conspiratorial approach to the economic crisis also helps Golden Dawn to present an image of economic populism without challenging the dominant capitalist strategies. After the eruption of the economic crisis, Golden Dawn has attempted to present itself as an anti-austerity Party in opposition to the policies of the European Union and the IMF. However, it has refrained from taking a clear position on the question of Greece's participation in the Eurozone, suggesting instead that a potential Greek exit can only be a bargaining tool of a "truly national leadership" (Golden Dawn 2012a). These positions have been combined with a careful pro-business approach. In Parliament, Golden Dawn has spoken in favour of innovative entrepreneurialism and has supported most government measures in favour of businesses, and there have been references in the Greek press to Golden Dawn being funded by major Greek corporations and particularly those related to ship-ownership and ship-repairs (Tsakanikas 2013).

In light of the above, the references to a "Nation in danger" by a global conspiracy, orchestrated by foreign powers, foreign bankers, "Zionism", and the surge of illegal immigrants endangering the supposed racial purity of the nation are also articulated with the economic proposals of Golden Dawn. The economics of Golden Dawn is a mixture of ideas that include market references to some form of protectionism plus a paternalistic state. Expelling immigrants and various forms of forced labour is presented as a solution to help the economy. References to "national wealth" exemplified in oil and mineral reserves are also common and Golden Dawn presents ambitious plans to exploit them (Golden Dawn 2012a). Consequently Golden Dawn's texts and intervention in the economy can be considered a variation of a certain anti-establishment populism that does not question capitalist social relations and in fact attempts "to pressure the state to manage an emergent contradiction between the transnational organization of globalized capital and the localized interests of native communities for whom there exists a single non-exchangeable cultural value: the nation-form" (Woodley 2013, 26).

The same element of an "anti-establishment discourse" that does not question private property or capitalist relations of production is evident in Golden Dawn's references to corrupt politicians that have to be brought to justice (Toumasis 2013), in an attempt to invest in the widespread distrust of mainstream politics. Accusing politicians of being "thieves" and "traitors" has been a recurring theme in Golden Dawn texts (Paraskeva-Veloudogianni 2013, 76). It is as if Golden Dawn were attempting to incorporate the disbelief and disillusionment of people regarding parliament within its own typically fascist anti-parliamentary stance. However, as Paraskeva-Veloudogianni has shown, this kind of discourse (re)produces a messianic image of Golden Dawn as "punisher-avenger" as part of a negative conception of politics which offers no other positive or creative solution to the audience than a belief "that the situation can only change through 'redemption' and the transfer of the 'enemy' to the situation the audience endures now" (Paraskeva-Veloudogianni 2013, 115). This, in its turn is also mixed with a certain nostalgia for the dictatorship period (Psarras 2012) and post-Civil War authoritarianism as concrete examples for their fantasy of a strong state.

3.5 The cult of leadership

Part of the core ideology of Golden Dawn has been a rejection of democracy in all its forms, including majority rule. Golden Dawn seeks an openly aristocratic conception of a "Popular State", with a "Leader" on top, presenting it as the state that incorporates the destiny of the Nation. Democracy is identified with demagogy and manipulation of Greece by "plutocrats", by foreign banks and by people of other nations and creeds (Papadakis 2012). In the original statute of the organization from the 1980s, there is explicit rejection of the "democratic form of governance" and instead the "leadership principle" (in a direct allusion to the Nazi Führerprinzip) is proposed as the basis of the decision making (Ios 2013).

This cult of leadership is also evident in the discursive strategies adopted by the leader of Golden Dawn, N. Michaloliakos, such as his use of the first person singular, the "I-You" polarity, and the constant attempt both to (self)present the "Leader" as having distinctive knowledge and expertise, while insisting that he is still one of the people in order to make sure that the audience can be identified with the leader (Paraskeva-Veloudogianni 2013, 142–44).

3.6 Social conservatism

An important aspect of the discourse and practice of Golden Dawn is articulated around social conservatism. First of all, this is evident in their relation to religion. Despite the historical association of Golden Dawn with occult traditions (Psarras 2012), Golden Dawn has attempted to present itself as a defender of Orthodox Christianity. This was evident in the many interventions it has made against supposedly "blasphemous" practices (Christopoulos 2013). This was also evident in the violent protests it organized against the Greek staging of Terrence McNally's Corpus Christi (Baboulias 2012). During these protests, Ilias Antonaros, a Golden Dawn member of parliament, was filmed shouting racist and homophobic insults against the director and the actors (Mason 2012), thus offering an example of the mixture of racism, homophobia, anti-intellectualism, and religious conservatism that has been the trademark of Golden Dawn.

Their positions on gender are marked by their opposition to feminism and theories of gender equality and by their insistence on family and motherhood being duties of a woman. "A woman who is a mother represents high merit by itself" and men and women "represent different substances with a different Duty against life" (Christou 2012). Motherhood is presented as a patriotic duty, as an obligation to the nation, justified in the name of the potential disappearance of the "Greek race" because of "Muslim women giving birth to six children in average" (Christou 2012). This discursive linking of patriarchy and nationalism follows, as Halkias (2004) has shown, a broader pattern in contemporary Greece, both in terms of ideology but also of the social production of a female body that is both heteronormatively sexualized and "nationalized". It is also worth noting their endorsement of a national-socialist position on the role of women, exemplified in their translation of NSDAP texts from the 1930s on the position of women in their website for women (http://whitewomenfront.blogspot.gr). To all these, we can also add the widespread projection of machismo in the form of Golden Dawn parades of athletic males and the adoption of a dress code that combines militarism and masculinity.

4. Economic crisis, crisis of hegemony and the changes in relations of representation

4.1 The history and emergence of Golden Dawn

To contextualize the discourse of Golden Dawn, it is necessary to situate it in the broader context of social and political developments in Greek society. What catapulted Golden Dawn, in terms of electoral results and political appeal, has been the social and political crisis that followed the full eruption of the Greek sovereign debt crisis and the imposition of extreme neoliberal austerity policies.

Golden Dawn began as an offspring of the traditions of the Greek Far Right. In other European countries neo-fascist groupings represented the defeated sides on WW-II, the fascist, Nazi and collaborationist regimes. In contrast, in Greece fascist and collaborationist elements became part of the political establishment. This is due to the particular evolution of the Greek Civil War, in all its long history from the first confrontations in 1943, to the post 1949 establishment of an anti-communist parliamentary "state of emergency", to the fall of the 1967–1974 democracy. The same goes with the authoritarian, anti-democratic, anticommunist ideology that formed the backbone not only of the Greek Far Right but also, in certain periods, of the Right itself and the state apparatuses (Charalambis 1985; Sakellaropoulos 1998; Kostopoulos 2005; Angouri and Wodak 2014). Only after 1974, did we witness a retreat of this authoritarian state discourse, with elements of anticommunism and anti-democratic authoritarianism remaining the official ideology of the forces of order. The initial core of Golden Dawn, including its leader Nicos Michaloliakos, comes from the most "radical" and violent currents of the post 1974 pro-Junta Far-Right; those tendencies that did not opt for some form of "re-absorption" within the political mainstream remained explicitly loyal to the memory of the 1967–1974 dictatorship and, for a short time, engaged in practices of Far-Right terrorism (Psarras 2012). In the 1980s, Golden Dawn emerged as a small openly neo-Nazi group, although its influence seemed rather marginal in relation to other formations of the Far-Right. In the 1990s, a series of racist attacks on immigrants but also against left-wing militants brought the spotlight upon Golden Dawn, especially after Dimitris Koussouris, a left-wing student activist, was almost beaten to death by a group of Golden Dawn members which included Antonios Androutsopoulos ("Periandros") who was at that time Golden Dawn's second in command. In the 2000s, Golden Dawn tried to consolidate its position investing in racist discourse and attacks against immigrants, especially undocumented immigrants and refugees. In the second half of the 2000s, Golden dawn tried to focus on certain neighbourhoods of Athens. They tried to form "citizens'" committees in those neighbourhoods and presented themselves as "angry citizens" demanding a solution to their problems. They tried to put the blame on increased immigration, despite the fact that in reality the problems of the centre of Athens had to do with the crisis and the changing economic and social landscape and not immigration (Maloutas et al. 2013). Consequently, despite their low electoral result in the general elections of 2009, they had better results in the 2010 municipal and regional elections, with Michaloliakos getting 5.29% of the vote in the first round of the election for the Mayor of Athens (Psarras 2012). Also in the 2000s, Golden Dawn invested politically into infiltrating associations of football fun clubs, using football as a means to expand their political appeal and a way to recruit new members (Zoumi and Louka 2013). It was in the context of the social and political crisis in Greece after 2010 that Golden Dawn managed to have an impressive rise in votes, reaching 6.97% in the national elections of May 2012 and 6.92% in the June 2012 and 9.39% in the 2014 European elections (despite the ongoing judicial process against the leadership).

4.2 The Greek economic and social crisis

The full eruption of the Greek sovereign debt crisis brought forward all the contradictions of Greek capitalism and Greece's participation in the Eurozone (Kouvelakis 2011; Lapavitsas *et al.* 2012). This led to the placement of the Greek economy under the supervision of the so-called Troika (EU-IMF-ECB), and the imposition, in return for bail-out loans, of a series of extreme austerity packages (the terms of which were expressed in the "Memoranda of Understanding" accompanying each bail-out), beginning in May 2010, as part of a necessary "internal devaluation process" (Ioakeimoglou 2012). These had devastating results for Greek society. Unemployment reached 27.6% in June 2013 with youth unemployment at 55% (ELSTAT 2013). The economy plunged into a prolonged recession (with a cumulative contraction of the economy estimated at -23.5% for the 2008–2013 period), real average wages were slashed by more than 25%, health indicators started to deteriorate, and labour legislation was drastically altered undermining any right to collective bargaining and increasing labour flexibility (Bank of Greece 2012, 2013; INE GSEE 2013; Stuckler and Basu 2013). Moreover, this whole process was implemented through the constant invocation of a "state of economic emergency", with measures practically being dictated by the representatives of the Troika and then passed through parliament without previous debate. Members of parliament have publicly admitted that they did not even read the laws they had voted for, since they were told this was what was demanded by the Troika. In this sense, large segments of Greek society have viewed the austerity packages not simply as a deterioration of social conditions, but as a direct attack on popular sovereignty and democracy. This, in turn, turned into an open political crisis (Kouvelakis 2011), with ruptures in traditional relations of representation, leading to the inability of mainstream political parties to gain consent for their austerity policies. Moreover, mainstream parties could not offer a plausible narrative for society, except neoliberal cynicism and "collective guilt" exemplified, in the statement by Theodoros Pangalos, a minister in PASOK governments, that "we all ate it together".

4.3 From mass protest to political crisis

The catalyst for this deep political crisis was a series of mass protests, rioting, and other forms of contentious practices of an almost insurrectionary character. First, there was an impressive series of general strikes, beginning in May 2010. Then, there was the "Movement in the Squares", in May — June 2011, which coincided with the Indignados 15M movement in Spain. The "Movement in the Squares" was a massive display of protest and which for the first time united people already militant in social movements with people with no prior experience of collective action (Sotiris 2011a). This mass protest sequence was followed by the strikes in autumn 2011 and the disruption of military parades on 28 October 2011 and mass rioting on 12 February 2012 (Sotiris 2012a). It also took other forms, such as the impressive struggle of the inhabitants of Keratea, a town in the greater Attica region that successfully resisted, despite military-style attacks by special police forces, the construction of a landfill in their vicinity, or the struggle of the inhabitants of Chalkidiki against environmentally disastrous gold-mining in that area. These protests also galvanized a certain form of community in struggle, exemplified in the proliferation of various forms of "democracy from below", such as popular assemblies in neighbourhoods and a myriad of solidarity initiatives to cope with the emerging humanitarian crisis that resulted from the economic crisis: food kitchens, social medicine centres and free tutorial lessons.

These protests not only intensified the political crisis, but also created the material conditions for impressive shifts in relations of political representation. The crisis of traditional political representation materialized in alternative forms of political belonging, at least during the protests themselves. This deepened the political crisis, in the sense of the ruling parties being unable to rule and the large masses of the citizenry refusing to be ruled in this way. This created a situation close to what Antonio Gramsci defined as "organic crisis" or "crisis of hegemony" (Gramsci 1971; Kouvelakis 2011).This fact can account for the impressive left-wing shift in electoral results, exemplified in the rise of SYRIZA (Coalition of the Radical Left) to the second position, with 16.8% in the May 6, 2012 elections. This opened up, for the first time, the possibility of a left-wing government in the country. In the follow-up June 2012 election, SYRIZA got 26.9%, the biggest electoral result of the Left in Greece. However, New Democracy got 29.7% and managed to form a pro-austerity government (Mavris 2012).

4.4 The rise of Golden Dawn

However, the rise of SYRIZA and the Left in general was not the only shift. The open crisis of systemic parties, mainly PASOK, but also New Democracy, also led to the rise of the Far Right and especially Golden Dawn, which managed to gain almost 7% of the vote, enter parliament for the first time, and come under the spotlight as more than a marginal political force.

A crucial factor for this development was the participation of New Democracy and LAOS in the Papademos pro-austerity government in 2011–12. LAOS is a far-right party ideologically close to the Front National in France. For some years, LAOS was the main far-right party in Greece (Psarras 2010). Papademos was a former governor of the Bank of Greece and a member of the board of the European Central Bank. The formation of this three-party government (PASOK — New Democracy — LAOS) was in effect dictated by the Troika, in a process that exemplified a condition of limited sovereignty (Sotiris 2011b). This government marked a turning point since New Democracy, which until then had opposed austerity, became part of the government. Consequently, the pro-Memoranda / anti-Memoranda divide was not a divide between mainstream parties but a dividing line within the electorate of the mainstream parties. Whereas the main beneficiaries of these shifts were to be the Left and the "Independent Greeks", a splinter from New Democracy, Golden Dawn was also a beneficiary.

For Golden Dawn, such a conjuncture of deep social and political crisis offered an opportunity to present itself as an anti-Memoranda, populist, "anti-establishment" party. It did not abandon the core of its racist and neo-fascist discourse, but attempted to attract people who were disillusioned with the political establishment, especially people from the traditions of the Greek right.

The Far-Right has long historical roots in Greek society. The appeal of a mixture of authoritarianism, patriarchy, sexism, social conservatism, and love of authority has always had significant appeal for a segment of the population historically associated with traditional conservative political patronage. There has been a continuous presence of Far-Right elements in the State apparatuses, from the integration of collaborationists into the State after the German Occupation (Kostopoulos 2005), to the vast mechanism of surveillance implemented after the 1946–49 Civil War, to the persistence of Far Right ideology in the security forces (Charalambis 1985; Sakellaropoulos 1998). The crisis of both New Democracy and LAOS, because of their participation in the austerity government, created an open space for the electoral representation of the Far-Right voters. However, thinking only in terms of a displacement of the traditional far-right vote cannot account for the dynamics of Golden Dawn. Particularly, it cannot account for the appeal of Golden Dawn in urban areas, in working class neighbourhoods, and in areas traditionally associated with the Left.

Consequently, the crucial determining factors in the emergence of Golden Dawn have been the large shifts in relations of representation in a conjuncture marked by a violent change in the social and economic paradigm. The experience of a massive deterioration of social conditions, the destruction of traditional petty bourgeois strata, and mass unemployment also contributed to it. Therefore, it is impossible to explain the rise of Golden Dawn without reference to this conjuncture.

Golden Dawn adopted a populist anti-memoranda and anti-austerity discourse, accusing governments of betrayal, treating politicians as traitors, and demanding national sovereignty. We must also stress the appeal not only of their discourse but also of their aggressive public style. The emphasis on verbal and physical aggression (including the attack by a Golden Dawn member of Parliament against two other left-wing members during a live morning TV news show), was combined with the adoption of an openly sexist — militarist aesthetic exemplified in the parades of athletic males in military fatigues. This was enhanced by the rather conscious choice of a segment of the Mass Media to promote them (Psarras 2012). This mixture of sexism, racism, and bravado was similar to certain aspects of the spontaneous ideology of certain segments of the working and petty-bourgeois classes, especially those segments that did not participate in collective practices of struggle and solidarity. Individualized despair could easily be turned into support for neo-fascist political forces (Sotiris 2013). Apart from that, we should also not underestimate the importance of the ties of Golden Dawn with the forces of order and of the fact that especially special police forces (riot police etc.) massively voted in favour of Golden Dawn (Psarras 2012). Moreover, as recent research on internet postings has shown (Angouri and Wodak 2014), Golden Dawn has managed to place itself at the centre of the complex nexus of conflicting discourses regarding the attribution of blame for the Greek crisis.

4.5 Golden Dawn and the authoritarian turn of mainstream politics

Although Golden Dawn has attempted to present itself as an anti-systemic force, there are strong analogies between the authoritarian politics of Golden Dawn and the authoritarian turn of neoliberal capitalism in general and of Greek politics in particular during the period of the austerity packages.

The imposition of austerity measures as part of the bailout agreements was combined with disregard of parliamentary procedure, with excessive police violence exemplified in the attacks on protestors during mass demonstrations, and with a dismantling of legislation guaranteeing basic rights such as collective bargaining and employment protection. At the same time, pro-austerity parties turned to a "law and order" rhetoric, including anti-immigrant policies and racist overtones. In 2011, a heroic hunger strike by 300 immigrants received many openly racist attacks from pro-austerity political parties and by corporate Media. In 2012, the then Health Minister, Andreas Loverdos, at the time a member of PASOK, cynically accused HIV-positive sex workers of having caused an HIV epidemic that was in fact the result of health cuts he had orchestrated (Stuckler and Basu 2013).

This also reflects a more general trend within the EU, where limited sovereignty and democracy are becoming the norm, in the sense of important decisions being made without any form of democratic control. European political elites seem to forget that politics cannot be some form of "auto-pilot" of dictating measures out of neoliberal textbooks and of simply attempting to impose a "consensus" around neoliberal policies regardless of the actual balance of forces. This tactic can only exacerbate a crisis of legitimacy. This "post-democratic" (Crouch 2004) and "post-hegemonic" form of neo-liberal governance might seem as the best conduit for neoliberal "social engineering", but, in reality, it opens the way for social explosions and open political crisis.

In this sense, the rise of Golden Dawn can also be attributed to a prevailing authoritarian and conservative climate. Therefore, instead of being anti-systemic, in reality Golden Dawn was acting as an extreme and perverse version of contemporary systemic politics.

5. Can we treat Golden Dawn as the result of the nationalist and populist overtones in the anti-austerity movement?

The "anti-memoranda" discourse of Golden Dawn has led many commentators to present the rise of Golden Dawn as the outcome of the movement against austerity or even as the direct result of the supposedly nationalist, populist, and anti-parliamentary character of this movement, especially in the form it took during the so-called "Movement of the Squares".

Those whose support this position have attempted to justify it by appealing to a certain political division within the so-called "Movement of the Squares". It is true that during the May-July 2011 protests alongside left-wing, radical left, anarchist-autonomist militants one could also see the militants of what was self-described as an "anti-memoranda patriotic political space" which combined the resistance to austerity and anti-democratic measures, with patriotic references to the need for reclaiming sovereignty. Within this particular political milieu and its "public sphere" of discussions, websites and blogs, one could find a mixture of people coming from different political traditions, including the tradition of PASOK, the Left, or splinter groups from New Democracy such as the Independent Greeks. Spitha ('Spark'), a political movement led by Mikis Theodorakis, a composer and historical figure of the Left, was also part of this political milieu. Despite the presence of people coming from the Right and the extended use of Greek national flags, (this use of the national flag was also observed during the 2001 protests in Argentina), it would be far from the truth to describe this contradictory political milieu as "proto-fascist". Moreover, Golden Dawn was not only absent from the "Movement of the Squares", but also explicitly condemned it. We do not want to underestimate the persistence of nationalism, but as we will try to explain, it would be wrong to treat all these "national — popular" references as opening up the way to fascism and racism.

5.1 The attempt to present Golden Dawn as a result of the "national-populism" of the anti-austerity movement

However, there have been many references in the Greek press, and also in theoretical texts, that the supposedly anomic forms of protest against austerity with their nationalist, populist and anti-parliamentary overtones provided the breeding ground for Golden Dawn's electoral rise. Consequently, we now turn our attention to those theorists who have recently suggested that the rise of Golden Dawn was the result of the prevalence of nationalist and populist discourses within anti-austerity movements.

For Anna Frangoudaki (2013), the problem has its roots in the specific history of nationalism in Greece beginning with 19th century irredentism, which has also taken the form of a feeling of "cultural insecurity and underrated national identity" that can account for the "contradictory and ambiguous relation of Greeks with the EU" (Frangoudaki 2013, 176). At the same time, this was combined with a crisis of institutions and anomic social reactions. Of particular importance have been the "erosion of the institution of Parliament" (Frangoudaki 2013, 198) and the emphasis by the Left on "disobedience" and "unruliness" (Frangoudaki 2013, 208) against austerity measures. All these led to the "Movement of the Squares", which, according to Frangoudaki, was marked by the perception of the economic crisis as a "purely national matter" (Frangoudaki 2013, 218). Moreover, the dominance of populist overtones within the movement and the "nationalist rhetoric on independence and national sovereignty" (Frangoudaki 2013, 220) legitimized the discourse of the Far-Right, of Golden Dawn in particular, and the discourse of politicians as traitors of the nation, while also fuelling a nationalist, anti-European discourse. Frangoudaki suggests that what is needed, instead, is a social-democratic approach, within the European Union, based upon assuming responsibility instead of nationalist and populist attacks on institutions.

A similar line of reasoning can be found in Pantazopoulos' writings. Pantazopoulos follows Taguieff's theorization of the "new national-populism" (Taguieff 2013). For Taguieff populism has been the basic defining element of the recent rise of far-right parties. He attributes it to the erosion of the appeal of the European Integration project, which seems like an elitist, impersonal, economic, technocratic process. For Taguieff populism is based upon a messianic conception of the people set against the "elites" or "capital", combined with nationalism, racism and xenophobia. Anti-elitism also takes the form of "conspiracy theory" (Taguieff 2013, 82) and can be combined with references to direct democracy. This combination of "anti-political", "anti-systemic" populism and xenophobic nationalism leads Taguieff to argue that the current form of populism, exemplified in the rise of Far-Right formations such the French National Front, is a form of "national-populism" (Taguieff 2013, 93). However, what is also important is that for Taguieff there is also a left-wing demagogy, which combines populism and miserabilism (Taguieff 2013, 118). For Taguieff, contemporary movements of indignation, such as the Spanish Indignados 15M Movement, the "Movement of the Squares" in Greece and the protests associated with what has been termed the "Arab Spring", can all be considered to be examples of populist movements. The reason is that they are based upon a simplistic demonization of the "opponents" exemplified for Taguieff by Greek protesters' portrayal of Sarkozy or Merkel as "Nazis" (Taguieff 2013, 125). For Taguieff, the common element of all forms of populism is that "they undermine the basic consensus upon which pluralist democracies are based" (Taguieff 2013, 146). Therefore, we find in Taguieff the basic argument of how contemporary movements can lead to forms of populism and national-populism.

Taguieff's theorization of national-populism offers the basis of Pantazopoulos' (2013) analysis of what he defines as the nationalist-populist discourse of protest movements in Greece since the December 2008 youth revolt. For Pantazopoulos, current protests in Greece have been characterized by a nihilistic culture, by resentment, by a national-populist opposition of the people to its enemies, and by an emphasis on "conspiracy theory" (Pantazopoulos 2013, 33).He describes the December 2008 riots as the moment of nihilism and the "Movement of the Squares" as the moment of national-populism exemplified in the extended use of the Greek national flag, the demands for national sovereignty and what he defines as a "wave of "anti-Memoranda" national-populist radicalization" (Pantazopoulos 2013, 46). Anti-austerity protests such as the "Movement of the Squares" are treated as a "miserabilist national-populist mobilization" (Pantazopoulos 2013, 57), combining nationalism with a populism that is no longer progressive, since it mainly expresses the resentment of the downtrodden. Pantazopoulos traces the roots of Greek national-populism in both the rhetoric of PASOK and Andreas Papandreou in the 1970s and 1980s, but also locates it in the contemporary discourse of SYRIZA and the "ideological PASOKization of the Left" (Pantazopoulos 2013, 130). These national-populist discourses, with their "anti-neoliberal and anti-western political culture" and "synoptic anti-capitalism and anti-plutocracy" (Pantazopoulos 2012) formed also part of the agenda of the Far Right and paved the way for the rise of Golden Dawn. This argument has been widely circulated. For Marantzidis (2012), it was the anti-liberalism and anti-parliamentarism of the "Movement of the Squares" that increased the appeal of Golden Dawn. Members of Parliament from the current government coalition, such as A. Georgiadis and P. Sachinidis, have publicly linked the rise of Golden Dawn to the anti-austerity protests. Even the Communist Party of Greece seems to accept this position (B.N. 2013).

5.2 Discourses as ideological contested terrains

I disagree with the argument that the reason for the rise of Golden Dawn is the persistence of nationalist and populist discourses in recent anti-austerity protests. I do not want to deny the nationalist, racist and populist character of the discourse and politics of Golden Dawn as is the case with most far-right and neo-fascist organizations (Ellinas 2013). Nor do I want to underestimate the importance of the social, political and economic crisis in Greece as a contributing factor to the rise of Golden Dawn. As I have already mentioned, it was exactly the political crisis and, in particular, the sharp ruptures in relations of political representation that helped the rise of Golden Dawn. What I would like to suggest is that this cannot be directly linked to the "national" and "popular" references in the discourses and aesthetics of the movements and protests in Greece. In contrast to this position, my contention is that the discourses coming from the movement have been mainly democratic and egalitarian and what have been described as "national-populist" references should not be equated with nationalism because they are more complex and contradictory.

Theoretically, I base my argument upon those theorists that insist on the contradictory ideological connotations of discursive practices and formations, including national-popular references, particularly those of Marxist perspectives that have attempted to treat discursive formations as inherently contradictory. In this theoretical tradition, there is always a struggle, a battle for words, concepts, phrases, their meanings, their connotations, their appeals. In Antonio Gramsci's prison writings, the whole concept of hegemony refers exactly to the complexity of the workings of power in capitalist society. Hegemony refers not only to a combination of coercion and consent but also to the many ways a social class can become leading, namely able to present itself, both in terms of its politics and its discourses, as representing the interests or the historical destiny of society (Gramsci 1971; Ives 2004). This is particularly true of concepts such as the nation or the people and the whole history of struggles and aspirations they carry with them. For Gramsci, the potential hegemony of a class also includes its ability to impose its strategy as a strategy for the whole of society, and thus for the whole nation. In this reading, the national and popular references cannot be taken as a priori references to nationalism and populism, but much more like contested discursive terrains where part of the struggle for hegemony is waged. In a similar line, Michel Pêcheux has insisted upon the necessarily contradictory character of ideological (and consequently discursive) formations: "an ideology is not identical to itself, it only exists under the modality of division, it is only realized in the contradiction that organizes in it the unity and the struggle of opposites" (Pêcheux 1977, 255). Regarding nationalism, Balibar (1991) has stressed that despite the obvious link between nationalism and racism, not all nationalisms have led to racism or have been historically reactionary and undemocratic and Anderson (1991) has insisted that that there have been nationalisms, especially anti-colonial, that were emancipatory and inclusive. At the same time, whatever reservations one might have regarding Laclau's delinking of ideological representations and class positions, he nevertheless offered some important points in his theorization of populism as an expression of the people/power bloc divide (Laclau 1979). More recently, D'Eramo (2013) has reminded us that populism did not always have the negative connotations it has acquired in the last decades. Contemporary mass movements, from the Arab Spring to Occupy! offer a terrain to rethink notions such as the "the people" or hegemony and have fuelled the relevant debates (Kioupkolis and Katsabekis 2014).

5.3 A counter-argument: the democratic and egalitarian character of the movement as an answer to fascism

I am using all these references in order to refute the argument that the rise of Golden Dawn has been the direct result of the supposedly nationalist and populist character and discourse of the protests against authority. In my view, not all of the references echoed nationalist or populist themes. A great deal of the discourses and demands of the movements was actually pointing to increased inequalities, job precariousness, dismantling of the welfare state, and erosion of democracy. Their more radical version can be considered as anti-capitalist not proto-fascist.

The anti-parliamentary discourses expressed in the movement were different than the particular anti-parliamentary discourse of fascist and neo-Nazi groups that tend to contrast the supposed democratic impasse to the advantages of authoritarian strong leadership by a charismatic leader. Rather they express an opposition to the way the parliament has been in the past years a theatre of undemocratic practices. On the contrary, the discourse of the movement was openly democratic, rightly accusing the government of performing parliamentary coup d'états and of resorting to extreme forms of police violence. The evocation of national references was also an expression of the appreciation of the importance of the loss of national and popular sovereignty following the placing of the Greek economy under the Troika's supervision. Therefore, we must say that the national-popular references in the discourse of the anti-austerity movement were democratic and egalitarian, rather than exclusive and authoritarian.

Therefore, there were no direct linkages to the discourse of fascism. On the contrary, the fascists tried to incorporate elements of this discourse emanating from the movement. Their aim was to attract electorally exactly those people who, while affected by austerity and aiming for a protest vote, were still influenced by conservative and racist/xenophobic discourses. In a way, Golden Dawn tried to "revamp" itself as an anti-austerity protest party, while remaining in its core a neo-Nazi or Far-Right party.

At the same time, the attempt by analysts to link Golden Dawn to the supposedly nationalist overtones of the anti-austerity protest movement is in itself a political strategy. Its latent theoretical premise is that democracy and progress are identical to neo-liberalism and the current version of parliamentary affairs. This makes them not only incapable of comprehending the dynamics of the movement, but also of seeing all forms of protest or anti-systemic discourse as inherently irrational and in a way proto-fascist. A common trait in recent theorizing on the "Greek problem" by pro-reform (that is pro-austerity) theorists has been to treat protests as obstacles to progress and modernization (Kalyvas et al. 2012).

I am not underestimating the importance of fighting against nationalism, xenophobia, and racism, and I think that we really need a new internationalism. However, this reaction to references to national or popular democratic aspirations should not be seen as simply a rejection of nationalism and populism. It also reflects important shifts in the politics of systemic, pro-austerity forces, particularly referring to Greece's relation to international organizations and the internationalization of economics and politics. Of particular importance has been the tendency towards reduced sovereignty in contemporary globalized capitalism. On the one hand, this is the result of the growing importance of international markets and capital flows and the increased dependence of national economies on global economic tendencies. On the other hand, we have specific institutional arrangements, such as the ones gradually implemented as part of the European Integration project that lead towards a condition of limited sovereignty and reduced democratic control of social and economic developments. A telling example is exactly the imposition of a reduced sovereignty condition in countries such as Greece (Sotiris 2012b).

Moreover, the theoretical position that the rise of nationalism and national-populism led to the rise of fascism is based upon a prescriptive and not a descriptive or analytical perspective. By this, I mean that most of the analysts that insist on the "national-populism" thesis in reality project their disapproval of the anti-austerity movement and radical contentious politics in general.

This does not mean that Golden Dawn has not resorted to nationalist or populist discourse. On the contrary, this has been a major aspect of its political strategy. The main point I would like to make is that this is not a projection of the discourse of the movement.

Golden Dawn was in no way a part of the movement. The political and discursive dynamics of the movement clearly opposed Golden Dawn. Golden Dawn appealed to people that wanted to protest but had not taken part in protests, having experienced the crisis in an individual, atomized way, and thus wanted someone to protest for them. This logic of substitution is at work here. Golden Dawn's theatrics in parliament or in the street, including displays of violence and masculine bravado act as a substitute: the party acts out the protest on their behalf. That is why Golden Dawn has not organized any major anti-government or anti-Troika protests, with the exception of simple pro-Golden Dawn rallies and ritualistic displays of force. Moreover, the absence of mass protests against the arrests of its leadership shows that Golden Dawn, despite its electoral results, cannot mobilize large numbers and act as the centre of a mass movement.

On the contrary, the basic tone of protests and movements since 2010 has been democratic, egalitarian and emancipatory. Especially the "Movement of the Squares" exemplified this tone, since it presented a call for real democracy, an opposition to austerity policies and an expression of strong disagreement with dominant policies, both within Greece and within international organizations such as the European Union or the IMF (Douzinas 2013). Moreover, it was a process that led to the re-politicization of society and to the proliferation of critical and oppositional discourses. This was in contrast to the dominance of pro-austerity discourses in corporate Media and the official "public sphere". This was helped by the fact that these movements are not only examples of instrumental goal-oriented practices; they also represent a process of re-appropriation of public space (Stavridis 2010).

Therefore, the eruption of mass protests in Greece against austerity, against the erosion of democracy and against the neoliberal supervision by the EU-IMF-ECB Troika helped create alternative spaces, alternative public spheres, and new discursive practices. Within the movement, critical and oppositional discourses flourished, in all their polyphonic and necessarily contradictory dynamics. The co-existence of discourses referring to social classes and alliances with "national

— popular" representations is an indication of these dynamics. As such, it created the terrain for the potential hegemony of radical, democratic, anti-capitalist discourses for social emancipation. This includes the transformation and re-articulation of "national — popular" representations into demands for social justice, solidarity, tolerance and democratic popular sovereignty as collective will for social change against the violence of contemporary capitalism (Dean 2014). In a sense, it is a process of re-inventing the "people" not as the imagined community of the "nation", but as the active collective subject of social and political emancipation, a collective subject that includes both Greeks and immigrants.

Consequently, it was not the movement that fuelled Golden Dawn and its discourse, but the limits of the movement. These limits refer to the fact that large segments of the subaltern classes have experienced a devastating social situation in terms of individualized despair and the fact that the dynamics of the movement did not manage to uproot deep-rooted sexist, authoritarian and xenophobic ideological representations, traditionally associated with the Right and Far-Right in Greece.

That is why the answer to the rise of neo-fascism cannot be found within the dominant logic of a disciplinary neo-liberalism that treats social movements and mass protests as obstacles for progress, but only through a proliferation and expansion of the collective practices associated with these movements. The dominant neoliberal logic, as it is expressed in the Troika's directives and the politics of pro-austerity parties, will only intensify the current crisis of hegemony, thus offering the material ground for the appeal of neo-fascist ideology. Only a radical perspective of social justice, solidarity and democracy, as potential (counter) hegemony, can offer an alternative to both the hegemonic crisis and the rise of neo-fascism.

6. Conclusion

The rise of Golden Dawn has been the outcome of the contradictory dynamics of social, political, and ideological crisis in Greece in a conjuncture marked by the imposition of extreme austerity and a violent change in the social paradigm that undermined historically formed relations of political representation. In this sense, the rise of Golden Dawn can be considered as an aspect of the crisis of hegemony.

Moreover, one can say that the authoritarian and conservative character of the ideology and discourse of Golden Dawn also reflected a more general turn towards authoritarian post-democratic institutional and political arrangements within contemporary capitalist societies, especially in light of the economic crisis and the dominant reaction to it as a "state of constant economic emergency".

The discourse of Golden Dawn has been a mixture of openly fascist and neo-Nazi elements (racism, anti-Semitism, authoritarianism, admiration of leadership, anti-parliamentarism) with an anti-austerity, anti-memoranda discourse that attempted to echo the grievances of people suffering from austerity. However, Golden Dawn was never a part of the anti-austerity movement, nor did it share the democratic culture of struggle, resistance and solidarity of the movement.

In contrast, the discourses coming from the movement combined democratic, egalitarian and anti-capitalist elements. The "national — popular" elements of the discourses of certain segments of the movement referred more to a democratic demand for social justice and popular sovereignty than to nationalism. Therefore, the recent attempt by some theorists to link the rise of Golden Dawn to the supposedly "national-populist" discourses and practices of the anti-austerity protests are unjustified. On the contrary, one can attribute the rise of Golden Dawn to the limits of the anti-austerity movement and the fact that it did not manage to reach all segments of the subaltern classes.

This is the challenge: the only potential answer to the rise of neo-fascism, in all its variations, means exactly articulating discourses and interpellations that can turn individualized despair into collective resistance and creating collective political projects that can transform an alliance of the subaltern classes into a collective subject of emancipation.

References

Althusser, Louis. 2014. *On the Reproduction of Capitalism. Ideology and Ideological Apparatuses of the State*. London: Verso.

Anderson, Benedict. 1991. *Imagined Communities*. London: Verso.

Angouri, Jo and Ruth Wodak. 2014. "They became big in the shadow of the crisis': The Greek success story and the rise of the far right". *Discourse and Society* 25(4): 540–565. doi: 10.1177/0957926514536955

Antepithesi 2014. "The eternal enmity between Hellenism and Zionism", http://www.xryshaygh.com/index.php/enimerosi/view/h-aiwnia-echthra-ellhnismou-siwnismou-ana-tous-ai-wnes (Last accessed, August, 25 2014).

B.N. 2013. "When the "egg of the snake" was warmed in the Squares." (In Greek). *Rizospastis* 30 September 2013. http://www.rizospastis.gr/page.do?id=14807&publDate=29%2F9%2F2013&direction=&pageNo=11 (Last Accessed October 5 2013).

Baboulias, Yiannis. 2012. "Greece, in 2012: fascists beating up people while the police look on". Guardian 12 October 2012. http://www.theguardian.com/commentisfree/2012/oct/12/greece-fascists-beating-people-police (Last accessed October 1 2013).

Balibar, Étienne. 1991. "The Nation Form. History and Ideology". In Étienne Balibar and Immanuel Wallerstein, *Race, Nation, Class: Ambiguous Identities*. Verso: London.

Bank of Greece. 2012. *Monetary Policy. Interim Report*. Bank of Greece (2013). *Annual Report 2012*. (in Greek). Athens: Bank of Greece.

Bank of Greece. 2013. *Annual Report 2012*. (In Greek). Athens: Bank of Greece.

Charalambis, Dimitris. 1985. *Army and Political Power. The Structure of Power in Post-Civil War Greece*. (In Greek). Athens: Exantas.

Chasapopoulos, Nicos. 2013. *Golden Dawn. The History, the Faces and the Truth*. (In Greek). Athens: Livanis.

Christou, Evgenia. 2012. "Woman and the Modern Way of Life", http://whitewomenfront.blogspot.gr/2012/04/blog-post_29.html (Last accessed, August 30, 2014).

Christopoulos, Dimitris (ed.) 2013. *God Does Not Need a Prosecutor. Church, Blasphemy and the Golden Dawn*. (In Greek). Hellenic League for Human Rights / Athens: Nepheli.

Costopoulos, Tasos. 2005. *Self-censored Memory*. Athens: Filistor.

Crouch, Colin. 2004. *Post-Democracy*. Polity: London.

Dean, Jodi. 2014. "Sovereignty of the People". In Alexandros Kioupkolis and Giorgos Karzambekis (eds.). *Radical Democracy and Collective Movements Today. The Biopolitics of the Multitude versus the Hegemony of the People*. Farnham: Ashgate

D'Eramo, Marco. 2013. "Populism and the New Oligarchy". *New Left Review* 82:5–28.

Douzinas, Costas. 2013. *Philosophy and Resistance in the Crisis. Greece and the Future of Europe*. London: Polity.

Ellinas, Antonis. 2013. "The Rise of Golden Dawn: The New Face of the Far Right in Greece." *South European Society and Politics* http://www.tandfonline.com/doi/abs/10.1080/13608746.2013.782838#.Uk7kMxA2PIU

ELSTAT (Hellenic Statistical Authority). 2013. "Press Release. Labour Force Survey. June 2013. http://www.statistics.gr/portal/page/portal/ESYE/BUCKET/A0101/PressReleases/A0101_SJO02_DT_MM_07_2013_01_F_EN.pdf (Last accessed, October 10, 2013).

Epitideios, Giorgos. 2012. "The Contemporary Genocide against Greeks." (In Greek). http://www.xryshaygh.com/index.php/enimerosi/view/h-sugchronh-genoktonia-kata-twn-ellhnwn-leipei-fwto#.Uk0Z0xA2PIU (Last accessed, October 1, 2013).

Fairclough, Norman. 1989. *Language and Power*. London: Longman.

Fairclough, Norman. 1995. *Critical Discourse Analysis: The Critical Study of Language*. London: Longman.

Frangoudaki, Anna. 2013. *Nationalism and the Rise of the Far-Right*. (In Greek). Athens: Alexandreia.

Georgiadou, Vasiliki. 2008. *The Far-Right and the Consequences of Consensus. Denmark, Norway, Holland, Switzerland, Austria, Germany*. (In Greek). Athens: Kastaniotis.

Golden Dawn. 2012a. *Golden Dawn. An Ideological Movement*. (In Greek). Athens: Golden Dawn.

Golden Dawn. 2012b. *Political Positions for the Golden Dawn of Hellenism* (In Greek). Athens: Golden Dawn.

Gramsci, Antonio. 1971. *Selections from the Prison Notebooks*. London: Lawrence and Wishart.

Hainsworth, Paul. 2008. *The Extreme Right in Western Europe*. London: Routledge.

Halkias, Alexandra. 2004. *The Empty Cradle of Democracy, Sex, Abortion, and Nationalism in Modern Greece*. Durham: Duke UP. doi:10.1215/9780822386049

Ios. 2013. "The Statute of Neonazi Golden Dawn". (In Greek). *Efimerida ton Syntakton*, 26 September 2013.

INE-GSEE. 2013. *Greek Economy and Employment. Annual Survey*. (In Greek). Athens: INE-GSEE.

Ioakeimoglou, Ilias. 2012. *Internal Devaluation and Capital Accumulation. A Critical Approach.* (In Greek). Athens: INE GSEE/ADEDY.

Ives, Peter. 2004. *Language and Hegemony in Gramsci*. London: Pluto.

Kalyvas, Stathis, George Pagoulatos, and Haridimos Tsoukas (eds.). 2012. *From Stagnation to Forced Adjustment. Reforms in Greece* 1974–2010. London: Hurst.

Karaiskos, Spyros. 2012. "Zionism and Globalization". (In Greek). http://www.xryshaygh.com/index.php/enimerosi/view/siwnismos-kai-pagkosmiopoihsh#.Uk0caRA2PIU (Last accessed, October 1 2013).

Kioupkolis, Alexandros, and Giorgos Katsambekis (eds.) 2014. *Radical Democracy and Collective Movements Today. The Biopolitics of the Multitude versus the Hegemony of the People*. Farnham: Ashgate.

Kohl, Diane. 2011. "The Presentation of "Self" and "Other" in Nazi Propaganda". *Psychology & Society*. Vol. 4(1):7–26.

Kouvelakis, Stathis. 2011. "The Greek Cauldron". *New Left Review* 72:17–32.

Kristeva, Julia. 1993. *Nations without Nationalism*. New York: Columbia University Press.

Laclau, Ernesto. 1979. *Politics and Ideology in Marxist Theory. Capitalism-Fascism-Populism.* London: Verso.

Lapavitas, Costas *et al.* 2012. *Crisis in the Euro-zone*. London: Verso.

Lecercle, Jean-Jacques. 2006. *A Marxist Philosophy of Language*. Leiden: Brill.

Maloutas, Thomas, Giorgos Kondylis, Michalis Petrou, and Nicos Souliotis (eds.). 2013. *The Centre of Athens as a Political Stake*. (In Greek). Athens: National Centre for Social Research and Harokopio University.

Marantizidis, Nicos. 2012. "Time for a Democratic Crescent" (In Greek). Kathimerini 22 September 2012. http://news.kathimerini.gr/4dcgi/_w_articles_columns_2_22/09/2013_534353 (Last accessed, October 5 2013).

Mason, Paul. 2012. "Alarm at Greek Police 'Collusion' with Far-right Golden Dawn". BBC, http://www.bbc.co.uk/news/world-19976841 (Last accessed, October 10 2013).

Mastoris, Giorgos. 2013. "The Actually Existing Racism against Greeks". http://www.xryshaygh.com/index.php/enimerosi/view/o-uparktos-ratsismos-kata-twn-ellhnwn?COLLCC=1141557050&#.Uk0jWhA2PIU (Last accessed, October 1 2013).

Mavris, Yiannis. 2012. "Greece's Austerity Election". *New Left Review* 76: 95–107.

Meintanas, Christos. 2013. "The Murderous Plan 'Greek Crisis'. Why was Greece chosen?". http://www.xryshaygh.com/index.php/enimerosi/view/to-anthrwpoktono-schedio-ellh-nikh-krish-giati-epilechthhke-h-ellada#.Uk0lsRA2PIU (Last accessed, October 1 2013).

Musolff, Andreas. 2004. *Metaphor and Political Discourse. Analogical Reasoning in Discourses about Europe*. London: Palgrave Macmillan.

Musolff, Andreas. 2007. "What Role Do Metaphors Play in Racial Prejudice? The Function of Antisemitic Imagery in Hitler's Mein Kampf". *Patterns of Prejudice*, 41(1):21–43. doi: 10.1080/00313220601118744

Musolff, Andreas. 2008. "What Can Critical Metaphor Analysis Add to the Understanding of Racist Ideology? Recent Studies of Hitler's Anti-Semitic Metaphors". *Critical Approaches to Discourse Analysis across Disciplines*. 2(2):1–10.

Pantazopoulos, Andreas. 2012. "Wishing Alone will not Deal with Golden Dawn". http://tvxs.gr/news/egrapsan-eipan/erga-kai-oxi-eyxologia-kata-tis-xrysis-aygis-toy-andrea-pantazo-poyloy (Last accessed, October 5 2013).

Pantazopoulos, Andreas. 2013. *Left-wing National-populism 2008-2013. From the "December Rebellion", the Greek "Indignados" and the 2012 Elections to the New Cyprus Question.* Athens: Epikentro.

Papadakis, Spyros. 2012. "Parliamentary Democracy: The Illusion of Popular sovereignty". (In Greek). http://www.xryshaygh.com/index.php/enimerosi/view/koinobouleutikh-dh-mokratia-h-fenakh-ths-laikhs-kuriarchias#.Uk0arRA2PIU (Last accessed, October 1 2013).

Papaioannou, Kostis. 2013. *The "Clean Hands" of Golden Dawn. Application of Nazi Purity.* Athens: Metaixmio.

Paraskeva-Veloudoyanni, Despoina. 2013. *The Enemy, the Blood, the Punisher. 13 Speeches of the 'Leader' of Golden Dawn.* (In Greek). MA thesis, Department of Political Science, University of Athens.

Pêcheux, Michel. 1977. "Remontos de Foucault à Spinoza". In *L' inquiétude de discours*, texts de Michel Pêcheux choisis et presents par Denise Maldidier. Paris: Editions des Cendres.

Pêcheux, Michel. 1982. *Language, Semantics and Ideology. Stating the Obvious.* London: Macmillan.

Psarras, Dimitris. 2010. *The Black Hand of Karatzaferis. The TV Revival of the Greek Far-Right.* (In Greek). Athens: Alexandreia.

Psarras, Dimitris. 2012. *The Black Bible of Golden Dawn.* (In Greek). Athens: Polis.

RED (Rights, Equality and Diversity European Network) 2012. "Neo-Nazi Golden Dawn Party Organizes Greek-only Blood Bank and Food Delivery". http://www.red-network.eu/?i=red-network.en.news.307 (Last accessed, October 2 2013).

Sakellaropoulos, Spyros. 1998. *The Reasons for the April Coup D'Etat. 1949-1967. The Social Context of the Road to Dictatorship.* (In Greek). Athens: Livanis.

Sotiris, Panagiotis. 2011a. "Greece: Crisis and Unrest", New Left Project http://www.newleft-project.org/index.php/site/article_comments/greece_crisis_and_unrest (Last accessed, October 1 2013).

Sotiris, Panagiotis. 2011b. "Rethinking the Notions of 'People' and 'Popular Sovereignty'". Greek Left Review. http://greekleftreview.wordpress.com/2011/11/15/rethinking-the-notions-of-%E2%80%98people%E2%80%99-and-%E2%80%98popular-sovereignty%E2%80%99/ (Last accessed, October 8 2013).

Sotiris, Panagiotis. 2012a. "Greece: From Despair to Resistance". The Bullet. Socialist Project. E-Bulletin No 598. http://www.socialistproject.ca/bullet/598.php (Last accessed, October 1 2013).

Sotiris, Panagiotis. 2012b. "Austerity. Limited Sovereignty and Social Devastation. Greece and the Dark Side of European Integration". LuXemburg http://www.zeitschrift-luxemburg.de/austerity-limited-sovereignty-and-social-devastation-greece-and-the-dark-side-of-euro-pean-integration/ (Last accessed, October 1 2013).

Sotiris, Panagiotis. 2013. "The Dark Dawn of Greek Neo-fascism". *Overland* 210:32–37.

Stavridis, Stavros. 2010. *Towards the City of Thresholds.* Trento: Professional Dreamers.

Stuckler, David, and Sunjay Basu. 2013. *The Body Economic. How Austerity Kills. Recessions, Budget Battles, and the Politics of Life and Death.* New York: Basic Books.

Taguieff, Pierre-André. 2013. *The New National-Populism.* (In Greek). Translated in Greek by Anastasia Iliadeli and Andreas Pantazopoulos. Athens: Epikentro.

Toumasis, Makis. 2013. "A Rotten Political System Breeds Corruption". http://www.xry-shaygh.com/index.php/enimerosi/view/h-diafthora-mesa-apo-to-politiko-susthma#.UlRsfRCbz2c (Last accessed, October 6 2013).

Tsakanikas, Nikos. 2013. "The 'Trade-unionism' of Golden Dawn in Perama". *(In Greek) Unfollow* 22:62–68.

van Dijk, Teun A. 1991. *Racism and the Press*. London: Routledge.

van Dijk, Teun A. (ed.) 1997. *Discourse as Structure and Process. Discourse Studies: A Multidisciplinary Approach*. Volume 1. London: Sage.

van Dijk Teun A. 2006. "Discourse and Manipulation". *Discourse and Society* 17(2): 359–383. doi:10.1177/0957926506060250

Weiss, Gilbert, and Ruth Wodak. (eds.) 2003. *Critical Discourse Analysis: Theory and Inrerdisciplinarity*. London: Palgrave Macmillan.

Wodak, Ruth, and Michael Meyer. (eds.) 2001. *Methods of Critical Discourse Analysis*. London: Sage.

Wodak, Ruth, Rudolf de Cillia, Martin Reisigl, and Karin Liebhart. 2009. *The Discursive Construction of National Identity*. 2nd ed. Edinburgh: Edinburgh University Press.

Woodley, Daniel. 2009. *Fascism and Political theory. Critical perspectives on fascist ideology*. London: Routledge.

Woodley, Daniel. 2013. "Radical Right Discourse Contra State-based Authoritarian Populism. Neoliberalism, Identity and Exclusion after the Crisis". In *Analysing Fascist Discourse. European Fascism in Talk and Text*, edited by Ruth E. Wodak, and John E. Richardson, 17–41.

Xenakis, Sappho. 2012. "A New Dawn. Change and Continuity in Political Violence in Greece". *Terrorism and Political Violence* 24:437–464. doi:10.1080/09546553.2011.633133

Zoumi, Aleka, and Maria Louka. 2013. "The Blackshirts at the Football Stadiums". http://stokok-kino.gr/article/2712/Oi-melanoxitones-sto-gipedo (Last accessed, October 11 2013).

Discursive violence and responsibility

Notes on the pragmatics of Dutch populism

Michiel Leezenberg
University of Amsterdam

This chapter discusses the discursive strategies of the Freedom Party (PVV), a contemporary Dutch populist and Islamophobic party. After tracing its ideological roots to mainstream liberalism rather than earlier forms of extreme right political movements, I will discuss its discourse about Muslims. It will appear that this discourse goes far beyond the legitimate expression of opinion. Using some of Judith Butler's ideas about the performativity of hate speech, I will attempt to describe how PVV leader Geert Wilders's language is not only a discourse *about* violence, but is also itself a discourse *of* violence. Simultaneously, however, Wilders systematically denied responsibility for any violence his words might contain, imply, or provoke; instead, he and his sympathizers blamed both Muslims and his political opponents for whatever violence might occur in the wake of his utterances. This appears most clearly in the discussion following Norwegian Anders Breivik's murderous 2011 assault on the Utøya island, an act which he himself claimed was in part inspired by Wilders's political rhetoric.

Keywords: hate speech, performativity, speech acts, discursive violence

In memoriam Niels Helsloot

1. Introduction

The discourse of early 21st-century Western European populist parties raises novel questions about free speech and censorship, and about the possible effects of radical discourse, or what is less neutrally called "hate speech". One famous and influential case of such populist discourse is that of the Dutch Freedom Party (Partij Voor de Vrijheid, PVV) headed by Geert Wilders. Ever since its foundation in 2004, PVV, and in particular its leader, Geert Wilders, has strongly influenced, indeed increasingly dominated, both the style and content of Dutch political debate. A long-time member of parliament for the liberal Volkspartij voor Vrijheid en

DOI 10.1075/bct.93.09lee

Democratie (VVD), Wilders had in the 1990s been active on behalf of the rights of minorities in Eastern Europe; after the September 11, 2001 assaults, however, he followed in the footsteps of maverick politicians Pim Fortuyn (who had run for parliament on a strongly Islamophobic ticket until he was assassinated by an animal rights activist right before national elections in May 2002) and Ayaan Hirsi Ali (who after a meteoric rise to political stardom in the Netherlands left for the United States in 2006), and started targeting Muslim population groups living in the Netherlands. Wilders's increasingly provocative rhetoric posed as a legitimate critique of Islam as a religion, but — as I hope to show below — was carefully crafted in such a way as to denigrate or offend Muslims and to antagonize political opponents.

Unlike a number of earlier populist parties, the PVV advertises itself as a bona fide liberal party: it legitimizes itself by appealing to liberal-democratic values of free speech, the rule of law, and a state monopoly on legitimate violence; and it places itself in an Enlightenment tradition of secularism, critique of religious authority, and rational debate. On the one hand, it successfully (though not necessarily correctly) represents itself as acting against a political and journalistic elite claimed to be "leftist", while at the same time, and significantly, remaining largely silent about the business and financial elites. On the other, it (again, largely successfully) presents its statements not as xenophobic discourse about immigrant workers but as a legitimate liberal-secular critique of a religion. Yet, as I will argue, in its very appeal to liberal values, it paradoxically and systematically undermines liberal principles such as tolerance and equality before the law.

Below, after a more theoretical introduction, I will discuss, first, the ideological roots of Wilders's particular brand of populism, which lie less in the xenophobic fringe parties of earlier decades than in the liberal, and neoliberal, political mainstream; second, basing myself on a number of his more famous interventions and interviews, I will zoom in on Wilders's language use, with an eye on his use of vocabulary and discursive strategies, and on the intended and unintended effects of those; third, I will discuss a number of issues concerning radical discourse and responsibility, issues that arose in the context of Wilders's 2010–2011 hate speech trial and Anders Breivik's July 2011 assaults; and finally, I will tackle some more general questions concerning the pragmatics of violence.[1]

1. The selection of samples from Wilders's public pronouncements until December 2012 is admittedly somewhat arbitrary, focusing on statements that have generated further debate. More elaborate searches in, or discussion of, a corpus that is as repetitive as it is extensive would not, I think, fundamentally affect the claims made below. Part of the material employed here also appears in Leezenberg (forthcoming), and is incorporated by permission of the publisher.

2. Free speech, censorship, performativity

In order to explore these paradoxical effects, one should sidestep the usual, and increasingly repetitive, polemics surrounding Wilders's anti-Islam rhetoric, and the equally repetitive debates whether or not Wilders's right to free speech should be curtailed. Opponents of the PVV have, with little more sophistication or factual accuracy than Wilders himself, brandished the party's ideology as "racist" or "fascist", and have dubbed its leader a new Hitler. Such criticisms have not only proved largely ineffective; they also appear to miss what is novel about the PVV, and about contemporary populism more generally. Wilders and his followers routinely deny being racist, claiming that they are not talking about race but about culture, and not offending people but criticizing a religion, or rather, a political ideology disguised as a religion. Moreover, unlike pre-war parties like the Italian fascists or the German national socialists, and like many another contemporary populist party in Western Europe, the PVV by and large accepts — indeed, insists upon — the rules of the game of the liberal state, including free speech, gender equality, rule of law, and secularism. Further, unlike twentieth-century fascist parties, it claims to accept the liberal state's monopoly on violence and does not resort to physical coercion as a political strategy: there are no bands of PVV thugs. One central question to be addressed below, however, is whether and to what extent PVV's discourse — which presents and legitimizes itself as the mere expression of opinions or as the courageous speaking out on uncomfortable societal truths — amounts to *verbal*, or discursive, violence.

In the public debate, a relation between words and violence is firmly established in the discussions surrounding Wilders and his party, but it hardly, if ever, reflects questions of whether and how Wilders's words *themselves* involve any kind of violence. In recent years, theorists like Judith Butler have questioned the apparently obvious distinction between physical and verbal violence, and the — initially equally plausible — assumption that acts of verbal violence, like abuse or hate speech, are "mere words", and, as such, have no physical consequences. Butler raises the question whether humans are a kind of "linguistic beings", who need language to exist: hence, she argues, a determinate social existence of the body becomes possible only in virtue of the linguistic process of naming.[2] Thus, the intuitive and initially self-evident distinctions between verbal and physical violence, and between utterances between speakers, become problematic.

Although Butler focuses much of her discussion on pornography and the statement "I am gay" in the U.S. army, she aims at nothing less than a "general theory of the performativity of political discourse" (1997, 72). Employing Althusser's

2. See in particular Butler (1997).

idea of naming (*appellation*) as constitutive of subjects and Derrida's notion of iteration as undermining the idea of the meaning of utterances being determined by speakers' intentions, she argues that speakers are never in sovereign control over their words. On the other hand, she claims, as a speech act's illocutionary force only becomes determinate against the background of the "complete speech situation", which can never be completely delimited, the force of words can no more unproblematically be located in the words themselves than in speaking subjects held to be sovereign. Put differently, hate speech is not in *itself* an act of violence, nor is any violent effect it may have simply *caused* by its being uttered.

With this emphasis on language as constitutive of subjects, Butler tries to avoid the appeal both to the "sovereign [*sic*] freedom of the individual" to express opinions and to state-supported censorship of hate speech by laws and regulations (1997, 41). On her account, the problematization of the distinction between words and actions avoids the implicit censorship of juridical regulation that can qualify (and hence censor) some utterances as "mere words" (1997, 127–164). State censorship, she claims, not only reiterates and reproduces hate speech in its very attempt to regulate it; it also produces subjects as much as it regulates words.

This radical reformulation of speech act-theoretical ideas forces us to pose anew various questions concerning speakers' responsibility and censorship, as it problematizes any attempt to unambiguously locate the effect of statements in either a force residing in the words themselves or in the intentions and social power of speakers. Its immediate political (and juridical) implications are not directly clear; but for a number of reasons, it seems particularly promising in the case of PVV's discourse. Not only does it help us escape the sterile and misleading opposition between free speech and the rights of minorities that has dominated public debate in the Netherlands; it may also do more justice to some of the idiosyncrasies and apparent contradictions of this discourse. To mention but a few of these: first, most of this discourse does not in fact originate with Wilders himself, but merely repeats claims and concepts of foreign Islamophobic circles; on occasion — as with Wilders's notorious short film, *Fitna* — it even boils down to outright plagiarism. Second, PVV's discourse does not always follow the expected chronological sequence of an utterance and its effects: thus, in the run-up to *Fitna's* 2008 release, Dutch media pundits and politicians hotly debated the contents and possible effects and consequences of a movie that nobody had even seen yet, reverting the usual temporal relation between the utterance of a sign and its effect on the audience. Finally, and most tragically, in July 2011, barely a month after a Dutch court acquitted Wilders from inciting hatred, a horrendous hate crime was committed in Norway that explicitly named him as a source of inspiration. These and other developments raise broader questions about power and violence, and about agency and responsibility, surrounding radical political discourse like the PVV's.

3. The ideology of the Freedom Party

The ideology of Wilders's PVV is clearly rooted in the new Dutch populism of actors like Frits Bolkestein, Pim Fortuyn, and Ayaan Hirsi Ali. In part, it involves familiar populist themes, in its attempt to blend elements of liberal free-market thinking and dislike of state interference with populist measures to protect lower-income groups (albeit specifically those of ethnically Dutch origins) and the elderly, two groups for whom the party's profound Euroscepticism is a welcome idea.[3] For years, however, the PVV's ideological hallmark has been less a socio-economic nationalism and populism than a consistent Islamophobia: thus, it was on a primarily anti-Islamic ticket that the PVV entered, and made substantial gains in, the 2006 and 2010 elections. Wilders sees Islam not as a religion but as a totalitarian political ideology, and thus undeserving of the respect and legal protection that other religions deserve. Likewise, he consistently describes the Qur'an as inciting hatred of, and violence towards, women and non-Muslims. In a 2007 op-ed, he even called for the Qur'an, which he called "the *Mein Kampf* of a religion out to eliminate others", to be banned: "in different suras, Muslims are called upon to repress, persecute or kill Jews, Christians, adherents of other faiths and non-believers, to beat and rape women, and to establish by violent means a worldwide Islamic state. Plenty of suras incite Muslims to death and destruction".[4]

This Islamophobic ideology does not, of course, originate with Wilders: it is not only indebted to earlier Dutch populists, but more importantly to "Islam critics" in the United States and elsewhere, like Daniel Pipes and Egyptian-born Bat Ye'or. The latter's alleged criticism of Islam is implicitly or even explicitly shaped by an unfailingly and uncritically pro-Israel ideology, which is likewise shared by Wilders.[5] Crucial elements of this ideology are, first, Ye'or's notion of *dhimmitude*,

3. I will not elaborate here on the (complex if not contradictory) neoliberal backgrounds of Dutch populism, or on Wilders's main sources of inspiration in figures like Margaret Thatcher in the UK and the former Italian prime minister Silvio Berlusconi. The major difference with the latter is, of course, the fact that Wilders, unlike Berlusconi, managed to dominate the national media even without actually owning them.

4. "In verschillende soera's worden moslims opgeroepen joden, christenen, andersgelovigen en niet-gelovigen te onderdrukken, vervolgen of vermoorden, vrouwen te slaan en te verkrachten en met geweld een wereldwijde islamitische staat te vestigen. Soera's te over die moslims oproepen en aanzetten tot dood en verderf." 'Genoeg is genoeg: verbied de Koran'. *De Volkskrant*, August 3, 2007, see http://www.volkskrant.nl/vk/nl/2686/Binnenland/article/detail/870859/2007/08/08/Genoeg-is-genoeg-verbied-de-Koran.dhtml (accessed April 29, 2013).

5. Thus, the party's 2012 electoral program states: "Israel, the sole democracy in the Middle East, deserves our enthusiastic support. Especially now that the country is continually threatened by the Mullah loonies in Iran. For the Freedom Party, Israel always is a beacon of hope,

which turns the Islamic notion of *dhimmi* or "protected peoples" into a sweeping argument that Islam in fact oppresses rather than protects minorities. In a European context, this notion is invoked to brandish every concession to Muslim demands or sensibilities as an act of defeat or self-effacement that will inevitably lead to the eventual imposition of the *sharîʿa*, or Islamic religious law. PVV voices claim that this *dhimmi* attitude is especially pronounced in progressive, or as they consistently call them, "leftist" or "socialist", circles.[6]

A second key ingredient of PVV ideology is Ye'or's (2005) notion of *Eurabia*, which points to an alleged conspiracy between the European Union and the Arab League to Islamicize Europe in the wake of the 1973 Yom Kippur war and the ensuing oil crisis; this conspiracy included a deliberate wave of immigration of Arab Muslims that aimed at changing the ethnographic balance of Europe. Ye'or herself has jokingly referred to her book as the 'Protocols of the Elders of Brussels', but it is clearly taken very seriously by followers like Wilders. Although it is hailed as fully backed by documentary evidence by its admirers, *Eurabia* does not in fact succeed in documenting any of its more dramatic claims.[7] Moreover, Ye'or's hypothesis of a Eurabian conspiracy is nonsensical both chronologically, as the major waves of Muslim labour migration had already started in the 1960s, and geographically, as these waves involved Turks at least as much as (Moroccan, Tunisian, and Algerian) Arabs; and Turks are not known for their pro-Arab sentiments.

A third and final element of the PVV's Islamophobic ideology is the concept of *taqiyya* or dissimulation. Originally developed in Shiʿite jurisprudence as a way of allowing Shiʿites to lie about their sectarian affiliation if their life was in danger, this notion has been reinterpreted in Islamophobic circles as a generic injunction to Muslims of whatever sectarian background to lie about their true intentions

progress, and civilization. On all forums, cheap Israel bashing by the combined forces of Islam and the Left should be countered" ("Israël, de enige democratie in het Midden-Oosten, verdient onze enthousiaste steun. Zeker nu het land steeds bedreigd wordt door de knotsgekke moellahs in Iran. Voor de Partij voor de Vrijheid is de Joodse staat altijd een baken van hoop, vooruitgang en westerse beschaving. Op alle podia moet het goedkope Israël-bashen van de gecombineerde krachten van islam en links worden tegengegaan."). PVV electoral program *Hún Brussel, óns Nederland*. 2012, p. 5; http://pvv.nl/index.php/visie/verkiezingsprogramma-2012.html (accessed September 23, 2014).

6. See Ye'or (1985). The anti-leftist strain is even more marked in the book by Wilders's ideological right hand, Martin Bosma (2011), *De schijn-élite van de valse munters* [The counterfeiters' fake elite]. In this work, all the evils of twentieth-century Europe (most notably, Nazism) are conveniently blamed on one entity labelled "socialism", which stretches from Leninism to post-war social democracy.

7. For a more detailed assessment of the argumentative strength of *Eurabia*, see my review in *INAMO*, no. 53 (2008).

(which, invariably, are said or implied to amount to the worldwide spread of Islam and to violent jihad against all unbelievers). Although unknown to the vast majority of Muslims, this notion is claimed as a key element of Islam by its critics; needless to say, it raises suspicions even against apparently assimilated or secularized Muslims, while simultaneously rendering Islamophobic discourse itself impossible to refute.

In short, the Islamophobic ideology of the PVV and its main sources of inspiration express a paranoid and unfalsifiable worldview of conspiracies, violent jihad and attempts to conquer the world, which goes far beyond any theological critique of Islam as a religion: it places all individuals of Islamic background, no matter how apparently secularized or assimilated, under permanent suspicion of secretly waging or planning a jihad against non-believers. This ideology is not only immune to falsification, but also remarkably silent on possible solutions; in fact, it implies that the only way of dealing with the alleged Islamic threat is either the permanent surveillance or the physical removal, not only of radical Muslims or of youthful troublemakers, but of *all* Muslims. Given the dogma of *taqiyya*, not even the assimilation or mass conversion of Muslims (an idea once floated by Hirsi Ali) will permanently remove the threat allegedly posed by the Muslim presence in Europe, as even converted, assimilated, or secularized individuals with a Muslim background may be merely hiding their jihadist intentions. Hence, taken to its logical conclusions, the PVV's ideology would require not only a stop to all immigration from Muslim countries, but also the expulsion of Muslims already living in the Netherlands, and more generally in Europe. These more radical conclusions are rarely drawn explicitly; but they certainly inform many an Islamophobic author, and as we will see, Wilders repeatedly hints at them.

As PVV statements hardly even pretend to add up to a systematic or coherent whole, it may be somewhat misleading to call them an 'ideology'; thus, the free speech demanded for Wilders is routinely denied to those who would speak on behalf of Islam or of Muslim population groups. This inconsistency, however, may have unexpected implications when extended to other minorities, as became painfully clear when the PVV supported a bill banning the ritual slaughter of animals, which had originally been proposed by the animal-rights and animal-welfare Partij voor de Dieren (PvdD). Ostensibly a bill against the unnecessary suffering of animals, the bill clearly targeted Muslim practices of *halal* butchering. Ultimately, however, the bill was rejected in parliament: it was not only rendered a dead letter by people's realization that they could simply import halal meat from abroad if it were to be banned in the Netherlands; but the bill also, and inadvertently, targeted Jewish practices of kosher butchering, thus undermining the PVV's staunchly pro-Jewish and pro-Israel stance.

4. The language of the Freedom Party

Wilders and his PVV have not just become famous, or notorious, for their anti-Islamic and anti-European and pro-Israel ideology, however, but also — and perhaps more importantly — for their rude and systematically provocative verbal strategies. This aspect of Freedom Party discourse is such a novel phenomenon in the Dutch political landscape that in 2010, Jan Kuitenbrouwer, a prominent Dutch journalist with a keen ear for linguistic trends and fashions, even published a book-length study of Wilders's vocabulary and framing strategies. In the same year, another, more academic book-length study was published, which similarly focused on framing but paid more attention to Wilders's argumentative style.[8] Kuitenbrouwer partly bases his analysis of the ways in which Wilders characterizes opponents and frames debates on George Lakoff's notion of political framing; as such, he may be said to focus on the semantics of Wilders's language and the conceptual tools underlying the rhetorical success of his vocabulary. In what follows, however, I would like to shift attention to questions that belong to pragmatics rather than semantics: exactly what audience are Wilders's statements actually addressed to? What effects are they intended to achieve? What linguistic ideologies do they presuppose or reproduce? The most difficult question to answer of all concerns violence: is PVV discourse a call to arms against Muslim violence, or does it instead provoke or incite physical violence, or perhaps even amount to verbal or discursive violence itself? I do not pretend to have a full-blown answer to these questions, which I will tackle with the aid of Speech Act Theory and some of its offshoots, in particular Judith Butler's approach to hate speech; but I hope to make clear that it is important to raise them.

One initial pragmatic question is exactly who is the intended audience or addressees of Wilders's utterances. For the most part, Wilders's remarks, although *about* Muslims, are clearly not directed *at* the Muslim population of the Netherlands, despite their occasional rhetorical appeal to abide by the law or to accept Western values. Nor do they simply target the Dutch electorate at large, as their tone and style antagonize a large part of the electorate. Rather, as will appear below, they almost seem intended to have a polarizing effect, and to aim at a clear separation between opponents and sympathizers. This becomes especially clear from the novel phenomenon of the tweet, a genre in which Wilders excels: tweets are typically brief, to the point, and undiplomatic; they are not directly addressed

8. Kuitenbrouwer (2010); De Bruijn (2010). Kuitenbrouwer employs George Lakoff's ideas about framing as expressed in e.g, Lakoff (2004).

to anyone in particular, and invite similarly pointed responses rather than a debate with arguments and counterarguments.[9]

In other words, despite its claim to form part of a rational debate, PVV discourse typically leaves little or no room for a reasoned exchange of arguments and justifications. But what *does* it aim at, then? One hesitates to speak of "rhetoric" here, a term that may carry associations of eloquence, elegance, and persuasion that are a far cry from Wilders's verbal style and tactics. Rather, he often uses a rude, crude, and systematically confrontational language that targets both Muslims and leftists for ridicule, and revels in insulting if not discriminatory remarks. This verbal style or strategy primarily consists of a deliberate flouting of unwritten rules of orderly parliamentary debate (and of polite conversation more generally), though not necessarily of any formal legal rules prohibiting discrimination and inciting hatred. Thus, on one occasion, Wilders called the speaker of parliament "raving mad" ("knettergek"); on another, he ridiculed the leader of the social democrat fraction as a "toleration poodle" ("gedoogpoedel") because of his support for the cabinet, even though at the time, it was the PVV itself rather than the social democrats that formally supported, or "tolerated", the minority cabinet of Liberals and Christian Democrats.

The cumulative effect of this provocative and polarizing discourse will be discussed below, but there are indications that it is used as a carefully thought-ought and implemented communicative strategy: not even maverick politician Pim Fortuyn had as systematically engaged in the insulting or provoking of both his political opponents and Muslims living in the Netherlands. Kuitenbrouwer (2010, 20ff.) suggests that the more picturesque of Wilders's characterizations have been jointly coined by Wilders himself and his aide, Martin Bosma, and virtually amount to a form of stand-up comedy. He further observes that Wilders's language is decidedly 1950s in vocabulary, and that, as coarse as it is, never becomes obscene in the way that much present-day debates include sexually explicit terms of abuse.

In general, Wilders appears careful not to make sweeping claims about population groups, as this might easily be construed as amounting to insult or discrimination of groups or individuals. In practice, of course, the distinction among Islam as a religion, political Islam as an ideology, and Muslims as a population group is not always easy to make, and Wilders systematically exploits this blurred

9. To mention but one among many examples that are as numerous as they are repetitive, on October 1, 2013, Wilders twittered about the new parliamentary speaker, Khadija Arib: "We'll never get used to it. This afternoon, a Moroccan (Arib) as speaker of parliament with the Qur'an in front of her, in the Dutch parliament" ("Het zal nooit wennen. Een Marokkaanse (Arib) vanmiddag als Kamervoorzitter met de Koran voor haar neus in de Nederlandse Tweede Kamer."). Wilders's tweets can be found at https://twitter.com/geertwilderspvv (accessed December 22, 2014).

distinction. In fact, some of his most notorious statements deliberately straddle the demarcation lines between Islam, Islamism, and Muslims, as when he proposed a special tax on headscarves during the opening of the parliamentary year in September 2009:

> A *better environment* starts with yourself. Many Dutchmen are irritated by Islam's *pollution* of public space. In some places, our streets start looking more and more like Mecca or Tehran. Headscarves, hate beards, burkas, men in weird long white dresses… Let us *reconquer* our streets and ensure that Holland starts looking like Holland again. Those headscarves are a symbol of an ideology that is out to *colonize us*. Therefore: high time for a *major cleansing* of our streets… Why not raise levies on headscarves? A head rag tax… The *polluter* pays."[10]

In this statement, Wilders clearly crosses the line between criticizing a religion and calling attention to its adherents because of their physical appearance, which he characterizes not only in derogatory terms like "hate beards", "head rags" and "weird long white dresses", but also in the more sinister vocabulary of dirt, pollution, and cleansing; and even in a discourse of violence, war, conquest, and colonization. It is not clear if the term *haatbaard* actually originated in PVV circles, but clearly, it was Wilders who made it popular. *Kopvod* may be a translation of the English *head rag*, as it occurs in, among others, William Faulkner's *Absalom! Absalom!* or Alice Walker's *The Color Purple*;[11] significantly, both uses have clearly racist contexts and connotations. Kuitenbrouwer (2010, 34), however, suggests that in Wilders's native province of Limburg, the term *kopvod* was a traditional vulgar and derogatory term for the head covering worn by catholic nuns. But whatever its origins, its effects were clearly not what Wilders had hoped or expected: the proposal not only, and predictably, met with unanimous disapproval in parliament, but also caused the PVV to drop significantly in local opinion polls. As a result of the latter, both terms were quietly dropped. Although repeatedly challenged to elaborate and formally launch their plan of taxing headscarves, Wilders and his

10. "Een *beter milieu* begint bij jezelf. Heel veel Nederlanders ergeren zich aan de *vervuiling* van de publieke ruimte door de Islam. Ons straatbeeld gaat op sommige plekken steeds meer lijken op Mekka en Teheran. Hoofddoekjes, haatbaarden, boerka's, mannen in rare lange witte jurken… Laten we onze straten *terugveroveren*, en zorgen dat Nederland er weer gaat uitzien als Nederland. Die hoofddoekjes zijn een symbool van een ideologie die erop uit is om ons te *koloniseren*. Daarom: tijd voor een *grote schoonmaak* van onze straten… Waarom dan niet een hoofddoekjesbelasting? Een kopvoddentaks… De *vervuiler* betaalt." Emph. added; quoted in Kuitenbrouwer (2010, 32).

11. The literary and other antecedents were noted by Dutch journalist Frits Abrahams, in his column, "Kopvod" verklaard, *NRC Handelsblad*, 22 September 2009 (http://weblogs.nrc.nl/dag/2009/09/22/%E2%80%98kopvod%E2%80%99-verklaard/#more-1149, accessed May 2, 2013).

colleagues generally evaded such challenges. The term *kopvoddentaks* did return in the PVV's 2012 electoral program, but not as a major policy item.

Wilders's self-censorship involving the term *haatbaard* is even more remarkable. Both on video footage of the original parliament session and in the parliamentary transcripts (which are approved by representatives before publication), Wilders appears to use the term *haardbaarden* ("hearth beards"), an expression which is simply meaningless. When uttering this term, Wilders was reading from a prepared text; this suggests that his wording may not have been a slip of the tongue but a deliberate malapropism for *haatbaard*, the word sounding closest to it, and indeed the word he was universally understood to have used. Thus, a quick internet search in Spring 2012 revealed 79,600 hits for *haatbaard* and a mere 311 for *haardbaard*, most of which clearly function as a euphemism or stand-in for the former. This act of self-censorship may suggest that Wilders, at this stage, still took some care to avoid language that indiscriminately targeted groups rather than beliefs, possibly with an eye to legal implications.

In a television debate, party ideologue Bosma did not disown terms like *haatbaard* and *kopvoddentaks*, but trivialized their possible effects, calling them "offensive but clear" (*kwetsend maar helder*).[12] The jocular tone in which Bosma conducted the entire discussion and more generally the readiness of PVV politicians to both introduce and drop items for debate strongly suggest that, almost irrespectively of its speakers' actual political and other beliefs, PVV discourse in large part consists of simply trying out which words "work", in the sense of attracting media attention and provoking public debate. Thus, at one point, the party also proposed a merger with the Flemish-speaking North of Belgium (which had broken away from the Netherlands in the early 19th century); on another occasion, it protested against the alleged undermining of the local Saint Nicholas celebration by politically correct foreign activists; these statements, however, met with indifference or ridicule, and were quietly dropped.

Wilders's statements may originate as a form of stand-up comedy intended to provoke laughter, if we are to believe Kuitenbrouwer (2010, 25); but they often revolve around violence. Although they are most obviously *about* the violence allegedly inherent to Islam, they have also led to substantial concerns that their *effect* may be one of violence. In public debate, questions were raised whether they amount to inciting hatred and may trigger violence *against* Muslims; rather more often, however, fears were expressed that they could provoke violent retaliations *by* Muslims. On this point, PVV discourse clearly involves two contradictory

12. *Pauw & Witteman*, 29 October 2010. http://pauwenwitteman.vara.nl/Uitzending-detail.113.0.html?&tx_ttnews[tt_news]=18416&tx_ttnews[backPid]=1546&cHash=e202233af4c289b82415f5b9a03209de (accessed April 3, 2012).

language ideologies: on the one hand, as will appear below, Wilders construes his own words as words rather than actions, and as constructive contributions to a political and public debate: thus, he implies that his words are *just* words, i.e., that they are legitimate and harmless expressions of opinions.[13] Others' words, however — whether Muslims' or ethnically Dutch opponents' — he tends to construe as actions rather than just words, and more specifically as threats or demonizations, that is, as inherently violent actions; likewise, he sees the language of the Qur'an as a call for violent action, rather than as the legitimate expression of a bona fide religious faith. We will return to this asymmetry below.

Thus, when confronted with protest that his remarks are offensive to Muslims, Wilders (like his populist predecessors) claims the right to offend as a crucial ingredient of public debate in a democratic society, disregarding any further effects that derogatory language might have on either its addressee or on a third party; more generally, he routinely denies that his polarizing language has, or could have, any violent effect at all. Put differently, he denies any responsibility for his own words, or attempts to shift the responsibility for any violent effects on others. Thus, he elaborated his 2007 call for banning the Qur'an as follows:

> It is not me who propagates hatred, it is the Qur'an. It is a fascist book. It is not a book we should have over here. Perhaps [it is admissible] if you take out all those nasty verses, but then little will remain; then the Qur'an will be as voluminous as a Donald Duck magazine.[14]

This comment does not only suggest that Wilders intends to depict any resulting polarization, discord, hatred or violence as not being caused by his own words but rather by the Qur'anic text itself.[15] At the same time, his comparisons of the Qur'an to Hitler's *Mein Kampf* and the *Donald Duck* magazine are carefully calculated to humiliate, irritate and/or provoke his opponents, and at the same time to provoke the laughter of his sympathizers. Predictably, both the cabinet and the other parties in parliament rejected Wilders's call for a ban, giving him the opportunity to

13. For more detailed discussion of this point, see. Leezenberg (forthcoming).

14. "Ik zaai geen haat, dat doet de Koran. Het is een fascistisch boek. Dit is geen boek dat we hier moeten hebben. Misschien als je al die foute verzen eruit haalt, maar dan blijft er weinig over; dan is de Koran net zo dik als de Donald Duck." Interview, "Mensen zijn islamisering spuugzat" ("People are sick and tired of Islamization"), *Algemeen Dagblad*, August 17, 2007 http://www.ad.nl/ad/nl/1012/Nederland/article/detail/2237022/2007/08/17/Mensen-zijn-islamisering-spuugzat.dhtml (accessed April 29, 2013).

15. As with many another element of PVV ideology, this factual claim is demonstrably nonsensical: the text of the Qur'an contains very few calls to political action, and even fewer law-like violent sanctions of inappropriate behaviour, let alone calls to violence against unbelievers outside of narrative contexts; cf. Woltering & Leezenberg (2010): ch. 7.

call his fellow politicians "cowards" and "scaredy-cats who do not talk straight" ("angsthazen die met meel in de mond praten"). Wilders's call led to a barrage of calls to prosecute him for inciting hatred; at the same time, his party skyrocketed in opinion polls, which proved that, this time at least, Wilders's polarizing tactics had paid off in electoral terms.

The question of whether Wilders's utterances merely call attention to violence, or instead may provoke (physical) violence by or against Muslims, or even amount to a form of verbal violence in themselves, becomes even more central in the overheated debates surrounding his 15-minute documentary, *Fitna*. Intriguingly, there was far more public debate in the months preceding the movie's actual release than in the weeks after, with Wilders demanding that his movie be broadcast on national public television in the interest of freedom of expression, and the Dutch government hesitatingly trying to restrict its circulation in the name of public security. Indeed, (fear of) violence by Muslims rather than a concern about discrimination was the main framing factor in the discussion surrounding the movie, long before its actual release. If we take *Fitna* as a sort of macro speech act, one might say that its effect of calling attention to violence in the name of Islam *preceded* its actually being uttered, in a reversal of the usual chronological order of an utterance and its effect. This reversal of temporality constitutes one of the most remarkable pragmatic oddities of PVV discourse.

The "fear of Muslim violence" framing proved very powerful indeed. When *Fitna* was finally released in March 2008, the main reaction was one of relief that no violent reactions had occurred among Muslims either in Holland or abroad — implying a tacit acceptance of the movie's suggestion that Muslims are prone to violence. Discussion hardly if at all addressed the movie's factual accuracy or its editing techniques, despite, for example, the demonstrably erroneous or tendentious translation of *all* Qur'anic verses, without exception, quoted in the movie,[16] and despite its breathtakingly crude propagandistic editing that juxtaposed any expression of a Muslim identity in Europe with images of murderous, terrorist violence. This kind of suggestive editing, moreover, was nothing very new: already in 1989, British poet Tony Harrison had written a poem in defence of Salman Rushdie, "The Blasphemers' Banquet", which had been broadcast to equally suggestively edited and reductionist video footage that generically associated Islam with violence much like *Fitna* did.[17] More remarkably, *Fitna* appears to have copied entire scenes — including music and subtitles — from *Obsession: Radical Islam's*

16. For a more detailed analysis of the adequacy of *Fitna's* Qur'anic translations, see "Slotwoord: heilig boek of haatpamflet?" (Woltering and Leezenberg 2010, 89–93).

17. The broadcast does not appear to be available on the internet; the poem itself is reprinted in Harrison (2007)'s *Collected Film Poetry* (London 2007).

War against the West, a 2005 pro-Israeli propaganda movie by Wayne Kopping and Raphael Shore. Surprisingly, Kopping did not make any objections against this obvious plagiarism; clearly, both movies use material, and even footage, originating in the same pro-Israeli sources, like Palestinian Media Watch and the Middle East Media Research Institute.[18]

What is perhaps most striking about *Fitna* is the discrepancy between the documentary's apparent meaning and its actual pragmatic effects. In an interview published shortly before its eventual release, Judith Butler correctly observed that public debate about the movie no longer concerned the factual correctness, quality or novelty of *Fitna* as a documentary, but had turned it into a sign for the freedom of speech;[19] the interesting thing being, of course, that for months, that sign was *not being uttered*. Moreover, *Fitna* became a sign or emblem not only for the liberal and secular right to free speech, but also — and in the same gesture — a sign of the violence allegedly inherent in Islam. As a sign or speech act of violence, however, the movie raises rather different questions: should it be seen as a descriptive statement or as a performative utterance, which aims at bringing about the very violence it represents? Can it be considered to have been successful or felicitous on either account? Clearly, the uptake of this speech act has not been one of either discussing its propositional content or factual accuracy or actually practicing physical violence (either by or against Muslims); but what *did* this utterance bring about, and what was it intended to bring about?

It is impossible to determine whether Wilders actually hoped or intended for the film, and his various other remarks, to provoke violence by Muslims; but they clearly seem to be phrased and framed in such a way as to provoke; and undoubtedly, he would have taken any resulting violence as proof of the point he was claiming to make. Intriguingly, the media followed suit: in the mainstream Dutch press, questions of whether the film was discriminatory or incited hatred were drowned out by heated discussions of whether it should be banned in the name of public order, and whether showing it would lead to social unrest or riots among Muslims in the Netherlands, or to economic or physical retaliation against Dutch citizens and interests abroad.

But one may go beyond the claim that Wilders's utterances may aspire at performatively bringing about the very violence by Muslims they claim to be

18. See "De Israel-connectie van Geert Wilders", *Vrij Nederland*, 15 October 2009 (http://www.vn.nl/Archief/Politiek/Artikel-Politiek/De-Israelconnectie-van-Geert-Wilders.htm, accessed April 29, 2013).

19. See "Ik snap niet dat de regering zo bang is", *Vrij Nederland*, March 15, 2008 (http://www.vn.nl/Archief/Wetenschapmilieu/Artikel-Wetenschapmilieu/Filosofe-Judith-Butler-Ik-snap-niet-dat-de-regering-zo-bang-is.htm, accessed March 31, 2012).

representing. One might well argue that these utterances *themselves* involve, or amount to, specific forms of discursive violence, or to what in juridical vocabulary would be called "hate speech", realizing that they involve not just the expression of individual opinions, but amount to a discourse that is simultaneously sustained by, and reinforces or reproduces, existing power relations and patterns of domination and exclusion. Like Hirsi Ali, Wilders has lived under permanent police protection since the assassination of Theo van Gogh in November 2004; thus, he is not simply a brave individual standing up for free speech, but a seasoned politician whose freedom of speech and movement require the repressive power of the state. Thus, he not only presupposes the power of the modern state as the precondition for his statements by demanding permanent police protection and claiming parliamentary immunity, but he also reproduces, reinforces, and legitimizes the repressive powers of that state in his frequent appeals for state censorship of "hate imams", as he consistently calls them, and for "radical" imams to be deported or not allowed to speak in public; in his calls for an outright prohibition of the Qur'an; in his frequent criminal complaints filed against real or perceived threats against him; and last but not least in his proposals to send in the Dutch military in urban quarters having problems with immigrant youths[20] or to have police troops shoot with live ammunition at rioters.[21] On his account, the state, having a mo-

20. 'Wilders: stuur het leger naar Gouda' (*Telegraaf*, 15 September 2008), http://www.telegraaf.nl/binnenland/20660379/__Wilders___Stuur_het_leger_naar_Gouda___.html (accessed April 29, 2013).

21. Various Dutch media, September 15, 2007. Wilders elaborated his comments in a column (accessible at http://www.pvv.nl/index.php?option=com_content&task=view&id=579, accessed April 29, 2013): "I propose to shoot with live ammunition during serious riots. First, a clear warning should be given, then a warning shot should be fired; subsequently, the police should deactivate rioters, preferably by shooting them in the legs. The unambiguous providing of legally binding impunity for the police in such cases will take away any hesitation on the side of policemen to rigorously engage with and to effectively counter rioters. It doesn't make any difference whether rioters are soccer hooligans (whether or not Moroccan), squatters, antiglobalists and other despicable scum" [Ik stel voor] om bij ernstige rellen met scherp te schieten. Hieraan voorafgaand moet er eerst een duidelijke waarschuwing gegeven worden, daarna een waarschuwingsschot en vervolgens dient de politie relschoppers uit te schakelen middels een schot bij voorkeur in het been. Het onomwonden wettelijk vastleggen dat bij het volgen van deze procedure de politie straffeloos is, zal aarzeling bij agenten om relschoppers hard aan te pakken wegnemen en de relschoppers effectief bestrijden. Het maakt overigens geen verschil of de relschoppers bestaan uit voetbalhooligans (Marokkaans of niet), krakers, antiglobalisten of ander verwerpelijk tuig." Note the final sentence, in which Wilders disingenuously suggests that his language has no ethnic dimension, simultaneously and oddly singling out Moroccans as soccer hooligans.

nopoly on legitimate violence, should not hesitate to resort to violence in dealing with unruly population groups.

On occasion, Wilders has even openly called for the deportation and ethnic cleansing of Muslim population groups at large, not only from Western Europe but even from their native lands. Thus, in December 2008, referring to then-ongoing clashes between Palestinians and the Israeli army, Wilders openly propagated ethnic cleansing as the only solution to the problem: referring to the Palestinians, he declared: "knikker de hele bende maar de Sinai in" ("just toss the entire bunch into the Sinai desert").[22] Likewise, in an interview with Danish television, Wilders openly said that Muslims who fail to abide by Western norms should be deported from Europe. Returning to his earlier image of a tsunami of Muslims flooding Europe, he argues that if the percentage of Muslims in a society increases, the remaining population will be deprived of its freedom, suggesting a direct causal link between demographic change, rising crime rates, the alleged Islamization of society, and the alleged disappearance of liberal values. Asked how many Muslims in Europe do in fact represent such a threat, he mentioned that "tens of millions" of Muslim immigrants are causing problems, and added what he called "a very clear message" to Europe's Muslim population:

> if you commit a crime, or if you start thinking about jihad or sharī'a, then it is very clear we will send you away, we will send you packing, we will strip you of the Dutch or Danish nationality, and we will send you away… At the same time, we want a stop of the immigration from Muslim countries, from any Muslim countries, to our societies.[23]

Note that Wilders does not refer to Muslims who have actually transgressed the law, but to Muslims who "start thinking" about doing so, apparently introducing a category of thought crime in the process. Equally remarkable is the recurrent, and apparently deliberate, slippage from criminality to caliphate and from immigration to Islamization in these remarks, which turns alleged evidence for the one automatically into evidence for the other.

22. "De aanleiding is blinde haat. Daar helpt helaas geen dialoog tegen. Als je volk en land in zijn bestaan wordt bedreigd en beschoten door terroristen, schiet je terug… Knikker de hele bende maar de Sinaï in" ("The motive is blind hatred. Unfortunately no dialogue helps against that. When your people and land are threatened in their existence and shot at by terrorists, you shoot back… Toss the entire bunch into the Sinai". *De Telegraaf*, 28 December 2008; see http://www.telegraaf.nl/binnenland/2878429/__Wilders_achter_Israel__.html (accessed March 31, 2012).

23. For footage of the interview, see http://www.youtube.com/watch?v=IoeVcslBwgg (accessed March 31, 2013).

In short, Wilders's discourse is clearly not only *about* violence, it is also itself a discourse *of* violence: he employs a vocabulary of war and physical violence rather than political debate, and openly calls for state violence against unruly Muslims (and to a lesser extent others), apparently presuming that state violence is legitimate by definition. It is, however, a moot question with serious juridical implications exactly *how* his words involve violence: can they be said to provoke or invite violence, not only on the part of the state but also on the part of Muslims, who are ostensibly the people talked about, or of the non-Muslim Dutch population, who are ostensibly the audience addressed? Are they *intended* to provoke such violence, and if so, how can this intent be proven? Such questions are of a juridical as much as of a pragmatic nature; and soon after, they were to acquire a tragic urgency.

5. Criminal responsibility? The hate speech trial and the Breivik assaults

There seem to be good *prima facie* reasons for thinking that Wilders's remarks go far beyond merely criticizing Islam as a religion and amount to the discrimination of, or inciting hatred against, Muslims as a group, and even amount to a call for physical violence to be exercised by the state. Various actors in the Netherlands have indeed drawn this conclusion, and over the years, a number of criminal complaints have been filed against Wilders; in particular the release of *Fitna* led to a barrage of calls for criminal prosecution; but in June 2008, the Dutch State Attorney decided to drop these cases, arguing that Wilders's remarks were "perhaps hurtful, coarse or lacking nuance, but did not amount to insult punishable by law" ("wellicht kwetsend, grof of ongenuanceerd, maar geen strafbare belediging").[24] After a group of lawyers had initiated a so-called 'Artikel 12 Strafvordering' (article 12 criminal proceedings) procedure — which allows victims to protest against State Attorney decisions not to prosecute — however, the Amsterdam court ruled in January 2009 that, because of their inflammatory tone and one-sided content, Wilders's remarks did indeed amount to inciting hatred against and discrimination of Muslims, and to criminal insult; accordingly, it ordered a trial, clearly against the preference of the State Attorney.[25]

In one of the more conspicuous ironies of the ensuing trial, Wilders decided to defend his claims to free speech by exercising his right to silence. In doing so, he once again indicated that he did not want to consider his beliefs or statements

24. For the June 30, 2008 ruling, see http://www.om.nl/onderwerpen/discriminatie/@148328/wilders_niet/ (accessed 11 May 2013).

25. For the court ruling, see http://zoeken.rechtspraak.nl/resultpage.aspx?snelzoeken=true&searchtype=ljn&ljn=BH0496 (accessed 2 May 2013).

as in any way open to criticism, debate, or justification; that is, he did not treat them as moves in a rational debate of providing, and listening to, arguments and justifications of differing viewpoints. Initially, Wilders's defence tried to divert the case from the *language* Wilders had been using to the *ideology* expressed by that language, which it presented as a politically inconvenient but scientifically established truth about Islam. For this line of defence, it had called in a large number of alleged expert witnesses, all of whom in fact hailed from the Dutch and international Islamophobic circles described above; but when all but three of these experts were rejected by the court, it switched tactics. Now, Wilders's lawyer, Bram Moszkowicz, repeatedly and ultimately successfully challenged the judges assigned to the case: as a result, a rerun of the trial with different judges was ordered in October 2010. By such and other stalling and diverting tactics, the defence managed to shift attention away from what had originally been the trial's main concern: the question of whether Wilders's remarks transgressed any legal boundaries of discrimination and sowed hatred. After a new trial had started in February 2011, the State Attorney demanded Wilders's acquittal in May, and on June 23, Wilders was indeed acquitted on all counts, with the judges apparently, and uncritically, following the line of defence that Wilders's words were meant as a criticism of Islam as a religion and did not speak out against Muslims as individuals or as a group, even though a good many of his remarks both inside and outside of parliament, like those about the allegedly polluting effect of Muslims and their physical appearance in public space, would seem to suggest otherwise.[26]

As we will see below, the court's ruling may be criticized on juridical grounds; but the most dramatic refutation of the court's conclusion that Wilders's discourse did not amount to hate speech came barely a month after Wilders's acquittal. On July 22, 2011, Norwegian activist Anders Breivik carried out a twin attack in the Norwegian capital Oslo and on the nearby island of Utøya, where the youth organisation of the Norwegian Labor Party had organized a summer camp, explicitly claiming Wilders as a source of inspiration for his actions. Breivik's attack left a total number of 77 people dead, and a further 110 injured. Although Breivik's actions were clearly ideologically motivated, and explained in detail in his 1500-page manifesto entitled *2083: A European Declaration of Independence*,[27] there was substantial discussion of whether Breivik could be held accountable for his actions.

26. http://www.rechtspraak.nl/Organisatie/Rechtbanken/Amsterdam/Nieuws/Pages/Uitspraak-van-de-rechtbank-AmsterdamindezaakWilders,23juni2011.aspx (accessed April 29, 2013).

27. For a summary of Breivik's manifesto, see e.g. "The Oslo Terrorist in His Own Words," *Washington Post*, July 23, 2011 (http://www.washingtontimes.com/blog/robbins-report/2011/jul/23/oslo-terrorist-his-own-words/ (accessed March 30, 2011). A more detailed analysis, in

Initially, forensic psychiatrists concluded that he was criminally insane, and hence could not be condemned to prison, partly on the basis of his writings, which, they held, expressed a universe of bizarre, grandiose, and delusional thoughts. No one, however, has to my knowledge ever seriously claimed that similarly radical discourse like the PVV's, which as noted above shares a good many of the paranoia and conspiracy theories that also shape Breivik's ideas (including those of a Eurabian conspiracy), is pathological.

Locating the ideological motivation and responsibility of Breivik's deeds was found to be difficult. In an interview with *Der Spiegel*, Norwegian peace researcher Johan Galtung stated that European rightist parties are indeed accessories to Breivik's crime and bear a shared guilt (*Mitschuld*), but added, in a slightly contradictory manner: "they are responsible for hatred emerging against Muslims; but they are not responsible for Breivik's hatred… His hatred of the alleged alliance between social democrats and Islamists has no example."[28] The latter claim is demonstrably wrong, however; as Dutch journalist Eildert Mulder has shown in detail, there are various ideological antecedents to Breivik's theories, although many of them stop short of explicitly proclaiming a violent solution.

The question of (direct and indirect) responsibility for Breivik's actions is of course a sensitive one. Breivik himself admitted to carrying out the killings, but pleaded not guilty, instead shifting responsibility to the Norwegian Labor Party: "As long as the Labor Party follows its ideological line and continues to deconstruct Norwegian culture and import Muslims en masse so they must take responsibility for this treason."[29] In his final plea in the hate speech trial, Wilders had likewise declared that he would continue to speak out, stating that silence on Islam and Islamization amounted to treason.[30] Breivik's words resonate with those of Wilders. Furthermore, a similar conclusion emerged from Ayaan Hirsi Ali. In July 2012, in a classical case of blaming the victims, Hirsi Ali declared in her acceptance speech for the *Bild Zeitung* prize that the causes of Breivik's deeds should not be sought in extremist Islamophobic ideology but in an alleged politically correct repression of open discussion. In an interview following her speech, she elaborated:

Dutch, can be found in Mulder (2012). See also Bangstad (2014), which unfortunately appeared too late to be included in the present discussion.

28. "Wir müssen verstehen, wie Breivik denkt" (interview, *Der Spiegel*, August 3, 2011). Available on http://www.spiegel.de/politik/ausland/0,1518,777942,00.html (accessed March 30, 2012).

29. http://www.bloomberg.com/news/2011-07-24/norway-killing-suspect-may-explain-motives.html (accessed March 30, 2013).

30. ""Ik wil mijn land beschermen tegen de islam, dus zwijgen is verraad." http://www.rtl.nl/components/actueel/rtlnieuws/2011/06_juni/01/binnenland/Zwijgen-is-verraad.xml (accessed April 29, 2013).

> *Q: Do you mean: Breivik's assaults are actually caused by the suppression of societal problems?*
> A: That is what he says in his manifesto. He also says it in the court case which is now public. So the theory that was initially proposed, that he was inspired by people who are against jihad is wrong. He says: I wanted to use violence because I saw no other way out. Well, I have heard that sentiment before, starting from the year 2000. I have heard it in the Netherlands, Germany, France, Australia: anywhere I went, people complained about political correctness, and so political correctness is not good.[31]

In other words, Hirsi Ali sees not a dehumanizing ideology, but rather the attempt to banish or silence that ideology, as the real cause of Breivik's violence. Thus, she not only uncritically reproduces one part of Breivik's ideological self-justifications while simultaneously downplaying his appeals to Wilders and herself; she also, and disingenuously, downplays the fact that Islamophobes like Wilders and herself had been using a rhetoric of war, violence and disease rather than a rational debate conducted in a peaceful democratic environment, and that they themselves had presented violent means such as forced assimilation or conversion, deportation and/or ethnic cleansing as the only viable solutions.

Despite the obvious similarities in ideology and language, Wilders issued a predictable, and predictably strongly worded, denial of any direct or indirect responsibility for the actions committed by Breivik, whom he called a "lunatic" and a "psychopath":

> Neither the PVV nor me are responsible for a solitary nutty idiot who has abused the freedom-loving anti-Islamization ideals in a violent manner… We are democrats in heart and soul. *The Freedom Party has never called for violence and never will.*[32]

31. *V: Bedoelt u daarmee: de aanslagen van Breivik zijn eigenlijk het gevolg van het stilzwijgen van maatschappelijke problemen?*
A: Dat zegt hij in zijn manifest. Dat zegt hij ook in de rechtszaak die nu publiek is. Dus de theorie die naar voren werd geschoven in het begin dat hij geïnspireerd zou zijn door mensen die tegen de jihad zijn dat klopt niet. Hij zegt: ik wilde geweld gebruiken omdat ik geen andere uitweg zag. Nou, dat sentiment heb ik vaker gehoord. Vanaf 2000. Ik hoorde het in Nederland, Duitsland, Frankrijk, Australië, waar ik ook naar toe ging, mensen klaagden voortdurend over politieke correctheid. En politieke correctheid is dus niet goed." http://www.joop.nl/wereld/detail/artikel/13954_hirsi_ali_breivik_is_product_van_politieke_correctheid/ (accessed 27 april 2013).

32. "De PVV noch ik zijn verantwoordelijk voor een eenzame verknipte idioot die de vrijheidslievende anti-islamiseringsidealen op gewelddadige manier misbruikt… Wij zijn democraten in hart en nieren. *De Partij voor de Vrijheid heeft nooit en te nimmer opgeroepen tot geweld en zal dat ook nooit doen*". PVV Press statement, 26 July 2011. http://www.pvv.nl/index.

Once more, Wilders poses as a bona fide liberal, by emphasizing his party's peaceful character and love of freedom, and by implicitly reaffirming that the state has a monopoly on legitimate violence; simultaneously, however, he once again lashes out at "leftists" for "demonizing" him by suggesting he might be indirectly responsible for the assaults. It was not only leftist politicians, however, that were unconvinced by Wilders's denials. His erstwhile ally Bart Jan Spruyt publicly called Wilders indirectly responsible for the assaults, blaming him for insufficiently distancing himself from the assaults and for creating an apocalyptic atmosphere of conflict and impending Islamic doom that left no room for politics.[33]

In the wake of the assaults, many Islamophobic websites toned down their rhetoric or removed some of their more incendiary pages. For several months, Wilders, too, displayed a noticeable shift away from anti-Muslim rhetoric to bashing the Labour Party (which was not even part of the governing coalition) and to rousing popular opinion against migrant workers from Eastern European countries, opening a website where people could file complaints against Eastern Europeans living in the Netherlands. He did not make any substantial changes to his Islamophobic discourse; however, in a lengthy television interview in December 2012, Wilders stated that he would not give up his fight against Islam, stating that "the biggest disease that our country has known in this century is called Islam", perhaps not coincidentally using precisely the discourse of disease that had been explicitly sanctioned by the Supreme Court.[34] In this interview, he once again described Islam as being a racist totalitarian ideology in essence, and (departing somewhat from his earlier invective) Muslims primarily as victims being oppressed by the yoke of Islam. This does not mean, of course, that Wilders had finally toned down his rhetoric: in the same breath, he stated that the Netherlands had a "Moroccans problem".[35]

The attempt to depict Breivik as an isolated lunatic and the denial of the ideological character of his assaults appear to have been largely successful: the Utøya massacres have hardly led to an enduring delegitimation of the radical Islamophobic discourse of Wilders and his allies. Thus, in March 2012, Dutch

---

php/component/content/article/36-geert-wilders/4529-verklaring-geert-wilders-noorwegen.html (emph. added; accessed April 29, 2013).

33. 'Wilders indirect verantwoordelijk voor Breivik', http://nos.nl/artikel/259288-wilders-indirect-verantwoordelijk-voor-breivik.html (accessed May 2, 2013).

34. As will be discussed below, in 2009 the Dutch Supreme Court had ruled that a public sign reading "Stop the tumor called Islam" did not amount to group insult; the court trying Wilders explicitly referred to this ruling in its acquittal.

35. Interview with NOS television, 20 December 2013, (http://nos.nl/video/455679-gehele-interview-met-pvvleider-wilders.html (accessed April 29, 2013).

author Theodor Holman staged a play, *Breivik ontmoet Wilders* (Breivik Meets Wilders), that openly expressed sympathy for part of Breivik's ideas, agreeing with the latter's analyses about the dangers of Islam for the Western world but rejecting his violent solutions. In an interview prior to the performance of the play, Holman openly acknowledged this agreement: "Now we had this killer, who had killed children. I am very sorry, but I find that extremely interesting. Here you see someone who thinks more or less as I do. I feel an affinity with Breivik, and I am not ashamed of it. And yet he took a totally different decision".[36] All of this suggests that the extreme Islamophobic rhetoric, involving claims that Muslims as well as their leftist Western apologists are beyond the pale of rational debate — and indeed of humanity — and are not to be seen as reasonable people with whom a dialogue can be conducted, had by then very much entered mainstream discourse and had by no means been delegitimized by the assaults in Norway.

6. Speech acts and violence

The successful disconnection between PVV discourse and Breivik's assaults brings us to broader questions concerning the pragmatics of violence. Clearly, Wilders bears no direct responsibility for the actions of others; but does that mean his words have no relation to Breivik's deeds at all? The above suggests that existing juridical frameworks may not be adequately equipped to deal with discourse like Wilders's. Both sympathizers and opponents of Wilders have by and large agreed on the principle of free speech, which is generally seen as an innocuous, not to say essential, aspect of a functioning liberal and secular democracy. In the public debate, however, few if any observers systematically paid any attention to exactly what other effects Wilders's words might have, beyond putting up a reductionist and misleading opposition between expressing opinions and inciting hatred. As the above makes clear, 'expressing opinions' is hardly an adequate term to capture the intent and effect of a substantial part of PVV discourse.

In the academic juridical literature, there has been more sustained attention for the potential effects of Wilders's language. Thus, in an analysis of the 2009 supreme court decision concerning an alleged insult against Islam, to which Wilders's judges had referred as a basis for their acquittal, Wouter Veraart (2010)

36. "Nu hadden we deze moordenaar, en die had kinderen vermoord. Het spijt me erg, maar ik vind dat waanzinnig interessant. Hier zie je iemand die min of meer denkt zoals ik. Ik voel me verwant met Breivik. En daar schaam ik me ook niet voor. En toch heeft die een totaal andere beslissing genomen." http://www.dagelijksestandaard.nl/2012/03/theodor-holman-ik-voel-me-verwant-met-breivik (accessed April 3, 2012).

argues that the Supreme court's overruling of an earlier court condemnation of a man who had publicly posted a sign with the slogan "Stop the tumor called Islam" in the wake of Theo van Gogh's assassination in 2004, reflects a new and more restrictive approach to group insult, which is based on an overly literalist and decontextualized reading of the text. A more balanced judgment, Veraart argues, should also take into account the context in which the statement was made. In his opinion, this context includes not only a critical public debate about the position of Islam as a religion in a multicultural society, but also acts of physical violence like the wave of arson attacks against mosques and Islamic schools following the assassination.

Veraart notes that if the Supreme Court had not focused on article 137c of the Dutch criminal code, which specifies group offence, but also looked at article 137d, which concerns inciting hatred against persons because of their race or religious beliefs, this context — which included not only a public debate but also acts of violence against Muslim targets — would also have been acknowledged in its ruling.[37] Against the Supreme Court ruling, Veraart further argues that the distinction between legitimate critique and illegitimate offence (let alone hate speech) cannot be drawn in an abstract and decontextualized manner: a decision whether or not an utterance amounts to hate speech should take into account not only the wider societal context but also the intentions with which the speaker made his utterance. Veraart notes that the Supreme Court's explicit denial that the case under jurisdiction concerns inciting hatred is odd for several reasons: first, it is highly unusual for a court — let alone the supreme court — to explicate what a court case is *not* about; second, the prosecution had in fact charged the defendant with inciting hatred, subsidiary to inflammatory speech and group offence; third, a fuller discussion of whether the slogan concerned amounted to inciting hatred rather than group offence would also have more systematically drawn attention to the context of physical violence against Islamic institutions. This suggests that pragmatic considerations concerning contexts and speaker's intentions of an utterance may become legally relevant in cases like the above. Against earlier

37. The text of articles 137c and 137d of the Dutch penal code call for the prosecution of, respectively "he who publicly, in speaking or in writing, expresses himself in a deliberately offensive manner about a group of people because of their race or religion" ("Hij die zich in het openbaar, mondeling of bij geschrift of afbeelding, opzettelijk beledigend uitlaat over een groep mensen wegens hun ras, godsdienst (enz.)") and "he who incites hatred against or discrimination of people, or violent action against people's person or property because of their race or religion" ("Hij die in het openbaar, mondeling of bij geschrift of afbeelding, aanzet tot haat tegen of discriminatie van mensen of gewelddadig optreden tegen persoon of goed van mensen wegens hun ras, geloof… (etc.)") (http://wetten.overheid.nl/BWBR0001854/TweedeBoek/TitelV/Artikel137c/geldigheidsdatum_02-05-2013, accessed May 2, 2013).

juridical analyses, Veraart rejects any strict distinction between an "offensive utterance in itself" and the "intended communication", because, he argues, no utterances are offensive in and of themselves, that is, outside a particular context. This is certainly an important point to make, but perhaps a difficult one to elaborate or apply in practice; on the one hand, it is notoriously difficult to use non-observable intentions as a means of explaining observable verbal behavior, and, on the other, Veraart's line of argument implies that an utterance that is at first blush completely innocuous could be turned into an offence, or even into the incitement of hatred, by the appropriate circumstances, regardless of the speaker's actual intentions.

All this indicates just how complex is the relation between utterances, contexts, and intended effects and possible unintended consequences on and for speaker, addressee, or possible third parties. Another, closely related question is exactly who or what *causes* the offence: is the effect of hate speech to be located in the words used, in the ideas or ideology expressed, in the context of the utterance, or in the speaker's intentions? Here, some of the ideas developed by Butler, as already discussed above, become relevant. In *Excitable Speech*, Butler (1997) develops an account of hate speech that proceeds from her Derridean take on speech act theory; thus, she proposes to treat speech acts as embodied actions that are not guided by an antecedently and independently given subjectivity or intentionality of the speaker, but by what Derrida (year) calls "iteration"; that is, by a logic of quotation in new contexts which inevitably and systematically exceed the speaker's intentions. From such a perspective, she argues, censorship is not simply a repressive form of state power that represses or constrains the sovereign utterances of antecedently given subjects; rather, she claims, it is a productive form of power: "censorship seeks to produce subjects according to implicit and explicit norms, […] the production of the subject has everything to do with the regulation of speech" (1997, 133). Following Foucault's (1975) ideas of modern disciplinary power as productive of modern subjectivities, Butler then argues that censorship produces both subjects and forms of acceptable speech. As such, she continues, it posits implicit and explicit norms; these norms, however, involve not so much explicit and codified rules but rather bodily dispositions, or what the French sociologist Bourdieu has called a "habitus", and hence cannot be fully accounted for in a quasi-legalist vocabulary that assumes both subjects as sovereign over their words and explicit rules as codified in laws. Thus, on her account, the effects of speech, and in particular the effects of hate speech, cannot exclusively be understood — let alone regulated — in terms of juridical power. Hate speech, she provocatively suggests, is produced by the state itself: not only does the state, in the guise of the court or more generally the judiciary, determine which utterances qualify as hate speech; hate speech as a sovereign and effective (or as Austin would say “felicitous”) speech act is also modelled on the speaking of the sovereign state (1997: 16, 81).

Butler next discusses whether and how speech can be injurious, refusing to reduce the injury caused by hate speech to either a perlocutionary effect bearing no necessary link to the utterance or an illocutionary force bearing a strict causal relation to the words being uttered. Thus, she rejects both the belief that words themselves have a causal effect and the equally reductionist belief that utterances are governed by speakers' intentions in any determinate way. Instead, she treats these effects, unforeseeable and uncontrollable as they are, in Derridean terms of iteration. A psychic injury, she argues, may affect bodily doxa, “that lived and corporeally registered set of beliefs that constitute social reality” (1997, 159).

By thus undermining the strict and unproblematic distinction between body and soul, and between speaking and acting, Butler effectively exposes the hypocrisy involved in demands for the right to offend or verbally injure as demands for a freedom of expression that is not only harmless but also essential to democratic debate. Indeed, calling attention to the performative character of hate speech helps us understand how, in claiming the right to freedom of expression, the perpetrators of such discourse try to position themselves as the victims of state repression or popular hatred, and the victims of hate speech as perpetrators. As the above discussion suggests, however, it may not be so much the injurious effects on the addressee as much as the possibly inflammatory effects on third parties that matter most in discussing the effects of Islamophobic discourse. Put differently, a critique of Islamophobic discourse should not only discuss the question of whether and how it causes any injury to Muslims; it should also, and perhaps more importantly, explore what Searle (2010, 187–191) has recently discussed under the heading of “libel and slander”. It is to a large extent up to me, Searle argues, to decide to what extent I am hurt by a hurtful utterance directed *against me*; but false or slanderous language *about me* spread to others can do great damage to me in a way that is wholly beyond my control. Hence, according to Searle, existing laws concerning slander should in fact be strengthened.[38] Butler (1997) would undoubtedly not agree with Searle's call for tightened legislation, and hence for greater repressive powers of the state, but the main juridical question at stake here is whether Islamophobic discourse amounts to what in America would be called

38. Recently, other authors from a broadly liberal background have similarly called for tightening the laws on hate speech. Thus, Waldron (2012) makes an eloquent case for increasing the legal restrictions on group defamation in the United States, which, he argues, threatens the basic dignity of individual members of society and undermines their freedom from fear, discrimination, and violence; according to Waldron, in Europe, existing laws are much better tailored to deal with hate speech. For some comments on Waldron's argument with a focus on the situation in the United Kingdom, see Modood a.o. (2014); see also Herz and Molnar (eds.) (2012).

hate speech, or rather qualifies as libel and slander; or to put the question in more analytical terms: does it primarily have its effects on the apparent addressee (i.e., the Muslim population groups in the Netherlands, or more generally Europe), or rather on a third party, specifically the Dutch public or electorate at large?[39] As noted, Wilders's predecessors like Theo van Gogh and Ayaan Hirsi Ali had also demanded a 'right to offend' as essential to enlightened or rational democratic debate; the question of what the beneficial effects of such offence are supposed to be, apart from an assumed undermining of religious authority and, more importantly, the question of exactly how such offence is supposed to further the emancipation of Muslim immigrants in general and of Muslim immigrant women in particular, rather than reproducing contempt for Muslims on the side of the majority population, are never even addressed. To my knowledge, not a single Muslim woman in the Netherlands has declared, whether in public or in private, to have been liberated from the tutelage of Islam thanks to Hirsi Ali's or Wilders's criticisms. In the case of the PVV, it is even clearer that Wilders's discourse is hardly if at all addressed to Muslims living in the Netherlands but primarily to those parts of the Dutch electorate that share, or are susceptible to, xenophobic sentiments.

7. Conclusions

For all its radicalism, PVV's discourse differs from other kinds of past and present populism in that it accepts, indeed insists on, the political and legal principles and values of liberal-secular democracies. It does not amount to a full-fledged, consistent political or linguistic ideology; however, PVV members habitually deny others the rights to free speech, respectability and the rule of law that they demand for themselves, and they systematically construe their own utterances as legitimate expressions of legitimate opinions, that is, as *mere* words; and the utterances of their opponents as illegitimate gestures of discursive or physical violence, that is, as *actions*. Moreover, Wilders routinely denies responsibility for his own words and attempts to shift any responsibility for possible violence that might result from them to Islam as a religion or to Muslim population groups. This asymmetry, or inconsistency, is not an accidental oversight but an integral, if not essential, prerequisite for the functioning of PVV discourse, which thus undermines liberal rights and values by its very act of appealing to them.

39. In a preface written especially for the Dutch translation of *Excitable Speech*, Butler argues against the Freedom Party's alleged instrumentalization of gay rights for promoting intolerance against religious minorities. On the whole, however, gay rights are hardly a dominant item in PVV discourse. See Butler (2007), esp. pp. 7–11.

The PVV's insistence on liberal-secular values in the face of the alleged threat from a fascist ideology posing as a bona fide religion goes a long way in explaining the ineffectiveness of liberal opposition against Wilders: by accepting his discourse as the expression of opinion and ignoring any further effects it may have, and by enshrining the right to freedom of expression as the most important, if not the sole, good to be protected by the laws and institutions of the state, one almost inevitably cedes the entire argument in advance. Paying systematic attention to the pragmatics of Wilders's language may help us transcend the sterile yes-no debate about whether or not his or others' rights to free expression should be curtailed for the sake of Muslim sensibilities or public security; it helps to refocus discussion on the diffuse range of effects of such discourse, not only on the speaker and the apparent addressee but also — and perhaps most importantly — on third parties. Put differently: we should see Wilders's utterances as primarily performative, rather than as either descriptive of facts or expressive of opinions. They are not descriptive: the truth content of most of Wilders's claims, like those of Hirsi Ali and other Islamophobes, is minimal, his statements about Eurabian conspiracies and Muslim *taqiyya* are irrefutable and hence uninformative, and his remarks about 'hearth beards' are completely meaningless. Thus, semantic content, factual truth or descriptive accuracy is obviously not what these statements are about. They are not simply expressive of opinions in a public debate either; they are not presented as negotiable moves in an orderly attempt to reach consensus. Instead, their provocative wording is carefully crafted to offend or humiliate, and to polarize and sow discord. PVV discourse is a language not of rational discussion but of violence and war, and of pollution and disease; moreover, it implicitly — and on occasion explicitly — suggests that the only solution to the societal ills it claims to have uncovered is an escalation of the repressive powers of the state, in the guise of either the forced assimilation of Muslims, deportation, or even ethnic cleansing. Thus, despite the liberal values it claims to presuppose and defend, it amounts to the decidedly illiberal rejection of the principle of equality before the law; that is, it is not only a discourse *about* violence but also a discourse *of* violence.

Language use may help in performatively bringing about what it appears to be describing, and this certainly seems to apply to PVV discourse: the very words Wilders uses aim at bringing about the social polarization he claims to be describing and at bringing about a social reality characterized by a polarization between Muslims and non-Muslims and by (the threat of) violence of different kinds. Thus, Wilders's Islamophobic discourse reflects the performative power of language to exclude groups of people, precisely in the name of liberal normative ideals like liberty and equality.

References

Bangstad, Sindre. 2014. *Anders Breivik and the Rise of Islamophobia*. London: Zed Books.

Bosma, Martin. 2011. *De schijn-élite van de valse munters: Drees, extreem rechts, nuttige idioten, Groep Wilders en ik*. Amsterdam: Prometheus.

Butler, Judith. 1997. *Excitable Speech: A Politics of the Performative*. London: Routledge. Dutch translation by Niels Helsloot, 2007. *Opgefokte taal: Een politiek van de performatief*. Amsterdam: Parrhèsia.

Foucault, Michel. 1975. *Surveiller et Punir: Naissance de la prison*. Paris: Gallimard.

Harrison, Tony. 2007. *Collected Film Poetry*. London: Faber & Faber.

Kuitenbrouwer, Jan. 2010. *De woorden van Wilders en hoe ze werken*. Amsterdam: De Bezige Bij

De Bruijn, Hans. 2010. *Geert Wilders in debat: over de framing en reframing van een politieke boodschap*. Den Haag: LEMMA.

Herz, Michael, and Peter Molnar (eds.). 2012. *The Content and Context of Hate Speech: Rethinking Regulation and Responses*. Cambridge: Cambridge University Press. doi:10.1017/CBO9781139042871

Lakoff, George. 2004. *Don't Think of an Elephant! Know your Values and Frame the Debate*. White River Junction VT: Chelsea Green Publishing Company.

Leezenberg, Michiel. Forthcoming. Free speech, hate speech, and hate beards: Language ideologies of Dutch populism. In D. Silva (ed.). *Language and Violence* (Amsterdam: Benjamins).

Modood, Tariq, a.o. 2013. Critical Exchange: Understanding and regulating hate speech. *A symposium on Jeremy Waldron's The Harm in Hate Speech. Contemporary Political Theory* 13 (2014): 88–109.

Mulder, Eildert. 2010. *Anders Breivik is niet alleen*. Zoetermeer: Meinema.

Searle, John. 2010. *Making the Social World: The Structure of Human Civilization*. Oxford: Oxford University Press.

Veraart, Wouter. 2010. Beledigen kan alleen in context. *Nederlands Juristenblad*, 591 : 724–730.

Waldron, Jeremy. 2012. *The Harm in Hate Speech*. Cambridge MA: Harvard University Press. doi:10.4159/harvard.9780674065086

Woltering, Robbert, and Michiel Leezenberg. 2010. *De Koran voor beginners*. Amsterdam: Bert Bakker.

Ye'or, Bat. 1985. *The Dhimmi: Christians and Jews under Islam*. Rutherford NJ: Fairleigh Dickinson University Press.

Ye'or, Bat. 2005 *Eurabia: The Euro-Arab Axis*. Rutherford NJ: Farleigh Dickinson University Press.

About the contributors

Paul Baker is Professor of English Language at Lancaster University. His research involves applications of corpus linguistics and his recent books including *Using Corpora to Analyze Gender* (2014), *Discourse Analysis and Media Attitudes* (2013) and *Sociolinguistics and Corpus Linguistics* (2010). He is the commissioning editor of the journal *Corpora*.

Matthew Evans is an English Language Ph.D. candidate at the University of Huddersfield. He currently works as a research assistant on the University of Huddersfield's Language in Conflict project, which looks at the role of language in the context of conflict and conflict resolution. His research interests include the media portrayal of various political concepts such as "choice" and the semantic meaning of terms such as "feminism".

Łukasz Grabowski is Associate Professor at the Institute of English, University of Opole, Poland. His research interests include corpus linguistics, phraseology, formulaic language, translation studies and lexicography. He is also interested in computer-assisted methods of text analysis. He has published internationally in such journals as *International Journal of Corpus Linguistics* and *English for Specific Purposes*, among others. He is also Managing Editor of the journal *Explorations: A Journal of Language and Literature*. Currently, he is working on a project targeted at mapping Polish wordnet (*Słowosieć*) onto Princeton wordnet on the level of lexical units (in collaboration with Maciej Piasecki, Ewa Rudnicka, Tadeusz Piotrowski and Francis Bond).

Adam Hodges is author of *The 'War on Terror' Narrative: Discourse and Intertextuality in the Construction and Contestation of Sociopolitical Reality* (2011, Oxford University Press), editor of *Discourses of War and Peace* (2013, Oxford University Press), and co-editor (with Chad Nilep) of *Discourse, War and Terrorism* (2007, John Benjamins). His work examines the social, cultural, and political dimensions of language use.

Zohar Kampf is Associate Professor of Communication at the Hebrew University of Jerusalem. His main research interest lies in the linkage among language, media and politics. He is the author of *Transforming Media Coverage of Violent Conflicts:*

The New Face of War (2013, Palgrave McMillan, with Tamar Liebes) and of articles in leading communication journals, including the *International Journal of Press/Politics, Political Communication, Media, Culture and Society, Discourse and Society, Communication Theory*, and *Journal of Pragmatics.*

Monika Kopytowska received her Ph.D. from the University of Lodz, Poland, where she is currently affiliated with the Department of Pragmatics. Her research interests revolve around identity, media discourse and the pragma-rhetorical aspects of the mass-mediated representation of conflict/terrorism, ethnicity, and religion. She has published internationally in linguistic journals and volumes (e.g. with Yusuf Kalyango (eds.) *Why Discourse Matters*, Peter Lang Publishers 2014 with Christian Karner (eds.) National Identity and Europe in times of Crisis, Emerald Publishing) and is now working on the dynamics of proximization in news discourse (*Creating Context, Shaping Cognition: Africa, Conflict and the Media*, forthcoming) and the mediatization of religion (with Paul Chilton (eds.) *Religion, Language and Human Mind.* New York: Oxford University Press, forthcoming). She is the co-editor of *Lodz Papers in Pragmatics* (de Gruyter), the assistant editor of *CADAAD Journal,* and editorial board member of *The University of Nairobi Journal of Language and Linguistics.* She is the board member of the European Network for Intercultural Education Activities.

Michiel Leezenberg teaches in the department of philosophy of the University of Amsterdam. He has published numerous articles on pragmatics and power, on the contemporary Middle East, on the intellectual history of the Islamic world, and more recently a book on sexuality and politics in Islam. With Robbert Woltering, he has also published a popularizing work, *The Qur'an for Beginners* (in Dutch).

Robbie Love is a PhD Research Student at the ESRC-funded Centre for Corpus Approaches to Social Science (CASS) at Lancaster University. His research interests include interfaces between corpus linguistics, sociolinguistics and (critical) discourse analysis.

Andreas Musolff is Professor of Intercultural Communication at the University of East Anglia in Norwich (UK). He has published on the History of Political Discourse, Metaphor Theory and the History of Pragmatics. His monographs include *Metaphor, Nation and the Holocaust* (2010), *Metaphor and Political Discourse* (2004), *Mirror Images of Europe* (2000) and *War against the Public: The Language of Terrorism* (1996, in German), and he has co-edited further volumes on political discourse in Europe as well as articles and book chapters on metaphor theory.

Simone Schuller studied Political Science at the University of Vienna and Conflict Resolution at the University of Bradford. She currently works as a research assistant on the University of Huddersfield's Language in Conflict project, which looks at the role of language in the context of conflict and conflict resolution. Her research interests include post-conflict peacebuilding, transitional justice and human rights.

Panagiotis Sotiris is currently doing research at the Laboratory of Arts and Cultural Management of the Department of Communication and Media Studies at the University of Athens. He has taught social theory and social and political philosophy at the Department of Sociology at the University of the Aegean. He has published widely on social philosophy, modern social theory and social and political developments in Greece.

Anna Szilágyi teaches communication at the Savannah College of Art and Design in Hong Kong. She earned her Ph.D. in Media and Communication at City University of Hong Kong. She holds an M.A. in Hungarian Language and Literature from Eötvös Loránd University and an M.A. in Political Science from Central European University (both in Budapest, Hungary). She is a multilingual discourse analyst whose research concerns politics, political discourses, media and journalism in post-communist Central and Eastern Europe and Russia, especially the rhetoric of nationalism, populism and far-right radicalism. Her recent publications include: "Variations on a Theme: the Jewish "Other" in Old and New Antisemitic Media Discourses in Hungary in the 1940s and 2011," (co-author with András Kovács) in Ruth Wodak and John E. Richardson (eds.), Analyzing Fascist Discourse, European Fascism in Talk and Text, New York: Routledge, 2013.

Ruth Wodak is Distinguished Professor of Discourse Studies at Lancaster University, UK. Besides various other prizes, she was awarded the Wittgenstein Prize for Elite Researchers in 1996 and an Honorary Doctorate from University of Örebro in Sweden in 2010. In 2011, she was awarded the Grand Decoration of Honour in Silver for Services to the Republic of Austria.

Her research interests focus on discourse studies; gender studies; language and/in politics; prejudice and discrimination. She is member of the editorial board of a range of linguistic journals and co-editor of the journals *Discourse and Society*, *Critical Discourse Studies*, and *Language and Politics*. She has held visiting professorships in University of Uppsala, Stanford University, University Minnesota, University of East Anglia, and Georgetown University. She is Fellow of the British Academy of Social Sciences and member of the *Academia Europaea*. In 2008, she was awarded the Kerstin Hesselgren Chair of the Swedish Parliament (at University Örebrö).

Recent book publications include *The Politics of Fear: What Right-Wing Populist Discourses Mean* (Sage 2015); *The Discourse of Politics in Action: 'Politics as Usual'* (Palgrave), revised edition (2011); *The Politics of Exclusion. Debating Migration in Austria* (with M. Krzyżanowski, Transaction Press, 2009); *The SAGE Handbook of Sociolinguistics* (with B. Johnstone, P. Kerswill, Sage 2010); *Analyzing Fascist Discourse. Fascism in Talk and Text* (with J. Richardson, Routledge 2013), and *Rightwing Populism in Europe: Politics and Discourse* (with M. KhosraviNik, B. Mral, Bloomsbury 2013). See http://www.ling.lancs.ac.uk/profiles/Ruth-Wodak for more information on on-going research projects and recent publications.

Julita Woźniak received Ph.D. from the University of Łódź after completing Interdisciplinary Interfaculty Doctoral Studies in the Humanities. Her research interests revolve around Critical Discourse Analysis, migration discourse and intercultural communication. Currently she conducts research on online hate speech within the EU project "C.O.N.T.A.C.T." — "Creating On-line Network, Monitoring Team and Phone App to Counter Hate Crime Tactics". She is also an intercultural trainer, global educator and active member of SIETAR Polska.

Index